THE CIVILIZATION OF THE AMERICAN INDIAN SERIES
(Complete list on page 364)

THE SHOSHONIS: *Sentinels of the Rockies*

The Shoshonis

SENTINELS OF THE ROCKIES

By *Virginia Cole Trenholm*
and *Maurine Carley*

UNIVERSITY OF OKLAHOMA PRESS
NORMAN

By Virginia Cole Trenholm

Footprints on the Frontier (Douglas, Wyoming, 1945)

The Arapahoes, Our People (Norman, 1970)

By Virginia Cole Trenholm and Maurine Carley

Wyoming Pageant (Casper, Wyoming, 1958)

The Shoshonis: Sentinels of the Rockies (Norman, 1964)

International Standard Book Numbers: 1–8061–0628–x (cloth); 1–8061–1055–4 (paper)

Library of Congress Catalog Card Number: 64–20770

The Shoshonis: Sentinels of the Rockies is Volume 74 in *The Civilization of the American Indian Series*.

Preface

WHEN THE WIND RIVER SHOSHONIS gaze toward Gannett, Fremont, or some lesser peak on the southwestern fringe of their reservation in Wyoming, or across the rich farm lands in Warm Valley to the east, they seem strangely introspective. Could it be that in their imaginations they are reliving the days when their people were in constant conflict with the Plains tribes, when as "Horse Indians" they knew no boundaries? Theirs is a colorful past, conducive to meditation.

The stocky-built, dark-skinned, full-featured highlanders were not always sedentary. Like their relatives, the Comanches, they were a marginal tribe when they first came into history. Their homeland was where the basin country and the buffalo plains meet, although they originated in the arid country to the west— the "land beyond the setting sun," as they call it.

They were the Sentinels of the Rockies, who eventually established themselves in naturally fortified positions from which they warred their enemies. Their reputed ferocity turned back the French explorers before they were able to reach the mountains. The highlanders did not merely contribute a chapter to the history of the West; they were an intricate part of it from the time of the arrival of the first white man.

Cultural changes had taken place since they left their native habitat. According to tradition, they had reached the Plains by way of the upper reaches of the Snake River. Some no doubt became familiar with Plateau culture during their prolonged migration. And yet their eventual contact with the Indians of the Plains caused them to be recognized as a distinct branch of the nation. In this case, the branch, known as the Northern, became more significant historically than the body from which it stemmed, namely the Western. While the Indians retained many of their legends and customs, they were receptive to their new environment and to the way of life of enemy tribes whose background was far different from their own. Resistance was lacking since Plains culture was not forced upon them, and the change was gradual, if never complete. In fact, these Basin aborigines were unaware that they were adjusting to their surroundings sufficiently to be called Plains Shoshonis.

In late prehistoric times, a further division took place, no doubt as a result of warfare with raiding tribes. Evidence points to the fact that enemies, possibly the Blackfeet, drove a wedge in their ranks. Those to the north fled to the mountains and westward into Idaho, where they came, perhaps for a second time, under the influence of their Plateau neighbors. Although the term did not originate until a half-century later, they have gone down in history as Lemhi Indians. When a woman of their number led the first Americans through their country, they were won over completely. They met in council with the white men on the friendliest of terms, and they guided them through their mountain passes.

Some of the Northern Shoshonis forced from the Plains found their way into southern Idaho and northern Utah. Others, in the largest and most significant segment, eventually became associated with the Green River area and are considered as a separate branch—the Eastern or Wyoming Shoshonis. These Indians threw wide the gate at South Pass and allowed fur trappers and traders, Oregon settlers, religious zealots, and California gold seekers to stream through to expand the American frontier. By so doing, they exposed themselves to yet another culture, that of the white man, who forced them to accept his way of life. Oddly enough, this forced acculturation proved more complicated for the Plains Shoshonis than for their Basin kinsmen for the reason that they were a warfaring people.

Unfortunately, the Indians who played such a significant role in Western history were illiterate, with no recorded language.

The white man, in his relentless effort to impose his culture, has done his utmost to discourage the use of the native language. It is preserved only by interpreters' obsolete vocabularies, no two of which are alike, and by leaflets prepared by resident missionaries.

Since the Indian point of view is obscure, it is difficult to maintain a proper perspective. Records destroyed in a fire at the agency at Fort Washakie might have clarified the Shoshoni attitude toward tribal matters. Unquestionably they would have contributed to the theory that Sacajawea, who accompanied the Lewis and Clark Expedition, was buried at Fort Washakie, Wyoming. Without these records, we rely upon the documents of the white man.

Excellent, though isolated, field studies and ethnological works contribute to an understanding of the background and acculturation of the Shoshonis. Government documents, old newspapers, and unprinted materials are likewise rich in information, but no investigation of this nature would be worth while without a sympathetic knowledge of the people involved. This has necessitated many interviews with the Indians during the years that we have been engaged in research for this project.

Having been exploited in the past, the Shoshonis were at first reticent, but soon they became our warm friends, making every effort in their power to contribute to this endeavor. They hope not only for a book that will be read with understanding by the white man but also for a record which will show their descendants their rich heritage.

While it would be impossible to name all of those whose patience and co-operation have made this book possible, we wish, nevertheless, to express to them our sincere appreciation for the help and encouragement they have given. We are grateful to Frank H. H. Roberts, of the Bureau of American Ethnology; to our Indian friends; to the personnel at the Wind River (Wyoming), the Fort Hall (Idaho), and the Western Shoshoni (Nevada) reservations; and to Will J. Pitner, area director, Bureau of Indian Affairs, Anadarko, Oklahoma. The librarians and their assistants in the University of Wyoming Library, Laramie; the

State Library, Cheyenne; and the Platte County Library, Wheatland, Wyoming, have helped immeasurably in this project.

Sven Liljeblad, authority on the Shoshonis and Bannocks of Idaho, has granted permission for the use of his unpublished materials, and Francis A. Riddell, archaeologist, of Sacramento, has kindly made his unpublished notes on the Lone Pine (California) Indians available. Clara S. Beatty, of Reno, director of the Nevada State Historical Society, has most graciously placed at our disposal the records and pictures which she had planned to use in the preparation of a history of the Western Shoshonis. Besides, Mrs. Beatty has pointed the way to helpful sources in California as well as in Nevada. Priscilla Knuth, of Portland; Dorothy C. Cragen, of Independence, California; A. R. Mortensen of Salt Lake City; and Merle W. Wells, of Boise, Idaho, have given helpful guidance in their areas.

To Angie Debo, author and historian, we wish especially to express our deep gratitude. First as impersonal critic and later as technical adviser, she has shown a professional but friendly interest in the Shoshoni project. Her keen perception and orderly way of thinking have influenced both the organization and the writing of this book.

We are indebted to the following: T. A. Larson, authority on Western history, for reading the manuscript and offering encouragement as well as helpful suggestions; William Mulloy, eminent archaeologist, for evaluating data relative to prehistoric times; and E. O. Fuller, authority on Indian cases, for making his files available to us. Furthermore, for the able assistance they have given in the research, we wish to thank Lenore Harrington, librarian, Missouri Historical Society; Lola Homsher, director, Wyoming State Archives and Historical Department; Ruby Preuit, past president, Wyoming Library Association; and Gene Gressley, archivist, University of Wyoming.

VIRGINIA COLE TRENHOLM
MAURINE CARLEY

Contents

Illustrations

THE SHOSHONIS: *Sentinels of the Rockies*

CHAPTER ONE

In the Basin

THE VAST TERRITORY belonging to the Shoshonean linguistic stock of the large Uto-Aztecan family once stretched from the
rugged Cascades and Sierra Nevadas to the northern Plains, then
southward almost to Mexico. With the exception of the Washos
of California, it included all of the Indians in the Great Basin area
—the Shoshonis, the Paiutes (Paviotsos), the Bannocks (Northern
Paiutes), and the Utes. There was a variety of dialects, but the
natives had little difficulty understanding each other.

With their linguistic bond and cultural similarity, they were
not readily distinguishable. Yet the Shoshoni (Snake) Indians,
bearing the linguistic name and speaking the Shoshoni-Comanche
dialect, are unique in that they show the influence of three distinct cultures—namely, the Basin, the Plateau, and the Plains. Their
territory, separate from that of their kinsmen, the Paiutes and
Utes, stretched continuously from the desert area of California,
across central and northeastern Nevada, then across Utah and
Idaho into Wyoming, over the Rockies and on to the Plains, with
the Comanche branch pushing southeastward through Colorado
deep into Texas.[1]

Just why they were called Shoshonis we do not know, for the
significance of the term has been lost.[2] They were known to the
Mandans, Omahas, Poncas, and Teton Dakotas as Snakes; to the
Atsinas and Yankton Dakotas as Rattlesnakes; to the Crows and
Hidatsas as Grass Lodges; and to the Kiowas as Grass House
People. Their Arapaho name, *E-wu-há-wu-si* (People-Who-
Use-Grass-or-Bark-for-Their-Lodges), probably comes nearer

---

[1] A. L. Kroeber, *Handbook of the Indians of California*, 587.
[2] John R. Swanton, *The Indian Tribes of North America*, 405.

explaining their tribal sign—a serpentine gesture—in reality the in-and-out motion used in weaving their shelters. There is little foundation for the assumption that they were snakelike in their manner and that their name signified that they were the lowliest of creatures, slithering into the brush from which they would emerge to attack their enemies.

Since all Shoshoneans originated in the Basin, the major division of the Shoshoni Nation into Western and Northern is more cultural than geographic. The Western Shoshonis, who had little contact with the outside world, clung to their original way of life while the Northern Shoshonis show the influence of the Plains and Plateau. The flexibility of the designation Shoshoni (Northern) and Shoshoko (Western) makes an exact demarcation impossible. A contemporary writer stated that when an Indian acquired a horse (the emblem of Plains culture) he was considered a Shoshoni; if he found himself deprived of it, he was once again a Shoshoko (Walker or Digger).

The Western Shoshonis (Shoshokos) were recognized as such because they lacked organized bands as well as horses before the arrival of the white man. To them warfare was practically nonexistent. They included the little-known Snakes in the Blue Mountains of Oregon; the Panamints (Kosos) of California; the Shoshonis of Nevada; the Gosiutes, Weber Utes (Cumumbahs),[3] and Shoshonis in Utah, as well as the Snake River Indians of Idaho. These Indians were loosely grouped according to the principal type of food found in their diet. They were known by such names as Root, Squirrel, Sunflower Seed, Salmon, Sheep, Pine Nut, and Dust or Earth Eaters.

Although the most primitive types of Indians were found among the Basin natives, they were a practical people, surprisingly adaptable to their surroundings. This alone accounts for their survival. Since vegetable and animal life was scarce in the arid country, shut away from the moisture of the sea by mountains, they had to range in family groups and sometimes alone in

---

[3] The names Gosiute and Weber Ute are confusing, as they suggest the Ute tribe. Brigham Young and some of the early agents called the Weber Utes Cumumbahs.

their constant search for food. It was so limited that it was a matter of the survival of the fittest.

Throughout the Basin area the Shoshokos—unexcelled in basketry—gathered seeds in large woven baskets, winnowed them on fiber trays, and ground them into meal with their metates. They used the meal in making cakes, which they dried in the sun and stored in the ground for winter use, if there were any left beyond their immediate need. They were usually in a starving condition by spring.

The Utes, who were active in the Indian-Mexican slave trade, would time their raids when they knew they would find these Indians in such a weakened state they would be unable to run away. Then they would capture them, take them to their camp, fatten them, and sell them in slavery. As the Shoshonis had neither weapons of war nor the inclination to fight, they were considered easy prey.[4]

They were, however, a resourceful as well as practical people. Their most useful possession was their pointed stick, with which they pried roots and native vegetables from the ground. This caused them to be known by the vague term "Digger," a name which they shared with the other Shoshoneans on a similar subsistence level. Besides gathering seeds and digging roots, they made intricate snares and fiber nets for trapping rodents, birds, and fish. After catching small game they would either kill it with stones or club it to death. Snares used to trap wildcats, coyotes, and other animals were often ingenious.[5] The Indians sometimes put a log across the trail and a brush fence obstruction on each side to force the animal to jump the log so that a foot might become caught in an obscured pit and trigger mechanism, well camouflaged on the opposite side.

Whenever possible, the natives would organize communal

[4] Julian H. Steward, "Basin-Plateau Aboriginal Sociopolitical Groups" (hereinafter cited as "Basin-Plateau Groups"), *Bulletin 120*, Bureau of American Ethnology (hereinafter cited as B.A.E.); also, Joseph J. Hill, "Spanish and Mexican Exploration and Trade Northwest from New Mexico into the Great Basin," *Utah Historical Quarterly* (hereinafter cited as *U.H.Q.*), Vol. III (1930), 3–22.

[5] Francis A. Riddell, unpublished field notes on the Lone Pine Indians of California.

drives in their food-gathering activities. A grasshopper drive among the Shoshokos of Utah was described by Pierre Jean de Smet,[6] the first priest to visit the area. He observed that they went to a place where grasshoppers swarmed by myriads, a place often visited by the Indians (probably Gosiutes):

> They begin by digging a hole, ten or twelve feet in diameter by four or five feet deep; then, armed with long branches . . . they surround a field of four or five acres, more or less, according to the number of persons who are engaged in it. They stand about twenty feet apart, and their whole work is to beat the ground, so as to frighten up the grasshoppers and make them bound forward. They chase them toward the center by degrees—that is, into the hole prepared for their reception. Their number is so considerable that frequently three or four acres furnish grasshoppers sufficient to fill the reservoir or hole.

He said that the Shoshokos, "like other mortals," had their tastes. Some ate the grasshoppers boiled in soup; others crushed them into a paste which they dried in the sun or before a fire. Still others strung the largest ones on a pointed stick, which they stuck in the ground in such a way that the insects were roasted in a campfire.

Since procuring food was a problem, it sometimes involved shamanistic practices. Certain medicine men possessed the power to charm antelope, their only big game except sheep in the mountain areas. Such communal drives amounted to a religious ceremony, involving the Indians in ritual and song. Unlike the Paiutes,[7] the Shoshoni participants sometimes included women, though no one menstruating was allowed to be present as she might break the charm and cause the antelope to run away.

The natives were lacking in clothing as well as food. In warm weather the men wore only a breechcloth and the women a fiber double apron, usually woven from sagebrush which had been pounded into a fringe. They were even known to take green scum

---

[6] *Life, Letters, and Travels of Father Pierre-Jean De Smet*, III, 1033.

[7] For details of the shamanistic antelope drive, *see* Sarah Winnemucca Hopkins, *Life among the Piutes*, 55–57.

from a stagnant water hole and tear it into the desired size for an apron. Had they been without this necessary shield, they would have violated an old taboo. Those looking upon a woman entirely unclothed would become blind.

In winter, men and women alike wore a woven garment of strips of rabbitskins. Since it took about forty rabbits for a single robe, one who could boast of a complete covering was fortunate. The robe or blanket was the greatest luxury in the basin. Those having only a few skins would use them to wrap their feet and legs.

Although some writers describe the Diggers as living in the lowliest state, little better than an animal, the idea that they hibernated in a hole in winter and crawled forth in spring to eat grass is highly exaggerated. It may be attributed to an early historian who described them in the following manner:

> Lying in a state of semi-torpor in holes in the ground during the winter, and in spring, crawling forth and eating grass on their hands and knees, until able to regain their feet; having no clothes, scarcely any cooked food, in many instances no weapons, with merely a few vague imaginings for religion, living in the utmost squalor and filth, putting no bridle on their passions, there is surely room for no missing link between them and the brutes.[8]

Their housing was temporary. While moving about during the food-gathering season, they had to carry with them the branches and mats used in the framework of their shelters. In winter they lived underground. Their mound-like earthen structures[9] had an opening at the top that was used by the Indians in coming and going and for the smoke to escape from their sage-brush fires. At a distance, a cluster of these dwellings resembled a prairie dog town.

All natural resources, with the sole exception of privately owned eagle nests,[10] were free to anyone. Though food was scarce, there seemed to be little contention between the indi-

[8] Hubert Howe Bancroft, "Wild Tribes," *Native Races*, I, 440.
[9] Alice Marriott, *The Ten Grandmothers*, 201–202.
[10] Steward, "Basin-Plateau Groups," 254.

viduals or neighboring tribes while they were acquiring it. When cannibalism was practiced, the lazy drones were the victims. As one student of the Western Shoshonis says, they were usually "fatter and more economically obnoxious."[11]

The "vague imaginings for religion" amounted to a simple faith dependent upon the spirit, the *mugua,* and the ghost, the *tsoap.* The Buhagant, the medicine man and spiritual leader, derived his power usually in some material way, perhaps by a feather or some other insignificant article, from Apo (the Sun), corresponding to what some Indians called the Great Spirit. The Shoshonis believed in the transmigration of the soul. Their father, Coyote—the Shoshokos thought—made them from clay when he was a man. After death their spirit would go to the land of Coyote. Halfway up, it would be met by another spirit that would escort it to its proper place. Until Wolf (Coyote's brother) had washed and revived it, only the medicine man could see it.

Since their belief in immortality was strong, the Western Shoshonis were sometimes known to practice sutteeism. Jules Remy,[12] traveling through the Basin area in 1861, was witness to an incident in Carson Valley, Nevada, where an Indian woman was killed so that her spirit might accompany her husband's into the next world. There is one recorded tale[13] of an Indian who experienced life after death. When the Sun told him that he was to die, his tribesmen built him a separate lodge and left him alone, as was their custom.

> I was still breathing [he said]. I thought of seeing my dead father and mother, brother and other relatives. I wished to die immediately. For three days and four nights I lay in the tent. At last on the fourth day, my soul came out of my thigh, made a step forward and glanced back at my body. The *mugua* (spirit) was about as large as this (ten inches).

[11] Jack Harris, "The White Knife Shoshoni of Nevada" (hereinafter cited as "The White Knife Shoshoni"), in *Acculturation in Seven American Indian Tribes,* 52.

[12] Jules Remy and Julius Brenchley, *A Journey to Great Salt Lake,* I, 131.

[13] Robert H. Lowie, "The Northern Shoshone," *Anthropological Papers* (hereinafter cited as *A.P.*), Vol. II, Pt. 2 (1924), 233.

My body was not yet lifeless. When the *mugua* had made three steps forward, my body dropped, cold and dead. I looked at it for some time; it made no movement at all.

Suddenly something came down and went clean through my soul. My soul began to go downward. It did not ascend. I reached another world and followed a trail there. I beheld a helper of the Father who was making some dead men over again. I thought I might see the Father, but could only hear him.

He was saying to me, "You don't look very ill." A kind of thin wire was making a noise at the time. The Father had a buckskin bag; out of its contents he makes everything. He tapped the wire three times. Then I was able to see his hand, which was as small and clean as a baby's, then the whole world opened up and I could see the earth plainly. I saw everything there. I saw my own body lying there dead.

The Sun told me I would be restored to life. I did not walk back and I don't know how I returned. Suddenly I was back alive. For a few moments, I had seen the Father. He was a handsome Indian. My familiar spirit left me when I fell sick and never returned after that.

On another occasion, I went up to the clouds. The people I met there were nothing but skeletons. I saw some of my friends there. In this other world there was a great deal of sagebrush.

In this legend, the Father is referred to as a "handsome Indian," not as Coyote, which suggests the possibility of the soul's going from man to Coyote and then back again. The Indians in their beliefs and mythology personified many animals and birds which could assume human characteristics and sometimes talk to them. Coyote, Wolf, Rabbit, Bear, and tiny Chickadee which made the world were held in awe. It was bad luck to kill a chickadee, but a coyote's howl at full moon was a good omen.

Legendary characters were as real to the imaginative Shoshonis as if they had seen them. The stories about them were repeated so often that no one even questioned the existence of the *NunumBi, "Little People."* These frightening dwarfs, roaming at large, would shoot invisible arrows of misfortune into anyone displeasing them.

9

Then, too, there were the red-haired cannibals of the Humboldt about whom all Shoshoneans knew. The legends concerning them are traceable to the red-haired remains of Indians found in Lovelock Cave (Nevada). Scientists say that the color of the hair was caused by chemical change after death, but the Indians are convinced that red-haired cannibals actually roamed in menacing numbers in their region.

According to Paiute accounts, they lived many hundreds of years ago. They would waylay the Indians, then kill and devour them. Not only that, they would come among them and carry away their dead for food. These barbarians, who were considered great fighters, could jump into the air and catch an arrow and hurl it back. The only way to get rid of them was all-out war, which Chief Truckee's Paiutes were finally forced to wage.

They surrounded them on Humboldt Lake and began killing them as they landed their bulrush boats. One night while the Paiutes were sleeping, the remainder of the barbarians on the lake came ashore and hid in a cave near the mountains. Refusing to come out and agree to live like Indians instead of beasts, they allowed themselves to be trapped in the cave, the Paiutes blocking the entrance with timber. When the barbarians still refused to behave, the Pine Nut Eaters (Paiutes) set fire to the wood and destroyed the tribe, thereby winning for themselves the name *Say-do-carah*, Conquerors.[14]

Another significant story,[15] involving a sixteen-year-old Lone Pine (California) Shoshoni girl, is told by a Paiute. The girl, he said, would become frightened from some unknown cause and cry until she was ill. Her parents finally consulted a medicine man from Death Valley. He laid her on a blanket near a small fire. Then he constructed a brush enclosure large enough to accommodate the visitors who were to witness the ceremony.

After two days of singing and circling the girl and the fire, the medicine man was ready to diagnose the case. He told the parents that they had at one time dreamed of a mountain lion as their

[14] Hopkins, *Life among the Piutes*, 73–75.
[15] Riddell, field notes.

"pet." That was why the girl was afraid "something would get her." He insisted that the parents admit it, but they stoutly denied having had such a dream. Lighting a gunny sack at the fire, he beat them until they admitted their "guilt." The Paiute telling the story said that beating people in this manner was an old-time way of getting the stubborn to confess. They would not otherwise admit having witched anyone, even when the medicine man found that it had been the case.

In the absence of bands and chieftains among the early root-digging people, the family, the largest group that could subsist in any given area for any length of time, was the all-important unit. The role of the woman in food-gathering activities gave her an equal status with the man. As a result, both polyandry and polygamy were practiced. Although Basin economy[16] did not permit the luxury of several wives, it was not uncommon for a man to have two, or for a woman to have two husbands. Usually the husbands were brothers and the wives, sisters. When a man lost his wife, he became her sister's "Cry House," causing them to be related through sorrow.

Marriage was important since the family group took the place of the social and political structure found among many tribes. Besides it was a necessary economic alliance for the preservation of the adult as well as the child. Although some unions lasted but a short time, it behooved single Indians to cast about for mates.

The mystic nature of birth caused both parents to observe certain taboos. They did not eat grease or meat until after the child's birth. Furthermore, they were not supposed to touch their heads, the origin of the strength and wisdom to be transmitted to the baby. If their heads needed to be scratched, they used a stick. They also refrained from scratching their bodies at that time for fear they would leave black marks.

A girl baby was considered a blessing because the parents knew that some day she would attract a mate who would help the family in its never-ending quest for food. A Coming-of-Age Ceremony

[16] Lowie, "Notes on Shoshonean Ethnography," *A.P.*, Vol. XX, Pt. 3 (1924), 266.

was observed throughout the Basin for the girl as well as the boy. The emphasis seemed to have been on isolation during the "dangerous period" in the girl's life and upon giving her tasks to strengthen her for the hardships she must face. The boy, too, was prepared for his life's work of helping to provide for a family. He was not allowed to eat the first wild game he killed, as a lesson in abstinence.

Marriage among the Shoshonis took three forms: (1) the usual, when the man either stayed with the girl in her parent's lodge or took her with her consent to his camp; (2) inducement, whereby the girl's family selected a mate for their daughter and offered something in the way of gifts to procure him; and (3) abduction by capture or by rape.[17] In the third type, it mattered not if the woman already had a husband, for she had no say in the matter. If some other man saw her and wanted her, he could come with a band of his male friends and engage the husband and all of the helpers he could muster in a free-for-all fight. Such gang fights might last an entire day. During one affray when the woman in question was injured, the other members of her sex scattered the aggressors by throwing live coals upon them. If anyone was killed or if the wife was taken away, it was considered a hazard to be expected and nothing was done about it. The wife could return later if she wished.

Although there is little evidence that a marriage ceremony existed among the Shoshonis, Sarah Winnemucca, a Paiute, tells of one among her people. She says that when the prospective bride handed her brave a basket of food she had prepared for him, he would seize her wrist with his right hand and take the food with the left. This constituted the marriage ceremony, following which the father would remind the bride of all the wifely duties she must perform.[18] Among the Shoshonis, if a man stayed one night with a girl, in her lodge or his, the marriage was considered consummated. The couple would usually live with the girl's parents for about

[17] *Ibid.*, 213–15.
[18] Hopkins, *Life among the Piutes*, 48–51.

a year or until the first child was born. Then they would provide a dwelling of their own.

As the people were continually moving about, the sweat house, which plays an important role in the social life of many tribes, was incidental. The Paiutes, on the other hand, enjoyed their community sweat houses where men could congregate as in a club room, but the Shoshokos' were usually individually built structures, often earth covered, too small for meetings. Since they were of simple construction for purification rites only, an Indian might have several at different places, or none at all.

When even a few could congregate, they enjoyed their favorite amusement, the hand game, which they enlivened by gambling. It was a guessing game, and the objects were concealed under blankets or basketry trays. The Shoshokos were naturally gregarious, but for the most part they lived a lonely life, far removed from their friends and relatives. Even so, they managed to congregate at specified intervals during their festivals,[19] their only means of bringing groups of any size together.

The California Shoshonis, however, would sometimes band together from economic necessity. Prior to reservation days, they occupied the northern halves of Death and Panamint valleys, Saline Valley, the southern end of Eureka Valley, the southern shore of Owens Lake, the Koso Mountain area, the northern edge of the Mojave Desert, and the eastern slope of the Sierra Nevada Mountains.[20] Throughout this area they had communal rabbit hunts, or several families might combine their efforts in gathering pine nuts, an activity in which men as well as women took part. In the fall there was a concerted drive for food to provide for their needs during their annual festival, which was more social than religious in character.

Besides visiting, gambling, and dancing, some of those who had lost members of their families took part in mourning rites, terminating the period when custom decreed that those nearest

[19] The account of festivals is based on the authoritative study by Julian H. Steward, "Basin-Plateau Groups."

[20] *Ibid.*, 70–93.

13

to the deceased should grieve. The Shoshonean people of California, especially the Paiutes, required that mourners abstain from meat and grease of all kinds until the annual festival. They were not supposed to wash during their bereavement. A band leader presided at the ceremony when the mourners finally washed away their grief, burned relics that they had saved from the funeral, and placed newly acquired articles on the sacrificial fire. It was, nevertheless, the custom of most Basin Indians to destroy all property of the deceased that they did not bury with the body.

The Gosiutes (also called Southern or Mormon Snakes) held their celebrations at Skull Valley and at Deep Creek, on the Utah-Nevada border. These took place in the spring for the purpose of making the seeds grow. During a prosperous year the celebrations might be given in the summer and perhaps again in the fall. The dance director would send messengers great distances to invite neighboring groups to attend the five-day fertility ceremony of his people.

In Nevada the fall festivities and the communal rabbit drive were usually held jointly, lasting five days and nights. Hunting took place in the daytime, dancing at night. The Shoshokos in the Duckwater locality often had three celebrations during the year —one in the spring when plants began to grow, one in the midsummer when seeds began to ripen, and one in the fall at harvesttime.

Indians in the vicinity of Ruby Valley held a ceremony in the summer or in the fall. The natives along the Humboldt usually assembled at pine nut harvesttime, though they sometimes performed their dances in the spring. The celebration held at South Fork (near Elko, Nevada) drew Indians from as far away as Carlin and Beowawe. The Shoshonis from Beowawe, as well as those from Iron Point, also went to Battle Mountain to take part in their festivals. The Round Dance, of native origin, took place when the Indians assembled. The Bear Dance, borrowed from the Utes, was introduced in more recent years. Courtship also became a part of the ceremony.

The general plan of the Reese River Valley festival indicated that it might have been indirectly influenced by the Sun Dance of the Plains. The camp circle had an opening to the east, opposite the leader's temporary shelter. There was a center pole or pine tree in the middle of the circle. During the ceremony the chief would admonish his people not to steal or cause trouble.

While the Tosawis (White Knives) of Owyhee were still Basin root diggers, they, too, would meet at least once a year, usually in the spring. The White Knives were not a distinct tribe but rather the Shoshonis who made use of white flint from the mountains of northern Nevada. They ranged from Goose Creek to the Humboldt, in the radius of Battle Mountain. Although economic necessity limited the number congregating, they sometimes managed to have a festival of five and one-half days' duration. To them it seemed to have had more religious significance than some of the gatherings we have noted, perhaps because the dance leaders had learned of the Plains concepts through the Northern Shoshonis.

The temporary shelters of the participants were erected in a semicircle, with the opening to the east like that found at Reese Valley. The Buhagant, serving as an intermediary between the Indians and the Sun (Apo), would pray for the growth of vegetable and animal life so that there might be food. The green willow pole, emblem of fertility, served the same function as the pine tree around which some of the Indians danced.

In reservation days, when the necessity for searching for food was not so acute, these Indians began holding their festivals with greater frequency, even neglecting their crops in their enthusiasm. One of their agents suggested having the dance annually, on the Fourth of July. It finally became their highly popular fandango, with the American flag taking the place of the willow pole.

The Snake River (Idaho) Indians, whose life was of a more complex nature, depended primarily upon salmon, mountain sheep, deer, camasses, and wild fruits for food. Festivals were the only means of bringing the various villages together, but they were so infrequent that they did little to unify the people. They followed the usual pattern of those in the Nevada groups. Whenever food was sufficient and participants could be found, the chief might call a festival of five days' duration.

Once assembled, the Indians would play the hand game, football, and women's hockey during the day and dance the Round Dance at night. The slightly improved economy of the Snake River Indians, who probably helped introduce the general plan of the camp circle into northern Nevada, gave them the advantage of being able to hold a day-long feast following the third night of dancing.

The Western Shoshonis who faced their tipis toward the east and prayed to Apo did not link the name with their ceremonies. By opening their camp circle toward the rising sun, they recognized its life-giving rays, but otherwise their festivals showed little influence of the Sun Dance, an innovation of the Plains tribes.

CHAPTER TWO

On the Plains

THE HARDY BASIN NATIVES, finding their way across the Rockies and out on the Plains as early as the 1500's,[1] took with them their customs and traditions. Ranging eastward, some if not all of them lived for a time in the mountains. Finding themselves in a new environment with food more plentiful, they were able to group together into settlements, where they remained long enough to ply their art in pictographs and petroglyphs.[2] One such group may have been in the Dinwoody area, located in the northwestern edge of the Wind River Reservation in Wyoming. This was a natural habitat for the ancient people of the region. Wildlife was plentiful, and the immediate area was so secluded from winds and driving snows that the Indians could live in caves in comparative comfort.

Petroglyphs found there indicate exacting workmanship. Many of these are on Sleeping Ledge, a reddish sandstone cliff. The most ancient are of animal design, indicating a correlation between the art and mythology of the primitive people. Since no horses are recorded at Dinwoody, the work was obviously that of Walkers. Archaeologists are reluctant to name the Indians once

[1] D. B. Shimkin ("Some Interactions of Culture, Needs, and Personality among the Wind River Shoshone," Ph.D. dissertation, University of California) suggests that the Shoshonis may have roamed the Plains many generations before being driven back into the Rockies.

[2] E. B. Renaud, "Archaeological Survey of Eastern Wyoming," University of Denver and University of Wyoming *Bulletin* (1932); William Mulloy, "Archaeological Investigations in the Shoshone Basin of Wyoming," *University of Wyoming Publications*, Vol. XVIII, Nos. 1, 2, 3 (1954); David S. Gebhard and H. A. Cahn, "The Petroglyphs of Dinwoody, Wyoming," *American Antiquity*, Vol. XV, No. 3 (1950); L. C. Steege, "Petroglyphs of Dinwoody," Wyoming State Museum, Cheyenne, 1954.

living there, beyond saying that they were prehistoric. The aborigines may have been Mountain Crows or even Broken Moccasins who, according to Shoshoni legend, were some of their number destroyed by a convulsion of nature.[3] Attempts to associate the art work with the Sheep Eaters have proved futile. Any interpretation of its meaning is likewise impossible since it was known only to the Indian artists themselves or to their cultural group.

While they were still Walkers, some of the Shoshonis seem to have been able to engage in buffalo-hunting in a limited fashion and to have found subsistence on the native foods as far away as the northern Plains.[4] Ceramics found in the Yellowstone River region of Montana have been identified as Shoshonean in craftsmanship. A flat-bottomed, cylindrical-sided vessel, with opposite holes in the rim for suspension, is known to have been made by natives in the Basin-Plateau area. The Lemhis, the Bannocks, the Indians of Grouse Creek, Promontory Point, and Cache Valley, as well as the Paiutes of Owens Valley and the Shoshokos of Death Valley made a similar type of vessel.[5] Although the Shoshonis roamed over the northern Plains, some authorities believe that it is doubtful that they lived there with any degree of permanency.[6] In the Shoshoni Basin, petroglyph styles show the influence of both the Plains and Plateau cultures, indicating that they may be of a later period than those at Dinwoody.

According to legend the Blackfeet, commonly known as The Northern Raiders, first encountered the Shoshonis south of "Belly River" (South Saskatchewan), which placed them in southern Alberta along the Bow and Oldman rivers and in northwestern Montana, where they are thought to have roamed before the introduction of firearms. The Wind River Shoshonis still talk of

---

[3] Meriwether Lewis and William Clark, *Original Journals of the Lewis and Clark Expedition*, II, 381. The first mention of these Indians was made by Lewis, August 20, 1805.

[4] For methods used by horseless Indians in procuring food, see Mulloy, "A Preliminary Historical Outline for the Northwestern Plains," *University of Wyoming Publications*, Vol. XXII, No. 1 (July, 1958), 16–21.

[5] *Ibid.*, 201.

[6] Waldo R. Wedel, *Prehistoric Man on the Great Plains*, 243.

the days when their "fathers" took long treks as far north as Canada and as far south as Mexico.[7] The Piegans, the southernmost band of the Blackfeet, were their first formidable enemy, as they would come great distances on foot to make war upon them.

The early method of warfare consisted of lining up opposite each other and making a great show of their might.[8] Kneeling behind their rawhide shields, which were impervious to the weapons then known, they might fight an entire day without suffering many casualties. Satisfied at nightfall, they would call it a draw, and the aggressors would return to their camp.

For political as well as economic reasons the Shoshonis discovered that their strength lay in banding together. In late prehistoric times they were well established east of the Rockies. The non-Shoshonean Kiowas seem to have lived just west of the Black Hills (South Dakota), the Shoshonis between them and the Rockies, and the dashing Comanches immediately south of the Kiowas. These three tribes were united in a loose association. In the early 1700's, when the few white travelers ventured into the Western country with their Indian guides, they were frightened when they observed horse dung or abandoned camps which they thought might indicate the presence of "Snakes," a term erroneously used to include all three tribes.[9]

A reshuffling of the early Plains tribes began about 1700 when the Comanches started migrating southward, for what reason we are not sure. It has been suggested that there may have been dissension; but more plausibly the Comanches, after acquiring the horse, wanted to move southward to the source of the supply, the Spanish settlements. They were replaced along the Platte River by the Kiowas, with the Staitans (allies and forerunners of the Cheyennes) moving from the Black Hills into the country along the eastern slope of the Rockies.

In the early 1700's the Shoshonis came in possession of the

[7] Maud Clairmont, informant, Fort Washakie, Wyoming.

[8] David Thompson, *David Thompson's Narrative of His Explorations in Western America, 1784–1812*, 328–34.

[9] Clark Wissler, *Indians of the United States*, 222.

19

horse, probably through the Comanches or indirectly through the Utes. A half-century later the Blackfeet were still telling how the Shoshonis brought the first horses into their country.[10] They came riding into their midst, "swift as a deer," on an animal such as the Blackfeet had never seen. Before they could recover from their surprise, the Shoshonis had knocked several warriors on the head with clubs and had fled.

This so infuriated the Blackfeet that they enlisted the aid of their allies, the Crees and Assiniboines, in making war upon the enemy. The allies, arriving in great numbers, brought with them a weapon recently acquired from the Canadian trappers. It was a long hollow rod that made a terrific noise as it emitted a missile that traveled even more swiftly than the Shoshonis' four-footed steed. The Piegans and their allies lost no time trying out the secret weapon on an encampment of Shoshonis who apparently were without horses.

After some maneuvering, the Indians lined up as usual, and the Piegan chief ordered his warriors to advance. The Cree and Assiniboin gunmen concealed their weapons behind their shields, while each held two balls in his mouth for reloading. The unsuspecting Shoshonis were mowed down as fast as the enemy could fire. Terrified by this new magic, the survivors fled.

When the Blackfeet encountered a lone horseman mounted on a four-footed animal like the ones upon which the enemy had come charging into their camp, they killed it with arrows and marveled at its size.[11] Was it a stag that had lost its horns? No, it was more like a dog, the Blackfeet's only domesticated animal. Apparently it was a slave to man, so they decided to name it "Big Dog," later "Elk Dog."

Terrorized by the mysterious weapon in the hands of the Assiniboines and Crees, the Shoshonis fled southward, forsaking Red Deer Valley. The Piegans, taking it over, made an attack

10 Thompson, *Narrative*, 300. For importance of the horse in Plains culture, *see* Clark Wissler, "The Influence of the Horse in the Development of Plains Culture," *American Anthropologist* (hereinafter cited as *A.A.*), Vol. XVI (1914), 1–2.
11 Thompson, *Narrative*, 330–34.

upon a silent village of Shoshonis. Ripping open the lodge skins, they found the Indians unable to fight back. They were a "mass of corruption," with those not yet dead, dying. The Piegans, who knew nothing of contagion, believed that this was caused by a Bad Spirit that had come to destroy their enemy. They took the horses and all useful equipment and returned to their camp.

Soon the deadly smallpox spread from lodge to lodge. Even the Piegan medicine men were unable to stop it. Finally, humbled by their affliction and weakened in numbers, the survivors were ready for a medicine talk with their enemy, but the Shoshonis could not be found. Later it was discovered that after suffering losses from the dread disease, they had withdrawn southward to the Missouri and its headwaters. They had left the Bow and Oldman rivers forever. Thus it was that the score between the two tribes was evened, for although the Piegans gave the Shoshonis their first taste of the white man's gun, the Shoshonis gave the Piegans smallpox.

The Staitans or Kite Indians, who were replaced in the Black Hills by the Cheyennes, were a small but ferocious tribe. They and the Kiowa-Apaches who followed at their heels did not remain long enough on the Eastern Slope to have much influence on the region, which was soon to be overrun by more powerful tribes. Yet they, the Shoshonis, Comanches, and Kiowas, were the first to occupy the Plains just east of the Rockies.

Although the Blackfeet may have chased the Shoshonis into the mountains, the Crows and other hostile tribes, with their superior weapons, managed to keep them there. The Crows claimed all the area between the Rockies and the Black Hills, north of the Platte. They centered on three southern tributaries of the Yellowstone—Powder River and the Wind and Bighorn rivers. They were so similar to the Hidatsas (the Gros Ventres of the Missouri) that at one time they may have been a single people. They and the unrelated Atsinas (Gros Ventres of the Prairies) who raided the Shoshonis were both known as "Big Bellies," all of which is confusing.

The Hidatsas, the Crows, the Tetons (Southern Sioux), and the

Assiniboins were related Siouan tribes. The Mandans, whom the first American explorers encountered in North Dakota, once claimed the center of culture on the Upper Missouri, but their nine large villages were so ravaged by smallpox and cholera that the few survivors finally joined the Hidatsas.[12]

The Dakotas (Sioux), who came into the Black Hills at the encouragement of the Cheyennes, were a special menace to the Green River Snakes, as we will see later. The Arapahoes ("Dog Eaters," the Shoshones called them) were kinsmen of the Blackfeet and of the Cheyennes, who were probably on the Plains before America was discovered. The Arapahoes continued southward, finally coming to stop in northeastern Colorado, with part of their number going farther south to form the Southern division. It was the Northern branch of this family that opposed the Green River Snakes and was, ironically, placed on their reservation years later.

There is no record of the date or circumstance, but sometime in the early 1800's the "fighting" Cheyennes and the Arapahoes met and formed an alliance. Not long afterwards they were joined by the Sioux, who became the most powerful tribe in this group, which was later to be known as the Platte River Indians.

These Indians were bitter enemies of the Plains or Northern Shoshonis, known technically as the Agaidükas, the Pohogues, and the Kogohues. The Agaidükas (Salmon Eaters) were the Lemhis encountered by the first white explorers in the Bitterroot Mountains (Montana). They also occupied the Lemhi River Valley (Idaho), where they were associated closely with their Plateau neighbors, the Flatheads and the Nez Percés, who would join them to trade or to trek to Camas Prairie in Western Idaho. We are not sure just when the Northern Bannocks and the Tukadükas (Sheep Eaters) consolidated with the Agaidükas, but it was probably in late prehistoric times. The Bannocks, a branch of the Oregon Northern Paiutes, have resided so long in the general area that they have no knowledge of their Paiute connection.

The miserably poor Sheep Eaters kept well to the mountains,

[12] Wissler, *Indians of the United States*, 176–77.

as they were without horses to transport them into the buffalo country. The mixed bands of Shoshonis and Bannocks dwelt for the most part along the tributaries of the Columbia during the fishing season (May to September). When the fish disappeared they would join their friends the Flatheads and sometimes the Nez Percés for a hunting trip northeastward to the headwaters of the Missouri over what became known as the Great Bannock Trail through the northern part of Yellowstone Park.[13] The Tushepaws, a subdivision of the Flatheads, were their only constant allies.[14]

As the Lemhis dreaded their enemies, the Blackfeet and the Crows with whom they were intermittently at war, they tarried only long enough to replenish their food supply. This was later supplemented with camas and other roots and berries and with deer, antelope, and the small game they managed to snare in their homeland. Buffalo disappeared from the upper Snake River Valley about 1840.[15]

The Pohogues (People of the Sage) were later known as the Fort Hall Shoshonis. They were called by Schoolcraft the "Bannarks" or "Middle Shoshones."[16] Just when they became allied with the Bannocks is not known. Unlike the Lemhis to the north, who had a name to designate the consolidated group, they were considered "mixed bands of Shoshones and Bannocks" throughout most of their history. They were so similar in language and habits that they were not readily distinguishable. In fact, one of the early traders lived with them two years without even noting a difference in their dialect.

The Kogohues (Green River Snakes) would often join the Lemhis and mixed bands for communal hunting excursions into hostile territory, but when it came to actual warfare they had little help from their kinsmen. Just what the connection was

[13] For Little Moon's account of intermittent warfare between his tribe (the Nez Percé) and the Shoshonis, see L. V. McWhorter, *Hear Me, My Chiefs!* 41–46, 568–70.

[14] Steward, "Basin-Plateau Groups," 201.

[15] *Ibid.*, 201, 203.

[16] Henry R. Schoolcraft, *Indian Tribes of the United States*, II, 37–38.

between the Sheep Eaters of the Yellowstone Park area with the Sheep Eaters of Idaho who joined the Lemhis is not clear. Possibly they were some of the same Indians. On the other hand, it is more probable that they were stragglers from the Northern Shoshonis who were driven into the mountains by hostile forces.

Very little is known about these primitive people or their origin. Recent archaeological discoveries indicate that there were prehistoric cave men in the general area before the Shoshonis as we know them entered the Rockies. If so, they may not have been Shoshonean, although the Sheep Eaters have long been considered remnants of the tribe. Without horses and means of defense, they were furtive creatures, living in the heights away from contact with all other people.

Some authorities claim that they were cowards, hiding in the high country to avoid their enemies. With the fierce Piegans to the north and a large tribe of hostile Crows to the east, they probably had reason to confine themselves to the wastelands in the mountains. Stories are told of how they rolled rocks down upon their enemies. The pole frameworks of some of their wickiups or brush shelters still stand, though they were abandoned about a century ago. It is believed that the last Sheep Eaters may have left the park about 1879.[17]

The suggestion that they became extinct because of smallpox has little foundation in fact. It appears that the few who remained in the park found life among friendly neighboring tribes more desirable. One of the last independent Sheep Eaters was Togwotee, for whom a well-known pass is named. He became a sub-chief under the Shoshoni chief Washakie and was not only a feared medicine man but also a trusted guide during the Indian wars.

One writer reports an interview with an aged woman said to have been the lone survivor of her tribe.[18] Though her claim is doubtful, she gives a somewhat plausible account of the Great Medicine Wheel near Shell, Wyoming. The Northern Shoshonis

---

[17] Ake Hultkrantz, "The Indians in Yellowstone Park," *Annals of Wyoming*, Vol. XXIX, No. 2 (1957), 134–35.

[18] W. A. Allen, *The Sheep Eaters*, 9.

disclaim any knowledge of it; the Crows say that it was put there by their gods to show them how to build their tipis.

The account given by the old woman has one point in its favor: the prehistoric shrine shows all evidence of having been made by human hands. The giant horseshoe prints, one halfway up the mountainside and the other near the top, were made, the Shoshonis believe, by the first great medicine man who came riding over the crest. One hundred miles southwestward, a Great Arrow points toward the Medicine Wheel. Fifty-eight feet in length, it is believed to have directed the tribes to the ceremonials.

According to the Sheep Eater woman, the twenty-eight spokes in the mysterious wheel represent the tribes of her race.[19] She remembered the ceremony in which Red Eagle, chief of the Sheep Eaters in her time, took his place at the hub in a miniature house of stone. The god of plenty and the goddess of beauty were stationed near by. To the west was a granite-built structure dedicated to the sun god, who was supposed to direct the services. Standing along the spokes were the worshipers, chanting their songs of praise.

The shrine, high in the mountains, seems to have had as little connection with the Sun Dance of the Plains as the Sheep Eaters had, culturally, with the Northern Shoshonis. They were Shoshokos in Shoshoni territory. They had neither the horse nor the buffalo which materially altered the Indian way of life. The horse made it possible for large groups to travel and live together. In their excursions into enemy territory they could band together under chieftains for political and economic expediency.

The Northern Shoshonis lived in skin lodges resembling those of the Plains, as they gradually grew away from grass lodges. Yet they would sometimes have to resort to them in emergencies. The first white explorers found the Lemhis in grass shelters because their skin lodges had been stolen by the Blackfeet.

Those who are familiar with the Indian country maintain that they can tell from a buffalo skull whether or not it was an Indian kill. If there is a hole in the forehead, the animal is said to have

[19] *Ibid.,* 9-10.

25

been slaughtered by an Indian. It was through this opening that he extracted the brains, which, with a substance from boiled deer bones, he used in the treatment of the skins. Buffalo and elk hides were stretched out on the ground and pegged down, while deer-skin was fastened to a frame and hung up for drying.

Preparation of a hide was an arduous task, sometimes requiring the efforts of more than one person. As the hide was patiently scraped smooth, it was repeatedly immersed in water, then wrung out. After the lengthy process was completed, it was ready for tanning, which was accomplished by arranging it tipi-fashion over a smoldering fire.[20] The Shoshonis produced three types of buck-skin—the white, the yellow, and the brown. In the preparation of the first type, the hair was removed by rolling the hide in ashes, wet with warm water, for several days before scraping it. The yellow tint was obtained by drying the skin over a smoldering fire of dry willows; the brown, over green willows.

The Northern bands accepted the Plains style of buckskin dress. Women wore their hair unbraided and parted in the middle, with the parting row sometimes painted red after the custom of the Crows. They used pine cones and porcupine quills tied to a stick for grooming their hair. Their buckskin clothing, like that of the Crows, was usually ornamented with elk teeth but not with beadwork until later, when they used a floral design which distinguished their work from the geometric patterns used by the Arapahoes.[21] Before the introduction of French beads, the Shoshonis made primitive beads of bones. The Arikaras maintained that they learned how to make beads from their Shoshoni prisoners. The moccasins, separate from the leggings, were of one-piece buckskin before the Arapahoes introduced the custom of using hard soles made from the tough neck of the deer.

Both men and women wore ornaments that struck their fancy. They were usually of polished bones, animal claws, teeth, and

[20] O. T. Mason, "Aboriginal Skin Dressing," *Report*, U.S. National Museum (1891), 572.

[21] Lowie, "The Northern Shoshone," *loc. cit.*, 175.

porcupine quills. In their charms, borrowed from the Plains, a certain pattern can be found to show the nature of their beliefs. Many of the objects were considered of value in keeping the ghosts or evil spirits away. Weasel skin and eagle feathers in the hair were considered protective, while the tail feathers of a flicker worn as a headgear had curative effects. To assure good health, a small bag or amulet containing pulverized pine needles was hung around the baby's neck.[22]

Before the introduction of popular woven fabrics and commercial blankets, the Northern Shoshonis wore robes fashioned from the hides of buffalo, antelope, deer, or Bighorn sheep, with the hair or wool often remaining on for ornamentation or warmth. The blanket was worn over the buckskin clothing. Sometimes the more elaborate robes were made from the skin of the wolf or the beaver. They were thrown loosely over the shoulders.

We think of the buffalo hunters as living exclusively upon meat, but they had a variety in their diet, ranging from roasted pine nuts and juniper berries to bread made from a mixture of sunflower seeds, lamb's-quarters, and serviceberries pounded together. Chokecherries, seeds and all, were pulverized, but they were not ordinarily mixed with meat when stored in rawhide bags for winter use.[23] In season other berries such as wild strawberries, currants, and snowberries were plentiful.

For vegetables, there were the young shoots of firewood, used as asparagus; yamps, or wild carrots, eaten raw or cooked; cow parsnips, used as rutabaga; thistle taproots, prepared as turnips; and balsam roots, used several ways. Salads of vegetables, fruits, or greens as well as wild mint tea, sage, and prairie flax flavoring for meats and vegetables, and licorice rootstalk chewing gum were usually available in season.[24]

Native plants also had medicinal uses known to the Indians. Wild geranium was thought to heal stomach ulcers; Canadian

[22] *Ibid.*, 229–30; also, Sarah Emilia Olden, *Shoshone Folk Lore*, 33–34.

[23] *Ibid.*, 203.

[24] Wayne F. Replogle, "Living from the Land," *Yellowstone's Bannock Indian Trails*, 51.

violet emulsion, lung infection; skullcap, mild heart trouble; while selfheal was supposed to sharpen the eyesight. Snowberry tea helped a mother recover rapidly from childbirth.

The Wind River Shoshonis, who have always denied eating either dog or roasted ants, did not scorn small game. They drove ground hogs from their holes with sharp barbed sticks. They trapped a species of squirrel and ran rabbits into hollow logs. Then they plugged the hole with sagebrush and fanned smoke into the opening. When the victim stopped squealing, they unplugged the hole and took it out. Hunters also snared rabbits by hanging a noose of tough bark from trees.[25]

Since a buffalo-hunting economy elevated men to a higher plane than women, the latter were held in far less esteem than their relatives in the Basin. They were more subject to abduction and even to mass rape. Polygamy was practiced, but no polyandry was recognized beyond certain sex privileges extended to brothers by husbands.

The Western Shoshonis, as we have indicated, required young girls to live in separate huts in their Coming-of-Age Ceremony, but women did not live apart at any time. The reverse was true of the Northern Shoshonis. The menstrual lodge was an established institution,[26] but there was no special Coming-of-Age Ceremony. Men feared that they might die if they stayed in the same lodge with a menstruating woman. They could speak to one from a distance, but they would not dare go near the lodge, which in some instances amounted to a form of club house where women could assemble and visit undisturbed by men. Among the Northern groups the lodge was extended to use during childbirth. Meateating, especially fish-eating, was a taboo during the time the women were secluded.

When a baby was born an older woman served as midwife, with the mother being required to stay in seclusion about thirty

[25] Robert H. Lowie, "Indians of the Plains," *Anthropological Handbook*, Vol. I (1954), 199; also, D. B. Shimkin, "Wind River Shoshone Ethnogeography," *Anthropological Records* (hereinafter cited as *A.R.*), Vol. V, No. 4 (1947), 276–78.
[26] *Ibid.*, 274.

days. Her husband did not come to see either his wife or child during that time for fear that he might bleed to death from the nose. After the birth of the child, a messenger would inform the father and direct him to go to the stream and wash his genitals while the baby was being washed. The messenger also told him when the navel cord fell off so that he could again eat meat. In case of twins, if some time elapsed between births, the older would be spirited away to die before the younger could see it. In this way, the younger would be assured of a long life.[27]

The Northern Shoshonis did not bury their dead. Instead they carefully washed and securely wrapped the bodies in clean blankets before depositing them in deep crevasses or other places where the wild animals could not reach them. Only the Green River Snakes could afford burial moccasins with beadwork on the soles. Pocatello, Chief Washakie's contemporary and leader of the Bannock Creek Shoshonis, was said to have been pushed down into a spring when he was buried. The pole that was used for the purpose was left to mark the grave. If true, this was contrary to the usual custom.

Warfare was a Plains Shoshoni way of life. The bow and arrow, the pogamoggan or war club, and the shield made from the tough skin of a buffalo bull were standard equipment before the introduction of the gun. The method of poisoning arrows consisted of dipping the point into a mixture of pulverized ants and the spleen of an animal, which had been allowed to decay in the direct rays of the sun. Rattlesnake venom was likewise used.

The coup stick, sometimes decorated with scalp locks, beads, and feathers, was of great significance in warfare, for it was considered more meritorious to touch a live enemy than to kill him. As in Plains warfare, more than one warrior could count coup on the same person, with the first winning the most honor.

The "Foolish One" among the Shoshonis was someone who felt bold enough to disregard caution and ride up to an enemy and strike him with his only weapons, a quirt and a buffalo scrotum rattle. If he managed to escape death, he was then acclaimed a

27 *Ibid.*, 269.

war chief for his valor. In spite of many casualties, there were always those who were reckless enough to take this chance.

Among some of the bands, the Foolish Ones worked in pairs. Besides appearing to be unusually brave, they were constantly up to mischief. While performing their clownish caper, they rode the same horse. They were supposed to be invulnerable except for some insignificant spot on their bodies. When one was killed during an act of bravery, his partner was automatically released from his commitment and allowed to return to normal.[28]

Following a battle, the scalps of the enemy were carried to the village where they were elevated on poles, around which the Scalp Dance was staged, with women taking an active part. Sometimes they alone participated. Other times the men were seated, and three or four women alternately approached and receded from them.

The Green River Snakes had a system of societies borrowed from the Plains.[29] These societies, the Yellow Noses and Logs, had special political and well as social functions. Whenever the tribe was on the march or taking part in a communal hunt, the duties of the two groups were routine.

Anyone who chose could be a member of either society, for there were no special requirements. As a rule, the friends and relatives of members preferred one or the other society. If they felt that they were not sufficiently brave they could withdraw from the Yellow Noses and become Logs. There was no stigma attached to membership in the latter society, for serving as the rear guards, they also performed necessary functions. Their tasks, however, were beneath the dignity of the warriors and not menial enough for the women, who were never spared the drudgery of camp life. Specifically, the Logs were supposed to protect the women and children and instruct them as to where they should place their lodges. Furthermore, they were expected to keep order at the end of the line and repair or replace broken lodgepoles.

[28] Robert H. Lowie, "Dances and Societies of the Plains Shoshone," *A.P.*, Vol. XI (1915), 813–16.

[29] The discussion of societies is based on Lowie's study, *ibid*.

When starting on a mission, a Yellow Nose was not supposed to stop even to pick up an article he might have dropped. His other distinctive trait was that he must use inverted speech. He was supposed to say, "Yes," when he meant, "No," and conversely. The headman of the society would even give his orders in the negative. This inverted or backward speech, confusing to a novice, was accepted as a general practice among the Yellow Noses.

Ordinarily the two societies held their functions separately, although they used the same Big Horse Dance. Upon rare occasions they would unite. The dance would take place during the afternoon and terminate before sundown. It was performed inside a skin lodge erected for the occasion, and the sides were raised so that the audience seated on the outside could see what was going on and help with the singing. To the rear of the lodge sat several musicians and singers, equipped with hand drums. Dancing was mandatory. When the Big Horse song was intoned, the headman went around with a quirt, making the members present get to their feet and dance. They were allowed to sit only during intermission.

There were no special costumes worn upon this occasion, but a dancer might carry a tomahawk or stick an eagle feather in his hair as a good-luck charm, or he might wear two decorated sticks of unequal length, tied to the sides of his head to improve his appearance. The style of wearing the hair indicated to which society he belonged. Following the dance, he was given a chance to boast of his accomplishments in battle before joining the rest of the tribe in a feast of wild carrot stew.

The war chief of the Shonshonis could take upon himself the authority to organize a hostile group whether or not this met with the approval of the chief, whose powers were nominal. Because of this, a chieftain might be held accountable for hostile action when the warriors were in reality going against his will. The chieftain, respected for his bravery, was spokesman for his people. His war bonnet, prepared by the elders amidst song and ceremony, was his emblem of honor, for the headband above the forehead showed two holes for each great exploit. As his office was not hereditary, he had to prove his valor before being chosen as leader of his people.

Legend has it that a Fort Hall Shoshoni and a Crow, coming face to face in a cave, gambled in sign language to see which would scalp the other. The winner—the Shoshoni—had the pleasure of "lifting" the scalp.[30] This may not have been mere legend because the Indians have always been inveterate gamblers, even the women. They were particularly fond of the hand game, of Basin origin.

Strenuous sports had special appeal, and they took part in athletics of all sorts.[31] Their game of football, played with about forty men and boys on a side, little resembles the game as we know it. Running as fast as they could, the players kicked two balls toward the goal, which might be several miles from the starting point. The balls, made of buckskin stuffed with rabbit hair, were not to be touched by the hands. Betting added to the excitement.

Children enjoyed war games and held imaginary buffalo hunts. As a rule the one who was "It" would bellow like a bull, while the other children tried to catch him. The kicking game consisted chiefly of kicking the opponents on the legs and bodies for exercise. Spectators as well as players enjoyed a fire-stick game in which burning sticks were thrown at night like javelins. Adults and children liked to juggle mud balls, run races, and pitch arrows at a target. They had a game similar to "cat's cradle," where they used a piece of string made from sagebrush bark.

Dreams and visions gave the Indians power to foretell future events. By going to the mountains to meditate, or through prayer, they might obtain in addition to great wisdom an object which was ever to be their "medicine." It was carried in an amulet or medicine bag for safekeeping, for if it were lost, it would cause great difficulty. The medicine bag, unknown to the Shoshokos,

[30] Julian H. Steward, "Northern and Gosiute Shoshoni," *A.R.*, Vol. VIII, No. 3 (1943), 367.

[31] Helen Overholt, "The Warm Valley Folk," Wyoming State Museum, 24, 36–80.

was usually suspended from a pole outside the house, and it was taken inside when it rained.

The Northern Shoshonis, like the Indians of the Plains, had a fear of the dark because they thought that they might encounter the spirit of a departed enemy. Moreover, they were afraid of encountering the elfin *NunumBi,* known to all Shoshonean people as having an evil disposition. The miniature men lurked in the dark recesses of the mountains and watched for a chance to shoot arrows of misfortune at any Shoshonis who displeased them. The Indians considered themselves safe from them at night only when they were in their tipis, which the pygmies could not enter. The Eastern Shoshonis still insist that these little people can be found in unexplored areas in the Wind River Mountains.

The Indians tell an unbelievable tale of a number of old warriors whose mummified bodies, hunched in their blankets, still sit in council in a cave in the Dinwoody area. Some of the Indians claim that they know of souvenirs that were taken from this cave. When the blankets were touched they seemed to disintegrate. Since no proof can actually be found, it will have to remain a legend of Dinwoody.

It has been impossible to establish a connection between this legend and an unmarked photograph of a mummified Indian in the Archives at the University of Wyoming. The mummy, well dressed and probably a chieftain, is of a much later period than the approximately 1,285-year-old "Joe," an attraction at the Whitney Gallery of Western Art at Cody, Wyoming. A radiocarbon dating was made from fragments of the mountain sheepskin clothing in which the latter was buried, thus indicating that Joe, who was discovered in a cave between Yellowstone Park and Cody in the fall of 1963, was a Sheep Eater.

The Shoshonis put great stock in their Buhagant, or prophet, who even had unusual powers for a medicine man. They thought that their medicine man could accomplish spectacular feats. He could die and go in spirit form to recover a soul which might have departed from this life. After he had restored the wandering soul

33

or personality to its proper place, between the eyes, both he and the dead could return to life.

In order to become endowed with spiritual power, it was necessary for a Wind River medicine man first to sleep near Bull Lake all night. This was an endurance test since the lake was supposed to contain the ghost of a white buffalo that had been chased into the depths many years before, when a hunter sought his hide for a robe. The winds on the icy waters create a roaring sound effect, resembling the bellow of a bull. The ordeal has caused more than one young Indian to give up his plan of becoming a medicine man, although it was one of the most elevated positions in the tribe.

Besides knowing how to mix potions, the medicine man could perform acts of magic. He could turn the "black stone" into an emblem of good fortune or into a hex. In the case of the latter, it could be hidden in an Indian lodge to cause untold misery. Until the stone was found and cast out, little could be done to change the luck of the person for whom it was intended.

Local legends have a purely geographical significance, since the Indian's active imagination is capable of supplying explanations for any unknown phenomenon. An example is the legend of Split Rock, which with variations is perhaps the best known. The enormous rock, on a hilltop near Sweetwater River, is cleft vertically from top to bottom, evidence enough to prove to the Shoshonis that it must have been the work of a superhuman power. In one version, a trapper jumped into a depression in the ground to avoid being crushed by a tumbling stone. Crouching, he expected it to roll on, but to his horror, it came to rest immediately above him.

Nighthawk responded to his call for help and summoned Lightning, who with one swift stroke severed the rock and freed the trapper. The paleface showed his ingratitude by devouring the first object in sight—the unfortunate Nighthawk. In this interesting legend, the Indian actually had a threefold purpose. He explained the mystery of the cleft rock; he showed his distrust in the white man; and he gave reason for the unusual sound the night hawk makes as it darts about at dusk in search of bugs. According to the Indians, Nighthawk is still showing his grief as well as his shock over the behavior of the treacherous trapper.

From the white man's point of view, many of the Northern Shoshoni myths are cruel and immoral.[32] Coyote, the trickster, is usually the leading character. He is thought to have married a girl who had been in the habit of killing and eating people who came to her lodge. Whether he won her by the blue stone he carried or by the thorns he plucked from a rosebush is obscure. The Northern Shoshonis accept the fact that Coyote and this unnamed sorceress were their ancestors. Many children were born to this union—in fact, all of the tribes in the world at one time. The new mother, who certainly had her hands full, washed them all but the Shoshonis whom she left in the care of Coyote. Had he washed the others, all Indians would have been Shoshoni.

Coyote, father of the tribe, is far from an admirable character. However, the Plains Shoshonis were grateful to him for some of the things he taught them. For example, he showed them that they should cry and cut off their hair when one of their number dies. True, Coyote's jealousy caused his beloved brother Wolf (father of the Bannocks) to be killed, but he managed to retrieve his forelock at a Scalp Dance, the first in the Indians' knowledge. Furthermore, he brought him back to life. Through his devotion to Wolf, he demonstrated the deep affection that one brother should have for another—the strongest tie recognized in family relationship.

In the process of stealing fire in the Fire Theft legend, Coyote was killed and skinned, but Jack Rabbit saved the day by coming from his hole and bringing him back to life by hitting him with his whistle. Through Coyote the Indians not only found life, but they also learned of death and the hereafter.

In the story of the Flood, Coyote begged the wild geese for some feathers so that he could join them. They flew to a mountaintop for council. There they decided to "wash the whole

[32] The myths briefly mentioned here are samples of those found in Lowie, "The Northern Shoshone," *loc. cit.*, 233–302. *See* Lowie's, "Shoshone Tales," *Journal of American Folk Lore* (hereinafter cited as *J. of A.F.–L.*), Vol. XXXVII (1924), and "Shoshone and Comanche Tales," *J. of A.F.–L.*, Vol. XXII (1909); also Rupert Weeks, *Pachee Goyo.*

world," drowning everyone but Coyote and his companions. When the water receded—"Someone shut it off; no one knows who"—the survivors stuck twigs along the mountain slopes to make trees, and they created the fish and wild animals so that the Indians might eat.

Cottontail is given credit for saving the scorching earth from destruction in another popular legend. Unable to knock it from its position with an arrow, he used his fire drill. When the sun fell, it caused his neck and legs to be burned yellow. Cutting the dead sun open at its chest, he took out its gall and made a new sun as well as a moon. He instructed the sun to remain at a respectful distance and the moon "to shine only a little."

There are those who maintain that the storytelling period of the Shoshonis is during the months of December, January, and February and that they refuse to tell their stories at any other time. It is useless to try to inveigle a narrator into telling his tale out of season, for it might displease Coyote.[33] The stories told during the "snowy moons" are the only means of preserving their legends. Old people, usually men, tell the tales. Good storytellers are in demand, but they have no exclusive right to any particular stories. The only rule is that when the tale is once started it must be told to the end.[34]

Having no recorded language except the personal vocabularies of the interpreters and agents and the religious translations of their missionaries, the Indians depend on the old men's tales for their tribal records. The center fire during the long winter months and the smoke, from a mixture of kinnikinnick and the white man's tobacco, contribute to an atmosphere for leisurely storytelling.

Coyote, according to legend, taught the Shoshonis the Naroya or Ghost Dance, later to figure in the messiah craze which swept the Plains.[35] The purpose of the dance originally was to drive out

---

[33] Tissaguina (One Chicken), also known as "Happy Jack" Guina, earned his reputation as a good storyteller on the Wind River Reservation by using pantomime and sound effects representing various animals.

[34] D. B. Shimkin, "Wind River Shoshone Literary Forms," *Journal,* Washington Academy of Sciences, Vol. XXXVII, No. 10 (October 15, 1947), 329.

[35] Lowie, "Dances and Societies of the Plains Shoshone," *loc. cit.,* 817.

the ghost or evil spirit that brought illness to someone in the tribe. Long ago it was danced at any season of the year; then it became a simple ceremony performed during the winter months at full moon or two or three nights thereafter.[36]

Anyone having illness in his family might give the dance, with both men and women taking part. The men formed a circle. Then the women would step between them, and they would interlock fingers. There were sometimes so many dancers that a larger concentric circle was necessary. In the daytime the dancing took place around a pine tree, at night around a fire. Originally it lasted five consecutive nights, with only the final performance taking place in daytime.

There is no instrumental accompaniment in the Ghost Dance, but the dancers sing as they shuffle their feet sidewise and move constantly to the left. The only special article of dress is the blanket with which they drive away the evil ghost at the conclusion. As they shake it, they pound their breasts. They have been known to go into messianic frenzies.

The Sun Dance is also a dance of prayer, for everything about it, from the utterances of the leader to the eagle bone whistles in the mouths of the dancers, is interpreted as prayerful. The dance is believed to have originated among the Algonquian Plains tribes, probably the Arapahoes or Cheyennes, as late as the first half of the eighteenth century.[37] It spread southward from the northern Plains through the Kiowas and eastward through the Dakotas who remained in contact with their tribesmen in Minnesota. There was a secondary center of diffusion among the Arapahoes, Blackfeet, and Dakotas. The Wind River Shoshonis' Sun Dance was apparently derived from the Kiowas through a Comanche serving as chief of their tribe. It was influenced largely by the Arapahoes and to a lesser degree by the Blackfeet or perhaps the Crows.

The Sun Dance reached its peak as a sacred tribal ceremony by the middle of the nineteenth century. It then stretched from

[36] Shimkin, "Wind River Shoshone Literary Forms," *loc. cit., 349.*

[37] D. B. Shimkin, "Wind River Shoshone Sun Dance," *Bulletin 151,* B.A.E., 404–17.

Alberta to Texas and from Wyoming to Minnesota. It had died out or had been suppressed among most of the Indians of the Great Plains by the end of the century.[38]

A new center, this time with a Christianized modification of the ceremony, was found at Wind River, from which a more acceptable version has spread since 1890 to other Shoshonis, as well as to the Utes and Bannocks. The Sun Dance again was carried eastward in 1941. The Crows, instructed by a Wind River and a Lemhi shaman, revived the ritual with zest.[39]

A prominent young Comanche, Yellow Hand (Ohamagwaya), who may have brought the dance to the Shoshonis, had become acquainted with the Kiowa Sun Dance as well as with Christian concepts through the Spaniards, by about 1790. He is believed to have joined the Green River Snakes some ten years later and to have become their leader about 1820. Furthermore, he is thought to have introduced to them the new Christianized version of the dance.

The leadership concentrated largely in Yellow Hand's lineal descendants following his death. Bazil (Pa:si) is said to have been his son (through adoption if not blood) and Andrew Bresil his grandson. Evidence as to time and place points to the fact that Yellow Hand may have been the same as Ama-qui-em, identified by a contemporary writer as leader of the Shoshonis about 1820.[40] He seems to have died sometime prior to 1842, as Iron Wristbands, his successor, then became chief.

The first Wind River Shoshoni Sun Dance probably took place in the Green River region, just when we do not know. One of the Indians claimed it was first held in the Big Horn Mountains. This is unlikely, for the country was too dangerous because of marauding Blackfeet in the early 1800's to permit the Shoshonis to tarry long enough to participate in an organized dance of several days' duration.

[38] Leslie Spier, "The Sun Dance of the Plains Indians," *A.P.*, Vol. XVI, No. 7 (1921) 459; Robert H. Lowie, "Sun Dance of the Shoshone, Ute, and Hidatsa," *A.P.* Vol. XVI, Pt. 5 (1919), 5.
[39] Shimkin, "Wind River Shoshone Sun Dance," *loc. cit.*, 403.
[40] *Ibid.*, 409-13.

In the 1930's, Lynn St. Clair, a Wind River Shoshoni, prepared a paper explaining in detail the history and significance of the Sun Dance, or the *Dagoo Winode* as he called it.[41] His purpose, he said, was to help his white friends understand the Indians' way of worship and their symbols. His information was gained from old-timers still living on the reservation.

St. Clair believed that the Sun Dance originally came to his people long before the birth of Christ. By this, he no doubt meant before Christianity was brought to them. He attributed the first version of the dance to Grass Hut, a Shoshoni, who had a dream in which he saw himself sitting on a hill. When a buffalo approached, he became so frightened that he started to run, but the animal said:

> "Do not get scared of me. Do not be afraid. I will not harm you. I only bring you a message." . . . The buffalo came up to him and said, "I am sent to you to tell you about a dance. You will call it *Dagoo Winode*. It is a dance in which you do not eat or drink for three days and nights. You only worship. If you pray for your people, the sick ones in this dance, and the ones who are brought to you, will get well." And he told him that from time to time the Sun Dance will change.

In the vision the buffalo showed him, Grass Hut saw a brush structure in which four men were dancing. As they approached the center pole, two old women, sitting on each side, held bunches of willows with which they brushed out the footprints the dancers made in the dust.

A second vision came to the Shoshonis many years later, according to St. Clair. This time it was brought by Great Eagle or Thunderbird to Yellow Wrist (Yellow Hand). James McAdams, a Wind River Shoshoni, who claimed to be the great-great-grandson of Yellow Hand, quoted him as saying:

[41] Lynn St. Clair, "The So-called Shoshone Sun Dance, *Dagoo Winode*" (hereinafter cited as "Sun Dance"), Western Archives, University of Wyoming Library. St. Clair was Sun Dance informant for Trenholm and Carley's *Wyoming Pageant* and Marie Montabé's *This is the Sun Dance*. Shiela Hart and Vida F. Carlson give an account from the tourists' point of view in their pamphlet, *We Saw the Sun Dance.*

"I am going to look for Power." He had a buffalo robe, and he painted this grey with white clay. Then in the evening he went to a butte (near Rawlins, Wyoming) and slept there overnight. There were no pictographs (objects through which visionary power was supposed to be transmitted) there, but a man came from heaven and told him: "You are looking for great power. I'll tell you what to do. Get a center, forked cottonwood tree and twelve poles; build them like a tipi. Get willows and lean them against the poles. The center pole will represent God; the twelve posts, God's friends.

"Get a two-year-old buffalo; face it west. Get an eagle, face it east. If anyone sick goes in, the buffalo will help him, with good power from the Sun. So will the eagle. Keep the buffalo's hide in shape with a bundle of willows. The cross-sticks will represent the cross.

"The first time we're going to dance, only five men will dance."[42]

A Sun Dance doll, considered the central source of supernatural power by the Kiowas, played a part in the early history of the Sun Dance at Wind River.[43] Quentin Quay, a Shoshoni leader, ascribed the doll to Yellow Hand, who he said painted it the first time. Because of this fact, it became a custom to paint a doll each year and leave it hanging on the center pole. This practice was discontinued about 1900.

The second version of the dance is substantially the same as we see today. The medicine pole in the center, originally symbolic of Thunderbird, now represents God. The twelve upright poles, which meant "something good," are no longer Thunderbird's tail feathers but the apostles, "God's friends."

[42] Shimkin, "Wind River Shoshone Sun Dance," *loc. cit.*, 409–74.
[43] Mildred P. Mayhall, *The Kiowas*, 131–33. The fetish representing the Sun Dance medicine was acquired by the Kiowas, probably from the Crows, about 1765. *Ibid.*, 9. For a picture of the Sun Dance doll, *see ibid.*, after page 222.

CHAPTER THREE

White Invaders

THE SHOSHONIS were as awed by the white man as the Piegans had been by the horse. The story is told that when one of the braves reported contact with an "ashen-faced" stranger, the chief of his band threatened to kill him, not only because of his deception but also because of the possibility of bad medicine in the unusual articles given to him by the unknown "barbarian." All that saved him was the fact that the tale was found to be true. There were such men as he had described, for they were sighted on the northwestern Plains. Apparently these were Canadians who preceded the American explorers in the region north of the Missouri River.

In 1743 the French explorer, Chevalier de la Vérendrye, and his party were told that the Snakes, the *"Gens des Serpent,"* had destroyed seventeen Indian camps near the Black Hills shortly before their arrival.[1] Knowledge of this caused the Frenchmen and the Bow Indians accompanying them to flee in terror when they found evidence of the abandoned camp east of the Big Horn Mountains in present northeastern Wyoming.

The Bow Indians, probably Piegans living in the Bow River area, were said to be the only Indians who, by dint of their bravery, were not afraid of the Snakes. Vérendrye identified them merely as *Gens de l'Arc.* Although the Comanches had moved southward about forty years before, the Shoshonis were still firmly contesting their rights to the Plains.

[1] Chevalier de la Vérendrye, "Journal of the Voyage Made by Chevalier de la Vérendrye with One of His Brothers in Search of the Western Sea," in "Margry Papers," *Oregon Historical Quarterly* (hereafter cited as *O.H.Q.*), Vol. XXVI, No. 2 (June, 1925), 116–27.

The first white men to penetrate their country were Meriwether Lewis and William Clark, whose famous expedition spent the winter of 1804–1805 at Fort Mandan, near Bismarck, North Dakota.[2] There they made preparation for their expedition to push westward in the spring. At the fort they listened to reports concerning the Shoshonis. The chief of the Big Bellies (Hidatsas) told them that his son was then out at war against the Snake Indians.

Later the young war chief gave the explorers a chart showing the way to the Missouri and informed them that he intended to go to war again in the spring. Realizing that this would be disastrous to their plans, they tried to dissuade him. They urged him to consider the nations that had been destroyed by war and to think seriously of the welfare of his people. They stressed the importance of peaceful relations to assure further trade between the tribes. Then they concluded by reminding him that if he went to war against defenseless people he would incur the displeasure of his "great father."

The young chief, convinced by their argument, replied that if his going to war against the Snakes would be displeasing to the white man, he would not go. Naïvely, he added that he had plenty of horses anyway.

By this time the explorers realized that the Shoshonis might be of the utmost importance in the accomplishment of their mission. If the route to the Pacific proved to be by land instead of by water, they would need horses for the completion of their journey. In order to assure friendly relations with the tribe, they not only hired the French-Canadian Toussaint Charbonneau as a guide and interpreter, but they also allowed him to take with him his wife, Sacajawea. She was between sixteen and eighteen years old at the time and was one of two Shoshoni wives he had purchased from the Hidatsas. Six weeks before the expedition left Fort Mandan she gave birth to a son, whom she carried in a cradleboard on her back to and from the Pacific.

[2] Lewis and Clark, *Journals*, I, 210. Except where otherwise noted, the discussion of the expedition is based on *ibid.*, I, 249, 257–58, 271, 272–75, 290; II, 321, 329–86; III, 3–44.

The party set out on April 7, 1805, with Sacajawea the only woman in the party. The interest in her and in her baby may be traced through the journals of the explorers and their employees, as both Lewis and Clark encouraged their men to keep records. They proceeded upstream to where the Missouri is fed by three major branches, the Madison, Jefferson, and Gallatin rivers. There at the Three Forks area (in Montana) they found country familiar to Sacajawea, who was able to pick the right fork leading to the encampment of her people. Lewis and some of the men set out by land while Sacajawea remained with Clark's contingent that stayed with the flotilla.

Lewis was the first to catch sight of a Shoshoni, on August 11, when he discovered, about two miles away, an Indian on horseback, coming down the plain toward him. Through his field glasses Lewis noted that the Indian's dress differed from any that he had seen, so he was satisfed that he was a member of the Shoshoni tribe. For arms, the Indian carried a bow and quiver of arrows, and he was riding an "elegant" horse. A small string, attached to the under jaw of his mount, served as a bridle.

Overjoyed by the sight, Lewis did not doubt but that the explorers would be able to obtain a friendly introduction to the Shoshoni Nation, if only he could get near enough to convince the brave that they were white men. He proceeded toward him at his usual pace. When the two were within a mile of each other, the explorer halted and signaled his friendship.

He held two corners of his robe. Then throwing it up into the air higher than his head, he brought it to the earth as if in the act of spreading it for the comfort of a guest. He did this three times, but it did not have the desired effect. At that moment two of his companions, George Drewyer and John Shields, came in sight. Their presence aroused the Indian's suspicion. Lewis hastened to take some trinkets from a sack. Unarmed, he advanced toward the brave, who sat watching until Lewis was about two hundred paces from him. Then he turned his horse and moved slowly away.

"Tab-ba-bone!" Lewis called repeatedly. The term, intended

for "white man," probably did not have an equivalent in the Sho-shoni language. The brave, looking over his shoulder, kept his eye on Drewyer and Shields, neither having "segacity enough to recollect the impropriety of advancing" when they saw him in parley with the Indian. Lewis signaled for the men to halt, but Shields kept on.

The Indian stopped again, then turned his horse about as if waiting. Lewis, repeating the word "Tab-ba-bone," held up the trinkets in his hands and pushed up his sleeve to prove that he was a white man. When he was within about one hundred paces, the brave suddenly turned his horse again. Then whipping it, he jumped the creek and disappeared in the willows.

Two days later Lewis and his party observed two women, a man, and some dogs that proved "les shye" than their masters. Lewis again went through the process of trying to contact them, but like the mounted brave, they fled. He did, however, find a well-used trail that eventually led to the Indian encampment. On the way he encountered two women—one old, one young—and a girl about twelve years of age. The young woman ran away, but the other two, finding themselves trapped, sat down and bowed their heads in anticipation of a death blow. Lewis took the old woman by the hand and helped her to her feet.

"Tab-ba-bone," he said to her and again raised his sleeve. He won the friendship of the two instantly with some beads, awls, pewter looking glasses, and a little paint. When the younger woman was induced to return, Lewis painted her cheeks with vermilion, which to the Shoshonis was an emblem of peace. Fol-lowing the road along the river, they were met by a party of about sixty mounted warriors, coming toward them at top speed.

When the women exultantly showed their gifts and told that the strangers were white men, the braves advanced and embraced Lewis affectionately in their manner "by putting their left arm over you(r) wright sholder clasping your back, while they apply their left cheek to yours and frequently vociforate the word, 'Ah-hi-e, ah-hi-e,' their way of showing their pleasure." Both parties then set out for the Indian camp.

The guests were seated on green boughs covered with antelope skins. One of the warriors, pulling up the grass in the center of the lodge, cleared a circular space about two feet in diameter. Then the chief, Cameahwait, produced his pipe and native tobacco, and the long ceremony began.

The Shoshonis removed their moccasins, and the chief instructed the white men to do the same. He then lit his pipe at the fire, kindled in the magic circle. Standing on the opposite side, he uttered a speech, several minutes in length. At the conclusion, he pointed his pipestem to the four cardinal points of the heavens, first beginning at the east.[3]

He then presented the pipe to Lewis, but when the white man reached his hand to receive it, the chief drew it back and repeated the same process three times. After that he pointed the stem first to the heavens, then to the center of the magic circle. After taking three puffs, he held the pipe until Lewis had taken as many puffs as he thought proper. The chief then held it to each of the white men, following which he gave it to his braves.

While Lewis explained the object of his journey, all the women and children in the camp collected to stare at the white men, the first they had seen. They watched them shyly as they brought dried cakes of serviceberries and chokecherries, all they had to offer. For breakfast, Lewis made a pudding of the berries by adding flour. The chief, seeing the powdery commodity for the first time, tasted it and asked if it were made from roots.

Cameahwait, "his fierce eyes and lank jaws grown meager for want of food," agreed to take his men and thirty horses to the forks of the Jefferson River, where they would meet Clark and transport supplies to the Indian camp. On the hour of departure the Indians refused to move. No amount of haranguing on the part of Cameahwait or persuasion on the part of the white man seemed to have any result.

Finally Lewis remarked that there were surely some among

---

[3] Robert Lowie's informant ("Notes on Shoshonean Ethnography," *A.P.*, Vol. XX, Pt. 3 (1924), 215) said that the pipe was never offered in the cardinal directions. Apparently this practice was discontinued before his time.

them who were brave enough to risk their lives, some who would go with him to the forks of the river where they would find canoes loaded with provisions. Cameahwait, whose bravery had been put to the test, jumped on his horse and again harangued his people. He vowed that even though he knew he would be killed, he would go to satisfy himself of the truth of the white man's statement. He hoped there were others who were not afraid to die. Only a half-dozen possessed such bravery. Several old women, fearing that the death of their warriors was imminent, began imploring the great spirit to watch over them.

Before the party had gone far, others began joining them until it looked as if all of the men and many of their women were in the cavalcade. They stayed with Lewis until they reached the spot where they expected to find Clark. He was not there but they encamped anyway. After some strategy Lewis convinced the Indians that Clark had been detained and that it would be necessary to send a group to meet him.

When Sacajawea caught sight of her people, she danced with joy. She sucked her fingers to show that they were of her tribe.[4] As the party neared the encampment, a young woman rushed out to greet her. She proved to be a girl who had been captured with Sacajawea but had made her escape.

While Charbonneau's Indian wife was greeting her people, Clark was being honored by Cameahwait, who invited him to be seated on a white robe. The chief then tied six small pearllike shells in his hair. This was a great honor, for the shells, having come from the seacoast, were highly prized. Sacajawea was in the process of interpreting when she recognized Cameahwait as her brother. Running to him, she threw her blanket over him in a gesture of affection and wept profusely.

Lewis paints a savage picture of the Indians when Drewyer killed a deer. Unaware of their habit of eating the whole of a butchered animal, he was bewildered and repulsed by the scene. He watched the "poor starved devils" with compassion as they

[4] Nicholas Biddle, "Lewis and Clark Journal," in Bernard De Voto, *The Journals of Lewis and Clark*, 202–203.

dismounted and ran "tumbling over each other like a parcel of famished dogs," each seizing and tearing away a part of the intestines which had been thrown away. Eating ravenously, with blood running from the corners of their mouths, they devoured the kidneys, the spleen, and the liver.

The Indians were rich only in horses, as they still had about seven hundred. They had suffered recent losses from the Blackfeet, who robbed them of all of their skin lodges except two. These they gave over to the comfort of their white guests.

We are indebted to Lewis for the first analysis of the Shoshoni Indians and their problems. He expressed his surprise at finding this band of one hundred warriors with three times that number of women and children. There were many of the latter, even though subsistence was difficult. The few very old persons, he observed, were not shown much tenderness or respect. He found the man to be the sole proprietor of his wives and daughters, with the right to barter or dispose of either as he saw fit. Though polygamy was a general practice, the wives, as a rule, were not sisters as was the case in many Indian tribes.

The father, who had unquestioned authority, often disposed of his infant daughters in marriage to men who were grown or to those who had sons for whom they desired wives. The compensation given in such cases consisted of horses or mules given at the time of contract, with the daughter remaining in her father's household until reaching maturity at the age of thirteen or fourteen.[5] Sacajawea had thus been disposed of in her childhood, and she had been captured before reaching puberty. Her Indian husband, more than twice her age, was living with the band. He claimed her, but inasmuch as she had a child by another man, he did not want her. Besides, he had two wives.

Lewis observed that the Shoshonis never corrected their children. They explained that whipping would cow and break the

[5] Just when this practice was discontinued we do not know, but later records make no reference to it except in eastern California. There the parents arranged their children's marriages, with the man's parents paying shell money to the girl's parents, the latter reciprocating with buckskins and food. Steward, "Basin-Plateau Groups," 83.

spirit of a boy, and he would never recover his independence of mind. The men compelled their women to perform all acts of drudgery, while they had little regard for their chastity. The husband, for a trifle, might "barter the companion of his bed" for a night or longer if he were adequately rewarded. On the other hand, husbands considered clandestine relations disgraceful.

In his efforts to determine whether these people had "the venereal," Lewis made inquiry through Charbonneau and his wife. They reported that it sometimes occurred, with death the usual result, as the Indians knew of no cure.[6] Lewis considered this strong proof that venereal diseases were native American disorders. Although these people suffered from smallpox, known to be imported, he felt that they were so detached from all communication with the white man that it was unlikely that venereal disorders had been introduced directly from the whites or indirectly through other Indian tribes.

Cameahwait had a grievance. He blamed the Spaniards in Santa Fe for furnishing guns to other tribes and denying them to the Shoshonis. The Spaniards had been putting them off by telling them that if they had guns they would kill themselves. Thus their neighbors would plunder them of their horses, run them down, and murder them without respect to age or sex. Cameahwait was forced to remain most of the time in the interior of the mountains, where his people suffered for want of food.

Lewis told him that the explorers had effected a peace with the Hidatsas and that when the white men finally returned to their homes toward the rising sun, they would come again to the Shoshonis with an abundance of guns and every other article necessary to their defense and comfort. The Indians would be able to supply themselves with these articles on reasonable terms in exchange for the skins of the beaver, otter, and ermine, so abundant in their country. The chief, expressing his great pleasure, said that he had long been anxious to see the white men who traded in guns and that they could depend on his friendship.

He assured them that the Indians would do whatever they

[6] Lowie, "Indians of the Plains," *loc. cit.*, 310.

wished of them. Cameahwait thus made it possible for the white men to pass through the Rocky Mountain country without incident. With the use of Shoshoni horses, Lewis and Clark were able to reach the headwaters of the Columbia River which ultimately led them to their goal, the Pacific Ocean.

When the homeward-bound expedition reached the Knife River (north of Bismarck, North Dakota), John Colter, one of the explorers, left the party to join two Illinois hunters going to the Yellowstone. We know little of what transpired, but it is possible that Colter may again have encountered the Lemhis if not the Green River Snakes, who at that time considered the Yellowstone the northern boundary of their territory.

The following spring, as he was returning to St. Louis, Colter met the ambitious trader Manuel Lisa, who had lost little time in following the trail of Lewis and Clark. When Lewis told the Shoshonis in council, in 1805, that the white men would return to them with "guns and every article necessary to their defense and comfort" he aroused false hopes, for Lisa was not so benevolent; he did not come to supply the Indians with "necessary articles on reasonable terms," but rather to profit by their unfathomed riches. Furthermore, he had no desire to supply the Indians with guns, for he had not been assured of their friendly attitude.

Lisa built a new trading post at the mouth of the Bighorn River, and in dead of winter sent Colter to invite the Shoshonis, Crows, and Cheyennes to trade.[7] Undaunted by the cold, Colter, by now a seasoned trapper, strapped a thirty-pound pack on his back and set out alone on snowshoes to find the Indians to the south and east. On his five-hundred-mile history-making excursion, he discovered the Crows in the upper end of Bighorn Valley. Enlisting some of them to guide him through the mountains, he went in search of the Shoshonis.

The direction he was traveling would indicate that he might have sought the Fort Hall Indians, about whom he had learned through the Lemhis or Crows. Although he reached as far as

[7] Paul C. Phillips, *The Fur Trade*, II, 260; also Hiram M. Chittenden, *History of the American Fur Trade*, I, 119.

Pierre's Hole (Idaho), it is doubtful that he found them. The Crows guiding him were attacked by a war party of Blackfeet, who may also have been in search of the Shoshonis. Colter was forced by circumstance to fight with his companions, who routed the Blackfeet. Apparently they carried with them a mental picture of the white man who contributed to their defeat and were determined to make him pay dearly someday for the part he had played in the battle. Colter, unmindful of what was in store for him, made the return journey though wounded in one leg.

His excursion into Shoshoni country was significant, for he was the first known white man to explore the Shoshone River, tributary of the Bighorn. He called it "Stinking River" because of the sulphurous odor in the area. The Boiling Springs he indicated south of Shoshone River may have been the area he described so graphically that it was called "Colter's Hell," a legendary name that has become almost synonymous with that of Yellowstone Park. It is now questioned whether he ever set foot in the park.[8] Because of the weather and his injury, it is considered doubtful that he would go on an exploring tour that would have taken him out of his way, though he may have reached the crest of the Absaroka Mountains, along the eastern border.

The Blackfeet had their opportunity for revenge when Colter, some time later, fell into their hands. Stripping him of his clothing, they forced him to make a run for his life over cactus-studded prairie. His friends, whom he told about his ordeal, discounted much of what he said because they thought the experience had caused him to become demented.

We know even less about the "lost trappers," Ezekiel Williams and his nineteen companions, who next came into the Big Horns. Setting out from Lisa's fort in 1808, they traveled southward through much of the Green River Snake country, but we have no knowledge of their contacts with the tribe or exactly where their wanderings took them. We do know that in their

[8] Merrill J. Mattes, "Behind the Legend of Colter's Hell," *Missouri Valley Historical Review* (1949), 251–82.

party there were two colorful characters, Edward Rose, later credited as being the first settler in the Big Horns, and the mulatto James Beckwourth, son of a slaveowner. Both found life among the Indians so agreeable to their nature that they chose to live with them.

Rose, for a time, was guide for the westward-bound Wilson Price Hunt party in 1811, but was dismissed before it crossed the Big Horns because he was found plotting with the Crows to steal his employer's horses. Hunt, a St. Louis businessman, led a land expedition of "Astorians," employees of the fur magnate John Jacob Astor. He planned to meet a party sent by sea to the mouth of the Columbia River, the place later known as Astoria, Oregon.

On his way westward across northern Wyoming, Hunt met three trappers (Hoback, Robinson, and Reznor), formerly employed by the fur trader Andrew Henry, who had established a trading post at the Three Forks. The Blackfeet had become so troublesome there that Henry and his trappers had attempted to rally the Northern Shoshonis and the Flatheads to their defense. Before this could be accomplished, the Blackfeet forced Henry to abandon his post.

The three fearless trappers (one wore a kerchief over his head at all times because he had lost his scalp to Indians when serving with Daniel Boone) had been among Henry's men when they had moved south across the Continental Divide to establish themselves on the north fork of the Snake River. Finding the country rich in beaver, they built their trading post, the first in the valley of the Columbia, likewise the first American trading post west of the Continental Divide. There Henry and his men found more friendly Indians—the Snakes—but the winter was so severe that they had to eat horseflesh to survive. In the spring they separated into groups, each going its way.

Hunt's Astorians are believed to have followed a well-beaten Indian trail through the general area of Dubois, Wyoming, as they made their way westward. By means of this, they gained access to the mountains. From there they looked out across the vast Shoshoni country toward three glistening peaks which they believed to be landmarks denoting the source of the Columbia. Unaware that the snow-covered peaks to the south were the Tetons, they called them "Pilot Knobs."

Most of the Green River Snakes did not know that the white explorers had been so near, unless the small band encountered in the Big Horns reported their presence. Not long afterwards stories may have been passed around the council fires about the five white trappers who became lost from the Hunt party. The Snakes, who found them in a starving condition, gave them venison and taught them how to prepare camass so that it would not poison them. Hunt, little realizing that horse-stealing was an act of valor and not a disgrace, left his horses in the care of some Shoshonis when he and his party made a trip down the Snake. On their return, they found the Indians and the horses gone.

Robert Stuart and his small eastbound band of Astorians came through the Shoshoni country the following year.[9] He had been with the Astorians who had taken the water route to Oregon. Before encountering the Shoshonis, the party came across four hunters who reported trapping on Bear River. There they met a "southern band of Snakes," probably Digger Indians.

A short time afterwards the Crows stole the horses belonging to the Astorians, who were afoot when they came upon a village of 40 tipis and 130 Snakes. The Indians were temporarily poor, for they had also been robbed by the Crows, who managed to escape with most of their horses as well as some of their women. Nevertheless, they parted with their last horse in exchange for a pistol, a knife, a tin cup, two awls, and other small trinkets. With the Shoshoni horse carrying their meager possessions, Stuart and his men moved eastward to the Sweetwater and thence to the Platte, along a route which in years to come was to be known as the Oregon Trail. Stuart may have been the first to go through South Pass, which, during the migration period, was to serve as "the gateway to the West."

[9] Washington Irving, *Astoria*, 376; also Howard R. Driggs, *Westward America*, 13.

Thomas James, a member of the Henry party, and his men had reason to think well of the Snakes.[10] When they became snow-blind in the Three Forks area, thirty friendly members of the tribe came among them but did not harm them. In their desperation the trappers ate three dogs and two horses before recovering enough sight to enable them to hunt.

During the time the trappers and traders were filtering into the country from the north and east, plans were in the making to invade the fur scene from the west. In 1812, the year the North West Company took over Astoria, John Reed, who had been a member of Hunt's overland party, brought four Canadians and three Americans with him to the Snake River. There he established a base for trade with the Shoshonis, Bannocks, and other near-by tribes. Pierre Dorion, guide for the expedition, brought along his Sioux wife and three children. The party was joined by Hoback, Reznor, and Robinson after it had reached the Snake.

In January, 1814, the trading base was attacked by Indians and all of the men were killed. The "Dorion woman," one of the heroines of the West, escaped and finally made her way back to Walla Walla, Washington, where she reported that the deed had been committed by "bad Snakes, called the Dogrib Tribe," later identified as Bannocks.

The first Snake River Expedition of the North West Company, which left Fort Nez Percé (Fort Walla Walla) in the fall of 1818, was led by the fearless Scot, Donald McKenzie. His hope was to assure peace between the tribes along the Columbia River and its tributaries so that his company might exploit the fur resources of the area.

At one time when McKenzie had only three helpers with him, a suspicious-looking party of Bannocks appeared in camp.[11] After accepting gifts, they became so bold as to attempt to get behind the breastworks that had been built for the purpose of defense. McKenzie, springing forward, placed a keg of gunpowder between himself and the Indians. Lighting a match, he dared them

---

[10] Thomas James, *Three Years among the Indians and Mexicans*, 51.
[11] Alexander Ross, *The Fur Hunters of the Far West*, I, 219, 249–55.

to come near. His bravery, coupled with the fact that about two hundred Flatheads had come in sight, caused the visitors to leave.

Alexander Ross, chronicler for the party, identified the Mountain Snakes and Dogribs as Bannocks. Also, he was the first to try to distinguish between the various bands of Snake Indians. He called the first group the "Sherry-dikas, or Dog-Eaters." These were the "true" Shoshonis or the Indians of the Eastern band. In the second group were the "Rar-are-ree-kas, or Fish-eaters," the Lemhis, also known as Salmon Eaters. The third group, the "Ban-at-tees, or robbers," were mixed bands of Shoshonis and Bannocks.

We find the fractious Bannocks at this early date in disrepute. When McKenzie gathered the Snakes for a treaty council, Pee-eye-em, a chief of the Sherry-dikas, complained of their deviltry, at the same time admitting his inability to cope with them. He vowed that it would be just as easy "to hunt out and kill all the foxes in the country as to hunt out and punish every Ban-at-tee that does mischief."

Ama-qui-em, another chief of the Sherry-dikas, went even further by accusing them of the murder of the Reed party. According to Ross, after the Sherry-dikas left the conference, the Bannocks again started plaguing the trappers.

When Ross called the Eastern Shoshonis "Dog-Eaters," he was unaware that he was insulting them. The term is one that they have always used in derision for their traditional enemies, the Arapahoes. The Shoshonis pride themselves on the fact that they have never been known to eat dog meat.

Ross was impressed by their "primeval simplicity," which they had maintained in their inland habitat, seldom visited by the whites. At the same time, he recognized their precarious position in relation to other tribes. For nearly a century their enemies had been receiving weapons of war from the white man, to the "almost ruin of the poor and defenseless Snakes, who have had to defend their country and protect themselves with the simple bow and arrow, against the destructive missiles of their numerous enemies." He spoke of the Shoshoni country as a theater of war, in which the Snakes had been stigmatized as unskilled in the art of warfare. Then he made a significant deduction:

But arm the Shoshones, and put them upon an equal footing with their adversaries, and I will venture to say, from what I have seen of them, that few Indians surpass them in boldness or moral courage; my only wonder is that they have been able, under so many discouraging circumstances, to exist as a nation, and preserve their freedom and independence so long.

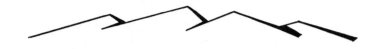

CHAPTER FOUR

Rendezvous

I N THE FALL AND WINTER OF 1823 the first organized trapping took place in the Wind River and Bighorn valleys by employees of the Ashley-Henry fur-trading company. William H. Ashley, a shrewd politician and businessman of St. Louis, was new to the West; but his partner, Andrew Henry, was the persevering fur man who carried the business to the Pacific side of the Rockies. The Ashley-Henry partnership employed some of the ablest mountain men ever to penetrate the rich beaver lands of the Rockies. Among them were James Bridger, Étienne Provost, Jedediah Smith, David E. Jackson, Thomas Fitzpatrick, William Sublette, James Clyman, and Edward Rose. The roster is impressive, for each man distinguished himself in the early history of the West.

The Ashley and Henry men worked in separate groups. One group, eleven in number if Clyman remembered correctly, set out from Fort Kiowa on the Missouri early in the fall.[1] Working the Wind River Valley, they may have reached the shadows of Fremont Peak before going down the Bighorn to winter with the Crows. There they were well treated by Rose's friends, who are thought to have directed them to a pass through which they could gain access to the rich beaver country beyond. This was the famous South Pass, leading to Green River, the Sisk-ke-dee (Prairie Hen), later to be the scene of approximately half of the annual rendezvous, all of which took place in lands claimed by the Shoshonis. There was no Sacajawea to pave the way toward an understanding between the Green River Snakes and the first trappers; there was no Cameahwait to serve as a friendly host.

[1] James Clyman, *James Clyman, American Frontiersman, 1792–1881*, 37.

Many of the Snakes, seeing the white men for the first time, viewed them in silent wonder. Unquestionably they had by now learned of the paleface explorers, but it was their first encounter with them deep in their homeland. Who were these *tibos* (barbarians) who had suddenly come into their midst to take possession of their streams as if they belonged to them? The Indians, as their myths indicate, had an attachment for all wildlife. When they made a kill it was from necessity, and they utilized every part of the carcass.

Although some authorities argue that the Indians were not the first conservationists, it is doubtful that they were guilty of wanton slaughter until after the fur traders had established a market for pelts and hides.[2] The destructive white man, with his steel traps and his guns, came killing and skinning not only the beaver but all other fur-bearing animals in his path. The system was so contrary to the Indian way of life, it is reasonable to assume that the redskins were not in sympathy with the first invaders.

The trappers, on the other hand, had reason to be displeased with the Indians, for after they had accepted food and hospitality, they disappeared with all of the trappers' horses. Clyman referred to them as "Digger Shoshone," a disrespectful name he had probably learned from the Crows. The white men, unable to locate the stolen animals, set their traps along the Green, where they worked until late spring. Then caching their furs and everything they were unable to carry, they started toward the Sweetwater.

Along the way they came upon a half-dozen braves mounted on several of their horses. The trappers forced the Indians at gun point to lead them to their camp, where they bluffed them into turning over all of the horses but one. Seizing the nearest Indian, the trappers tied him and threatened to shoot him if he did not produce the remaining horse. The frightened redskin hastened to carry out their orders. Galloping back to their cache, the trappers found their furs and other valuables and returned triumphantly to the Sweetwater. In this, their first encounter with the

[2] For George E. Hyde's opinion of Indians as conservationists, see Chapter 15 in this volume.

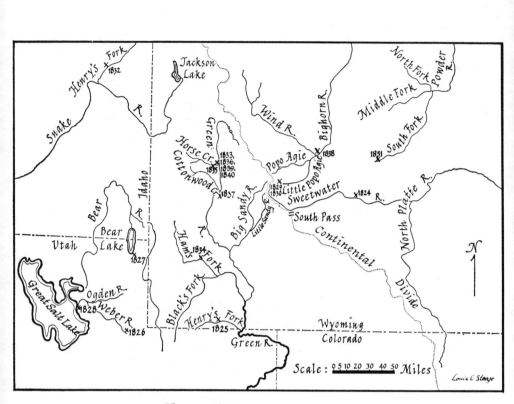

TRAPPERS' RENDEZVOUS, 1824–40

Snakes, they could pride themselves on the fact that they were the victors.

Breaking up into small hunting expeditions, they set out in different directions—one going to the upper Snake country, where they found the Canadian Hudson's Bay Company operating. Another crossed the Uinta Range to Weber River. When the latter reached Bear River, two members of the party had an argument concerning its course. Jim Bridger was selected to follow the stream and determine who was right. His journey took him to where the river passes through the mountains, and there he discovered the Great Salt Lake. After tasting the water and finding that it contained salt, he returned to the party to make his report.

The salt water caused the trappers to wonder if it might be an arm of the Pacific Ocean. The following spring, four men circled the lake in an attempt to discover the other streams emptying into it.

These trappers had few brushes with the Indians in the Green River area. Consequently, they left meager records. We find that an old Shoshoni Indian was credited with giving valuable advice while acting as guide for one of the trapping expeditions and that upon several occasions the Indians were mentioned as friendly in manner.[3]

The trappers characterized the Snakes as a "cowardly lot, easily routed by a show of numbers."[4] Actually the Indian with his bow and arrow was no match for the white man with a gun. The Snakes' only way of obtaining modern weapons was through theft or trade. At this early date they had been given little opportunity for either.

Provost had a disastrous encounter with an evil-minded Shoshoni chief, Mauvais Gauche,[5] on the shore of Utah Lake.[6] He had fallen in with a band of Snake Indians and had been invited to smoke the pipe. The treacherous chief said that it was contrary to his medicine to have anything of a metallic nature near by while a council was in progress, so he asked the white men to remove their weapons and place them outside the council ring.[7]

Provost, believing that it was better to humor the whims of the Indians than to cross them, did as directed. After placing their guns to one side, the trappers sat down in the circle to smoke. Suddenly at a prearranged signal the Indians seized knives and tomahawks, concealed under their clothing, and attacked the unsuspecting trappers, most of whom were killed. Provost, a man of great power, managed to fight his way out and, with three or

---

[3] Harrison C. Dale, *The Ashley-Smith Explorations*, 155.
[4] *Ibid.*, 110.
[5] Mauvais Gauche should not be confused with the Assiniboin chief Gauche for whom Gauche's Hole (Goshen Hole) was named in southeastern Wyoming.
[6] J. Cecil Alter, *James Bridger*, 45.
[7] Chittenden, *American Fur Trade*, I, 276.

four others, escaped. This unwarranted attack made a deep impression upon the mountain men, who vowed vengeance upon the wily chief, but he eluded their search.

In their wanderings, Jedediah Smith and his men obtained a large number of beavers on the tributaries of Green and Snake rivers. Late in the fall of 1824 they encountered Pierre, an old Iroquois, who with his party had been detached from the Hudson's Bay Company in June. "Old Pierre" was a leader of a group of Iroquois trappers hired from the neighborhood of Montreal. They were brought into the Oregon country by the Canadian trappers because of their exceptional hunting ability. Smith found the Indians destitute, for they had been overtaken by a war party of Snakes shortly before the white men arrived. They told him of their misfortune, in which they had lost their traps and guns as well as a large quantity of their furs.

They still had 900 pelts left. According to Pierre, Smith drove a shrewd bargain in which he relieved them of all of their furs practically in exchange for safe conveyance to the vicinity of Pierre's Hole, where they were supposed to meet Alexander Ross.[8] The details of the transaction are not certain, but it is known that Ross looked upon the American as a spy, and he felt that Smith might have entered into secret agreement with his men.[9]

Fearing that he and his trappers might suffer the same treatment as had the Iroquois at the hands of the Snakes, Smith accompanied the Ross party northward to Flathead House, in the vicinity of Thompson Falls (Montana). Here he obtained valuable information from Ross and Peter Skene Ogden, of the Hudson's Bay Company. He discovered that the British, employing some 60 trappers in the district claimed by the Shoshonis, had, within the last four years, taken out 80,000 beaver hides, weighing approximately 160,000 pounds.

William Ashley, informally called the "general" of the fur

---

[8] Dale, *Explorations*, 92–93. Pierre's Hole (Idaho) is on the opposite side of the mountains from the better known Jackson's Hole, Wyoming.

[9] Alexander Ross, "Journal of the Snake River Expedition, 1824," *O.H.Q.*, Vol. XLV (December, 1913), 385.

trade, gave an evaluation of the riches carried from the Shoshoni country by the white men. He said, "You can form some idea of the quantity of beaver that country once possessed, when I tell you that some of our hunters had taken upwards of one hundred in the last spring hunt out of streams which had been trapped, as I am informed, every season for the last four years. It appears from Mr. Smith's account that there is no scarcity of buffalo as he penetrated the country."[10]

This last statement of Ashley's is prophetic. The farsighted businessman was aware that at the feverish rate the trappers were working, the beaver would one day be exterminated, and the white man would have to look to the buffalo. Actually this meant cutting off the Indians' means of subsistence. The Shoshonis were not materially affected by the loss of the beaver, but a wholesale slaughter of the buffalo would seal their doom.

In spite of Provost's experiences with the Snakes, the Ashley-Henry trappers found them preferable to the Arikaras and the Blackfeet. This may have been one reason for their abandoning the Missouri River region—this coupled with the fact that in the fresh territory they no longer had to contend with a formidable rival, the Missouri Fur Company.

The vast Shoshoni area was not conducive to the establishment of trading posts; therefore, Ashley decided upon a plan whereby the trappers could comb the streams for peltries and bring them to a designated place once a year for transportation to St. Louis. A plan of like nature had been devised by the British companies in their Snake River expeditions on the headwaters of the Columbia, and the Shoshonis had held their grand encampment at three-year intervals. Yet Ashley originated the term "rendezvous" and perfected the plan.

An experimental gathering (not considered one of the regular rendezvous) was held at Three Crossings on the Sweetwater in 1824. It was a mild affair in comparison to those that were to follow, as there was no drinking, and there were no Indians. The trappers brought in a large shipment of furs, which were packed

[10] Dale, *Explorations*, 157–58.

and transported to St. Louis. Beckwourth described this event as lasting a week, during which the trappers spent their time "very pleasantly hunting, fishing, target-shooting, foot-racing and sundry other exercises."[11]

Now that the rendezvous had proved a success, a new route would be needed to shorten the distance between St. Louis, the fur capital, and the Shoshoni country, an important source of its wealth. Thomas Fitzpatrick, after returning to the mountains by way of the North Platte, reported a land route to be feasible. Theretofore, the navigable Missouri had been considered the only practical route.

Ashley was determined to follow the North Platte on his return to the mountains, for it was late in the season (November) and he wished to reach his destination with all possible speed. In 1824–25 he plotted the section of the Central Overland Route from St. Louis to Salt Lake, and from there Jedediah S. Smith marked out both a southern and a central route to the coast.[12] A great highway cutting ruthlessly through the Shoshoni country was no longer a possibility. It was a reality and the forerunner of dark days for the Indians.

Peter Skene Ogden, leader of the British Snake River Brigade, was no doubt the first white man to penetrate the Basin area, in 1825. He supposedly discovered the Humboldt and named it for his Shoshonean wife, Mary, sometimes called "The Sacajawea of Nevada."[13] Since the Humboldt country had so little to offer, Ogden returned to the beaver-rich land between Snake and Green rivers, thus bringing him into conflict with the Americans.

The mountain man Joe Meek tells of a time just prior to the first official rendezvous when Fitzpatrick, camping in the neighborhood of Ogden's company, opened a keg of whisky and obtained from the inebriated trappers the whole product of their year's hunt.[14] While feeling was running high, a stampede oc-

[11] T. D. Bonner, ed., *Life and Adventures of James P. Beckwourth*, 74.
[12] Dale, *Explorations*, 116, 156–57.
[13] Effie Mona Mack, *Nevada, a History of the State from the Earliest Times through the Civil War*, 41.
[14] Frances F. Victor, *The River of the West*, 95–97.

curred among the horses in Ogden's camp, and several animals ran into the camp of the rival company. Among them was a horse belonging to Ogden's wife Mary. It had escaped with Ogden's baby still hanging to the saddle. The mother fearlessly entered Fitzpatrick's camp and caught the bridle. There she espied one of her husband's pack horses, loaded with beaver skins.

The men were exulting over their windfall, as the furs had become theirs by the law of possession. Mounting her horse, the Indian woman seized the halter of the pack animal and led it from camp. The men were dumbfounded. While the baser ones wanted to shoot her, the rest cheered her for her bravery. "Let her go!" they shouted in admiration as she galloped away with her baby and her pack horse.

At the first official rendezvous (1825), 191 fur packs, each worth $1,000, were brought in by the trappers from the country belonging to the Shoshonis and Bannocks. Included in that year's shipment was a valuable cache of furs taken from the Hudson's Bay Company in such a mysterious manner that not even Ashley attempted to account for them.[15] While he seems not to have been directly implicated in the transaction, he was undoubtedly aware of the source of his wealth.

Some authorities believe that Ogden's party fell in with Ashley's and that twenty-nine men defected, taking with them their furs, which they disposed of for a mere trifle of their worth. Another theory is that Ashley's men stumbled upon the cache, and since they thought that the British had no right in the country, they proceeded to help themselves.

During a ten-month period the Snakes were reported to have killed thirteen whites besides stealing a large number of traps. In exasperation, Ogden stated: "The Americans swear to make an example of them; I do hope from my soul they may."[16] Without any specific reason for doing so, he classified these Indians as "Plains Snakes" and "Lower Snakes." He attributed one thou-

[15] Chittenden, *American Fur Trade*, I, 277.
[16] "The Peter Skene Ogden Journal, Snake Expedition, 1825–1826," *O.H.Q.*, Vol. XI, No. 4 (December, 1910), 357–62.

sand warriors to the former and fifteen hundred to the latter.[17] In view of the comparatively small number of trappers, the Snakes seem not to have been too troublesome.

During the winter of 1825–26, near the mouth of Weber River, a marauding band of Bannocks stole the horses belonging to a detachment of Ashley's men. When the loss was discovered, forty trappers were selected to follow on foot. Locating the Indian village, the trappers split forces—one group under the command of Fitzpatrick charging the camp, with the other under Bridger stampeding the horses. The trappers, without losing a man, not only recovered the ones they had lost—about 350—but they returned to their base with 40 Indian ponies.

When Ashley left with his cargo for St. Louis, he again followed the watercourse. After crossing South Pass, he went through Wind River Valley until he came to the canyon, where he constructed bullboats to descend the river. The stream, flowing north, enters the canyon as Wind River and comes out as the Bighorn. At the mouth of the Bighorn he found General Henry Atkinson with a large military force, which assured a safe convoy for the wealth of furs he carried from the Shoshoni country. Ashley made one last trip to the mountains, in March, 1826. Following the course of the Platte, he gained further distinction by taking over South Pass the first wheeled vehicle, a cannon on wheels. This was a more ominous threat to the defenseless Snakes than the first guns had been.

They had begun to acquire firearms by this time. Beckwourth recounted an incident in which they tried to talk him out of his gun while he and some Crow companions were trading for horses.[18] He told them that he would not sell it to anyone except his own people (the Crows). Declaring that "things were bad in camp," the Shoshonis told him to leave. Some Utes were apparently there to make trouble. The Crows, aware of this, sprang upon their horses and left. Soon they discovered that the Snakes had not sold them their swiftest horses as they had claimed, for

---

[17] *Ibid.,* 365.　　　　[18] Bonner, *Beckwourth,* 197–98.

they were overtaken and six of their "noble young [Crow] warriors" were killed and scalped.

Beckwourth, or Red Arm as the Crows knew him, called for five hundred warriors to "wipe out the stain" and chastise the Snakes for their duplicity. In the ensuing battle the Crows, according to Beckwourth, lifted one hundred scalps and captured a large number of guns and ammunition. The capture of the firearms seems unlikely, however, as most authorities maintain that the Shoshonis were without the necessary guns to defend themselves. Beckwourth claimed that this defeat brought them to their senses, and they immediately came to the Crow village to sue for peace.

While the trappers were in winter quarters near Salt Lake, early in 1826, a large band of Snakes moved in on them. There were so many Indians that the encampment entirely surrounded the trappers. This had long been a favorite camp-site of the Snakes, who saw no reason for changing their plans even though the white men had reached there first.

After pitching their tipis, they built a large lodge for their religious ceremonies. This medicine lodge, according to Beckwourth, was "the tabernacle of the wilderness, the habitation of the Great Spirit, the sacred ark of their faith." When it was completed the Buhagant began his operations. Beckwourth explained him as resembling a prophet in the Old Testament. He was a high priest or dreamer, and his dreams or prophecies were considered sacred. If they failed to materialize, the fault was not with the medicine man but with the Indian who had disregarded some of his instructions. On the other hand, if the dreams proved true, the Indians' confidence in him was boundless.

During the weeks the trappers spent with the Snakes, they had an excellent opportunity to study their character, but Beckwourth was the only one who recorded his observations. He said that the Indians often invited the trappers into their sacred lodge to witness their religious ceremonies and listen to their prophecies. The oracle at the time was Ohamagwaya (Yellow Hand) who was serving as Shoshoni chief. One evening he delivered the following prophecy:[19]

"I can see white people on Big Shell (Platte River); I see them boring a hole in a red bucket; I see them drawing out medicine water (whisky); I see them fighting each other; but Fate (Sublette) has gone down on the other side of the river; he does not see them. He has gone to the white lodges. Where are you going?" [This sudden question had nothing to do with the first prophecy, but it served to usher in a second.]

"We are going (Fitzpatrick told him) to trap on Bear Head and the other small streams in the country of the Blackfeet."

"No," said Ohamagwaya, "you will go to Sheep Mountain; there you will find the snow so deep that you cannot pass. You will then go down Port Neif to Snake River. If you are fortunate you will discover the Black Feet before they see you, and you will beat them. If they discover you first, they will rub you all out—kill you all. Bad Hand Fitzpatrick,[20] I tell you there is blood in your path this grass. If you beat the Black Feet, you will retrace your steps and go to Bear River, whose water you will follow until you come to Sage River. There you will meet two men who will give you news."

The trappers spent the weeks comfortably, and upon the opening of spring, whites and Indians alike moved to Cache Valley (Utah), where they left the seventy-five packs of furs then in their possession. While they were digging in an embankment, the earth caved in, killing two Canadians who were with the party. The Indians claimed the privilege of burying them. Beckwourth said that the ceremony consisted of "hoisting them up in trees."[21] He maintained that this was the method used "by most, if not all of the Rocky Mountain tribes" in disposing of their dead.

The body is securely wrapped in blankets and robes, fastened with thongs, in which are inclosed the war implements, pipes, and tobacco of the deceased. If he had been a warrior, his war-horse

[19] *Ibid.*, 94–96.
[20] The Indians called Fitzpatrick Bad Hand, Broken Hand, or Three Fingers because of an injury that resulted when a gun burst in his hand. LeRoy R. Hafen and W. J. Ghent, *Broken Hand, the Life Story of Thomas Fitzpatrick*, 71.
[21] Bonner, *Beckwourth*, 96–97.

IN THIS CAVALCADE at the Green River rendezvous Chief Ma-wo-ma
leads the Shoshonis in one of the grand parades for which they were
famous. From an oil painting by Alfred Jacob Miller.

Courtesy Oklahoma Historical Society

SHOSHONI ENCAMPMENT IN THE ROCKIES

Courtesy Bureau of American Ethnology

SHEEP EATER FAMILY encamped near the head of Medicine Lodge
Creek, Idaho. From a photograph by W. H. Jackson, 1871.

Courtesy Bureau of American Ethnology

BASIN INDIAN HOME NEAR DAYTON, NEVADA

Courtesy Nevada Historical Society

WESTERN SHOSHONI BASKET MAKERS

Courtesy Henry E. Huntington Library and Art Gallery

WASHAKIE, great chief of the Shoshonis, from an oil painting by
Henry H. Cross.

Courtesy Thomas Gilcrease Institute of American History and Art

John Enos, guide for Bonneville and Frémont,
from a photograph taken at Fort Washakie,
about 1900.

Courtesy J. K. Moore, Jr.

LITTLE SOLDIER, Weber Ute (Shoshoni) chief, copied by
A. Z. Shindler, Washington, D.C., in 1869.

Courtesy Bureau of American Ethnology

is killed and buried, together with the saddle and other implements, at the foot of the same tree.

The story sounds plausible except the burial by hoisting the bodies up in trees. This was a custom followed by most of the Plains Indians, but the Shoshonis never were known to have adopted it. Beckwourth seems to have attributed to them the manner of burial that he found among the Crows.

He acquired the widow of one of the Canadians as a "slave," whom he described as of light complexion for an Indian, "smart, trim and active, and never tired in her efforts to please" him. He admitted that the experience was new as he had not had a servant before. We can imagine how he, who had been born in slavery (of a Negro mother and a white landowner father), must have relished the idea of turning the tables. He found his Indian wife of great service in keeping his clothes in repair, making his bed, and caring for his weapons. To the mulatto she was but a passing fancy, although he did renew his contract for the coming year with the privilege of taking his "servant" with him. We assume that he remained with her for the duration of the contract.

Early accounts of the Shoshonis are so meager in diaries and memoirs that from time to time they seem to fade from sight. The chroniclers either fail to say enough to shed much light upon their history, or they leave it to the imaginative Beckwourth to supply the details, which he usually exaggerated. He gives us another bit of information which may not have been entirely fabricated. The incident occurred before the trappers left Cache Valley:

> One of our men was out hunting, and coming across an antelope, as he supposed, fired at the animal's head and killed it. On going to cut the animal's throat, to his surprise he found he had killed one of the Snake Indians, who had put on this disguise to decoy the antelope near him. This was an accident we deeply lamented, as the Snakes were very friendly towards us.
>
> Before the Indians discovered the accident, we held a council, and resolved to make a precipitate retreat, as we felt very distrustful of the consequences. While we were preparing to start, the chief came among us and was greatly surprised at our sudden de-

parture, especially as we had given him no previous notice. We excused ourselves by saying we were going to engage in hunting and trapping. He then asked what ailed us, saying we all looked terrified, and wished to know what had happened. Fitzpatrick at length told him what had taken place, and how it came to pass.

"Oh," said the chief, "if that is what you are alarmed at, take off your packs and stay. The Indian was a fool to use a decoy when he knew the antelope came into the sage every day, and that the white men shoot all they see."

He then made a speech to his warriors, telling them what had happened, and ordered some of his men to bring in the dead Indian. Then turning to us, he said, "You and the Snakes are brothers; we are all friends; we cannot at all times guard against accidents. You lost two of your warriors in the bank; the Snakes have lost one. Give me some red cloth to wrap up the body. We will bury the fallen brave."

We gave the chief a scarlet blanket as he had desired, and all was well.

After the trappers had left Cache Valley they proceeded to the land of the Blackfeet, where Ohamagwaya's prophecy proved true. Finding Sheep Mountain impassable, they changed their course and went down the Portneuf until they reached the junction with the Snake River. While on their way, they observed Blackfoot warriors coming down Snake River toward them. The trappers, seeing them first, were quick to prepare for an anticipated assault. Finding themselves at a disadvantage, the Blackfeet signaled their friendship. Soon a delegation made its appearance among the trappers, who viewed them with caution.

In spite of the vigilance of the guard, the enemy tried to drive away the horses at daybreak. The alarm was sounded and six were killed, including the chief. In the battle which followed four trappers were slain and seven wounded. Beckwourth, who admitted that he could not ascertain the exact number of Indian casualties because of their habit of carrying off their dead, thought that the Blackfeet might have lost about one hundred warriors.

The trappers were with the Snakes another time when the Blackfeet attacked. They began by killing and scalping five Shoshonis who were root-digging some distance from the camp. Ohamagwaya, hearing an alarm, held council with Sublette, whom he called "Cut Face" because of an obvious scar. Appealing to the white man for help, he cried, "Three of my warriors have been killed by the Black Feet. You say that your warriors can fight—that they are great braves. Now let me see them fight, that I may know your words are true."

Sublette answered, "You shall see them fight, and then you will know that they are all brave—that I have no cowards among my men, and that we are all ready to die for our Snake friends." He told his men that they must defeat the Blackfeet, not only to show the Snakes that they could fight but also to warn them indirectly so that they would be afraid to cause trouble. Three hundred mounted trappers, under the direction of Sublette, were joined by the Shoshoni warriors, "thirsting to take vengeance on the Blackfeet for the five scalps of their friends."

After fighting for six hours, the trappers became hungry. Sublette instructed his allies "to rub out" all of the foe while they moved back from the battle line to eat. The Snakes, having tired of the conflict, followed along, as they, too, wanted something to eat. The Blackfeet, seemingly unaware of the turn of events, must also have had enough, for in the absence of the trappers and their allies, they withdrew, leaving many of their dead on the battlefield.

The fruits of victory consisted of 173 scalps, with many quivers of arrows, war clubs, battle-axes, and lances. As the trappers and the Snakes had killed a number of the enemys' horses, this may have accounted for their unexpected departure. The trapper casualties amounted to 7 or 8 wounded, with none killed. Besides the 5 previously slain, the Snakes lost 11 in battle. The reason for their not being scalped might have been attributed to the haste with which the Blackfeet withdrew rather than to the fact that the enemy recognized their bravery. Since no Indian could enter the afterworld without his forelock, the warriors would sometimes refrain from scalping those who were outstandingly brave.

Beckwourth modestly stated: "Had this battle been fought in the open plain, but few of our foes could have escaped; and even as it was, had we continued to fight, not a dozen could have got away. But, considering that we were fighting for our allies, we did not exert ourselves."[22]

He explained how fighting could go on for many hours without heavy casualties. The secret lay in the Indians' mode of warfare. Killing with their arrows meant that they had to be near their object or the arrow would not take effect. When hunting buffalo, they trained their horses to keep by the side of their game until the arrow was discharged. Then springing away, the horse escaped the charge of the wounded animal. The red men were poor marksmen with guns, especially on horseback. The white men, on the other hand, would seldom fire unless they were sure of their man, thereby conserving their ammunition. Besides being better marksmen, the trappers felt that they had the Indian outclassed in hand-to-hand fighting. They usually considered three Indians to one white man a fair ratio.

General Ashley, after selling his interests to Smith, Jackson, and Sublette, gave a farewell speech on July 26, 1826, expressing his indebtedness to the loyal trappers who had risked their lives in his service. Not one word did he say for the Shoshonis whose land he had ravished. Though he minimized the number, many of his men died while helping him amass a fortune. Bowing out of the Rocky Mountain scene, he continued to handle the business end of the firm from St. Louis.

The trappers, after repeated difficulties with the Blackfeet, again came upon their friends the Snakes, who invited them to join them in their village 5 miles distant. After accepting the invitation, the fur men discovered a near-by encampment of Bannocks of approximately 185 lodges. These unpredictable Indians had fired upon 3 trappers the day before, killing 1 and wounding the other 2. All that saved the wounded from death was that Sublette heard the firing and dispatched his forces to their relief.

Beckwourth called the Bannocks "Pun-naks."[23] He described

22 *Ibid.*, 104–105.

23 "Punnacks" was the Shoshoni name for the Bannocks. It is from the word "Pa-naik-nia" meaning "someone who does not care about anything." Another

them as "a discarded band of the Snakes, very bad Indians, and very great thieves."[24] That they managed to maintain their individuality is surprising in view of the fact that they were frequently joined by outlaws and that they were closely allied to the scattered Shoshoni bands in their area. They were, however, the dominant group, often inducing their allies to take part in depredations which resulted in condemnation of the entire Shoshoni family.

Two trappers and a Snake, calling upon the Bannocks one evening, were attacked without provocation. The Indian was killed, his companions wounded. In the morning, 215 volunteers, with Jim Bridger as captain, set out to avenge the wrong. Arriving at the site of the village, they found that the Bannocks, fearing vengeance, had fled.

The trappers, following their trail over forty-five miles, encountered the Bannocks on Green River, where they had taken refuge on an island. Splitting forces in the same maneuver that they had found successful when they recovered their horses, the trappers managed to reach the opposite side of the stream, and they blocked all escape. The "withering" fire continued until there was "not one Pun-nak left of either sex or any age." Beckwourth boasted, "We carried back 488 scalps, and as we then supposed, annihilated the Pun-nak band."

Six or eight of the Bannock women, separated from their party, were captured and turned over to the Snakes, who were exuberant over the defeat of their kinsmen. Calling them "very bad Indians," the Snakes joyfully celebrated with a Scalp Dance. Beckwourth admitted that some of the old men, women, and children fled to the mountains for safety.[25]

The Bannocks said to have been annihilated on the island must have been but a small remnant of the tribe, as Ogden later found three hundred lodges (fifteen hundred persons) of the tribe on

explanation is "hair thrown back," referring to the pompadour style of hair arrangement used by Bannock men.

[24] Bonner, *Beckwourth*, 124.

[25] *Ibid.*, 124–25.

Camas Prairie (Idaho). Upon that occasion The Horse, chief of the tribe, carried an American flag when he came forward to meet Ogden. Regardless of the chief's professed friendship, depredations continued. Ogden was powerless to retaliate because of his company's policy toward the Indians. All he could do was fret and wish that "the Americans" would wage an all-out war against them.[26]

Soon after this a band of Crows, temporarily at peace with the Snakes, appeared in camp. They were delighted to see many Blackfeet scalps hanging on lodgepoles. After Beckwourth was pointed out as the hero of the battle, the visitors regarded him with profound admiration. One of the trappers, seeing an opportunity to spin a yarn equal to Beckwourth's, told the Crows that White-handled Knife (Beckwourth's Snake name) was a Crow. Knowing something of the history of the tribe, he referred to the time many years before when they had suffered severe defeat at the hands of the Cheyennes. The enemy had killed most of their warriors and carried off great numbers of women and children. Beckwourth was, according to the trapper, one of these children.

The tale, causing great excitement among the Indians, paved the way for the mulatto, who lost no time following up his advantage by going to the Crow country. There he was identified by a Mrs. Big Bowl as her son because of a mole on his eyelid. Basking in his new-found glory, he remained among the tribe, and he did not see a white man for the next three years. Beckwourth, with his usual braggadocio, claimed that after he became a great man in the tribe the Crow chief offered him his daughter for a wife. Like Manuel Lisa, who set the pattern for the squaw man, he was aware of the advantages such a union would give him.

> Considering this an alliance that would guarantee my life as well as enlarge my trade, I accepted his offer, and without any superfluous ceremony, became son-in-law to As-as-to, the head chief of the Black Feet. . . . To me the alliance was more offensive than defensive, but thrift was my object more than hymeneal enjoyment. Trade prospered greatly. I purchased beaver and horses

[26] Ogden, "Journal," *loc. cit.*, 362–72.

at my own price. Many times I bought a fine beaver-skin for a butcher knife or a plug of tobacco.[27]

The Snake country lost its most fantastic character, and the fur-trading period its most verbose narrator, when Beckwourth left. Though he was unquestionably guilty of gross exaggeration, all names, places, dates, and incidents were unchallenged when there were those living who knew the circumstances. Having lost our informant to the Crows, we find only a few details concerning the closing days of the 1820's.

The rendezvous of 1827 was held at Bear Lake (on the Utah-Idaho border), with Jedediah Smith, recently returned from his first trip to California, in charge. Satisfied by the take, a half-million dollars worth of furs, he again set out for the coast.

Little is known of the rendezvous of 1828, held on Weber River, but the one the following year took place on the Popo Agie (near Atlantic City, Wyoming). It was a gala affair, lasting a month, and it marked the year that John Jacob Astor and his American Fur Company entered into active competition with the Rocky Mountain Fur Company. The latter had been highly successful without too much interference from the British, who had been operating from the west into the Snake River region. With the appearance of Astor in the field as a formidable rival, the Rocky Mountain Fur Company monopoly was at an end. While all the rivalry was taking place, the Indians who really owned the furs passively watched.

[27] Bonner, *Beckwourth*, 111.

CHAPTER FIVE

Trapper Trails

For generations the Shoshoni trails had led from the Great Salt Lake to Green River, across the Sandy and over South Pass, toward Bighorn Valley and thence to the Yellowstone. Had the soil not been tilled, these trails could probably be traced to this day as definitely as the Great Bannock Trail that went through the northern part of Yellowstone Park.

Even if South Pass had not been pointed out to Ashley's men, they would soon have discovered it, for it was indelibly marked on the mountain slopes, through the valleys, and across the prairies. As surely as the Lemhis pointed the way for Lewis and Clark through the mountains to the north, these trails guided the white men to the only practical pass through the Rockies. The fact that this was in the heart of the Shoshoni territory did not deter the trappers when they went over the mountains to a land of wealth. In their greed for riches, they did not once consider Shoshoni rights.

South Pass is so broad, so gently sloping, so free of obstacles that it resembles an elevated plain with mountain peaks, like conical tipis, jutting up in the distance. Nature prepared the road and gave the Shoshonis the key to the gateway, and yet these Indians were not able even to collect the toll. Ironically, the Sentinels of the Rockies were armed only with primitive weapons. They could not have stopped the white man had they tried.

Let us consider for a moment what might have happened if the Spaniards had given them modern weapons. They already had a natural fortification, the Rocky Mountains. With guns, they could have driven out the trappers and stopped the westward migration through South Pass before it started. If the Americans had been turned back as effectively as the French had been, the Shoshonis could have concentrated their efforts on driving out the British.

By 1830 the Indian trail through South Pass had become the white man's ever-widening thoroughfare. When William Sublette arrived with supplies for the rendezvous, held that year thirty miles above the mouth of Popo Agie, he brought with him the first wagon train. We can well imagine the excitement which the appearance of Sublette's ten wagons, pulled by five mules each, must have caused among the Shoshonis.

The following year there was no summer rendezvous as Fitzpatrick, returning to the mountains through Santa Fe, was late in arriving. Sublette and Bridger had given up seeing him again and had gone to the Powder River country for the winter. There they soon became aware that William H. Vanderburgh, Andrew Dripps, and Lucien Fontenelle—Astor's scouts—were stalking them to learn the location of the best trapping areas.

Instead of settling down for a quiet winter of trapping in the Powder River country, the seasoned mountain men accordingly set out on a four-hundred-mile journey in an unsuccessful effort to elude their rivals. They remained free of them during the part of the winter they spent with the Flathead and Nez Percé Indians. Just how the American Fur Company men fared among the Snakes and Bannocks we are unable to say. We do know that they survived, for Bridger later found them in Bear River Valley looking for him.

While trying to elude Vanderburgh, the trappers stopped at Salt Lake. There they hired John Grey, an Iroquois chief, and seven of his tribesmen. Shortly afterwards, Grey's daughter complained to her father that she had been mistreated by one of the trappers, and a general melee ensued. Milton Sublette (William's brother) was severely stabbed by the chief. He remained in critical condition forty days while Joe Meek stayed faithfully at his side. Meanwhile, the other trappers managed to reach the upper Green.

According to Meek, Sublette was on the mend, and they had

started on their way when they encountered a band of warring Snakes.[1] They saved themselves by dashing into the village and entering the medicine lodge, where no blood could be shed. Gotia (probably Mauvais Gauche) caused the horses to be stampeded to divert his warriors. Then he directed the trappers into the forest, where they were met by a "beautiful Shoshone maiden" by the name of Umentucken (Mountain Lamb). She presented them with two lively horses upon which they escaped. Following her admonition to make all possible speed, they rode frantically to Pierre's Hole.

Not long afterwards, Umentucken became the wife of Sublette, thus giving him the distinction of being among the early squaw men in the Shoshoni country. When he was forced to go east for surgery, he left Mountain Lamb and his "little lambkin" in the care of his friend Joe Meek. After he failed to return, Meek modestly admitted that he won her over by stripping to the waist so that she might have cloth to wrap her baby in to keep it from freezing. Unused to such chivalry, Mountain Lamb became his dutiful wife, following him devotedly until her untimely death, as we shall see later. Meek admits his indulgence in describing her.

> She was the most beautiful Indian woman I ever saw, and when she was mounted on her dapple gray horse, which cost me three hundred dollars, she made a fine show. She wore a skirt of beautiful blue broadcloth, and a bodice and leggins of scarlet cloth, of the very finest make. Her hair was braided and fell over her shoulders, a scarlet silk handkerchief, tied on hood fashion, covered her head; and the finest embroidered moccasins her feet. She rode like the Indians, astride, and carried on one side of the saddle a tomahawk for war, and on the other the pipe of peace.
>
> The name of her horse was "All Fours." His accoutrements were as fine as his rider's. The saddle, crupper, and bust girths cost one hundred and fifty dollars; the bridle fifty dollars, and the muck-a-moots fifty dollars more. All of these articles were ornamented with fine cut glass beads, porcupine quills, and hawk's bells, that tinkled

---

[1] Victor, *The River of the West,* 104–105.

76

at every step. Her blankets were of scarlet and blue, and of the finest quality. Such was the outfit of the trapper's wife, Umentucken.[2]

The rendezvous was held in the summer of 1832 at Pierre's Hole. By now, there seemed to be as many white men as Indians in the high country. Besides the large number of American Fur Company representatives, Nathaniel J. Wyeth and his "New Englanders" had entered the field. There were also two other fur companies of importance, Gant and Blackwell and the Bonneville Company. In addition, there were about three hundred free trappers. To the Indians, it must have looked as if all the white tribesmen from the East were moving in upon them.

Just as the rendezvous was breaking up, the Blackfeet (or Gros Ventres as some authorities maintain) made an untimely appearance.[3] Dressed for battle, they were obviously in search of the Shoshonis. Had they realized the great number of white men in the immediate area at the time, they would probably have stayed out of the country. Little realizing what the consequence would be, they accosted a party of trappers and their Flathead and Nez Percé companions who were leaving the rendezvous together. Discovering themselves confronted with a superior force, the warriors signified their friendly intentions. The chief, unarmed, then came forward with his peace pipe.

Antoine Godin, one of the trappers whose father had been killed by Indians, and an unnamed Flathead, who may have suffered a similar loss, volunteered to go forth to meet the chief. Advancing, unarmed, he carried a peace pipe. Godin, instead of taking the pipe, ordered the Flathead to fire. As the chieftain, mortally wounded, fell to the ground, Godin grabbed his bright red blanket and returned to his lines to boast of his accomplishment. The warriors, now deprived of their leader, scattered into the timber. There they began to regroup. Hastily they made breastworks, consisting of a brush shelter, which they covered with blankets.

The trappers, barricading themselves behind their baggage

[2] *Ibid.*, 175.   [3] Zenas Leonard, *Adventures of Zenas Leonard*, 45.

and a horse that was sacrificed for the purpose, managed to get word to the main camp at the rendezvous. Hundreds of trappers and Indians rushed to their aid. Although the hostiles put up a savage fight, they did not have a chance. The battle was swift and decisive. After it was over and the surviving enemy had been routed, the Nez Percés were rewarded by being allowed to keep the blankets which they had daringly dragged from the fortress during the heat of the battle.

Enemy losses were undetermined, though the hostiles left ten bodies on the battlefield. Alexander Sinclair, one of the trappers, and seven Indians fighting with him lost their lives. Thirty-two dead horses were counted. John Ball, one of Wyeth's men, said that eight white men were killed, but he did not identify them. Sinclair was buried in the "horse pen" because it was so well trodden that his body could not be found by the Indians.[4]

Captain Benjamin L. E. Bonneville and Meek tell somewhat different versions of an incident following the battle.[5] The former maintains that a Blackfoot Indian woman was found grieving over her lover's body, which she refused to leave. Meek, however, says that her leg was broken and that she was unable to move from the spot.

"Kill me! Kill me!" she implored, as the white trappers came near. When they would not accommodate her, a vengeful Indian put an end to her suffering.

The same year Warren A. Ferris, of the American Fur Company, found the mixed bands of Bannocks and Shoshonis suffering from the results of a poor hunting season.[6] They were unkempt and on the point of freezing or starving to death. He contrasted them with the handsome and well-clad Flatheads, with whom he had been trading.

[4] John Ball, "Across the Continent Seventy Years Ago," *O.H.Q.*, Vol. III, No. 4 (1902) 82–92.

[5] Washington Irving, *The Adventures of Captain Bonneville*, 67; Victor, *The River of the West*, 116–17.

[6] "A Diary of Wanderings on the Sources of the Rivers Missouri, Columbia, and Colorado from February, 1830, to November, 1835," in Paul C. Phillips, *Life in the Rocky Mountains*, 132.

In the fall, the Rocky Mountain Fur Company trappers reported a successful engagement between the Bannocks and Shoshonis on the one hand and the Blackfeet on the other. When 150 Blackfeet attacked a Bannock-Shoshoni village, the Northern raiders were repulsed and driven into the willows. The defenders fired the prairie and almost roasted the enemy alive. When the Blackfeet tried to escape, they chased them three miles across the plain toward a forest at the base of the mountains. In this running battle, the Blackfeet lost 40 men and 5 women, the Bannocks and Shoshonis only 9. Among the nine was their leader, The Horse.[7]

Captain Bonneville found them mourning their loss. This chief was believed to have possessed a charmed life and to have been invulnerable. He had managed to deflect bullets of the "surest marksmen." His being killed did not cause the Indians to lose faith, for they maintained that the bullet was not lead but a bit of horn. Following his death there was no one with sufficient influence over the tribe "to restrain the wild and predatory propensities of the young men." In consequence they became troublesome and dangerous neighbors, "openly friendly for the sake of traffic, but disposed to commit secret depredations and to molest any small party that might fall within their reach."[8]

Bonneville, the "romantic captain" who joined forces with these Indians "to buffalo," gives an exciting account of their surround.[9] After posting a lookout on a hilltop, the hunters, on horseback and armed with bows and arrows, moved slowly and cautiously toward the herd. They stayed in the hollows and ravines, out of sight as much as possible. When the buffalo neared them, a signal was given, and they all rushed out "like a pack of hounds." Yelling and dashing into the midst of the herd, they "launched their arrows to the right and left." The plain seemed to shake under the tramp of many hoofs.

---

[7] *Ibid.*, 185–90.

[8] Irving, *Bonneville*, 126–27. The scattered bands of Shoshoni Indians who took part in Bannock depredations were seldom mentioned separately. As the Bannocks were more dominant, their Shoshoni allies were probably led by the same chieftains. Later, during the Shoshoni uprising the latter had their own recognized leaders.

[9] *Ibid.*, 206–209.

The cows were in headlong panic, the bulls furious with rage, uttering deep roars, and occasionally turning with a desperate rush upon their pursuers. Nothing could surpass the spirit, grace, and dexterity with which the Indians managed their horses; wheeling and coursing them among the affrighted herd, and launching their arrows with unerring aim.

In the midst of the apparent confusion, they selected their victims with perfect judgment, generally aiming at the fattest of the cows, the flesh of the bull being nearly worthless at this season of the year. In a few minutes, each of the hunters had crippled three or four cows. A single shot was sufficient for the purpose, and the animal, once maimed, was left to be completely dispatched at the end of the chase.

Frequently a cow was killed on the spot by a single arrow. In one instance, Captain Bonneville saw an Indian shoot his arrow completely through the body of a cow, so that it struck the ground beyond. The bulls, however, are not so easily killed, and always cost the hunter several arrows, sometimes making battle upon the horses, and chasing them furiously though severely wounded, with the darts still sticking in their flesh.

In proportion to the amount of meat with which they gorged themselves, the braves grew in stoutness of heart. "Ruffling and swelling, and snorting, and slapping their breasts, and brandishing their arms," they expostulated upon wrongs that had been done their people by the Blackfeet—"how they had drenched their villages in tears and blood!" They dared the enemy to come among them. Receiving no reply, they derided him with sneers and insults for not accepting the challenge. Having thus given themselves credit for their valor, the braves "gradually calmed down, lowered their crests, smoothed their ruffled feathers, and betook themselves to sleep, without placing a single guard over their camp, so that, had the Blackfeet taken them at their word, but few of these braggart heroes might have survived for any further boasting."

Bonneville avowed his friendship for the Shoshonis and Bannocks and his faith in their honesty, while Wyeth, who had difficulty distinguishing between them, had special praise for the latter. He found that each tribe branded the other as murderers of the whites, while they maintained their own innocence.

One of Wyeth's New Englanders, John K. Townsend, arriving at a Bannock-Shoshoni camp near Lost River Mountain (Idaho), found that these Indians had just completed a successful engagement with the Blackfeet. In fact, they had thirty-six "green" scalps to prove it. Consequently he felt that he and his men had narrowly escaped certain death at the hands of the northern raiders.[10]

His next adventure with the Indians was not as satisfactory.[11] While he was trading with them, the Bannock chief began stalling for time. Wyeth, finally losing patience, started to ride away. Whereupon the chief ordered the women to bring some fried fish, which they disdainfully threw upon the ground before the trappers. In a threatening tone of voice, the chief demanded a ridiculous price. Disgusted, the white men whirled to leave. As they turned, an Indian struck Townsend's horse over the head. Without thought of a consequence, the reckless trapper lashed him across the shoulders with a whip. As the white men dashed away, the scornful taunts of the Indians rang in their ears.

In the following months the hostile attitude of the Shoshonis was shown by the fact that they killed three of Bonneville's valiant trappers.[12] The Crows as well as the Shoshonis seem to have become demoralized by the ruthless competition between the white men in their desire for wealth. Apparently at the instigation of the American Fur Company, Fitzpatrick was robbed of all he had, even to his shirt. The fur company finally made restitution of all hides branded RMF.

Rival companies, using every effort to undermine the power of others, had lost all sense of honor in their dealings with each other as well as with the Indians. As a consequence the natives lost

[10] John K. Townsend, *Narrative of a Journey across the Rocky Mountains to the Columbia River*, 262–63.

[11] *Ibid.*, 326.

[12] Charles G. Coutant, *History of Wyoming*, I, 205.

faith. Why should they keep their promises when the white men did not keep theirs? The Snakes broke their record of friendship by killing William Small, of Bonneville's party, early in the fall while he was setting his traps. No details are available, but it is supposed that he was killed by straggling Indians as no attack was made upon the trappers by a war party.

During this time, so much was taking place in the fur country that the Basin Indians were almost forgotten in the records. However, we find mention made of them by Zenas Leonard, an early traveler to the West through the Basin. He gives us a rare glimpse of the Shoshokos as he observed them.[13] From his account, we see how little the white man had influenced the way of life of these primitive people, whose only weapons were still the bow and arrow.

> They [the Shoshokos] are generally of a more swarthy nature, small and cowardly, and travel in small gangs of from four to five families—this they are compelled to do in order to keep from starvation. They are always roving from plain to plain and from valley to valley—never remaining in one place longer than till game gets scarce. When on the move the women have to perform the most laborious part—having charge of the transportation of their baggage. While doing this, a female . . . will carry a load of perhaps a hundred weight a whole day without manifesting the least fatigue or complaint. . . .
>
> They [the Shoshokos] are no way ill disposed towards the whites or at least they never disturbed us—with the exception of stealing a few of our traps. . . . To get a beaver skin from these Indians worth eight or ten dollars, never cost more than an awl, a fish-hook, a knife, a string of beads, or something equally as trifling. . . . The manner and customs of the Snake Indians are very similar to those of the Flatheads, with the exception of stealing, which they consider no harm.

Timoak (Tümok), a Ruby Valley (Nevada) Shoshoni, was trapping sage hens when he saw his first white man.[14] The "dog face people" were three in number and they had long beards. He

---

[13] *Adventures*, 48-49.
[14] Steward, "Basin-Plateau Groups," 149-50.

had never seen anyone like them. They raised their hands in greeting, but he was frightened and started to run away. Curiosity caused him to tarry long enough to find out what they wanted. They sought directions, he discovered from their sign language. The accommodating Timoak, like the Shoshonis in the Rockies, pointed the way—this time to a pass through the Nevada mountains.

Timoak and Chief Truckee, of the Paiutes, became two of the most loyal friends whom the white man found in the Basin. Truckee was better known as "Captain" or "Pancho" to his fellow soldiers. He carried a "rag friend," as he called his honorable discharge, to show that he had served in the Mexican War.

Although both Timoak and Truckee spoke in glowing terms of the strangers, many of their tribesmen were terrified when they heard of the white-skinned people. In some way they identified them with the red-haired cannibals of the Humboldt. Sarah Winnemucca Hopkins, who claimed to be the daughter of Chief Winnemucca and the granddaughter of Truckee, tells dramatically the following experience of her childhood:

> Oh, what a fright we all got one morning to hear some white people were coming. Everyone ran as best they could. My poor mother was left with little sister and me. . . .
>
> My poor mother was carrying my little sister on her back, and trying to make me run; but I was so frightened I could not move my feet, and while my poor mother was trying to get me along my aunt overtook us, and she said to my mother:
>
> "Let us bury our girls, or we shall all be killed and eaten up."
>
> So they went to work and buried us, and told us if we heard any noise not to cry out, for if we did they would surely kill us and eat us. So our mothers buried me and my cousin, planted sage bushes over our faces to keep the sun from burning them, and there we were left all day.
>
> Oh, can anyone imagine my feelings, *buried alive*, thinking every minute that I was to be unburied and eaten by the people that my grandfather loved so much?[15]

[15] Hopkins, *Life among the Piutes*, 11–14. Some doubt is cast upon Sarah Winnemucca's claims. Paiutes related to Winnemucca say that she was from the

83

After dark the girls were uncovered by their parents. Later, when Sarah Winnemucca saw her first white man, she screamed, "Oh, Mother, the owls!" All night long she imagined that she could see "their big white eyes" staring from their hairy faces.[16]

Captain Bonneville, after watching some of the Salmon Eaters (Lemhis) spear their fish, invited himself to dinner. While conversing with an Indian family in their lodge, he felt something move behind him. By removing a buffalo robe, he found a young girl, about fourteen years of age, crouched beneath. Terrified, she stared into his face. When he attempted to gain her confidence by tying a bright ribbon around her neck, she drew back with a snarl. Just then a younger child of the family entered the lodge. Catching sight of the white man, he ran away screaming.[17]

Returning to Green River, we find that the last important rendezvous, held on Ham's Fork of Black's Fork, took place in 1834, a date which marks the end of the Rocky Mountain Fur Company. Although the rendezvous period was not over, the competition between rival buyers had become so keen that even the Indians were bewildered. Sublette and his partner, Robert Campbell, seeing that Ashley's form of trade was outmoded, built a trading post (Fort William, later to be known as Fort Laramie) at the mouth of Laramie River on the North Platte. A year later this was sold to Fitzpatrick, Sublette, and Bridger. With the establishment of this fort, a new era in the fur trade was in the making.

Meanwhile certain changes were taking place in the Shoshoni country. Although the trappers had a demoralizing influence upon the Indians, they also played an indirect role in their religious acculturation. Since Padre Escalante's influence had failed to reach north of the Uinta Mountains, it was left for the Iroquois trappers to introduce Christianity to the Salish tribes of the Plateau—the Flatheads and the Nez Percé Indians.

Winnemucca band but was not his daughter. Had she been, she could not have been the granddaughter of Truckee since the two unrelated chiefs were contemporaries, not father and son.

[16] *Ibid.*, 25. Among J. K. Moore's keepsakes at Lander, Wyoming, is "Washakie's razor," consisting of broad tweezers and a small heart-shaped mirror.

[17] Irving, *Bonneville*, 317–19.

The Shoshoni Chief, Hiding Bear (Pah-dasher-wah-un-dah), "a thinking man and a man of observation,"[18] noted that the Nez Percés had a superior rating with the white men. This he attributed to their acceptance of Christianity. Consequently, he decided to visit his Plateau friends to learn their code of religious morality and attend their devotional services. He then decided that through the acceptance of this new dogma his people might gain superiority over their "ignorant rivals," the Utes, with whom they were usually at odds. He was unaware of the fact that Escalante had attempted to Christianize them in the late 1700's.

Assembling his people, Hiding Bear taught them the mongrel doctrines and form of worship of the Nez Percés and recommended adoption of the new religious concept. The Shoshonis, struck by the novelty, entered into it with spirit. They began to observe Sundays and holidays and to have their devotional dances and ceremonials, about which the "ignorant" Utes knew nothing.

Osborne Russell, a twenty-year-old employee in Wyeth's second expedition, gives us our first definite knowledge of Hiding Bear, with whom he smoked the pipe in October, 1834.[19] His mention of him also as Iron Wristbands, the name the trappers called him, would indicate that he might have worn jewelry acquired through the Comanches, or on the other hand, he may have been a Comanche.

On this second expedition Wyeth erected Fort Hall (Idaho) in the heart of the Bannock-Shoshoni country. He had a grudge against Sublette for canceling a contract, and he threatened "to roll a stone in the garden." This fort apparently was the "stone," as it served as an obstacle to his business.

Following one of the many raids of the Blackfeet upon the Shoshonis and Bannocks at Fort Hall, Wyeth's men combed the area in an attempt to tabulate the number killed in battle.[20] To their surprise they found a thirteen-year-old girl, whose leg had been shattered by a ball. She had crawled under the brush and had

18 *Ibid.*, 335–38.
19 *Journal of a Trapper*, 114–16.
20 James B. Marsh, *Four Years in the Rockies*, 92–93.

pulled branches over her so that she would not be seen. The trappers nursed her back to health during the winter, and she became a great favorite among them. Her name was Chilsipee (The Antelope). While recovering from her injury, she spent her time making preparations for the coming rendezvous. We find this delightful description of the Indian girl—the mascot of Wyeth's men—on her way to Green River:

> Chilsipee was in the height of her glory, and she was indeed a picture worthy the pencil of one of the greatest masters. Her horse, the one belonging to [Isaac P.] Rose, was beautifully and tastefully caparisoned. A broad leathern belt, a foot wide, reached from the saddle across its breast; this was covered with fine red cloth, and tastefully ornamented with beads, which were worked into stars and other emblematical devices.
>
> Porcupine quills also formed part of the decorations, and the whole was fringed with a large number of girlews or small bells which yielded a jingling, musical sound as she galloped along. Her saddle and saddle cloth were ornamental in a similar manner, but Chilsipee herself was a picture; her fine beaver skin cap was bound with gold lace and girlews; her tight-fitting bodice was the finest red cloth, worked with beads and porcupine quills; her flowing blue skirt was also of the finest material, and this together with her red leggings and moccasins, like the rest of her dress, was elaborately embroidered.
>
> She rode as all Indian women do, man fashion, and the trappers were all delighted with and proud of their little pet. Chilsipee would ride at the head of the column, then, on rising ground, she would halt her horse and allow the cavalcade to pass by, like an army passing in review before a general. Then starting from the rear, she would gallop to the front at full speed, amid shouts of "Hurrah! for Chilsipee." "Go it, little un'!"[21]

Sometime later, when Wyeth's men were trapping in Blackfoot country, Chilsipee became unusually excited. Rose, seeing her look longingly toward her native hills, asked if she wanted to return to her people. She did not answer, but tears came to her eyes. A few nights later she disappeared. She had packed and taken

[21] *Ibid.*, 91, 134.

everything she owned as well as one of the company's best horses. It was thought that she might have been aided in her escape by an Indian or a white man.

Fort Hall, bought by the Hudson's Bay Company in 1837, was used as a further "stone," this time in the occupational process. The British at this way station attempted to discourage American expansion and settlement in the vast Oregon region. There was no other station between it and the trading post (Fort Laramie) on the North Platte until Fort Bridger was built on Black's Fork of Green River.

An early-day Wyoming historian once said, "God and humanity hardly entered into the prevailing conditions in the territory [later to be known as Wyoming] prior to 1835," when a new influence was introduced.[22] It was the year that two Presbyterian missionaries—the scholarly and fastidious Reverend Samuel Parker and the energetic Marcus Whitman—came westward over the trapper trail with the American Fur Company. Dr. Whitman, who became instantly popular at the rendezvous at Horse Creek (a tributary of the Green), so impressed Joe Meek that he felt he possessed the traits of a good mountain leader. The Indians were amazed by his skill when he removed a Blackfoot arrowhead which Bridger had carried in his back for three years.

Among those assembled at the rendezvous was the well-known scout, Kit Carson. Although he played a minor role in Shoshoni history, he was a squaw man, affiliated with the Shoshokos.[23] Isaac Rose and he were hunting one day in the Basin area when they startled a young girl from a clump of bushes. Rose says that she "ran like a deer, her long black hair streaming behind her in the wind." She appeared to be about fifteen years old, small and graceful. Carson vowed that she was the prettiest Indian he had ever seen. "I'm goin' to make a dicker fur that gal," he told Rose. "I'll have her if it takes the best horse I've got." He gave not only that but also a red blanket before the father of the girl was satisfied.

It was at the rendezvous of 1835 that Kit Carson had his

[22] Coutant, *History of Wyoming*, I, 207.
[23] Marsh, *Four Years in the Rockies*, 92–94.

famous duel with Shunar, the bully of the mountains. The braggart mounted his horse and with loaded rifle challenged "any Frenchman, American, Spaniard or Dutchman" to fight him in single combat. When Carson accepted the challenge as an American, Shunar continued to defy him. Carson jumped on his horse, and with loaded pistol, rushed into close contact. Both fired instantly. Carson's ball entered Shunar's hand, came out at the wrist, and passed through the arm above the elbow. Shunar's ball passed over the head of Carson. When the latter went for another pistol, Shunar begged that his life be spared.

Among the witnesses of the Carson-Shunar duel were some two hundred white man and about two thousand Indians, most of whom were of the Shoshoni tribe. Chiefs of the Utes were there with delegations of their people, but missionaries did not formally visit either tribe. They were guided by the Flathead and Nez Percé Indians on their way to the Oregon coast.

Shortly after this Meek fell into the hands of the Crows. Instead of killing him outright, the Indians agreed upon a parley. Little Gun, second in command, was sent as an emissary to meet Bridger. Stripped and unarmed, they were to stop halfway, embrace, and kiss each other according to Indian custom. The trappers managed to make a prisoner of Little Gun, for whom the Crows had to exchange Meek. Resentment was expressed later when a Crow struck Mountain Lamb with a whip; whereupon, Meek killed him. Before peace could be restored, three Indians and one trapper had lost their lives.

Following this incident the white men turned back toward Green River, for it was about time for the next rendezvous. Along the way Bridger was approached by a band of Nez Percés who complained that the Bannocks had stolen their horses. Forthwith, he helped recover them. He was reimbursed for this undertaking with a very fine animal, which apparently belonged to the Bannock chief who came to claim his property. Bridger was standing in front of his lodge when the chief rushed up and grabbed the lead rope from his hand. Noting the insult, "Negro Jim," the cook, seized his rifle and killed him. The Bannocks, disorganized by the loss of their chief, fled in confusion, with the trappers in pursuit. According to Meek's casual mention, an arrow shot at random struck his Shoshoni wife in the breast, "and the joys and sorrows of the Mountain Lamb were no more."[24]

Again the white men claimed that they had killed all of the braves. Meek says that toward morning an old woman came bearing the pipe of peace. "You have killed all our warriors, do you now want to kill the women?" she asked. "If you wish to smoke with women, I have the pipe." Meek demurred. He answered that he did not care either to fight or to smoke with "so feeble a representative of the Bannocks."

This was the last war party which that nation sent against the mountain men.[25] Nevertheless, the Bannocks avenged the losses by small-scale depredations which eventually erupted in the Bannock War of 1878.

The sharp edge of rivalry had worn off by 1836, and we find the old rivals, Fontenelle and Bridger, in charge of the rendezvous, held on Green River (near Daniel, Wyoming). An even greater surprise than this was in store for the Indians—the sight of the first white women in the region. They were Narcissa, the bride of Dr. Marcus Whitman, and Eliza, the bride of Dr. Henry J. Spalding. This was Whitman's second visit, for he had returned east and married after attending his first rendezvous. The Whitmans and Spaldings, en route to Oregon, reached South Pass on July 3, 1836. Here they spent the Fourth of July, while their companions pushed on. Spalding was impressed by the historic import of the occasion:

> The moral and physical scene was grand and thrilling. Hope and joy beamed on the face of my dear wife though pains racked her frame. She seemed to receive new strength. "Is it a reality or a dream," she exclaimed, "that after four months of hard and painful journeyings, I am alive and actually standing on the summit of the Rocky Mountains, where yet the foot of white woman has never trod?"[26]

24 Victor, *The River of the West*, 179–80, 193–97.
25 *Ibid.*, 197–98.   26 Myron Eells, *Marcus Whitman*, 34.

According to a story told in later years, Whitman, leader of the little band of missionaries, took his Bible and an American flag from the wagon. Spreading out a blanket on the ground, he stood with the flagstaff in his hand as he lifted his voice in prayer. While the members of his party knelt, there at the gateway to the West, Whitman prayed for his country and for the cause of Christ in Oregon. He then took possession of the territory which afterwards became Wyoming, and the country beyond, in the name of God and the United States. Mrs. Whitman, who was noted for her magnificent voice, led in a patriotic hymn, after which the missionaries followed the fur men.

The Indians, delighted with the first white women at the rendezvous, came bearing gifts of mountain trout and elk meat. The Shoshonis made an impressive show of their might when about six hundred warriors, bedecked in their finery, staged a mock attack upon the lodges occupied by the missionaries. The women were terrified by this form of entertainment. The war whoops did not stop until the Indians came within a few yards of the tents. Gracefully wheeling to the right, they disappeared across the prairie. This display of horsemanship was intended as an honor, the highest compliment which the Snakes could pay to the first white women they had ever seen.

In the closing days of the 1830's, travel along the trail to Oregon began to thicken. As it did, we find more frequent mention of incidents involving the Bannocks. Asahel Munger and wife, early travelers to the newly opened Oregon country, were among those who termed the Bannocks "very bad."[27] Thomas Farnham, the patriot who came bearing the placard "Oregon or the Grave," recognized the Bannocks as treacherous and a "dangerous race." Even so he credited them with sincere sorrow in the death of a tribesman. They had docked some of their horses' tails as part of their mourning, and the women were keening over the dead.[28]

The first missionary to travel to the rendezvous with that as

[27] Asahel Munger, "Diary of Asahel Munger and Wife," *O.H.Q.*, Vol. VIII (1907), 40.

[28] *Travels in the Great Western Prairies*, 76.

his specific destination was W. H. Gray, who had come west with the Whitmans and Spaldings. He had left the party to start a mission among the Flatheads whom he accompanied to Green River. He was apparently on an excursion, for he did not remain to do missionary work.

The rendezvous in 1837 was held on Green River, twelve miles south of Horse Creek. When the Indians pulled up stakes, a second Mrs. Meek, with her baby on a cradleboard, joined them. Meek followed her but was unable to prevail upon her to stay with him. She was homesick for her people.

That year Uncle Dick Wootton, veteran trapper, came near being killed by the usually friendly Snake Indians, though the details are unknown. At that he fared better than a trapper named La Bonte, a member of his party. La Bonte, according to local legend, was killed by the Utes, who cut his flesh from the bones and ate it.[29]

In the spring of 1839, Jim Bridger, upon one of his infrequent trips to St. Louis, became acquainted with Jim Baker. The twenty-year-old Baker accompanied him to the mountains, where he attended his first rendezvous, held that year on Horse Creek, near Fort Bonneville.[30] It was quiet compared to many that had gone before, and it was the last of consequence. Yet F. W. Wislizenus, a German physician, gives us one of the best firsthand descriptions to be found of the rendezvous:

> What first struck our eye was several long rows of Indian tents extending along the Green River for at least a mile. Indians and whites were mingled here in varied groups. Of the Indians there had come chiefly Snakes, Flatheads and Nez Perces, peaceful tribes, living beyond the Rocky Mountains. . . .

[29] Coutant, *History of Wyoming*, I, 698. La Bonte Station and La Bonte Creek in southeastern Wyoming may have been named for him. Since there were two trappers by the name of La Bonte, no one knows for whom the landmarks were named.

[30] Fort Bonneville (Fort Nonsense or Bonneville's Folly) was erected above the mouth of Horse Creek on the upper valley of Green River. Before the pickets and bastions were complete, Captain Bonneville realized that it was impractical because of high elevation. Used during this one rendezvous only, it was abandoned a month later. Chittenden, *American Fur Trade*, I, 400.

A pint of meal, for instance, costs from half a dollar to a dollar; a pint of coffee beans, cocoa beans or sugar, two dollars each; a pint dilute alcohol (the only spirituous liquor to be had), four dollars; a piece of chewing tobacco of the commonest sort, which is usually smoked, Indian fashion, mixed with herbs, one or two dollars. Guns and ammunition, bear traps, blankets, kerchiefs and gaudy finery for squaws, are sold at an enormous profit. . . .

The Indians who had come to the meeting were no less interesting than the trappers. There must have been some thousands of them. Their tents are sewed together, stretched in cone shape over a dozen poles, that are leaned against each other, their tops crossing. In front and on top (of) this, leather can be thrown back to form door and chimney.

The tents are about twelve feet high and twenty feet in circumference at the ground, and give sufficient protection in any kind of weather. I visited many tents, partly out of curiosity, partly to barter for trifles, and sought to make myself intelligible in the language of signs as far as possible.

An army of Indian dogs, very much resembling the wolf, usually beset the entrance. From some tents comes the sound of music. A virtuoso beats a sort of kettle drum with bells around, with all his might, and the chorus accompanies him with strange monotone untrained sound that shows strong tendency to the minor chords.

A similar heart rending song drew me to a troop of squaws that were engrossed in the game of "the hand," so popular with the Indians. Some small object, a bit of wood, for instance, is passed from hand to hand among the players seated in a circle; and it is some one's part to guess in whose hands the object is.

During the game, the chorus steadily sings some songs as monotonous as those to which bears dance. But the real object is to gamble in this way for some designated prize. It is a game of hazard. In this case, for example, a pile of beads and corals, which lay in the midst of the circle, was the object in question. Men and women were so carried away by the game that they often spent a whole day and night at it.

Other groups of whites and Indians were engaged in barter. The Indians had for the trade chiefly tanned skins, moccasins, thongs of buffalo leather, or braided buffalo hair, and fresh or dried buffalo meat. . . . The articles that attracted them most in exchange were powder and lead, knives, tobacco, cinnabar, gaily colored kerchiefs, pocket mirrors and all sorts of ornaments.

Before the Indian begins to trade he demands sight of everything that may be offered by the other party to the trade. If there is something there that attracts him, he, too, will produce his wares, but discovers very quickly how much or how little they are coveted. If he himself is not willed to dispose of some particular thing, he obstinately adheres to his refusal, though ten times the value be offered him.[31]

Before leaving the trapping period, further mention of the squaw man should be made. Bonneville presents an unforgettable picture of a long caravan which he saw passing through a "skirt of woodland" in the Upper Missouri River region.[32] He describes a train that stretched single file nearly half a mile:

> The mountaineers in their rude hunting dress, armed with rifles and roughly mounted, and leading their pack horses down a hill of the forest, looked like banditti returning with plunder. On the top of some of the packs were perched several half-breed children, perfect little imps, with black eyes glaring from among elf locks. These, I was told, were children of the trappers; pledges of love from their squaw spouses in the wilderness.

Bonneville, referring to the free trapper as if he were a different breed from the men regularly employed, says:

> ... In the eye of an Indian girl he [the free trapper] combines all that is dashing and heroic in a warrior of her own race—whose gait, and garb, and bravery he emulates—with all that is gallant and glorious in the white man. And then the indulgence with which he treats her, the finery in which he decks her out, the state in which she moves, the sway she enjoys over both his purse and person; instead of being the drudge and slave of an Indian husband, obliged to carry his pack, and build his lodge, and make his fire, and bear his cross humors and blows. No there is no comparison, in the eyes of an aspiring belle of the wilderness, between a free trapper and an Indian brave.[33]

[31] *A Journey to the Rocky Mountains in 1839*, 90.
[32] Irving, *Bonneville*, 81–82.
[33] *Ibid.*, 338–39.

An incident involving two free trappers, fresh from their winter encampment with the American Fur Company in the Green River country, was recounted by Bonneville.[34] These gay young blades, "arrayed in their savage finery and mounted on steeds as fine and as fiery as themselves, and all jingling with Hawks'-bells, came galloping, with whoop and halloo, into the camp." They immediately spotted two young Indian beauties, who caught their fancy. One was a "pert little Eutaw," recently taken prisoner by a Shoshoni brave, who readily ransomed her for a few trifles. The other was a slave—subject to the will of the favorite wife—of one of the Snakes who refused to part with her at any price. In her subordinate position, she naturally preferred the dashing young trapper to her husband. After the jealous Snake had beaten her for arousing the white man's interest, she escaped with the free trapper on his horse. When the enraged husband finally caught up with them, he settled for two horses, which he considered fair exchange for a bad wife.

The squaw man—whether he be free trapper, regularly employed trapper, or trader—played a leading male role in the Western scene. True, he was often selfish in his motives, but some of those who established Indian families became the first settlers in the West. Four outstanding fur traders in the Snake country were squaw men, loyal to their Indian wives. They were Thomas Fitzpatrick, Jim Bridger, Jim Baker, and Jack Robertson.

When he was fifty years old, Fitzpatrick married a half-blood, Margaret Poisal, an interpreter, whose father was a French-Canadian trapper and whose mother (Snake Woman) was an Arapaho. A son, Andrew Jackson, and a posthumous daughter, Virginia Thomasine, were born to this union. Fitzpatrick provided in his will for any children born within nine months after his death. Virginia, who was widely known for her work in schools in Oklahoma and Colorado, had "a charming manner and a lively and adventurous disposition."[35]

Jim Bridger had three wives—a Flathead, a Ute, and a Shoshoni

[34] *Ibid.*, 340–41.
[35] Hafen and Ghent, *Broken Hand*, 220, 261–62.

—each taken successively after the death of the former.[36] His children, Felix and Josephine (half-Flathead), were sent to St. Louis to school. Mary Ann, their older sister, and Josephine Mar Meek (Joe Meek's half–Nez Percé daughter) lost their lives in a Cayuse uprising (the Whitman Massacre in Oregon), in which the Indians blamed the white man for not stopping a measles epidemic. The Whitmans were among those slain.

When Bridger lost his Ute wife in childbirth, he raised his infant daughter Virginia on buffalo milk. She was taken to St. Louis by Robert Campbell when she was five years old and two years later placed in a convent. She had a brother John, two years older. When Bridger returned to his native Missouri to live, he took with him his Shoshoni wife, whom he named Mary Washakie and married in the white man's manner. They had two children, Mary and William.

Jim Baker, one of the most celebrated pioneers in Wyoming and Colorado, lived with his half-blood children in the Dixon, Wyoming, vicinity until his death.[37] Meateetse (Little Traveler), his Shoshoni wife, came originally from the Fort Bridger country. Following a Sioux attack, a soldier, reportedly in Gen. O. O. Howard's command, found two small children, Meateetse and her brother. He took them to Denver where Meateetse grew to maturity and married Jim Baker.

As his wife, she remained with him until shortly before her tenth child was born. Then depressed by personal sorrow, she returned to the Shoshonis, where she stayed until her death. She spent her last days with a daughter Isabel, wife of Napoleon Bonaparte Kinnear (of Mayflower descent), who as an engineer settled in the Wind River Valley. Their two daughters, Irene (Mrs. Lawrence J. Meade) and Kate (Mrs. Frank Erickson), were both sent to college in California.

Jack Robertson, or "Uncle Jack Robinson" as he was usually called, was the only one of the above mentioned who remained in the Fort Bridger country until his death. He, his Shoshoni wife

[36] Alter, *James Bridger*, 101, 518–20.
[37] Nolie Mumey, *The Life of Jim Baker*, 206–33.

("Madame Jack"), and their children rounded out their lives in the area, where their descendants are still living.

Regardless of his many faults, the bearded squaw man, with his flowing locks, remains one of the most picturesque type characters in the early West. Though often crude, he fed and clothed his children in the white man's manner. Through him the Indians gained a basic knowledge of the white man's culture. His half-blood children often had educational advantages that he himself had lacked, for many of the squaw men were illiterate.

CHAPTER SIX

Emigrant Road

THE YEAR 1840, which ushered in one of the most trying decades in Shoshoni history, marked a transition from the
fur-trade era to the migration period. The last rendezvous, which
took place on the Sisk-ke-dee where the first official gathering
had been held a brief but eventful fifteen years before, sounded a
death knell to an industry that had probed deep into the hearts of
the Shoshonis and their country. Never again could anyone call
it an unexplored wilderness, for a great highway was by now
established from the Platte to the Sweetwater, by Independence
Rock and Devil's Gate, over South Pass, across Big Sandy, thence
to Green River, on to Fort Hall, and westward to the coastal settlements of Oregon. The land of the Shoshonis had lost its isolation.

During the forties, as the Master Trail, or the Emigrant Road
to Oregon, gradually changed to the Mormon, then to the California Trail, the Shoshonis were still destined to play a significant
if passive role. While the general purpose of the main trail through
their country was shifting, the Snake Indians were finding themselves confronted by momentous decisions, their problems being
political as well as economic.

We are not sure just why the Indians had become dissatisfied
with Pah-dasher-wah-un-dah, but by the year 1840 there were
so many malcontents in the tribe that his brother Moh-woom-hah
was on the verge of taking over. He had enlisted a following of
three hundred lodges and had rallied to his support three of the
"pillars of the nation," Ink-a-tosh-a-pop, Fibe-to-un-to-wat-see,
and Washakie.[1]

Osborn Russell, whose records comprise the first mention that

[1] Russell, *Journal of a Trapper*, 114–16.

97

can be found of Washakie, enjoyed a Christmas Day feast with the Shoshonis on Weber River. There Russell had a chance to observe the political uncertainty of Pah-dasher-wah-un-dah and the rising popularity of the three young warriors, "at a mention of whose names the Blackfeet quaked in fear." We have no way of knowing why the Blackfeet should "quake" at the mention of the other two names but they, as well as the Sioux, were aware of the warlike ability of Washakie.

At the time of his birth, he was named Pina Quanah (Smell of Sugar), which he was called until he earned the name by which he was to be known throughout his lifetime.[2] Washakie is variously interpreted to mean Rawhide Rattle, Shoots Straight, Shoots-on-the-Fly, Sure Shot, and Gambler's Gourd.[3] Although it was customary for a Shoshoni to have at least three names during his lifetime, we are unable to find mention of a third. D. B. Huntington, who compiled a vocabulary of the Shoshoni language while acting as an interpreter among the Utes and Shoshonis, tells how he acquired his name Washakie:

> The first buffalo he ever killed, he skinned the pate, took the hair off, puckered it up, and tied it around a stick with a hole in it, so that he could blow it up like a bladder. He put some stones in it, and when it became perfectly dry, it would rattle, and when the Sioux came to war with them, he would ride in among them and scare their horses; so they called him Wash-a-ki, "The Rattle."[4]

Washakie was born about the turn of the century. His father Paseego was a Flathead and his mother Shoshonean. It is reasonable to assume that she was a Lemhi of a neighboring band. As near as the story can be pieced together, the family was living with Paseego's people when the Blackfeet attacked their village and killed the father. The survivors, who became widely scattered, included the mother with her small children, five-year-old Pina

2 W. F. Lander, *Report* (hereinafter cited as Lander's report), *Sen. Exec. Doc. 42*, 36 Cong., 1 sess. (1033), 121–39.

3 Grace Raymond Hebard, *Washakie*, 48–51.

4 *Vocabulary of the Ute and Sho-sho-ne or Snake Tribe.*

Quanah, his two brothers and two sisters. They wandered until they found a band of Lemhis on the banks of the Salmon River.

The family stayed with these Indians until after Washakie had grown to be a young man, tall of stature and lighter complexioned than the average Shoshoni. In appearance, he resembled his father's people. He and a sister remained with their benefactors even after a band of visiting Flatheads had persuaded his mother and the rest of the family to return to their tribe. His sister married a Lemhi, while Washakie joined the Bannocks and lived with them about five years.

Since he was distinguished throughout the rest of his life for his friendship to the white man, his stay among the hostile Bannocks has puzzled some historians.[5] And yet it is obvious from the length of time he spent with them that he must have been in sympathy with their ways at least while he was there. Whether their attitude had anything to do with his ultimately leaving them and taking up residence among the friendly Green River Snakes, we have no way of knowing. We are not even sure just when he went from one tribe to the other, though it was probably in the late twenties or early thirties. As one of the "pillars of the nation" in 1840, he could not have been a newcomer.

Sometime prior to 1840 he took part in an engagement which might have given the Blackfeet reason to fear him. According to a well-known local legend, he not only followed them from the Green River to the Missouri to recover stolen horses, but he also returned with most of the scalps belonging to the marauders. Ink-a-tosh-a-pop and Fibe-to-un-to-wat-see may have accompanied him on this mission. The training he received among the Bannocks no doubt prepared him for this exploit and others in which he proved his great courage.

Father Pierre Jean de Smet, the first "Black Robe" (Catholic missionary), arrived in the Rockies in 1840. As in the case of the first women along the trail, members of the American Fur Company furnished safe transportation. After leaving the Platte, De Smet paused to engrave his name on "Rock Independence," which

5 Hebard, *Washakie,* 49–50.

he aptly termed "The Great Register of the Desert." Moving on westward, he encountered a band of Flatheads and Pend d'Oreilles, whom he greeted as long-lost children. Pausing in the Wind River country, he conducted the first Mass in the Rockies, *"La Prairie de la Messe,"* on July 5.[6] At Green River, De Smet found the rendezvous in progress. He observed many "Shoshones, or Rootdiggers, also called Snakes," whom he described:

> They inhabit the southern part of the territory of Oregon, in the vicinity of upper California. Their population of about 10,000 souls is divided into several bands, scattered here and there over the barrenest country in all the region west of the mountains. . . . Occasionally a hunting party will come east of the mountains to hunt buffalo, and at the season when the fish come up from the sea, they go down to the banks of Salmon River and its tributaries to lay in their winter stock. They are pretty well provided with horses.
>
> At the rendezvous, they gave a parade to greet the whites that were there. Three hundred of their warriors came up in good order and at full gallop into the midst of our camp. They were hideously painted, armed with war clubs and covered all over with feathers, pearls, wolves' tails, teeth and claws of animals, outlandish adornments, with which each one had decked himself out according to his fancy.
>
> Those who had wounds received in war, and those who had killed the enemies of their tribe, displayed their scars ostentatiously and waved the scalps they had taken on the end of poles, after the manner of standards. After riding a few times around the camp, uttering at intervals shouts of joy, they dismounted and all came to shake hands with the whites in sign of friendship.[7]

De Smet felt little enthusiasm for their method of entertainment, the same as they had accorded the first women to follow the trail. Unlike the Protestant missionaries who had preceded him, he made an effort to discuss religious matters with the Green River

---

[6] Patrick A. McGovern, *History of the Diocese of Cheyenne*, 243–44.

[7] *Letters and Sketches*, 163–164. The Green River Snakes may have been "Rootdiggers" because of scarcity of game in the Green River area. Meeting the Indians for the first time, De Smet could not recognize the difference between Digger and Horse Indians.

Snakes in council, where he explained that he had come to save
their souls. After the Indians had had a chance to debate the matter
thoroughly, Pah-dasher-wah-un-dah addressed the priest. "Black-
gown," he said, "your words have entered our hearts, they will
never go out from them."

Then he told the priest that his country was open to him, that
he could settle wherever he pleased. After discussing the matter
with the elders of his tribe, the chief announced that he had created
a law whereby anyone who stole from the white man or "committed any other scandal" would be punished publicly. De Smet
observed that the Snakes believed that the Great Spirit resided in
the sun, in the fire, and in the earth, all of which they called upon
to witness their pledge of good behavior.

The priest was less favorably impressed by the Bannocks,
whom he considered "the most perfidious nation" next to the
Blackfeet, although in the following year he made many converts
among them. He first learned of their treachery from Little Chief
of the Flatheads, who would not smoke the pipe with them because of an experience he had had some time before, when they
attempted to wipe out his band after professing their friendship.
Learning of their plan in time, he drove them off, at the same time
inflicting several casualties. He would probably have killed more
had he not realized that it was Sunday. In respect for the day,
he called off his warriors, and they knelt in prayer.[8]

When Oregon-bound Joseph Williams traveled west two
years later, the captain of his emigrant train told him not to be
afraid of Indians who approached openly, for they were coming
out of curiosity with no evil intent.[9] Not all white men were as
perceptive. Will Drannan, whose many exploits fill two volumes,[10]
tells of spotting a column of young braves not far from Green
River.[11] In recounting the story, he admitted that they were not

---

[8] *Ibid.*, 288–89.

[9] Joseph Williams, *Narrative of a Tour from the State of Indiana to the Oregon Territory in the Years 1841–1842*, 45.

[10] W. F. Drannan, *Thirty-One Years on the Plains and in the Mountains*
and *Chief of Scouts Piloting Emigrants across the Plains.*

[11] *Ibid.*, 131–33.

on the warpath but on a hunting excursion. Nevertheless, he called his scouts to him and cautioned them to have their guns and pistols ready. When the Indians rounded the point, each man was instructed to get an Indian—"to shout and shoot to kill."

When he ordered, "Charge!" every man "did his duty." Although Drannan claimed that he had been in several Indian fights before, he said that he had never seen Indians so completely taken by surprise. When the scouts fired upon them, they whirled and went at least two hundred yards before even attempting to shoot an arrow. Fourteen were killed in the first charge, and within three hundred yards, six more were slain. After the rest escaped in the willows, the white men caught sixteen of their horses, all with good hair ropes around their necks.

Drannan instructed his companions to "lift the scalps," but to his surprise, they did not know what he meant. So he demonstrated. When asked what he was going to do with the bloody trophies, he said that he intended to make "guards" of them. They would be placed on poles, elevated above the wagons as warning to the natives. The Indians were incensed by such atrocities.

Open hostility on the part of the Cheyennes and the Sioux broke out east of the Rockies in the spring of 1841. Reports of their outrages reached Bridger, then on Henry's Fork. In deep concern for the safety of the veteran trapper Henry Fraeb, he sent Jim Baker to warn him, for he was then on the upper Little Snake River, on the west side of the Laramie Mountains, just inside the border of Shoshoni territory.

Baker and the Sioux arrived at approximately the same time, the latter firing upon Fraeb's scouts. Although they caused no further trouble for the next two weeks, the white men, knowing that they would come again, hastily constructed a fortress. The sight of it so infuriated the Indians that they fired upon it relentlessly, killing four of the trappers, including Fraeb. The others escaped and made their way to Henry's Fork.[12]

[12] LeRoy R. Hafen, "Fraeb's Last Fight and How Battle Mountain Got Its Name," *Colorado Magazine*, Vol. VII, No. 3 (May, 1930), 97–101.

The following year Pah-dasher-wah-un-dah, still chief of the Shoshonis, died of natural causes. He was succeeded by Moh-woom-hah, who lived but a few months to enjoy his honor. The cause of his death is unknown, but the result amounted to chaos. The Shoshonis scattered in small, disorganized bands, which were easy prey for their enemies. Word of their unsettled condition soon reached the Plains.

Elijah White, a missionary recently appointed Indian agent for Oregon, was the first to report a brush with the Sioux inside Shoshoni territory. Fitzpatrick, who led White's party of more than one hundred settlers bound for Oregon, guided them from Fort Laramie to Fort Hall. He is credited with saving the life of at least two members of the party—Lansford W. Hastings and A. L. Lovejoy, who made the mistake of dropping behind to carve their names on Independence Rock.[13] They were seized by a band of Sioux warriors and stripped of their clothing. The Indians held them captive two hours while trying to make up their minds what to do with them. Meanwhile, the white men prepared for battle.

When the Sioux approached, Fitzpatrick went forward, signifying his desire for peace, but they did not stop until they were within gunshot. Then as if impressed by the warlike preparations of the camp, they released their two victims, who were joyfully reunited with their friends. Before the white men moved on, the Indians again showed signs of hostility. A second time Fitzpatrick went forward as moderator. He prevailed upon the chief and his warriors to pay a visit to the white men. Satisfied by the gifts and entertainment they received from the emigrants, the Indians withdrew without further trouble.

The possibility of incursions of Sioux caused White to designate "the dangerous Indian country" as lying between Fort Laramie and Fort Hall. He felt safe in the thought that he had obtained

---

[13] Lansford W. Hastings, *The Emigrant's Guide to Oregon and California*, 9–10; A. L. Lovejoy, "Lovejoy's Own Story," *O.H.Q.*, Vol. XXXI, No. 3 (1930), 240–50.

Fitzpatrick as his guide to conduct him beyond the dangers of the "savages," who were on every hand, "as subtle as the devil himself."[14]

The year 1842 had further significance, for gold was discovered in the South Pass area, although it was not until almost twenty years later that the finds were sufficient to warrant a gold rush. Also that year John Charles Frémont, "the Pathfinder," appeared in the Rockies. He had quickly won the respect if not the friendship of the Sioux at Fort Laramie, where he let it be known to the warriors that he had no fear of them.[15] The force of his statement which follows served better than a banner of scalps to impress the Indians that he meant what he said:

> We are few and you are many, and may kill us all; but there will be much crying in your villages, for many of your young men will stay behind and forget to return with your warriors from the mountains. Do you think that our great chief will let his soldiers die and forget to cover their graves? Before the snow melts again, his warriors will sweep away your villages as the fire does the prairies in the autumn. See! I have pulled down my white houses, and my people are ready. When the sun is ten paces higher, we will be on the march.

Frémont proceeded westward without incident. When he reached Wind River, he scaled what he thought to be the highest peak (Fremont Peak) in the mountain range. After unfurling an American flag at the top, he and his companion viewed with awe the headwaters of the famous rivers of the Northwest.[16] Although Frémont was in error regarding the peak, he made such a great contribution to the early period of migration that he justified his title, "the Pathfinder." The designation came so many years after the paths had actually been found that it seems out of place, and yet with his maps and travel aids he popularized the trail.

Jim Bridger informed Frémont of the exceedingly dangerous

[14] A. J. Allen, *Ten Years in Oregon*, 153.
[15] John Charles Frémont, *Memoirs of My Life*, 201.
[16] Later Henry Gannett (see Richard A. Bartlett, *Great Surveys of the American West*, 60), a member of the Hayden Expedition, discovered that another peak in the Wind River Range was higher. It bears the name Gannett.

conditions of the time.[17] He said that the Sioux had broken into open hostility, and that the preceding autumn his party had met them in an engagement in which a number of lives had been lost on both sides. He stated that the Sioux, united with the Cheyenne and Gros Ventre Indians, were scouring the upper country in large war parties, and were, at the time, in the neighborhood of "the famous landmark," Red Buttes (near Casper, Wyoming). Furthermore, they had declared war on every living thing to be found west of that point, their main object being an attack on a large camp of whites and Snake Indians in Sweetwater Valley.

There is no record to show exactly when Washakie took over as chief of the Shoshonis, but the enemy war parties mentioned by Bridger may have brought his people to the realization that they must have strong leadership. Their only chance for survival would be in banding together under a young chieftain who would lead them in war as well as in peace. The major decision to make Washakie their head chief may have been reached while the Indians were in the encampment at Sweetwater.

The establishment of Fort Bridger (1843) was important to the Shoshonis, as it was later to prove a popular trading post and campground, but it offered little protection during its first year. A party of New York emigrants who had planned to remain at the Bridger-Vasquez Fort (Fort Bridger) two weeks "to make meat" changed their minds when they found that the Sioux and Cheyennes had run all of the buffalo out of the country. Besides, previous to the arrival of the emigrants, they had killed three Snake Indians and stolen sixty horses. [18]

Louis Vasquez, Bridger's partner, was thoroughly familiar with the mountains after many years of experience as trapper and trader. He came originally from St. Louis, where he was born to a French mother and a Spanish father. Later he became copartner of the Bridger and Vasquez business in Salt Lake City, which he operated as Bridger preferred to live among the Snakes.

[17] Charles Pruess, *Exploring with Frémont*, 25–26.

[18] Alter quotes from the privately owned manuscript of John Boardman in *James Bridger*, 176.

Soon after establishing the fort, Bridger dictated a letter to the famous fur-trading firm, Pierre Chouteau, Jr., & Company of St. Louis. In it he said, "I have established a small fort, with a blacksmith shop and a supply of iron in the road of the emigrants on Black Fork of Green River, which promises fairly."[19]

Joel Palmer, leader of an Oregon emigrant train, called Fort Bridger "a shabby concern," of poles daubed with mud.[20] When he visited there on July 25, 1845, he saw twenty-five lodges occupied by squaw men and their families. The traders had a good supply of Indian goods, ranging from robes to moccasins "and other Indian fixens." These they would trade for commodities such as flour, sugar, and gunpowder. The Indian wives of the traders were mostly Shoshonis and Paiutes, with probably several Utes included in the number.

Another emigrant, Edwin C. Bryant, who came along the trail a year later, reported conditions still unsettled.[21] He and his party found about five hundred Snake Indians encamped near Fort Bridger, but when he gave them news respecting the movement of the Sioux, most of them left. He said he supposed that they were going elsewhere to organize a war party to resist the threatened invasion from the large number of Sioux warriors whom he had observed heading their way.

About this time Bill Hamilton, chronicler with the expedition of the colorful mountain man Old Bill Williams, arrived in the Wind River area.[22] He claimed that it was constantly being invaded by war parties of Blackfeet and Crows. After discovering moccasin tracks, the white men slept with arms at their sides. During the night, the expected attack was made by the Blackfeet, who retreated after losing several of their number. The next morning the trappers found that some of their horses had been wounded; consequently, they tracked the enemy down and wiped them out.

Four days later the trappers encountered the Shoshonis, who

[19] *Ibid.*, 177.
[20] *Journal of Travels over the Rocky Mountains*, 74.
[21] *What I Saw in California; Or Rocky Mountain Adventures*, 136–43.
[22] William T. Hamilton, *My Sixty Years on the Plains*, 78–98.

were wild with joy at the sight of Blackfeet scalps and were glad to pay handsomely for them. Later Washakie arrived with a body-guard of twenty well-armed braves. He greeted Williams warmly for the two had long been friends. The chief's son (probably Ko-na-ya), after buying a good horse, presented it to Hamilton, who obligingly gave him the scalp he had been admiring.

The trappers, somewhat later, taught the bothersome Utes a bitter lesson regarding the fighting ability of white men by over-whelming a large number of them. The Utes had attacked their camp just before daylight, as was their custom. A Bannock band was likewise defeated when the trappers reached Camas Prairie. The deadly Colts in the hands of the white men took a merciless toll. Each trapper acquired a scalp or two, besides flintlock guns and horses.

The trapping party next joined the Green River Snakes on one of their hunting excursions into the Big Horns. In spite of their constant fear of encountering an enemy, Hamilton described the Indians as leading a carefree life. The young people would sing and dance until midnight while the elders of the tribe would sit in council and debate over which foe they were most likely to meet next. There were one hundred lodges in their village.

As the Indians proceeded to Shoshone River, Washakie pointed out the Big Hot Springs which he prized highly. He was later to turn them over to the government with the stipulation that the Indians might always be allowed to camp there without charge.

The Crows were apparently at peace with the Shoshonis at the time Bill Williams was with them, as a friendly party came to call. During a horse race the Shoshonis held back their best racers until after the Crows had bet all that they had. Then they en-tered their best horses and easily won the stakes. Crestfallen, though lacking in bitterness over their defeat, the guests left with the promise of returning at a later date. Hamilton stated that In-dians were good losers. When he defeated a Shoshoni brave in a horse race, the young man took it in good spirit, "as the Indians are always known to do."[23]

[23] *Ibid.*, 136-37.

On June 28, 1847, Jim Bridger met Brigham Young on the Big Sandy. There, in answer to the Mormon leader's questions regarding the nature of the country, he reputedly made his celebrated remark that he would give a thousand dollars for a bushel of corn raised in the Great Salt Lake Basin. Proof that the statement was ever made lies in the contemporary records of the Latter-day Saint Church Historian who said, "He [Bridger] considered it imprudent to bring a large population into the Great Basin until it was ascertained that grain could be raised; he said he would give one thousand dollars for a bushel of corn raised in the basin."[24]

This statement, oft quoted and misquoted, sometimes reads an ear of corn, a bushel of wheat, or a bushel of grain. It later served as an impetus to the determined settlers, and it was used by church authorities to encourage its members to persevere through hardship and even to suggest to them the probability of altering the climate to fit their needs.[25] No one knew the country better than Jim Bridger, but he obviously underestimated the Mormons.

He seemed oblivious of the fact that he might have offended them. When he met in council with the Twelve Apostles, he generously shared his knowledge of the Great Salt Lake Basin and the surrounding area. He told them about the country itself, the lake (it had taken his men three months by canoe to circle it), the climate, the minerals, the timber, and the Indians. He did not mention the friendlies (the Shoshonis), but he did warn them to be on guard against the treacherous Utes, the "bad people around Utah Lake." Though most of the so-called bad Indians were armed, he said that they would not molest large parties. They might, however, rob, abuse, or even kill anyone caught alone.

He made the noteworthy comment that a farmer had already settled in the Bear River Valley (1847). While Bridger considered the soil fertile, he felt that the nights were too cold for growing corn. He spoke vaguely of a "land at the north end of the Cali-

[24] William Richards, "History of Brigham Young," Latter-day Saints (hereinafter cited as L.D.S.) Church Historian's Office, 95.

[25] Alter, *James Bridger*, 189–92.

fornia mountains," where there was good timber, and where grain and fruit could be grown profitably. Southeast of the barren desert (stretching between Salt Lake and the Gulf of California) there was a tribe of Indians, he said, "unknown to either travelers or geographers." He described them as raising abundant crops of every kind, but he did not identify them.

He was most definitely referring to the area claimed by Shoshonean Pine Nut Eaters when he said, "There is a kind of cedar grows on it [the land of his description] which bears fruit something like juniper berries, of a yellow color and about the size of an ordinary plum. The Indians grind the fruit and make the best kind of meal." He added that he could "easily gather a hundred bushels off one tree." "Blanket Chief" Bridger, the entertainer, was undeniably stretching the fact. The Mormon leader William Clayton, who listened skeptically to his remarks, stated that the Saints would know more about the country after they had seen it for themselves.[26]

Wilford Woodruff, another member of the Mormon party, stated that Bridger told the Saints that if they decided to settle he would go with them.[27] Nevertheless, as the wagons rolled westward, the informant seems not to have been invited to go along. The Saints, like Astor's scouts, were profiting by his excellent experience, though they were not too sure of his veracity. The mountain man was to find in the following years that he could not rid himself of the Mormons as easily as he had of Vanderburgh, whom he had led into the Blackfoot country where he was killed. The Mormons had come to found an empire, regardless of Bridger and his warnings or of the Indians who claimed the country.

A week after the Mormons had taken up residence in the Great Salt Lake Basin, a band of Shoshonis made their appearance. They came to advise the white men that the land belonged to them, but that they would sell for guns and ammunition. Furthermore, they wished to complain against the Utes for usurping their rights by coming into their territory to trade. Peace was restored when the two tribes met in council to talk over their difficulties and feast

[26] *William Clayton's Journal*, 276.   [27] *Journal and Life History*, 15–16.

on uncooked crickets. This was the first known medicine talk between the Shoshonis and the Utes at Salt Lake.

The Saints, undeterred by Bridger, found their Promised Land. Their trail, branching from the Emigrant Road to Oregon at Fort Bridger, was well traveled by the time gold was discovered at Sutter's Mill in California. The feverish gold seekers pouring through Shoshoni country caused the old trail to be widened and new trails to be made to shorten the distance to the gold fields.

When De Smet brought a group of Indians from the upper Missouri to Fort Laramie (1851), they were astounded by the trail:

> Our Indian companions, who had never seen but the narrow hunting paths by which they transport themselves and their lodges, were filled with admiration on seeing this noble highway, which is as smooth as a bare floor swept by the winds, and not a blade of grass can shoot up on it on account of the continual passing.
>
> They conceived a high idea of the "Countless White Nation," as they expressed it. They fancied that all had gone over that road, and that an immense void must exist in the land of the rising sun. Their countenances testified evident incredulity when I told them that their exit was in no wise perceived in the land of the whites. They styled the route the "Great Medicine Road of the Whites."[28]

Every mile of this road was represented by heartache and suffering. It became lined with graves of those unable to reach their goal: a new life in Oregon, spiritual fulfillment in the Promised Land of Utah, or wealth at the "diggings" in California. The fate of the Donner Party (1846–47), in which forty-two lost their lives in the deep Sierra snows of California, is well known.

Also, we are familiar with the details of the Death Valley tragedy, three years later. Many accounts are based on the records of William Lewis Manly, who rescued the starving remnants of a once large party of emigrants. In the Valley of Death, the horrors and privations were well known to the Panamints, who for generations had brought their sick and aged there to perish. Such stories are detailed but infrequent, for little is known about the countless unmarked graves along the Emigrant Road.

[28] De Smet, *Life and Letters*, II, 671–72.

CHAPTER SEVEN

Great White Father

THE SHOSHONIS viewed with alarm the continual traffic along the Emigrant Road. Would it never cease? They were gravely concerned over the ever widening "river of destruction," for the white man devoured their game while his horses fed upon the grass which had once nourished large herds of buffalo. Additional roads and cutoffs continued to be made, disregarding Indian rights. Would the country to the west some day be filled, and would the impoverished hunting grounds next be coveted by the white man?

Captain Howard Stansbury, of the corps of Topographical Engineers of the army, hired Bridger to guide him over a new trail from Black's Fork to Salt Lake (1849). According to Stansbury's report, there were already two emigrant routes from Fort Bridger to the Humboldt River in Nevada.[1] The first followed the Bear and Portneuf rivers and passed southwestward, while the second went by way of Echo and Weber canyons and the north end of Great Salt Lake to a junction with the main California road on the Humboldt, below Point of Rocks. Since one went too far north, the other too far south, the impatient gold seekers felt that they needed a shortened route between the two.

Trails going through the heart of the Basin country blotted out the already sparse vegetation and even caused loss of life among the natives. An example of the reckless nature of the white men is found in the following note penned by a member of an emigrant party going along the Humboldt Valley route to California. "None of our company was killed by the Indians; but John

[1] (Hereinafter cited as Stansbury's report), *Sen. Exec. Doc. 3*, 32 Cong., spec. sess. (587), II, 77.

Greenwood, son of the pilot, shot down an Indian by the roadside and afterwards boasted of it."[2] Lacking means of defense, the Basin natives found themselves at the mercy of the white man. Many incidents caused resentment to mount among the Shoshokos of Utah and Nevada who sought means of retaliation.

Captain Stansbury and Bridger were joined by Lieutenant John W. Gunnison for a reconnaissance trip over the new road westward. Their first camp was a spot well known to the Indians, for it was one to which they had formerly been in the habit of going to consult their oracle, whose medicine lodge had been located in the area. Although the sacred lodge had apparently been moved, there was still a small encampment of Snakes on the opposite side of the stream.

Stansbury tells us that an ox, strayed from some "unfortunate emigrant," was found in such capital condition that it was shot, "and such portions as the white men could not carry with them were most generously presented to the Indians."[3] He noted how every portion of the animal was used, even the paunch and entrails, which were washed thoroughly. The women, serving as butchers, showed their skill "while the men lounged about leaning lazily upon their rifles and looking listlessly on as if it were a matter in which they were in no manner interested." When Stansbury and his party crossed Ogden Valley, they came upon eight to ten Indian women and girls who, with baskets on their backs, were gathering seeds. Bridger called them "Snake Diggers." Stansbury stated:

> The instant they discovered us, an immediate and precipitate flight took place, nor could all the remonstrance of the guide, who called loudly after them in their own language, induce them to halt for a single moment. Those who were too close to escape by running hid themselves in the bushes and grass so effectively that in less time than it has taken to narrate the circumstances, only two of them were to be seen.
> These were a couple of girls of twelve or thirteen years of age,

[2] Harris, "The White Knife Shoshoni," *loc. cit.*, 74.
[3] Stansbury's report (587), 82.

who, with their baskets dangling at their backs, set off at their utmost speed for the mountains, and continued to run as long as we could see them, without stopping or so much as turning their heads to look behind them. The whole party was entirely naked.

After they had disappeared, we came near riding over two girls of sixteen or seventeen who had "cached" themselves behind a fallen tree. They started up, gazed upon us for a second, waved us to continue our journey and then fled with a rapidity that soon carried them beyond our sight.

If these young women were Snake Diggers as Bridger claimed, Stansbury's statement that they were "entirely naked" should probably have been qualified to read that they were "entirely naked except for the double apron," which was a necessary garment of the women. The women did not realize until after the arrival of the white man that modesty required them to cover their breasts.

The White Knife Shoshonis in recent times proved that although many of the taboos had been discarded, the Indians still had their own idea about what constitutes modesty.[4] A baby show was held at the agency hospital at Owyhee, Nevada, where the nurses made the mistake of completely unclothing the female babies. Such consternation resulted that the affair was not repeated.

Stansbury, with Bridger as his guide, next went eastward to found a new trail to the south of the old roadway along the Sweetwater. Leaving the established emigrant road near Church Butte (below the mouth of Ham's Fork), Bridger led the way to Pilot Butte (near Green River, Wyoming). Then, after descending Rabbit Hollow, he crossed Green River and entered Bitter Creek Basin as he proceeded eastward toward the North Platte.

Just before crossing the river, Stansbury and his men saw a war party of Shoshonis come charging toward them. The warriors had mistaken them for the enemies, the Utes. Recognizing Bridger, they allowed the white men to pass unmolested. Stansbury described them as having an assortment of weapons, including old bayonets attached to the end of long poles.

[4] Harris, "The White Knife Shoshoni," *loc. cit.*, 105.

The explorers proceeded toward Little Snake River and crossed the Continental Divide at Bridger's Pass. Although the route they found between Bridger and Fort Laramie was more direct, the original trail—the trail of the Oregon, Mormon, and California emigrants—continued to be used. The Pony Express (1860), which lasted only eighteen months, until the Overland Telegraph (1861) was completed, followed the Master Trail to Oregon. Because of the Overland Telegraph and the Overland Stage lines, it became known as the Overland Trail.

The white man, however, was finally forced, in 1862, to turn the old route along the Platte back to the Sioux in order to gain passage of the railroad through southern Wyoming (1868). The new route—the Overland Trail or Overland Stage Route in Wyoming—went southward to the Cherokee Trail (Colorado) and back northward to the Laramie Plains. Then it followed the course charted by Stansbury and Bridger to Green River. While satisfying the Sioux by withdrawing from their area, the government did not consider the Shoshonis, through whose territory another major highway was then established.

Frémont, back in 1842, had recommended that forts be constructed and maintained for the protection of emigrants along the trails, but it was not until 1849 that the government bought Fort Laramie and Fort Hall for this purpose. That same year the Great White Father in Washington assumed the problem of administering the affairs of the Indians in the Far West.[5]

The Oregon Superintendency was supposed to serve the vast Oregon Territory which extended from the Pacific Coast to the Continental Divide. It included all Shoshoni lands north of the

[5] Dale L. Morgan, "Washakie and the Shoshoni," *Annals of Wyoming*, Vol. 25, No. 2 (July, 1953), 141–45. A transcript of selected letters of the Utah Superintendency in the National Archives was made and edited by Dale L. Morgan and subsequently published in serial form in the *Annals of Wyoming* (July, 1953, to April, 1958), under the above title. Documents and incoming correspondence of the Bureau of Indian Affairs from agencies and superintendencies (1824–80) are now on microfilm. They are found in their original form in Record Group 75, Office of Indian Affairs, Washington, D.C., Indian Office Records (hereinafter cited as I.O.R.).

territorial line at 42°. From the east, the Central Superintendency at St. Louis reached as far as the Oregon boundary at South Pass. Even before the Utah Superintendency (extending eastward over the Uinta Mountains of Colorado and Bridger Valley of Wyoming) was created, John Wilson, a Missourian, was appointed Salt Lake Indian agent.

In his first official report, dated at Fort Bridger, August 22, 1849, he mentioned the chiefs of the various bands of Shoshonis as Mono (Lots of Sons-in-law), Wiskin (Cut-Hair), Oapiche (Big Man), and Washakie (Gourd Rattle). He made a distinction between the Shoshonis and Shoshokos and gave the name Augutasipa as the "most noted chief" of the latter. These Indians had now begun to acquire the horse and the gun, and they were consolidating for purposes of depredation. They were uniting into bands for the first time in their history. Raiding parties, sometimes instigated by unscrupulous white men who had affiliated themselves with the Indians, were beginning to prey upon the emigrants along the trail.

Wilson made a significant distinction between the Shoshonis and Shoshokos by saying: "Of the relative portion of each band, no definite account can be given; for as soon as a Sho-sho-nie becomes too poor or does not own a horse, he is at once called a Sho-sho-coe; but as soon as a Sho-sho-coe can or does own a horse he is again a riding Indian and therefore a Sho-sho-nie."[6] His division into Shoshonis (Snakes) and Shoshokos represents the two main branches of the tribe—the Northern and the Western. Washakie's followers had long since assumed a superficial Plains culture, changing them from typical Basin type Indians even though they still continued to share the same taboos and legends.

We regret that Wilson did not tell the nature of his interview with Washakie on his official visit. He merely alluded to it. Then he outlined the territory claimed by the various bands. In his opinion the land occupied by the Green River Snakes had too high an elevation ever to be useful for cultivation. For food, he

[6] John Wilson to Secretary of the Interior, August 22, 1849, I.O.R.

said, the Shoshonis depended largely on game and roots. He spoke of camass as "rank poison" in its native state, but it became a wholesome diet after the natives had put it in a hole in the ground and built a large fire over it.

He urged the government to "put in practice some mode of relief for these unfortunate people." He stated that the fish in Utah Lake and its sources had been "greatly diminished" by the settlement in Salt Lake Valley and that the emigrants along the trails had driven away the game.

The agent outlined a plan for a council at Fort Bridger that met with Washakie's hearty approval, but the council which the chief had reason to look forward to did not materialize until 1851. Then ironically it was not held in his country but at Fort Laramie, where the energetic Fitzpatrick was serving as agent for the Platte River Indians—the Sioux, Arapahoes, and Cheyennes.

With the creation of Utah Territory in 1850, the governor (Brigham Young) was made ex officio superintendent of Indian affairs. On July 21, 1851, he issued his first proclamation as superintendent.[7] In it he created three agencies to handle Indian matters in the newly formed territory.

All Snakes or Shoshonis were assigned to the Uinta Agency, "along with the Uinta, Yampa, and all other tribes South, within said Territory, and east of the Eastern rim of the Great Basin." Jacob H. Holeman, a Kentucky gentile, was the agent and Stephen B. Rose, a Mormon from New Jersey, was the subagent assigned to the Uinta Agency. Brigham Young felt that the Uinta Valley would be a suitable location for an agency as it had "the greatest facilities for exercising a favorable influence for uniting the various tribes and bands in one common interest."

The long-anticipated council was scheduled to meet in Fort Laramie on September 1, 1851. Holeman planned to pick up Jim Bridger along the way and join the Shoshonis, as previously arranged, at Sweetwater.[8] Both Young and Holeman urged the sub-

---

[7] "Proclamation," *Deseret News* (August 8, 1851).
[8] Jacob Holeman to Young, August 11, 1851, I.O.R.

agents to go on this mission and take some of the chiefs under their jurisdiction. Holeman suggested that it might be well to convey the Ute chiefs through the Snake and Crow territory in carriages "as privately as possible." Young replied:

> I have sent a letter with the messengers to some of the Utah [Ute] Chiefs, inducing them to go; Indian Walker [better known as the Ute war chief Walkara] and in fact many others of the chiefs are at war with the Shoshones and other tribes who will probably be en masse at Laramie. It will, therefore, be of the utmost importance, if Walker and others of the Tribes should go (which I apprehend will be an exploit not easily accomplished) to take such measures as to ensure their safe return to their various tribes, free from the molestation of other Indians.
>
> I do most earnestly recommend that they go as privately as possible, in citizens dress, such as white men wear. They will of course be furnished rations; and I think should go in carriages or covered wagons; and when they shall arrive at Laramie, have a room where they can remain in safety, unless they will of their own accord go out and mix with other tribes.[9]

The Mormon leader recommended that Sowiette go with the group as he, unlike Walkara, was one of the most peaceful and influential chiefs among the Utes. Young warned Holeman to watch over the aged chieftain closely because of his advanced years and the fact that the Shoshonis, having good cause to remember him, might try to lift his scalp.

Agent Holeman met the Shoshonis at Sweetwater on August 22. The opportunity to talk with the Great White Father at his council evoked such great excitement that the whole band of Green River Snakes planned to go. But they had scarcely begun their trek the next day when two of their number were discovered at the roadside, killed and scalped. Great confusion ensued. The infuriated Indians were undecided for the moment whether to blame the white men or the Cheyennes, who had committed the atrocity. In any event, they told the agent that they would go no

---

[9] Young to Holeman, August 11, 1851, I.O.R.

farther. They said that their oracle had advised them not to go—
that they would surely be murdered, for the white men were leading them into the hands of their enemies.

They were now sure that the oracle had been correct. Abandoning their plan to attend the treaty council, the warriors set out
to find the guilty Cheyennes. Meanwhile, the agent put up his
strongest arguments for their going on to Fort Laramie. He feared
that if he gave up the plan when they were in such a hostile state
of mind, it might be difficult to negotiate with them in the future.
While the warriors unsuccessfully scoured the country, he and
the elders parleyed. The latter explained that they had a friendly
feeling toward their white brothers, but they felt that if they were
going through enemy country they might unknowingly do something wrong and that the other Indian tribes might attack and
abuse them. It was not until Holeman had rushed two white men
to Fort Laramie to ask for a military escort that they reconsidered.

That night at council they consulted their medicine and decided that they should not go as a village, but that they would
send eighty of their leading men as spokesmen for the tribe. These
men, with their retinue of women, children, and guards who
accompanied them, amounted to a delegation of perhaps two
hundred Indians. Jim Bridger made sure that each warrior had a
gun. By arming the Indians, he was unconsciously driving a
further wedge between himself and the Mormons, for guns in the
hands of the Shoshonis threatened the peace of the settlers. The
old mountaineer's motives would inevitably be questioned.

The Shoshonis followed the general course of the "Medicine
Road of the Whites" along the Sweetwater to the North Platte
River, which they crossed west of present Casper, Wyoming.
From there on, they followed the south side of the stream. Emigrants were advised at Fort Laramie and Fort Bridger to be on
the lookout for a friendly band of Indians, so that a reckless white
man would not fire upon them.

It was a novel experience for the Shoshonis to be traveling
peacefully into the heart of the country claimed by the Platte

River Indians. The warriors had been there before on a different kind of mission. Now they were going fearlessly into a country that once belonged to their fathers and their allies, the Kiowas and Comanches. It was the territory from which they had been driven by the Blackfeet, the Crows, and the powerful Platte River federation—the Sioux, Arapahoes, and Cheyennes.

The Shoshonis proceeded without incident until they came in sight of the famous fort at the mouth of the Laramie—Fort William it had been called at the time of its construction as a fur-trading post in 1834. The American Fur Company had bought it two years later and had replaced the decaying log fortress with a more permanent adobe structure (1841), renamed Fort John. Eight years later it had been bought by the government and given the permanent title Laramie. La Ramie, for whom the fort was indirectly named, was a fur trapper thought to have been killed by the Arapahoes in 1821.

As the Shoshonis were filing in single column down the slope to the west, they heard the sound of wailing from the Sioux encampment to the south, along the river. The women were keening for their loved ones, killed at some time in the past by the Shoshonis. Soldiers had come out to watch the drama. Washakie and his Indians, disregarding the commotion they had aroused, continued to advance slowly. Recognizing the tenseness of the situation, the officer in charge on the post had "Boots and Saddles" sounded to alert the soldiers for possible trouble.

The Shoshonis silently rode forward. Before them stretched a panoramic view with so many tipis dotting the area along the river that it was impossible to count them all. Washakie could see the old fur-trading post—Fort John—still standing. New buildings had been constructed outside the adobe walls since Laramie had become a military post. It was a busy sight, with people coming forward to watch the arrival.

If Washakie had any thought of the prediction of the oracle, he did not waver. Bridger had already reported the approach of the Snakes and had been instructed to lead them to the fort. Private Percival Lowe, one of the Dragoons stationed there, afterwards described the long line as it moved forward, the warriors in their battle array with "arms ready for use and every man apparently expectant, the women and children and baggage bringing up the rear, well guarded. . . . They were dressed in their best, riding fine horses, and made a grandly savage appearance."[10]

When the Shoshonis were less than a mile away, a Sioux, bow and arrow in hand, sprang upon his pony and rushed toward Washakie. The hostile apparently was attempting to seek revenge because the chief had killed a relative in battle. An interpreter, foreseeing trouble, gave chase. The long column stopped abruptly, and Washakie calmly lifted his gun to his shoulder. When the interpreter reached the Sioux, he pulled him from his horse and disarmed him. The Shoshonis held their ground while he was led away.

Lowe, who later talked to Bridger about the incident, concluded that all that saved the Sioux was the brave work of the interpreter. He quoted Bridger as saying:

> My chief would 'er killed him quick, and then the fool Sioux would 'er got their backs up, and there wouldn't a been room to camp 'round here fer dead Sioux. You Dragoons acted nice, but you wouldn't have had no show if the fight had commenced—no makin' peace then.
>
> And I tell you another thing: the Sioux ain't goin' to try it again. They saw how the Snakes are armed. I got them guns fer 'um and they are good ones. It'll be a proud day for the Snakes if any of these prairie tribes pitch into 'um, and they are not a bit afraid. Uncle Sam told 'um to come down here and they'd be safe, but they aren't takin' his word for it altogether.[11]

The thousands of ponies in the already overgrazed radius of the fort necessitated moving the council, even before it convened, to the mouth of Horse Creek, near Lyman, Nebraska. The assembly there is sometimes known as the Horse Creek Council, differentiating it from other treaty councils held with the Platte

[10] *Five Years a Dragoon*, 79–81.
[11] *Ibid.*, 82.

River tribes at Fort Laramie.[12] During the move from Fort Laramie to Horse Creek, one of the most unusual cavalcades in Western history, a certain decorum was observed. Two companies of troops led the way. Then came government dignitaries from the Central Superintendency. Their carriages were followed by a long supply train.

Next came the Indians. The column, some two miles in length, included chiefs made handsome by war bonnets, warriors with their accouterments ready for battle, women with cradleboards strapped to their backs, children enjoying the luxury of a travois ride behind broken-down war ponies, and dogs—some with miniature travois dragging behind them. There was merit in the move, for all of the Indians were diverted from their grievances by the urgency of the moment. They were too busy for contention. In fact, the activity seemed to engender good will, which spread from one tribe to another.

Colonel D. D. Mitchell, of the Central Superintendency, failed to include the Shoshonis in the treaty. The reason he gave was that the Indians were not under his jurisdiction, but rather under the Utah Superintendency. He did, however, express his pleasure that they had come and promised to give them gifts along with the rest. Agent Holeman did not disguise his disappointment.

Washakie was soon aware of the fact that he was only a guest at the treaty council. His speech, which showed an undertone of disappointment, lacked his natural eloquence:

> Grand Father [he said], I have come a great distance to see you and hear you. I threw my family, too, away to come and listen, and I am glad and my people are glad that we have come. Our hearts are full; all our hearts are full of your words. We will talk them over again.

His remarks do not have the ring of assurance found in the speech of Chief Cut Nose of the Arapaho tribe, which still proudly claimed the Plains in conjunction with its allies, the Sioux and the

[12] A transcript of news reports published in the *St. Louis Missouri Republican*, September 26–November 30, 1851, is on file in the Western Archives, University of Wyoming Library. This account is based on these reports.

Cheyennes. In literary merit, the speech of Cut Nose ranks with the orations of Washakie at a later date. It follows:

> Grand Father, I thank the Great Spirit, the Sun and the Moon, for putting me on this earth. It is a good earth, and I hope there will be no more fighting on it—that the grass will grow and the water fall, and plenty of buffalo. You, Grand Father, are doing well for your children, in coming so far and taking so much trouble about them.
>
> I think you will do us much good; I will go home satisfied. I will sleep sound, and not have to watch my horses in the night, or be afraid for my squaws and children. We have to live on these streams and in the hills, and I would be glad if the whites would pick out a place for themselves and not come into our grounds; but if they must pass through our country, they should give us game for what they drive off.

Washakie had reason to be uneasy and unhappy, for he had not forgotten the outrage which the Cheyennes had committed on the first day of his journey. He stubbornly refused to smoke the pipe with them until they "covered the body," which meant that they must return the scalps taken near South Pass. After this was reluctantly done, he still refused to smoke until the Cheyennes had assured him that they had not celebrated with a Scalp Dance. After they had complied with his wishes, the Cheyennes entertained with a corn feast in deference to the Shoshonis who would not eat dog meat. The celebration lasted all night.

There is a related incident of a Cheyenne woman who appeared in the midst of a council session with her son, astride a horse. The boy, about twelve years of age, had been orphaned when his father was killed in battle by Washakie. The woman interrupted proceedings to present him to the chief, who, according to custom, was obligated to adopt him as his son with all rights and privileges. Washakie could not refuse.

The Horse Creek Council was thoroughly unsatisfactory from Washakie's point of view. In the first place, he had been wanting a council of his own in Bridger Valley as agent Wilson had suggested. There he could have given utterance to his complaints against the Crows for invading his hunting grounds. He could have told the Great Father that the Medicine Road of the Whites had brought such suffering to his people in the Green River region, and that he wished to claim Warm Valley (Wind River Valley) for his homeland. He did not have a voice at the Horse Creek Council nor did he have the privilege of refusing to sign the treaty which, if explained to him, was far from his desires. He was power-less to do anything about it when the white men gave the Big Horns down to Wind River to the Crows. Keeping his own council, he bided the day when he would have a chance to settle his right to the land in his own way.

From bits of information, we find that Tavendu-wets (White Man's Child),[13] another Shoshoni Indian, was recognized by the white man as leader of the tribe at Horse Creek. Could Washakie and Fitzpatrick have had difficulties, and was the slight intended? Or might it have been an error on the part of some irresponsible white man? There is even a possibility that Tavendu-wets spoke the English language better and, therefore, was a more satisfac-tory communicant. Washakie had some knowledge of English and French, though he seldom spoke either.

It seems incredible that an insignificant Indian should be named chieftain deliberately to undermine Washakie's already recog-nized power among his people—a power for peace. One authority, dismissing Tavendu-wets as a myth, points out that such men as Fitzpatrick were present and that they knew the prestige which Washakie had won.[14] True, and yet might the white men have feared this prestige, which had welded the Shoshonis into a pow-erful people? There was a lack of trust on the part of the white men as well as the Indians. The former were known to have rec-ognized minor individuals in other tribes for a similar reason. We have no knowledge of Tavendu-wets' background, but he appears to have been brought to the attention of his tribesmen for the first time.

[13] Tavendu-wets is an Anglicized form of Tibo-deapa (Tibo=white man+deapa=son).

[14] Hebard, *Washakie*, 82–83.

James S. Brown, Mormon missionary to the Shoshonis, in 1854, found a sad and thoughtful Washakie who claimed that he was no longer head chief but that the agent at Fort Laramie had bestowed the title upon another—Tavendu-wets.[15] At the time of his meeting with Washakie, Brown said that the chief claimed that when the agent at Fort Laramie designated Tavendu-wets as head of the Shoshonis he told them that they must accept him as their chief. Not only that, but the agent distributed blankets and other goods through the appointed leader, whom the Indians never recognized as their chief.

> That act of the government agents [said Brown] was the opening wedge to divide the Shoshone tribe into discontented factions, and thereby weaken it. Possibly that was the purpose in view, for before that the tribe was very powerful, with a chief at their head unexcelled for bravery, skill, and farsightedness. Chief Washakie was a bold, noble, hospitable, and honorable man. As an orator, I think he surpassed any man I ever met.

After the missionaries expressed themselves as wanting to visit the camp of Tavendu-wets, Washakie replied, "Maybe that is good, maybe not. I don't know. I hear there are bad men over there. I don't know."

Because there was no trail, the missionaries asked for a guide. One of the braves led them twenty miles, then disappeared over a ridge. By this time, the white men had found tracks which led them to the camp. In spite of a feeling of impending trouble, they pressed on. Soon they heard a drum and many voices in a war song. Rounding a point, they looked upon a village of what appeared to be thousands of Indians, dancing and singing. The missionaries had "a heavy feeling," as if "murder lurked in the offing." This was not surprising, for the garb as well as the expression in the eyes of the Indians they met indicated clearly that the Shoshonis were on the warpath.[16]

> The chief came slowly out, coolly shook hands with us, ordered our stock taken care of, and a dish of boiled meat set before us.

[15] Brown, *Life of a Pioneer*, 319. [16] *Ibid.*, 321.

Then his family left the lodge, taking their effects, leaving only three robes for us. The sun was just setting, and the chief said we could occupy his lodge that night, as he was going away, being afraid to stop there, as there were men in camp that he could not control. Then he walked off and out of sight.

Three braves, stripped and painted for battle, took a "sharp look" at the white men, then went to join in the War Dance. Heavyhearted, the missionaries seated themselves around the campfire. They were surrounded by about three hundred lodges, possibly fifteen hundred to two thousand Indians, mostly Shoshonis, though there were some Cheyenne and Arapaho traders among them. How could four white men defend themselves when the chief sought safer quarters? The missionaries discovered that L. B. Ryan, a white man and an avowed enemy of all Mormons, was chief of the organized band of desperadoes and Indians.

Escape was out of the question, especially since the missionaries were now without horses and food. They said their evening prayers, put their trust in God, and went to bed. The sound of the drum came nearer, and at length Ryan and seven young warriors paused just outside the lodge. Entering, the leader of the desperadoes squatted, cut off pieces from a stick of wood with his cutlass, and kindled the fire for a bright light. Then he demanded to know the missionaries' business. At the same time he told them that he had been robbed by the Mormons of his "bottom dollar," and that by "the eternal gods" he intended to have revenge. He smote the billet of wood in signal for his braves to enter. They came, "bows tightly corded and arrows in hand." Finding the white men with revolvers, they withdrew.

Against the fire outside, the white men could see the silhouettes of Indians circling the lodge in their fiendish dancing. Clutching their revolvers, Brown and his three companions planned to shoot the first warrior who entered and kill as many as possible before their lives were claimed. With their scalping knives, some of the warriors slashed a number of places in the side of the lodge as they danced by, but they did not re-enter. With a final war whoop they passed up the creek in the direction from which they came.

Thus we still lived, and were spared the awful necessity of shedding man's blood, even in self-defense, thanks be to God for His protection and mercies. Still the clouds hung so low, and so thickly around, that we could not feel safe in an attempt to leave the camp.[17]

Next morning Tavendu-wets sent the missionaries some boiled buffalo meat. Then he came to call. He emphasized the fact that until the danger was over they should remain in his lodge, where they would be relatively safe. All day they listened to the drum, the wild shouts, and "the whistling reeds of the war party," while "The Spirit whispered" for them "to stay in place."

In the early afternoon of the next day, the chief came with their horses and told them that it was a good time to move. Even Ryan and his henchmen appeared, with their manner more friendly. Ryan wanted to know which road the white men planned to take. When they told him that they intended to return to Washakie's camp, Tavendu-wets disappeared into the brush. As the white men rounded the bend, he appeared in their pathway and warned them not to go in the direction they had indicated. Again he told them that there were men in his camp whom he could not control.

This incident shows that Tavendu-wets, the Great White Father's hand-picked leader, was not altogether bad, just unable to cope with problems of leadership. Though capricious and troublemaking, he later proved to be a crafty and efficient band leader while Washakie and his warriors were away fighting the Crows in the disputed Wind River area.

[17] *Ibid.*, 324.

CHAPTER EIGHT

Troublesome Utes

IN AN EFFORT TO COMPLY with the wishes of Governor Young, Henry R. Day of the Pahvant Agency had purchased a carriage to convey the Ute chiefs to the Horse Creek Council.[1] Furthermore, he had sent an interpreter to the Indians in his district to prevail upon their chiefs to accompany him to Fort Laramie, but not one appeared. A band chief named Gro-se-pene and his sister were the only notables accepting the invitation. Sowiette sent his son Quon-di-ats; Walkara, Tomey (To-ma); and Wanship, Sou-ette. Young, believing that these delegates did not properly represent the different tribes, ordered Day to abandon the trip and buy each a suit of clothing, knives, tobacco, and other gifts for their willingness to attend the council.[2]

Sowiette and Walkara gave as their reason for not going the fact that they feared a trap on the part of the Mormons to kill them. Before the Indians had time to forget the white man's generosity, Day tried to negotiate a peaceful settlement of difficulties between the Shoshonis and the Utes. He sent for Cut Nose, a subchief, as Washakie was then at the Horse Creek Treaty Council. He asked that he and Sowiette, together with their warriors, meet him at Fort Bridger in late September for an important medicine talk. Day found that the two tribes had been warring for years. The council was perhaps of greater importance to the Shoshonis than the treaty arranged for the Platte River Indians because they were direct participants. How Washakie would have enjoyed the

[1] The Pahvants comprised a branch of the Utes who ranged in the desert country west of the Wasatch Mountains almost to the Utah-Nevada border. For discussion of the Pahvant Utes, *see* Steward, "Basin-Plateau Groups," 222, 224, 226–27.

[2] Henry R. Day to Commissioner of Indian Affairs, January 2, 1852, I.O.R.

opportunity of talking over his personal problems in council! But he had not yet returned from Horse Creek.

Coming together to discuss their tribal difficulties, the Utes and Shoshonis found themselves in agreement upon a common issue, the settlers. Nothing could have diverted them from their usual animosities more than a chance to concentrate their wrath upon the encroaching white men. Sowiette, rising to give full forcefulness to his words, exclaimed, "American—good! Mormon —no good! American—friend—! Mormon—Kill—Steal . . . ."

The chief vowed that they and their people had claimed all the lands upon which the Mormons had settled and that the Saints were driving them back farther each year. They were helping themselves not only to the soil but also to their timber. The Indians asked, if the Great Father were so powerful, why did he not keep the Mormons from taking their valleys and driving them into the mountains to starve? After the leaders of the two tribes had been given an opportunity to talk over their troubles, Day told them that the Great Father wished them to be at peace with the different nations of Indians and with the whites. Furthermore, they must not steal. After smoking the pipe again, the Indians clasped hands and agreed to be harmonious.

Agent Jacob H. Holeman, after returning from Horse Creek, expressed himself as encouraged by the feelings that the council had engendered.[3] He believed that the Shoshonis were so well pleased with the trip and the evidences of friendship which they received that they would use their influence with other tribes to make peace between themselves and to establish friendly relations with the whites. Commenting upon the Green River Snakes who attended the council, he said that they showed a profound respect for their Great Father. He referred to other Indians as scattered widely and split into small bands, each ruled by some favorite chief. He was impressed by the unified nature of the Shoshoni Nation, although he made no reference to the wedge which the white man had already driven.

[3] Holeman to Commissioner of Indian Affairs, March 29, 1852, I.O.R.

Two months after his return, Holeman met with a deputation of Ute Indians from Uinta Valley at Fort Bridger. Coming with overtures of friendship, they asked to have traders sent among them. Furthermore, they seemed determined to meet the Snakes in council so that they could sign a peace treaty.[4] Apparently they considered Day's informal meeting merely a preliminary to a conference.

The council was held in March, 1852, but details are lacking. Holeman reported that they were "now engaged in that laudable object." He had assurance from both the Utes and the Snakes that they would make a treaty which would place their friendly relations upon a lasting basis, but there were no white men present to report what took place.

The conflicting opinions of Agent Holeman and Young present a confusing picture. The former told of unrest and trouble along the trail through the Shoshoni country while Young indicated that all was serene.

Though Holeman had only words of the highest praise for the Green River Snakes, he reported that the Indians along the Humboldt were murdering and plundering every train that passed along the road. It was his hope to establish an agency in that vicinity in order to make the emigrants secure in their travel from Missouri to the West Coast. He gave as an example the attack upon the November mail from California, when four men were killed and a fifth wounded.[5] The wounded man, captured by the Indians, made his escape but was later found dead. Apparently, he had died from his wounds or from exhaustion.

Holeman explained the cause of these depredations. First, he said, the Indians were bitter toward the white men because trappers and traders cheated them out of their few possessions. Second, the Mormons took possession of their country, often driving off their game and even killing some of the natives. Third, emigrants were guilty of committing depredations on those who were in-

[4] Holeman to Young, March 30, 1852, I.O.R.
[5] Holeman to Commissioner of Indian Affairs, April 29, 1852, I.O.R.

clined to be friendly. Too many considered all Indians potential enemies. It was frequently stated that "the only good Indian is a dead one."

Young, denying Holeman's charges, defended the Mormons, the Indians, and even the "Freemen" (mountain men) at Green River, with whom he was later to have great difficulty. He said of the Shoshonis:

> There seems to be a mistaken idea in relation to the Shoshone Indians committing depredations, murders, etc., upon the emigrants. It has been and is the universal practice of emigrants upon reaching the country of these Indians, to relax their vigilance and usually dispense with their guard. This feeling of safety and sense of security is induced from the known friendly disposition of the Shoshones in whose country the weary traveler can repose in safety and the emigrant pass with impunity. As long as my acquaintance with them has existed, this is the first time that I have heard of such charges coming against them.[6]

The Mormon leader attempted also to clear the records for the Utes, who lived "below the main line of travel." He admitted talking to some of the Fort Hall Indians regarding the possibility that Bannocks and Shoshonis might have taken part in the depredations on the Humboldt. The Indians whom he questioned denied having had any part in the attacks. At the same time they admitted that they had heard rumors that emigrants were being robbed and killed in that locality.

On August 6, 1852, six Shoshoni messengers arrived at Salt Lake to make inquiry regarding trade and the possibility of a treaty council with Walkara of the Utes.[7] The medicine talks engineered by Day the September before, and those between the two tribes the following March, had brought about little change in their relations. This time the Shoshonis took their troubles directly to Brigham Young, who made plans to bring the two tribes together.

When the Shoshonis—under the leadership of Washakie, To-

---

[6] Young to Commissioner of Indian Affairs, May 28, 1852, I.O.R.
[7] Young to Commissioner of Indian Affairs, September 29, 1852, I.O.R.

ter-mitch, Watche-namp, and Ter-ret-e-ma—arrived, there were twenty-six lodges of them. The Mormons gave them presents, but they had difficulty getting the Utes to come to the council. After several unsuccessful attempts, they finally tolled them to Salt Lake. On their arrival, the Utes appeared "wary and inclined to try the patience of the Shoshones to the utmost." They were represented by Sowiette, Walkara, Antaro, and Anker-howitch with thirty-four lodges.

The main difficulty, according to Young, was in getting the two tribes to meet on friendly terms. Finally succeeding, he began by asking Walkara and Washakie if they wished to make peace and be friendly toward each other. They signified that they did. They also expressed themselves as wanting a lasting peace. Young then instructed Walkara to tell his tribe what had been said and to ask them if they, too, wanted lasting peace. If so, they were to rise and hold up their right hands. All stood and raised their hands. The Shoshonis were informed by their chief that they also were to vote. Again the affirmative vote was unanimous. The Mormon leader told them that they must never fight again. By living in peace, they could travel and trade in each other's country.

Following this, Young asked the Utes if the Mormons had been their friends, and if they loved them. When the question was interpreted, the Indians answered, "Yes," with signs of joy and good feeling. When the Utes were asked if the Saints might settle on their lands, the affirmative vote was again unanimous. Sowiette replied that it was good to have them settle there and that he wanted "a house close beside them." The Indians' hearts had been "made glad" by the Saints' hospitality—so glad in fact that they had for the time forgotten their grievances against the settlers.

Young then asked the Shoshonis if they would like to have the Mormons settle in the Green River country. Their reply was surprising. They said that the country did not belong to them, for they now lived in the Wind River area and along the Sweetwater. This assertion was made although the Treaty of 1851 specifically designated the Big Horn country to Wind River as Crow territory. Washakie by his admission was relinquishing his right to the Green River country and claiming his hunting ground for the first time as his homeland. According to Young, he stated that if the Mormons would settle on Green River, his people would gladly trade with them. This invitation was later accepted, as we will find.

Young expressed his appreciation of the Shoshonis' friendship with the whites. He mentioned the feeling of safety with which the emigrants had been able to pass through their country, and he hoped that the Shoshonis would always make this possible. He also promised to return anything that the whites might steal from them if it could be found, and he admonished them to do the same.

The Shoshonis demanded ten horses of the Utes in payment for a like number of their Indians killed in a recent attack. After some discussion, they agreed to settle for nine, to be delivered at a later date at Fort Bridger. Walkara spoke at length, explaining why he had attacked the Shoshonis. It had been his belief that they had killed some of his people, but now he was convinced that he was wrong, and he was sorry. In conclusion he said, "I will hear now what Brigham says to me, me good." Placing his hand on his breast, he added, "Have been a fool but will do better in future."

The Shoshoni chief To-ter-mitch then vowed that his "ears were wide open to hear" and his "heart was good." Following his speech, the Mormon directed that clothes, ammunition, some beef cattle and flour be distributed among the Indians. Believing that the friendly spirit engendered by the Salt Lake council had paved the way for further expansion into the Indian country, Young addressed a letter, on August 30, 1852, "To the brethren who are emigrating to the valley of the mountains," in which he outlined his plans.[8] He said, "It has been our cherished object to have a good permanent settlement" at Green River.

His plan called for two toll bridges to be built during the fall and winter when the water was low. He believed Green River to be a good stock country, and he was sure that grain would

---

[8] Young to Huntington "and others at Green River," August 30, 1852, L.D.S. Church Historian's Office, Salt Lake City, Utah.

mature if planted in February or March. He also thought that it might be an ideal wayside stop for emigrants. No Mormon settlement, he stated, had been made on Shoshoni lands, though he was sure that the Indians would continue to be friendly "if correctly managed."

> ... the advantages which the place possesses in a pecuniary point of view for a settlement is not what we wish so particularly to present as the necessity for a settlement at that point, and the fact of its being calculated to be productive of much good in promoting the advancement of the cause which is dear to every Latter-day Saint. We therefore say unto you that we wish to have a sufficient number stop to organize a county at that place which was last winter named Green River County and attached to G.S.L. County for revenue, election and Indian purposes.[9]

The Mormons, arriving at Green River according to plan, did not receive the friendly welcome that they had anticipated. They were unaware of the strong affiliation between the Indians and the mountain men who ran the Green River ferries. Since many of the latter were squaw men, the Indians considered the interference of the Saints a personal affront. Subsequently, they met in council and decided to drive the white men out of the country. This seemed to apply only to the Mormons, for the squaw men were considered members of their tribe.

As a result of this attitude, the Saints were forced to abandon their plan of building toll bridges and to give up any hope that they may have had at this time of taking over the ferries. Young recalled the Saints from Green River on October 14, 1852, without specifically mentioning why.[10] He merely said that it was needless to urge the matter of settlement for the present. He made the following cautious statement: "We do not wish to lay the foundation for any difficulty which by a little foresight may be

[9] The Mormon empire, known as "The State of Deseret" (1846–57), stretched from eastern California into western Wyoming as far as South Pass. Ray Allen Billington, *A History of the American Frontier*, 544.

[10] Young to Huntington, Brigham H. Young, "and others" at Green River, October 14, 1852, L.D.S. Church Historian's Office.

avoided." He suggested that some of the missionaries join the Indians in hunting, so that "a good influence might be exerted among them, which it would not be in the power of anybody else to counteract."

Edward A. Bedell, a Mormon who succeeded Holeman, made no reference to the difficulties at Green River during the summer of 1853. Since Mormon accounts of the incident are vague there is no way of telling to what extent the Shoshonis were involved, but it seems that they were only indirectly concerned in a fight between the mountain men and the Mormons which will be mentioned in more detail later.

The trouble between the Shoshonis and Utes at this time was overshadowed by the Walker War. The unpredictable Walkara or Walker, with his brother Arrapeen, had been baptized into the Mormon church by Isaac Morley on March 13, 1850; he had been made an elder in June of the following year. Yet he continued to attack settlers and cause trouble among the Mormons as well as the Shoshonis. Attempting to calm him and put a stop to his depredations, Brigham Young wrote the following letter to him from "G.S.L. City, July 25, 1853":

CAPT. WACHER:

I send you some tobacco for you to smoke in the Mountains when you get lonesome. You are a fool for fighting your best friend for we are the best friends and the only friends that you have in the world. Everybody else would kill you if they could get a chance. If you get hungry send some friendly Indian down to the settlements or come yourself and we will give you some beef cattle and flour. If you are afraid of the Tobacco which I send you, you can let some of your prisoners try it first and then you will know that it is good. When you git good natured again I should like to see you don't you think that you would be ashamed. You know that I have always been your best friend.

B.Y.[11]

When Bedell talked with Walkara early in the spring of 1854,

[11] In Military Records Division, Utah State Historical Society.

he complained that the Shoshonis had stolen 150 Ute horses. He also disclaimed any connection with the murder of Captain John W. Gunnison the preceding fall.[12] The Pahvant warriors made an attack one morning when Gunnison's men—ten in number—were eating breakfast in their camp near Sevier River (Utah). Gunnison was shot down as he came from his tent. Four men managed to escape, and the Mormons buried the bodies of those slain several days later.

The Pahvants, who were considered a clever people, were more dependable than most tribes. The only outrage that they were ever known to commit was the killing of Captain Gunnison and his party. Kanosh, their chief, was called by an interpreter the most gentlemanly Indian he had ever met—"an excellent subject for civilization."[13]

During the course of the Walker War, the "Nauvoo Legion" or Mormon Militia mustered 18 companies, totaling 714 officers and men, for expeditionary services into territories affected by the hostilities. The difficulties were at their peak between July and October, 1853. Walkara sent in his peace emissaries the following March, and he and Kanosh entered into a formal treaty after a talk with Brigham Young at Chicken Creek, Juab County, Utah. Thus ended the Walker War in which 19 white men and an untold number of Indians lost their lives.

Walkara died from natural causes at Meadow Creek, Millard County, Utah, in 1855, bringing to an end some of the troubles of the Shoshonis as well as of the Mormon settlers. He was buried on a high mountain twelve miles southeast of Fillmore, Utah, with two of his wives who were killed so that they might accompany his spirit to the life beyond. Ten horses, ten blankets, and ten buckskins were thrown into the pit, and two Piede (Southern Paiute) children—a boy and a girl who had been taken prisoners by the Utes—were placed alive in a rocked-up cairn on top. Three days later the boy called out to passing Indians that he was hungry

12 LeRoy R. Hafen and Ann W. Hafen, *Colorado*, 100.
13 Pacific Wagon Road, *Report, Sen. Exec. Doc. 40*, 36 Cong., 2 sess. (984), 43.

and wanted to get out, but the Indians rode on. The Utes cried, sang, and lamented the death of Walkara for a period of twenty days.[14]

In June, 1854, Young spoke of rumored difficulties between the Shoshonis and Utes. Again in September he mentioned a small party of Shoshonis who the week before attacked some Utes near Provo when they were searching for horses said to have been stolen.[15] In the skirmish four Utes were killed and seven wounded. The Shoshonis returned to their camp after two of their warriors had been injured.

When the new agent, Garland Hurt, was on his way to the Humboldt the following year, he encountered a friendly band of Utes and gave them presents. The next evening as he and his companions were preparing to encamp, they were visited by a band of Shoshonis, who were in the same general neighborhood. He gave the following account of his experience:

> ... We camped at Willow Creek, and scarcely had time to un-harness when we discovered in the distance a perfect cloud of dust, which we perceived was produced by a large band of Shoshones, or Snakes proper, from the Green River country, numbering something over one hundred, who came over to the mouth of Bear river to fish; and hearing that we were in the neighborhood, said they supposed we had come to give presents, and I soon saw they were not disposed to leave disappointed. So I gave them some shirts and tobacco and some bits of calico for their squaws. These are a good looking band of Indians, and left a favorable impression of their friendly disposition towards the whites.[16]

Young made a "good peace" between the Shoshonis and Utes in 1855. The treaty council was especially significant because

[14] Paul Bailey, *Walkara, Hawk of the Mountains*, 169–73.

[15] *Deseret News* (July 20, 1854); Young to Commissioner of Indian Affairs, June 30 and September 30, 1854, I.O.R.

[16] Although Garland Hurt's original report was lost, Dale L. Morgan was able to recover it in other documentary records. See *Annals of Wyoming*, Vol. XXVI, Pt. 2, 172.

Tavendu-wets was in charge of the band of three hundred Green River Snakes at Salt Lake. Washakie, meanwhile, was in Crow country, where, as we learn later, he acquired in battle seventy-five head of horses and a large quantity of furs.

Agent Hurt selected campgrounds and supplied the Indians with provisions, fuel, and hay for their horses. In a few days they were joined by the Utes and the Cumumbahs, totaling about five hundred Indians. Hurt, in telling why his expenditures in presents and provisions seemed unnecessarily large, explained that in some way the Indians had been informed that large appropriations had been made by Congress for the purpose of making presents to and treaties with them. He was not prepared to say how they had come in possession of the facts, but they had been looking for something to be done for them all summer. This was the most adequately covered council yet held between the two tribes, for besides Young's and Hurt's reports we have the splendid account given by D. B. Huntington, the interpreter, printed in the *Deseret News:*

> ... The Snakes [with Tavendu-wets as their spokesman] complained that they had permitted the white people to make roads through all their lands and travel upon them in safety, use the grass and drink the water, and had never received anything for it, although the tribes around them had been getting presents. Under these circumstances, I saw no way to retain their confidence but to meet these expectations. And as they have succeeded in making peace among themselves, and renewed their pledges of friendship to the whites, we have reason to hope that harmony will prevail for a season.[17]

In describing the council, Huntington said that Ka-tat-o arrived as chief of a band of Snakes, presumably Cumumbahs. These Indians inhabited the central part of Utah Territory. Extending north, south, and west from Salt Lake, they bordered the desert country. According to Young, the Shoshonis (apparently the Green River Snakes) had at one time claimed a small tract of land at the mouth of Weber Canyon but had left as the buffalo

[17] September 19, 1855.

receded. It was then held by the Cumumbahs (Weber Utes) or Snake Diggers, united with a "broken off" band of Shoshonis.[18]

Several Ute chiefs were present when the tribes met, but Arra-peen, Walkara's successor, had not yet arrived. The Utes, reaching the governor's office about 10:00 A.M., were completely armed and painted black as if for battle. The Snakes, not knowing what to expect, lined up opposite the Tabernacle. They were unarmed, to signify their desire for peace.

The Utes ordered the Snakes to stop where they were. After pausing, they moved east to a position opposite the Deseret Store, where they met their adversaries. The Shoshonis were led by Huntington, who served as interpreter for both tribes. He instructed the Utes to place their weapons against the wall. All obeyed at once but Squash and To-ma, who were reluctant. As the Utes stacked their guns, many tried to conceal their bows and arrows beneath their blankets. One Batieste held on to his war spear. Kat-tat-osaw dramatically lifted his peace pipe toward the heavens and shouted, "This is the weapon I come to fight with!" Batieste began dancing the War Dance and singing as he thrust his spear toward the earth.

The interpreter urged the Utes to come forward and meet the Snakes in the same peaceful spirit which they had shown. Old Pe-teet-neet, one of the many Ute chiefs, was the first to lead out. Then the others followed. Pe-teet-neet offered to shake hands with Tavendu-wets, but the latter refused. Instead, he raised his hand toward the heavens. The Ute did likewise. After lowering their hands toward the earth, they straightened up, looked each other in the eye, then shook hands and embraced. The other chiefs followed their example. The Indians then adjourned to the encampment of the Snakes on Union Square. (The Utes had temporarily pitched their tents in Huntington's yard.)

Members of the two tribes formed parallel lines and sat on the grass facing each other. Tavendu-wets and Ka-tat-o, after filling two large pipes, began at the right of the line of Utes. Holding

[18] Washakie claimed that these Indians did not belong to his nation. See *Annals of Wyoming*, Vol. XXVI, No. 1, 76.

the pipe, they allowed each to smoke as long as he wished, but he was not permitted to touch the pipe with his hands. Anyone unaccustomed to smoke was excused. He would put his right hand on the shoulder of the Snake, and then draw it slowly down his arm and along the pipe. After the Shoshonis had passed their pipe to all the Utes, Pe-teet-neet and Tin-tick then went through the same formality in presenting it to them.

When Arrapeen finally arrived, on September 7, he and his band of Utes called at the Governor's office. Learning of their arrival, the Snakes went to meet them, "singing as usual." Arrapeen, hearing their war song, declared that it was "not good." As Huntington went out on the street to meet the Snakes he ordered them to stop singing.

> We met the Snakes in front of T. S. Williams & Co.'s store [Huntington said]. I introduced the two chiefs to each other, and after shaking hands, Ar-ra-pine took the Snake chief in his arms and gave him a tremendous hug, and raised him clear from the ground.
>
> They went through the usual compliment of shaking hands and then repaired to the Temple Block, and were seated under the bowery to smoke until the Governor should come to talk to them. I seated the two tribes in front of each other. Ar-ra-pine took the presidency of the meeting, and having requested the citizens to be seated, he called upon all his men to raise their hands toward Heaven as a token or covenant of peace.
>
> They did so twice; all the Utahs then knelt down, and Ar-ra-pine made a lengthy prayer. He prayed like unto the ancients, for his wives and children, flocks and herds, and for all that he could think of. The pipe of peace was passed around until the Governor arrived, when Ar-ra-pine requested all who wanted to speak to do so, reserving his own until last. Several spoke on both sides, expressing a desire to be on friendly terms with each other. The Governor gave them some good counsel.
>
> It was agreed that the Utahs should visit the Snakes, encamped on Union Square, and the Snakes agreed to take their lodges and move about four miles south, to where the Utahs were encamped. [By now they had moved out of Huntington's yard.]

The Indian Agent, Dr. Garland Hurt, kindly furnished them provisions, and gave the Utahs some presents; they appeared to be well satisfied. I visited the encampment the next day; they were enjoying themselves well. They say they have not had so good a treaty for twenty years. . . . The Utes and Snakes have agreed to meet on White River, and hunt buffalo together this winter.

Following this historic council, the fickle Tavendu-wets and his warriors caused trouble (October 18) at Fort Supply, which we will discuss more fully later. Singing their war songs, they threw down the fences and came charging across the wheat fields. When the white men tried to be friendly, the Indians vowed that they were "heap mad," for while they were in Salt Lake City the big Mormon captain (Brigham Young) "had written with blood on their children" and a number of them had died. Tavendu-wets firmly believed that "Brigham's talk" killed two of his children.[19]

Tavendu-wets and his men entered the fort but refused seats.[20] Several of the braves jumped on the beds and demanded pay for the death of their children. When two Indians stretched themselves out on James S. Brown's bed, he told them several times to move, but they only sneered at him. He jerked one of them off so quickly that the other preferred to leave of his own accord.

Tavendu-wets made extravagant demands. When Brown refused him, the Indian branded him a "wolf and a liar." The Shoshonis then turned their horses into the fields of shocked grain, and their women began digging and sacking potatoes. Brown sent several men out to order them from the patch, but they only laughed at them. He then went to see what he could do. Passing some brush he picked up a stick and started toward the women, who ran away screaming before he got near enough to touch them.

Soon two young braves rode up in front of the door and demanded to see the captain (Brown). When they found out who he was, they began taunting him with, "You heap fight squaw,

[19] Isaac Bullock to George A. Smith, October 20, 1855, L.D.S. Church Historian's Office.
[20] James S. Brown, *Life of a Pioneer*, 324; also George Armstrong's report, in *Report of Commissioner of Indian Affairs*, 1855, 204–206.

you no fight Injun!" When he ordered them to leave, an Indian aimed his arrow at him. One of Brown's men whirled his horse so that its head came between them while another man handed him a Colt's revolver.

Soon there were from seventy-five to one hundred warriors ready for battle. By managing to prevent bloodshed, Brown pleased the unpredictable Tavendu-wets, who forbade his men to shoot. Finally the Mormons barred the gates to the bastion so that the Indians could not enter. Brown parleyed through a porthole until he succeeded in getting them to leave.

About two o'clock the next afternoon a man at the lookout in the watchtower reported a great amount of dust to the north, while the herders came rushing in with the horses. It was a race between the herders and the Indians to see which could reach the fort first. The herders won, but as the Indians neared the bolted barrier they shouted, "Open the gates!" Three mountain men with them called out that they would be responsible—that the Indian agent (George Armstrong) was on his way and that the Indians only wanted to be there to receive the goods that he was bringing. It was true that Armstrong, whom the Indians called their "Great Father's Papoose," was arriving. He brought with him goods that gave the Shoshonis great satisfaction.

CHAPTER NINE

Lamanites

In a revelation that was supposed to have come to Joseph Smith in 1830, the Latter-day Saints were specifically obligated to take the message of the Book of Mormon to the natives, whom they called Lamanites, or "unbelievers." The forefathers of the aborigines, the Mormons claimed, belonged to a branch of the house of Israel, said to have fled from Jerusalem about 600 B.C., and to have ultimately found their way to the Western Hemisphere. Missionary efforts stretched west of the Rockies in 1847.

Six years later the first missionaries were sent to Fort Hall. In October a company of men with James S. Brown in charge was ordered north to protect and assist them. But the order—for a reason which Brown does not state—was countermanded.[1] Instead, he was chosen among others to take a mission to the Indian tribes east of Salt Lake Valley.

Elder Orson Hyde was to lead the company to the region of Green River, where he was instructed to select a place and build an outpost from which to operate. The purpose of the expedition was to preach Mormonism to the Indians, to attempt to civilize them, and to show them how to cultivate the soil. Furthermore, the missionaries were advised to establish friendly relations as a means of preventing trouble for the settlers. They were told to identify themselves with the interests of the natives, "even to marrying among them, if permitted to take the young daughters of the chief and leading men." Moreover, they were instructed to dress the wives like civilized, educated Americans.

With the blessings of Elders Orson Hyde, Parley P. Pratt, and Ezra T. Benson, twenty-nine missionaries set out for Green

[1] James S. Brown, *Life of a Pioneer*, 304–305.

River on November 2, 1853. Since they were authorized to serve in a military capacity if necessary, they must have been well armed. They went with every intent of settling, for they took with them 20 wagons, 110 head of cattle, horses, and mules, and each man had 300 pounds of flour, 75 pounds of seed wheat, and 40 pounds of seed potatoes for a start.[2]

After struggling through deep snows, they finally reached Fort Bridger on November 15. They found the place occupied by twelve or fifteen rough mountain men, "surly and suspicious," with "the spirit of murder and death lurking in their minds." The Saints were keenly aware of "the terrible influence." A duel had been fought the night before. Two of the desperadoes had slashed themselves to death, and had been thrown into a hole and covered up, "clasped in each other's arms." Brown alluded to the incident partly to explain the surly disposition of the mountain men.

In order to understand the chief reason for their lack of hospitality, we need only look back to the events which took place during the summer. Trouble had started when the Utah Territorial Legislature had granted a charter to a firm to operate the emigrant ferries at Green River, held to be in a part of Deseret. The mountaineers who had monopolized the business did not recognize the legal claim, and at gun-point they carried on business as usual. Consequently, the Saints sued them for the sum of $300,000, the approximate amount collected during the summer.

Bridger seems to have had no direct connection with the suit, but the Saints, thwarted at the ferries, turned their attention to him. Had he not boasted at Fort Laramie that he had furnished guns to the Shoshonis? Had he not been connected by marriage with the Utes, who, under Walkara, had dealt the settlers so much grief? If the Mormons could not settle their problems with the mountain men at the ferries, they would have the satisfaction of putting a stop to Bridger's interference. Therefore, they decided to clean out Fort Bridger, "lock, stock, and barrel."

Beginning with an affidavit charging him with furnishing the

2 This discussion is based on Brown, *ibid.*, 312–60, the best available source of information regarding Mormon missionary efforts among the Green River Snakes.

Indians guns to shoot Mormons, the sheriff and his posse of 150 select men went to the fort to arrest him. Finding the place deserted except for Rutta, Bridger's Shoshoni wife, they pitched camp near by. When they finally became tired of waiting for Blanket Chief's return, they made a drive upon his stronghold only to find that Rutta, too, had vanished.

Considering Bridger a fugitive criminal, the Saints took possession of the fort on August 26, 1853,[3] and they stripped the premises of everything they could carry. Going from there to Green River, they attacked the mountain men. After killing two or three of them, they confiscated several hundred head of livestock and other items and returned to Salt Lake City.[4] This incident explains why Brown's orders were countermanded, and he was sent to Green River instead of to Fort Hall. Furthermore, it shows the reason for the attitude of the mountain men whom Brown found occupying Fort Bridger.

The missionaries, unable to stay at the fort, made a temporary camp about a mile and a half away, along Black's Fork. From there they intended to go to Henry's Fork, but they changed their plans when they found that the place where they hoped to camp was already occupied by about one hundred mountain men, and that the Utes were soon to arrive to spend the winter with them. Without delay, they moved on to Smith's Fork, where "The Spirit" forbade their going farther. Between the forks of the stream they selected a spot, "the chosen ground," for winter quarters and proceeded to build a blockhouse, the nucleus of Fort Supply, the first authorized Mormon settlement in the Green River Snake country.[5]

Brown drew the plans, and no doubt urged on by the cold, the men completed the new fortress in two weeks. During the severe winter which followed, they studied the Shoshoni language diligently, with the help of Sally (the Indian wife of Elisha

[3] The date supplied by Dale L. Morgan (Mormon records do not mention it) was found in the diary of a California emigrant, Dr. Thomas Flint. Historical Society of Southern California, *Annual Publications*, Vol. XII, No. 3, 97.

[4] Alter, *James Bridger*, 248–49.

[5] *Ibid.*, 252.

B. Ward, one of the missionaries); her brother, Indian John; his wife, "Madame"; and a starving family that came to the fort for food. Only six of the Mormons, now numbering almost one hundred, made much progress. Of these, E. B. Ward, Isaac Bullock, and James S. Brown were chosen in April to go among the Indians for the purpose of furthering their cause. There, as we mentioned earlier, Brown learned of Tavendu-wets.

The Saints' object was to deliver in person a letter written to Washakie by Orson Hyde. Delivery had been delayed because of the weather. The letter attempted to justify the recent difficulties over the Green River ferries:

> When you learn all about what some white men have done on Green River you will not blame the "Mormons" for taking some of their stock, it was done according to the laws of our Great Father at Washington. Believe not all the bad things that some white men say of us but come and see us. We would like some Lamanites of your people to come and live in our little settlement so that we may talk with them and learn your language. I send you this letter by Bro. Barney Ward who has a Shoshone wife and some of our young men go with him to see you. I send you some tobacco and some shirts also and my best wishes.[6]

With great difficulty the small party finally managed to reach the headwaters of the Platte, where they had been told that they would find Washakie's camp. It was midafternoon when they met their first Shoshonis, who would not speak. In reply to questions they pointed to the chief's lodge. As Brown related it:

> That spirit of "mum" seemed to pervade the entire camp, and when we rode up in front of the chief's lodge, that Indian dignitary came out, bowed, and shook hands with each of us, but without uttering a word. By gestures [sign language] he invited us to dismount, come in, sit down, and tell the truth regarding our errand to his camp, but no lies.
> Then he had some clean, nice robes spread for us. At the same

[6] Orson Hyde to Washakeete, December 10, 1853, Lyman Stake Historical Records, L.D.S. Church Historian's Office.

time his women folks came out, taking our horses by the bits. We dismounted, and took seats as invited. The chief and ourselves were all "mum" until the horses had been unsaddled, and everything belonging to us had been put under the bottom of the lodge, just to the rear of where we sat.

These proceedings being over, the chief said: "Who are you, from where do you come, and what is your errand to my country?" Then by gestures, he said, "Tell me the truth; do not tell me any lies, nor talk any crooked talk." He paused, and, by motions, invited us to reply.[7]

After answering the chief's questions fully, the Saints manifested their friendship and the desire of the Great Father to see his children live in peace, one with another. They said that they hoped to improve their dialect so that they could tell the Indians what the Great Spirit had told their "big captain" (Joseph Smith). Furthermore, they wanted to warn the Indians that before many more snows the game would all be gone, and they would have to live in the white man's way by raising food from the ground to survive.

The chief interrupted. "Wait awhile," he urged. "My little children are very hungry for some of the white man's food, and they want some sugar." When the Saints handed over all the bread and sugar they had, Washakie gave the food to his wife, who distributed it to the children clustered around her. Without further ceremony, he walked out. When he returned, someone set a kettle of buffalo beef before the white men. After they had eaten, a council was called.

The account given by Brown reminds us of the Lewis and Clark journals of a half-century before. Little had changed in the Shoshoni way of life in the intervening years. The tribal leaders filed into their accustomed places. The pipe was lit, and "a rude figure of one of the planets was drawn in the ashes of the fire" in the center of the lodge.

Then the old man, sitting on the left of the chief, held the pipe, we having been seated on the right of the chief. The latter com-

[7] *Life of a Pioneer*, 347–50.

146

menced, and told the story of our visit, from the time we came into the lodge up to that moment. It was told without interruptions, and then the pipe was started on its way, following the course of the sun.

Every man except the one holding the pipe put his hand over his mouth, and sat perfectly silent and still. The one with the pipe took from one to three long draws, allowing the smoke from the last one to escape gradually through his nostrils, at the same time passing the pipe with his right hand to the next person; then if he had anything to say, he did it in as few words as possible, and put his hand over his mouth, thus signifying that he had no more to say.

Occasionally some old man, when he took the pipe, made some signs above and in front of him, struck himself on the breast and offered a few words of prayer.

After the Indians had all puffed the pipe for their allotted time, it was passed to the white men, who followed the same procedure. When it reached the chief, he looked around the circle, where all of his councilors had their mouths covered. He then spoke briefly.

All went well until the Saints suggested that some of their number might want to take some of the young Indian women for their wives. One elder protested. "No, for we have not got daughters enough for our own men, and we cannot afford to give our daughters to the white man, but we are willing to give him an Indian girl for a white girl. I cannot see why a white man wants an Indian girl. They are dirty, ugly, stubborn and cross, and it is a strange idea for white men to want such wives. But I can see why an Indian wants a white woman."

Washakie wisely carried the point to its conclusion. He told the white men that they might look around, and if they could find a girl who would go with them, it would be all right. However, he made one stipulation—that the Indian must have the same privilege in the white camp. With that, the council came to an end.

Brown later served as interpreter at the Green River ferries, which by now were being "legally" operated by the Mormons. Even so, the mountain men would sometimes daringly take over and collect the money at the so-called Upper Ferry. It would require all the force the Saints could muster to run them off. When

Brown was not busy helping with this task, he was assisting the drovers as they swam their cattle across the stream.

One day Washakie arrived with seven of his braves. They made a general inspection of the ferryboat and its fixtures. The chief then visited the store, the settlement, the blacksmith shop, and finally the saloon and gambling room where he watched the white man's money carelessly change hands. Following this, he stopped to see the ferry captain, who at the time was handling a quantity of money, including several fifty-dollar gold slugs. The chief admired the gold, which to the Indian way of thinking, the captain should have given to him. Instead, he turned a deaf ear. Then Washakie asked him for a slug. The captain laughed and indulgently handed him a silver dollar. The great chief of the Shoshonis was insulted. In some way he managed to get some liquor, which contributed further to his bad mood. When he finally located Brown at the water's edge, he lost no time expressing himself:

This is my country, and my people's country [he shouted]. My father lived here, and drank water from this river, while our ponies grazed on these bottoms. Our mothers gathered the dry wood from this land. The buffalo and elk came here to drink water and eat grass; but now they have been killed or driven back out of our land.

The grass is all eaten off by the white man's horses and cattle, and the dry wood has been burned; and sometimes, when our young men have been hunting, and got tired and hungry, they have come to the white man's camp, and have been ordered to get out, and they are slapped, or kicked, and called "damned Injuns." Then our young men get heap mad, and say as they have often, they will take revenge upon him.

Sometimes they have been so abused that they have threatened to kill all the white men they meet in our land. But I have always been a friend to the white man, and have told my people never to moisten our land with his blood; and to this day the white man can not show in all our country where the Shoshone has killed one of his people, though we can point to many abuses we have patiently suffered from him.

148

Now I can see that he only loves himself; he love his own flesh, and he does not think of us; he loves heap money; he had a big bag full of it; he got it on my land, and would not give me a little piece. I am mad, and you heap my good friend, and I will tell you what I am going to do.

Every white man, woman, and child, that I find on this side of that water (pointing to the river) at sunrise tomorrow I will wipe out (rubbing his hands together). You heap my friend; you stay here all right; you tell them to leave my land.

If they are on the other side of my water, all right, me no kill them, they go home to their country, no come back to my land. Tomorrow morning when the sun come up, you see me. My warriors come, heap damn mad, and wipe them all out, no one leave. Goodby, you tell him, chief, he mad!

With that final remark, he mounted his pony and rode angrily toward the Shoshoni village, then on Big Sandy. Consternation reigned in the white camp. Brown was offered a good horse and fifty dollars if he would go to the Indians and attempt a reconciliation, but it was too dark to find a horse. The night was spent moving possessions across the river, where the Mormons prepared for defense.

When Washakie returned at sunrise next day with fifteen armed warriors, he was sober and friendly. He appraised the situation and observed the disruption that had been caused by his threat. Then he said with compassion, "Tell them to come back. We will not hurt them. We will be good friends."

After Brown left the Green River country he served as interpreter for Brigham Young among the Shoshonis of Utah. Through him we have our first glimpse of Chief Little Soldier, who later played a significant role in the Shoshoni uprisings. The chief and his band had been causing trouble among the settlers in Weber County at the time of Brown's arrival. As a result the Mormons, during the winter, attempted to disarm the Indians and distribute them among families in the county. The most rebellious of the lot was Little Soldier's brother, unnamed in the records. He expressed the feeling of resentment of his people, who were being deprived of their freedom to roam as their fathers had before them.

He said in desperation, "Here are my wife, my children, my horses and everything that I have. Take it all and keep it, only give me back my gun and let me go free. I will cast all the rest away. There is my child." He pointed to a three-year-old. "Take it." When the baby held up its hands, he appeared to look upon it in disgust. "Go away," he ordered. "You are not mine, for I have thrown you away, and will not have you any more."

The Indians now considered themselves reduced to the status of women, unable to defend their families. Brown was sympathetic for he realized that it was difficult for them. Yet he felt that it was the only course open to the white man, whose stock was being killed and whose fences were being burned.

By spring (1855) plans were under way for a settlement in the country to the north, among the Lemhis and Flatheads. Young sent twenty-seven men to found it. Among the missionaries were David Moore (their chronicler) and G. W. Hill, who had studied the Shoshoni language in Brown's school along with thirty other adults. Hill was able to preach to the natives in their language.

Bannock recruits joined the expedition along the way and seemed to take kindly to Mormonism. On June 12 the delegation reached a branch of the Salmon River, which they named Limhi (Lemhi) after a neophyte king in the Book of Mormon.[8] Not only that, they gave the Indians their name Lemhi, which is used by historians for them from the time they first came into notice to distinguish them from other bands. Technically, these Indians were Agaidükas (Salmon Eaters) and Tukadükas (Sheep Eaters) affiliated with Bannocks, as we have previously mentioned. Although they were later consolidated under one head, at this time they had two chiefs—the 275-pound Le Grand Coquin (The Great Rogue), Bannock; and Tio-van-du-ah (Snag), Shoshoni.

Le Grand Coquin rode seventy-five miles to welcome the missionaries. He expressed the wish of his people to learn how to farm and his personal desire for ammunition. He is said to have talked the white men into settling on the Lemhi River, instead of going farther north into the Flathead and Nez Percé country. The lo-

[8] Brigham D. Madsen, *The Bannock of Idaho*, 84–110.

cation was ideal, for it was the spot where there had been Indian rendezvous many years before Ashley introduced the term into fur-trading history. Here the Northern Shoshonis and Bannocks had come each year to gamble and trade for horses with the Flatheads and Nez Percés.

By the time the mission was completed the Indians had begun to congregate. When the Saints held their prayer meetings, an old Nez Percé chief and Le Grand Coquin, who took to the services with enthusiasm, would join in the hymn-singing and would be most attentive during time of prayer. By July, 1856, one hundred Indians had been baptized, most of them Bannocks. Among the converts was Snag, who was baptized on November 11, 1855.[9]

While the Saints were establishing themselves at Fort Lemhi, Brown was making his last visit to Washakie's camp. There were eight Saints in his party. Having finished planting their crops at Fort Supply, they fitted themselves out and started, on May 29, 1855, to the Shoshoni camp. They had heard that it was on the headwaters of either the Green or the Snake river. On June 5 they reached the camp (twenty lodges) of Siveadus, a leader of a small band of Shoshonis. He proved inhospitable, but he gave them the desired information. Washakie, he said, could be found somewhere on the headwaters of Horse Creek.

Encouraged by a dream in which he saw a large band of friendly Indians pitch their camp near by, Brown was convinced that he would soon find Washakie. From a high point he observed smoke from campfires. Although unable to discover whether the Indians were Shoshonis, Crows, or Blackfeet, the Saints were forced to go forward. Soon they were surrounded by a score or more of warriors, painted for battle. "Green" scalps hung from their bridle bits. Though they were believed to be Shoshonis, there was no recognition from either side. Fearlessly, the white men spoke to them and offered their hands in greeting, but the warriors

9 David Moore, "Salmon River Mission Record" (hereinafter cited as "Salmon River Mission"), L.D.S. Church Historian's Office, 40, 60. Moore's record of the Lemhi Mission is no less informative than Brown's account of his experience among the Green River Snakes.

shook their heads and pointed the way to the lodge of their chief. Proudly they escorted the missionaries to Washakie, who stood waiting to receive them.

When they alighted, the chief shook hands. In sign language he signified that the Indians were moving camp and that he wished them to go with him. He explained that the day before they had had a successful encounter with the Crows and the Blackfeet, who were united against them, and that they were fleeing before their enemies had an opportunity to gain reinforcements.

As the Shoshonis moved forward, their advance guard in a flanking movement fanned out in such a way as to bag all wildlife in the path ahead. The missionaries, riding along, had much time to reflect upon the general pattern and purpose of their assignment:

> We thought of ancient Israel, of the Ten Tribes coming from the north country, and of the promises that had been made to the Indians by the prophets of their forefathers. To us this was a great day of thought and meditation, for at times it seemed to us that we could see the opening glories of a better day, and could declare, "Now is the dawn of the day of Israel," for we had a letter from that modern Moses [Brigham Young] to read and interpret to the red men, and also the *Book of Mormon* to introduce to them that very evening, for the first time; and the question was uppermost in our minds as to whether they would receive it or not, for there were many hard looking countenances in the throng, and we could see plainly from their frowns that they were not all friendly to us.[10]

After the chief's lodge had been pitched, clean robes were spread for the white men and preparations were made for the council. When the customary center fire was built, the councilors took their places, though many looked coldly upon the guests. In sign language Washakie demanded to know what they had to say. He told them that he would tolerate no "crooked talk." He wanted the truth.

The missionaries presented a letter from Brigham Young, which they read and translated. It expressed the friendship of the Mormons for the Indians as well as their desire to help them learn

[10] James S. Brown, *Life of a Pioneer*, 350–54.

to raise crops for survival. The Mormon leader said that he hoped for an understanding between the Shoshonis and the missionaries so that when they came to know each other better, the white men could tell them many things regarding the Great Spirit's dealings with their forefathers, and what He would do for them and their children.

The Saints then presented a copy of the Book of Mormon to Washakie. His left-hand man filled the pipe and drew a rude figure of the sun in the ashes of the center fire. The chief muttered some unintelligible words, smote his chest, took several whiffs from the pipe, passed it to the next man on his left, who reached for the book. He said, as he opened its pages, "No good for Indian; good only for white man."

Following the customary procedure, the book as well as the pipe passed around the circle repeatedly, as the elders were given a chance to express themselves. Each time the book made its round, the Indian on Washakie's left would draw a new figure representing a different planet. One man after another spoke, with all expressing their disapproval. One said, "This book is of no use. If the Mormon captain has nothing better to send than this, we had better send it, his letter, and these men back to him, and tell him they are no good to us, that we want powder, lead and caps, sugar, coffee, flour, paint, knives, and blankets, for these we can use. Send these men away to their own land."

Washakie listened attentively as the book made the circle more than twenty times, with no one speaking a word in its favor. When it finally returned to the hands of the Mormons, the chief reached for it. Turning its pages thoughtfully, he seemed to be studying it. Then he looked around the circle and wanted to know if everyone had had his say. All the councilors now sat with hands over their mouths. Then he reprimanded his people for their stupidity:

> You are all fools, you are blind, and cannot see; you have no ears, for you do not hear; you are fools for you do not understand. These men are our friends. The great Mormon captain has talked with our Father above the clouds, and He told the Mormon captain to send these men here to tell us the truth, and not a lie.

They have not got forked tongues. They talk straight, with one tongue, and tell us that after a few more snows the buffalo will be gone, and if we do not learn some other way to get something to eat, we will starve to death.

Now, we know that is the truth, for this country was once covered with buffalo, elk, deer and antelope, and we had plenty to eat, and also robes for bedding, and to make lodges. But now, since the white man has made a road across our land, and has killed off our game, we are hungry, and there is nothing for us to eat. Our women and children cry for food and we have no food to give them.

The time was when our Father, who lives above the clouds, loved our fathers, who lived long ago, and His face was bright, and He talked with our fathers. His face shone upon them, and their skins were white like the white man's. Then they were wise and wrote books, and the Great Father talked good to them; but after a while our people would not hear Him, and they quarreled and stole and fought, until the Great Father got mad, because His children would not hear Him talk.

Then He turned His face away from them, and His back to them, and that caused a shade to come over them, and that it why our skin is black and our minds dark. That darkness came because the Great Father's back was toward us, and now we cannot see as the white man sees. We can make a bow and arrow, but the white man's mind is strong and light.

The white man can make this (picking up a Colt's revolver), and a little thing that he carries in his pocket, so that he can tell where the sun is on a dark day, and when it is night he can tell when it will come daylight. This is because the face of the Father is towards him, and His back is towards us. But after a while the Great Father will quit being mad, and will turn his face towards us. Then our skin will be light.[11]

As Washakie continued his speech, he told in detail how much better than the Indian's was the white man's way of life. The elders sat quietly listening until he had finished. Their only comment was an occasional grunt of approval. When he had finally stopped talking, each man quietly withdrew, and a scanty meal was served before the Saints retired for the night.

[11] *Ibid.,* 354-60.

154

Before the missionaries left the next day, Washakie remarked that the wolves had written the Book of Mormon while they were men. Then they had become beasts. What Washakie meant is beyond interpretation, for Wolf, father of the Bannocks, and Coyote, father of the Shoshonis, were brothers. The Shoshonis could understand why the Bannocks were mean; it was the fault of Wolf. They sometimes explained their own misconduct by referring to the unsavory traits of Coyote.

Although the Lemhi missionaries were advised to marry native women to strengthen the ties of friendship, Young warned the brethren to refrain from marrying the "old vanigadoes" who might run off with the first man to come along.[12] We recall that Brown's party was also urged to marry the "young" daughters of the native leaders. Such marriages did not flourish among the mixed bands of Shoshonis and Bannocks any more than they did among the Green River Snakes for the simple reason that the chiefs did not approve.

During a period of unrest, horse-stealing, and war-dancing in the Lemhi country, the Saints somehow managed to keep on friendly terms with the Indians, then warring against each other —the Bannocks and Shoshonis, the Nez Percés, and the Pend d'Oreilles. In fact, they had made such a devout convert of Chief Snag that he began spreading the word of Brigham Young in his preaching. In his effort to dissuade the Nez Percés and Bannocks, planning to wage war over their age-old grievance, horse-stealing, he told them that the Lord would be displeased with those who fought.

Within the next two years, matters between the Mormons and the United States government became increasingly grave. Finally, in 1857, the citizens of Utah (more exactly, Deseret) were declared to be in open revolt, defying the government and taking the law into their own hands. Specifically they were accused of driving out federal officers, threatening a federal judge with violence, and destroying or withholding certain court records. Revoking

[12] Moore, "Salmon River Mission," 113; W. H. Daines, "Journal," L.D.S. Church Historian's Office.

the appointment of Brigham Young as governor and superintendent of Indian affairs, President James Buchanan appointed new Territorial officers and ordered the Utah Expedition to proceed with them to Salt Lake City.

Rumor had picked up Young's words to the effect that if troops dared to force the issue, he would "no longer hold the Indians by the wrist for the white men to shoot at. . . . If the issue comes [he reportedly said], you may tell the government to stop all emigration across the continent, for the Indians will kill all who attempt it."[13]

The Saints were celebrating their tenth anniversary, on July 24, 1857, when word reached them that the President planned to send an expeditionary force into Deseret. Great excitement followed, and the militia, estimated at approximately six thousand, began mobilizing. Five years before, Agent Holeman had warned the government. "God and the Governor command," were his words. He reported the Mormons as drilling for just such an emergency, and he quoted the commanding officer as saying that they had been in the habit of drilling in Nauvoo, Illinois, where they had only one state to oppose. Now that it was the whole United States, they should be "properly prepared."[14]

Brigham Young was highly conscious of what was taking place when he wrote his official report as superintendent of Indian affairs on September 12. After reviewing his activities, he mentioned hostility on the part of the Snake Diggers on the line of travel west of the settlements and difficulties arising from the fact that some of the emigrants were shooting at every Indian they could see—"a practice utterly abhorrent to all good people."[15] He added:

> The sound of war quickens the blood and nerves of an Indian. The report that troops are wending their way to this Territory has also had its influence upon them. In one or two instances this was the reason assigned why they made attacks which they did

[13] Bancroft, *History of Utah*, 507.
[14] Holeman to Commissioner of Indian Affairs, March 29, 1852, I.O.R.
[15] Young to Commissioner of Indian Affairs, September 12, 1857, I.O.R.

upon some herds of Cattle they seemed to think that if it was to be war they might as well commence and begin to lay in a Supply of food, when they had a chance.

The Mormon leader made three suggestions. First, that the emigrants discontinue their "infamous practice" of shooting at every Indian they happen to see. Second, that more liberal appropriations be made for presents. Third, that troops be kept away. He said that the greatest hostility among the Indians and the least security for persons and property could be found where there were troops.

While Young was writing his report, the army was on the march. At Fort Laramie the commanding officer found Jim Bridger, whom he hired as guide. It was Bridger's first trip back to his fort since being driven out by the Mormon posse. Although the fort had apparently been purchased by the Saints through his partner Vasquez, it must have given him a great deal of satisfaction to be returning with a military escort when he had left as a fugitive.

The Mormons set fire to one after another of their five mail stations connecting Fort Laramie and Salt Lake City as they fled before the advancing army. Had Bridger's advice been solicited, he would have said that the expedition was ill timed; for it was September, and no one who knew the high country would be starting out on such a venture that late in the season. The soldiers suffered untold hardships as they moved through the mountainous country.

Although Washakie is represented by some writers as being strictly neutral during the Mormon crisis, such was not the case. Captain Jesse A. Gove, with the Army for Utah, gives an account of his offering twelve hundred warriors to the cause.[16] Gove described the Green River Snakes as the most warlike tribe "this side of the mountains." He was at that time at Green River, on the Western Slope. Gove stated that the Shoshonis, "a splendid set of men," were "down on the Mormons." He regretted that their services were declined as he thought that the officer in charge should at least have hired about twenty-five of them as guides and hunters.

16 *Utah Expedition*, 66.

The Mormon War was unlike any conflict in the experience of the Indians. Not one shot was fired, nor were there any casualties, with the exception of a soldier who died of a heart attack. When the army reached Fort Bridger, they found nothing except the mortar and stones of the Mormon Wall[17] and the picket enclosure around the stockade. They soon rebuilt the fort and established Camp Scott near by, but they spent a disagreeable winter bogged down on Black's Fork.

In the spring Alfred Cumming, the newly appointed governor for Utah, made his way to Salt Lake. At the same time President Buchanan granted to the citizens of Deseret a pardon:

> ... being anxious to save the effusion of blood, and to avoid the indiscriminate punishment of a whole people for crimes of which it is not probable that all are equally guilty, I offer now a full and free pardon to all who will submit themselves to the authority of the federal government. If you refuse to accept it, let the consequences fall upon your heads. But I conjure you to pause deliberately and reflect well before you reject this tender of peace and good will.[18]

The pardon was accepted by the Mormons. Subsequently, thirty thousand Saints evacuated Salt Lake City and went to Provo before Johnston's army could march triumphantly through the capital of Deseret. Without stopping, Jim Bridger guided the army through the empty city and on to Camp Floyd, thirty miles south of Salt Lake City, where it bivouacked and soon built a permanent camp.

During the Mormon crisis, trouble was brewing in the Lemhi country. The day after Christmas, 1857, the Nez Percés went as far as to hold a War Dance at Fort Lemhi. Although the Mormons did all in their power to appease them, they left in a militant mood, taking with them about seventy head of horses belonging to the Shoshonis. The Lemhis donned their paint and feathers and made

[17] The Mormon wall, a fragment of which still stands, was built for defense after the Saints came in possession of Fort Bridger.

[18] *U.S. Statutes at Large*, from December 3, 1855, to March 3, 1859, 796–97.

ready to fight, while the Mormons attempted to calm them with a feast. According to Moore, it was not entirely successful, for some of the Indians who would not eat declared that they "were not dogs," hungry enough to sit down and eat from the ground. Accordingly, they "stood off and looked and acted quite mumpy."[19]

A few days later reports came to the uneasy Saints that one of the Bannock chiefs was advising his followers to wipe out the missionaries before settling the trouble with the Nez Percés. A number of warriors, painted for battle, boldly made their appearance. The Mormons, after giving them grain, sent them on their way. Then the usually friendly Le Grand Coquin aroused suspicion by making an inspection of the horse corral.

John W. Powell, who had been trading with the Lemhis, brought word to the Mormons that the Indians were preparing an attack. He told them that the Shoshonis had been reluctant to join their allies but that they had been forced, after being threatened by the Bannocks. The Saints were suspicious of Powell, for they knew that he had been buying cattle from the Lemhis to supply the army, and they were of the opinion that he might have started the trouble.

Midmorning, February 25, about 200 Bannock and Shoshoni warriors drove off 250 cattle and horses belonging to the Mormons. In the ensuing skirmish 2 Saints were killed, 5 wounded. The Mormons, anticipating a direct attack upon the fortress, excommunicated those converts who were known to be in the raiding party. The fickle Le Grand Coquin no doubt headed the list. Three Shoshoni representatives, desiring terms of peace, then offered to return 30 head of cattle in their possession. They maintained that the Bannocks, after a bitter quarrel, had taken the rest.

Orders were finally issued to close the Lemhi mission, and the disheartened Saints left the valley on April 1. Charges were hurled against Powell for instigating the trouble, against the soldiers in Johnston's army for encouraging the Indians to harass the mis-

[19] "Salmon River Mission," 79–90.

sionaries, and against the Mormons for aiding and abetting the Nez Percés by furnishing them arms with which to make war upon the Lemhis.[20]

It is possible, as one contemporary writer maintained, that the uprising was instigated by Pash-e-co (Sweet Root), a Bannock Digger, who was later to lead a costly Shoshoni uprising that was to involve Indians throughout the West.[21] His success in forcing the fort to be closed may have been the first step toward his rising power.

Among the government appointees for Utah was Jacob Forney, assigned to Fort Bridger. Taking over the duties of superintendent of Indian affairs, he succeeded Brigham Young. Chief Little Soldier with a small band of Cumumbahs was among his first visitors.[22] The chief was accompanied by Ben Simon, a half-blood interpreter, who seemed equally at home with the Mormons and the gentiles. His presence cast some doubt on Little Soldier's motives, even though he later maintained that he "always kept aloof from Mormon delusions." He had come to find out the object and destination of the soldiers. When this was explained to him, he seemed satisfied. Little Soldier showed no apparent resentment against the Mormons, and yet his band was the one disarmed at Ogden.

Game had been so scarce in the Green River region in the winter of 1857–58 that Washakie was forced to remain at Wind River. Nevertheless, he was aware of what was taking place. The new Superintendent reported that the Snakes were on friendly terms with the Utes, probably because they were separated by miles.

Forney's first visit to an Indian camp took place in April, fifty

---

[20] Madsen, *The Bannock of Idaho*, 101.

[21] C. H. Miller, *Report* (hereinafter cited as Miller's report), *Sen. Exec. Doc. 36*, 36 Cong., 2 sess. (984), 70–71.

[22] Little Soldier is reported variously as chief of the Utes, Paiutes, Shoshonis, Digger Snakes, and Digger Utes. Brown classified him with the Utes and Forney with the Shoshonis. Although he probably had some Utes in his band, his Indians, the Weber Utes (Cumumbahs), are classified by ethnologists as Shoshoni Indians.

miles from Fort Bridger, on Bear River.[23] He gave the following account of his experience:

> I promised the Chiefs of this Tribe [Little Soldier and Ben Simon] sometime ago and when yet encamped in Weber Valley, that whenever they had moved to Bear River, I would endeavor to visit them, consequently Tuesday evening of last week, two Chiefs, with seventy men, came to my place, all well mounted, to escort me to there camp. There was no backing out, on the following day we started. . . .
>
> I was decidedly pleased with the general appearance & appearently industrious habits of these people. I was informed by one of the Chiefs, Ben Simon, who acted as Interpreter, that they had out almost constantly hunting parties. They have killed this Winter, over a hundred elk, & a large quantity of small game—They have also commenced trapping in Bear River & have already Caught considerable Otter & Beaver. . . .
>
> This is one of the Tribes—B. Young, boasted, would assist him, in the event of conflict with the U. States. Several days intercourse, on my recent visit, enables me to say most confidently, that this Tribe is true to the Government, beyond all peradventure.

Young in his last official letter as superintendent of Indian affairs, dated June 30, 1858, said that he had continued to serve even though he was aware that Jacob Forney had been assigned to the post.[24] He stated that Forney "tho doubtless having been some time in the Territory and probably officiating partially in his office while at Camp Scott did not until quite recently sufficiently assume its duties" to the extent that he "could feel relieved therefrom." He concluded with the statement, "Being now at the scene of his duties, these matters will hereafter devolve upon him, thus closing my official intercourse with the department."

As he bowed out, he listed his expenditures. During the preceding August, $1,368.44 had been spent at Fort Bridger for presents for Washakie, Standing Rock, Tib-en-de-wah, and their

---

23 Jacob Forney to Acting Commissioner of Indian Affairs, April 17, 1858, I.O.R.

24 Young to Commissioner of Indian Affairs, June 30, 1858, I.O.R.

tribesmen. He said that the Indians had been relatively quiet, with the exception of the Utes under White-Eye, Antaro, Pe-teet-neet, San Pitch, and Tin-tick. With their bands numbering about six hundred, they came to the settlements from their camp in the vicinity of Fort Bridger, "very hostile in their feelings and apparently only awaiting the advance of the troops from that point to make a general attack." They committed many depredations, but after they learned "the peaceable advance of the troops," their hostile feelings seemed to subside.

The Mormon missionary influence, lasting a decade, did not have the desired effect upon the Shoshoni Indians, for they continued to be Lamanites (unbelievers). Even those who became converts were easily turned away. While some professed Mormonism and "got washed," they never discarded their native religion or ceremonials. They still had their oracle and Sun Dance.

The encroaching white man, who settled the valleys, killed off the game, and relentlessly pushed the natives into the less productive area, had little to offer to offset the material losses. He did, however, make an indirect though lasting contribution to the Indian way of life by showing through example how to till the soil, run water through irrigation ditches, and raise food from the ground.

Garland Hurt was the first agent employed by the government to introduce farming among the Indians in the area. He worked tirelessly at the "Indian Farms" in Utah, where his work was primarily with the Utes. He attempted to teach those seeking instruction, but few were interested. The venture was disheartening, but it did prove that with perseverance the Indians could be taught to raise their own food. The two farms, started in 1856, suffered from political pressure, but they paved the way for a solution to the Indian problem, as Jacob Forney pointed out.[25] He urged that reservations be established without delay, before the white man could settle upon every irrigable acre of land.

[25] Forney to Acting Commissioner of Indian Affairs, September 6, 1858, I.O.R.

CHAPTER TEN

Warm Valley

Iɴ ᴛʜᴇ ʏᴇᴀʀ ᴏꜰ ᴛʜᴇ Mᴏʀᴍᴏɴ Wᴀʀ, the Shoshonis may have been restless, as Young suggests, but they showed no intention of taking sides against the army. As Pocatello, chief of the Bannock Creek Shoshonis, said, "Big-um [Brigham] was as a little finger to the whole hand" compared to the Great White Father.[1] Nevertheless, the Mormons through the medium of the *Deseret News* brought accusations against John W. Powell and B. F. Ficklin, another trader sent by General Johnston[2] to buy cattle and horses as far away as Beaverhead (Montana).

Ficklin, in his own defense, made a statement before the Chief Justice of the Utah Supreme Court (then at Camp Scott) in which he declared that he had taken every opportunity to tell the Indians as well as the whites whom he met on the way that Johnston "did not desire, and would not permit, any interference from them."[3] William M. F. Magraw, who had been replaced by F. W. Lander in the construction of the Central Division of the Pacific Wagon Road (Lander's Cutoff), and Jim Bridger also made statements to the Adjutant General at Camp Scott in defense of Johnston's policy regarding the redskins.[4]

They maintained that upon two occasions the Shoshonis had made overtures to Johnston—the time mentioned by Gove when the chief offered twelve hundred warriors to the service of the army and another time when Little Soldier came with complaints

[1] Miller's report (984), 72.

[2] Colonel Albert Sidney Johnston, while on his march to Utah, was made brevet brigadier general on November 18, 1857.

[3] B. F. Ficklin, *Report* (hereinafter cited as Ficklin's report), *Sen. Exec. Doc. 1*, II, 35 Cong., 2 sess. (975), 79.

[4] W. M. F. Magraw and Bridger to F. J. Porter, April 28, 1858, *ibid.*, 82.

against the Mormons. Both times the Indians had been advised to have nothing to do with existing difficulties, but rather to take their people to the buffalo country and stay out of the trouble area.

Brigham Young complained to Governor Cumming that the Indians who used to visit among the Mormons on the friendliest terms would now "draw their bows on our wives and take blankets from our beds." They called the Mormons "squaws" because they would not fight.[5] Meanwhile, Washakie seems to have followed Johnston's advice and stayed far removed from the difficulty. The year of 1857 had naturally drawn many Shoshonis northward from the trail as it was the year of the grand encampment. We regret that there was no chronicler present to record the event or tell us just where or when it was held and what took place. It probably was much the same as the previous one, three years before, when the agenda included visiting, gambling, and horse racing.

An account of the encampment of 1854 was given us by twelve-year-old Nick Wilson, the adopted son of Washakie's mother.[6] "The white Indian boy" was not a captive but a voluntary exile, tolled away from his home in a settlement south of Salt Lake by adventure stories related by the Green River Snakes. He had learned the language from a Gosiute boy with whom he had herded sheep; thus he had no difficulty adjusting himself to nomadic Indian life, so appealing to a boy of his age.

That year the Shoshonis went northward from Salt Lake to the Snake River, which delayed them a week in crossing. The women spent much of the time making bulrush rafts in order to transport their goods across the stream. Washakie alone carried five hundred pounds of dried meat for the needs of his family.

The six thousand Indians who finally assembled in Deer Lodge Valley (Montana) comprised the bands recognizing Washakie as

[5] "Journal History," L.D.S. Church Historian's Office, April 14, 1858.

[6] E. N. Wilson, *The White Indian Boy*, 20–32. Wilson, one of the West's beloved pioneers, rounded out his full life in the Jackson Hole country where the name Wilson, Wyoming, pays tribute to his memory.

their head chief. They fairly well included all of the nation except the scattered Basin Indians. Conspicuous among those present was Pocatello, "a wicked looking Indian." Nick's Indian mother warned him to be on his guard; Pocatello might steal him and trade him to the cannibals who would kill and eat him. Her reference seems to be to the legend of the red-haired cannibals of the Humboldt.

The excitement of the encampment sounds like rendezvous days, although the object was recreation and sociability more than trade. Accidents were to be expected in the savage abandonment of the occasion. Two Indians were killed in a horse race, and a woman and her papoose run over. Besides spending much of their time gambling, the bands celebrated with their Scalp Dance.

Pocatello, jealous of Washakie's exalted position, considered him an "old woman" because he would not fight the white man. Unable to goad Washakie into action, Pocatello had been trying to poison the minds of his warriors and toll them away. The Scalp Dance held by these two chieftains had special import, for Washakie did not have the scalp of a white person among his trophies. On the other hand, Pocatello had at least six from emigrants whom he had recently killed. Besides that, he displayed new quilts, white men's clothing, and guns that he had taken in his last foray. The scalps were strung up on poles, and the Indians danced around them at intervals for a week.

Two years later Pocatello tried to stir up trouble between Washakie and the white man by reporting that the Shoshonis held Nick captive. He finally sent several braves to Washakie's camp with the word that an army was being sent against him. Neither the chief nor the boy believed this, for Nick had told his plans to an old Gosiute, who he was sure had informed his parents of his whereabouts. Since his father had done nothing toward recovering him during the time he had spent in the Shoshoni camp, Nick was sure that the report was false. Pocatello's Indians, feeling that they had accomplished nothing, left in a bad mood.

In council the war chief suggested sending the white boy home to clear the records. Washakie agreed that this should be done.

As always, he did not want to have trouble with the white man. He only asked that Nick tell the truth—that he was not a captive. Thus it was that the political enmity between Pocatello and Washakie caused Nick Wilson to be returned to his parents after many eventful experiences among the Indians.[7]

While the chief of the Green River Snakes endured every personal affront, even to being fired upon by emigrants, he was unwavering in his determination to remain peaceful. Some writers would have us think that he had an undying love for the paleface. On the contrary, while he admired the products of the white man's civilization, he had no illusions regarding the white man's selfish nature. Wilson quoted an old arrow maker, Morogonai, as saying that the chief advised him "to keep away from the road where the white men travel, and have nothing to do with them; 'for,' said he, 'they have crooked tongues; no one can believe what they have to say.' "

This the Shoshonis had learned through bitter experience. Pocatello once stated that he could not control the thoughts of his young men whose relatives had been killed by the emigrants. Washakie took no chances in controlling the thoughts and actions of his warriors in the vicinity of the trail. It was better to fight the Crows in the Big Horns than to involve his people in untold trouble with the Great White Father. Thus Washakie was considered a "camp mover" by his enemies, as he was constantly trying to keep his Indians busy in their quest for food, which was dwindling each year. He was not like Pocatello, who was openly hostile, or Little Soldier, who soon learned that personal gain lay in keeping in the good graces of the Indian agents. As a somewhat doubtful informant, Little Soldier always managed to be on hand to receive gratuitous gifts from the white man.

Washakie, by holding his followers in check, was able to spare the lives of countless emigrants. It may seem inconsistent to believe that he granted amnesty to the travelers when he had an inward bitterness brought about by injustices, broken promises, and the ruthless way the white man overran his country. There

7 *Ibid.,* 109–18.

can be only one explanation for his behavior. He was convinced that there was but one way out of the dilemma in which the Indians found themselves. That was to align themselves with the white man in spite of his faults and hope for crumbs of compassion at treaty councils.

He had the foresight to realize that the era of the red man was drawing to a close. With the gradual depletion of wild game and the plowing up of camass and other roots, the natural food supply would soon be gone; therefore, the Indian must inevitably accept the white man's way of life to survive. Furthermore, by keeping on friendly terms with the aggressor, the Indian might gain certain advantages.

The Indians, though group conscious, believed in individual responsibility. They could not see the justice of destroying a village because of the misconduct of some of the Indians. Since Washakie recognized good and bad members of his tribe, he constantly tried to weed out the miscreants, for he knew that they would bring nothing but discredit upon his people. If some of the vengeful Shoshonis chose to follow Pocatello or Tavendu-wets, he felt that he was not accountable for them.

On the other hand, the chief of the Shoshonis did not hold the Great White Father responsible for the misconduct of his wayward children. His faith in the Great White Father was strong though not unfaltering, as we will see. He believed that by maintaining a peaceful heart, he would receive his reward. This idea was so contrary to that of the average chieftain that it is no wonder that many of his warriors deserted his ranks to follow other leaders who permitted or encouraged them to give vent to their resentment.

This reduced the number in Washakie's ranks until Brigham Young voiced his concern. He wrote to Washakie, advising him not to let his people divide into small groups, for they would become the easy prey of enemy tribes.[8] This is ironic, for it will be remembered that at the Horse Creek Council the white man had seemingly tried to break up the solidarity in Washakie's ranks.

[8] "Journal History," *loc. cit.*, November 30, 1854.

167

This error in judgment was not long in showing itself. As nearly as Young could estimate, the Shoshonis had formerly numbered approximately three hundred lodges, but they had become broken up into so many different bands that it was difficult now to determine exactly how many there were.

The Green River Snakes were far more concerned over their claim to the Wind River hunting grounds than they had been over the difficulties between the gentiles and the Mormons. Washakie had no doubt been displeased by the trouble at Green River. When he had invited the Mormons to the area to establish a trading center, he did not know what the acceptance of such an invitation might involve. He did not realize that his friend Jim Bridger would, as a result of his long-standing difficulty with the Mormons, be driven from his fort. Washakie's displeasure had not been sufficient to cause him to break his vow by making war upon the Saints, but his resentment must have been deep for him to offer to go on the warpath with the Army for Utah. When Colonel Johnston urged him to go on a hunting trip and stay out of the trouble area, it was not difficult for him as this was in line with the policy he had been following.[9]

During the time that Nick Wilson was with the Shoshonis, they fought a fierce but apparently indecisive battle with the Crows over their buffalo grounds (1856).[10] After leaving Henry's Lake, at the head of the north fork of Snake River, they had bravely but somewhat cautiously traveled toward the Crow country. The boy had heard Washakie affirm that he was going through if it cost him half his tribe. He would no longer be intimidated. Apparently the Crows had forced the Snakes out of the country on other occasions, for the war chief indicated that they had retreated so often that the Crows had begun to believe they were cowards. He favored giving the enemy a lesson that they would never forget.

The fighting in this battle, which was the forerunner of a series of conflicts leading to "open war" two years later, was sav-

9 Ficklin's report (975), 82.
10 Wilson, *The White Indian Boy*, 81–97.

age, as the Snakes came up against an encampment of one thousand Crows. At the end of the first hour of fighting, the Shoshonis were pushed back over a hill, in sight of four hundred of their women and children who were being held a safe distance away. As the fighting came closer, the women armed themselves with butcher knives and prepared to take part. Wilson says that he watched the chief "on his big buckskin horse dashing around among the Indians and telling them what to do." Soon the tide of battle turned, and the warriors began again to disappear over the ridge. The boy could tell that the Shoshonis were beating the Crows.[11]

The women and children would probably have been in the midst of the action had they not been heavily guarded by about fifty old Indians who circled them on horseback to make sure that they stayed together. After six hours of fighting, a wounded warrior brought a message that the women were not to unpack until they had received further word from the war chief. Finally toward sundown the Crows retreated, with Washakie and half of his warriors following. Another messenger instructed the women to make camp. He brought word that fresh horses were being taken to the warriors who were pursuing the Crows. Also, he reported that 25 dead Shoshonis had been counted on the battlefield. Without knowledge of who they were, the women and children began wailing until they could be heard two miles away.

Many badly wounded warriors were brought to the temporary encampment during the night, and several old Indians were dispatched to the battlefield to keep the eagles and wolves from devouring the dead. When Washakie returned, he reported that the Crows had fled into the timber from which he was unable to rout them, but he believed that there were few left. His warriors returned with the spoils of war, including about 250 horses, besides saddles, buffalo robes, blankets, bows, arrows, and guns.

The next morning the Indians went to the battleground to bury the dead. They found 31 bodies on the field. The mourners carried them to a deep washout on the hillside, where they deposited them and covered them with rocks and dirt. Later 18 of

[11] *Ibid.*, 92.

the wounded died, making a total of 49 killed and 100 wounded. The Indians whom Washakie sent out to count the enemy dead reported 103, but they had no idea how many the Crows had carried away, nor how many had died of wounds.

In the summer of 1856, presumably after the battle with the Crows just described, J. Robert Brown, of Ohio, came to the Bridger country in company with E. R. Yates, a well-known trader in the vicinity of the fort. While they were preparing their breakfast one morning, an Indian came into their camp. He struck his breast in token of friendship and said, "Shoshone!" When another arrived, the white men could tell from his signs that Washakie was coming. After dividing their bread with the two Indians, the white men sat waiting with interest for the arrival of the chief. As Brown related it:

We all now listened, and these Indians said Wassakee, Wassakee, in a low voice. Very soon 7 or 8 Indians came around the point of the hill and partially held up, and came slowly up to camp. When they came up Yates recognized one of them as being Brazil [Bazil], whom he had seen often two years ago.

He shook hands and all dismounted and came to the fire, and Brazil and Wassakee shook hands all around. I soon picked out Wassakee by his appearance. We found out through Brazil which was Wassakee for certain; an Indian will not tell his own name. . . . Wassakee is a medium sized man . . . [with] a perfect form, straight, muscular, and firm, and possesses the most beautiful set of teeth I ever saw. He was out on a hunt, and was dressed in a kind of coat and pants made of an old white blanket.

Yates made the whisky flow freely now, and Wassakee drank much, but he would pour some into a tin cup and then fill it up with water, and then portion out a little to each Indian except Brazil, whom he allowed to take the raw material. I could not see that it affected Wassakee any; but Brazil's eye began to brighten. After the Indians had drank he would wave his hand, and the Indians would mount and away.

We had not left camp far this morning before Wassakee and Brazil, and another Indian, followed us. They had started up the road, but I suppose they had not yet had enough whisky, so Yates rode back and met them. When they came up, he stopped the wagons and filled a sardine box with whisky and gave it to W., who then called for a pipe and some tobacco, which was found and given to him, when they took their gifts and sat down beside the road.

Wassakee, before he left us, shook hands with me only, and spoke the word, "che-bungo," which Yates says means "good." We had not gone more than a mile before here came Brazil in a gallop. Yates now tried to hide himself in the wagons. Brazil came up and asked me, in American, "where's Yates? Mr. Yates." Says I, he's gone on.

"No," says he. Just then the wind raised the wagon cover and he saw Yates in the wagon. He made him get out and give him one more "leetle dram, Mr. Yates." Then he gave back the pipe and left us. He was getting very tight, and his tongue was thick; he promised us "antelope heap, much me." . . . Yates says Wassakee is rich and can dress as fine as any chieftain in the mountains.[12]

Brown's colorful account places Washakie's band on Black's Fork, where they no doubt spent as much time as the limited food supply permitted. From there they made repeated forays into the Wind River and Bighorn valleys, where their difficulty with the Crows seemed to mount. The battle described by Nick Wilson was but one in a series waged over the disputed hunting ground. The tempo increased until the climax was reached in the Battle of Crowheart Butte. Unfortunately Nick had long since been returned to his people, and there were no chroniclers present to tell us what actually happened. Consequently, much has been left to the imagination.

Even the date is uncertain. Edmo LeClair, a half-blood son of a fur trader in the Fort Bridger area, is quoted as giving it as March, 1866,[13] but this is most unlikely in view of the fact that the Indian agent, Luther Mann, Jr., writing his report for that year, stated: "The Shoshones have not been engaged in any warfare offensive

12 Reprint, *Annals of Wyoming*, Vol. XXVI, No. 2, 183–185.
13 Hebard, *Washakie*, 150–52.

or defensive, during the past year with the neighboring tribes, have been at peace with them, and, I am proud to say, continued faithful to their treaty stipulations."[14]

F. W. Lander, who succeeded Magraw as superintendent of the Central Division of the Pacific Wagon Road, constructed under the direction of the Department of the Interior (1857, 1858, and 1859), said in his report for the year 1858 that the Crows and Shoshonis had broken out in open war in the north.[15] As a result, he would not risk exposing the large stock of mules of the construction crew at the camp previously selected—the one used as wintering ground the year before.

Ficklin's report corroborates Lander's statement concerning warfare between the Shoshonis and Crows, for he said that the Snakes wintering on Wind River were from last accounts in a starving condition.[16] They were at war with the Crows and unable to go out in search of game. He affirmed that on October 27 they had had a battle in which they had killed ten Crows. We do not know whether this was a reference to a forerunner of the Crow-Heart Battle or to the battle itself. The Bannocks, no doubt aroused by war fever, probably burned Fort Thompson, the supply depot of the Pacific Wagon crew, at the same time—when excitement was at its peak. Ficklin also stated that Washakie had said that if Uncle Sam did not do better by his Indians, he would let them steal from the whites all they wished. He claimed that they were being cheated every year.

From this we see that Washakie's nerves were frayed and that he was on the verge of allowing his warriors to right the wrongs done to them. He was apparently in this desperate mood when he fought the Battle of Crowheart Butte. Although we cannot tell definitely the date when it occurred, we are reasonably sure that it climaxed the warfare between the Shoshonis and the Crows

[14] Luther Mann, Jr., to Commissioner of Indian Affairs, September 15, 1856, I.O.R.

[15] *Sen. Exec. Doc. 36*, 36 Cong., 2 sess. (984), 49.

[16] *Ibid.*, 69.

and that it happened between the fall of 1858 and the spring of 1859, when work was resumed on the Lander Cutoff.

While the details are lacking, we can reconstruct the battle scene from the accounts given by Indians in the area. The Crows, in open defiance of the Shoshonis, set up a large encampment in Big Wind River Valley near present Kinnear, Wyoming. Taghee and his Bannocks were encamped on the Big Popo Agie River, near Hudson, Wyoming, with the Shoshonis somewhere between. Washakie is said to have sent a peace envoy, a brave and his wife, to the Crow camp. Since Washakie was in a militant mood, it is more likely that the message was an emphatic demand that the Crows leave the country. At any rate, the enemy killed the brave, but his wife escaped to report the atrocity. Washakie did not rush headlong into battle as the Crows had anticipated. Instead, he sent a runner to Taghee for help.

Irene Kinnear Meade, who lived all of her life in the Wind River Valley, listened as a child to accounts of the battle. She said that while the war chiefs of the two tribes were sparring and Washakie was waiting for reinforcements, the Crow chief taunted him by calling him a "squaw and an old woman," and by telling him that he was too cowardly to fight. When Washakie lifted his hand to signal the attack, an arrow pierced it. Presumably Taghee and his warriors had arrived by this time, for they joined in the battle, which lasted four days. Mrs. Meade's elders would tell how the women and children, hiding in the cut-banks along the stream, set up such a howl that had the Crow warriors not been too busy to bother with them they could have found them without trouble.

The main part of the battle was fought on Black Mountain, near the head of Crow Creek. In a legendary version well known locally, the battle reached a stalemate on the third day. Then Washakie and Big Robber, chief of the Crows, settled the matter with a duel in which the latter was slain. Washakie is said by realistic writers to have eaten the Crow chief's heart to bolster his courage. This is not improbable when we recall that the Indians were still uncivilized, and cannibalism among the Shoshonis was not unknown. Other authorities prefer to think that Washakie merely carried the Crow heart on the end of his lance during the War Dance which followed.

Although we have no way of proving who is correct, we know that this battle was decisive. Washakie gained the respect of the Crows, and they were no longer a major problem. Besides settling his right to his hunting grounds in his own way, he also acquired as a battle trophy a girl, Ah-ah-why-per-sie (Crow Maiden), who later became one of his wives. Washakie's Indians who had long been called Green River Snakes were now Wind River Shoshonis, privileged to live in "Warm Valley," as Washakie called it, out of the way of the emigrants. The chief at this time was unaware that the white man was already making plans to follow him with still another destructive trail to bring further hardship to his people.

CHAPTER ELEVEN

Shoshoni Uprisings

W̶ITH THE MORMONS now in check and the Crows driven effectively from the Wind River area, the Shoshonis should have been able to attain a degree of serenity, but such was not the case. While the Mormon difficulties were resolving themselves, the Department of the Interior was pushing its plan for still another major highway through Shoshoni country—the Fort Kearney, South Pass, and Honey Lake Road, or the Pacific Wagon Road, to which we have alluded through the reports of Lander, Magraw, and others variously employed in the enterprise.

Lander, who was not new to the Rockies, had previously crossed the continent by way of South Pass in exploring a practical route for a railroad from the Mississippi River to the Pacific Coast. The proposed wagon road was designed to improve the old emigrant road from Independence Rock to South Pass. Then after leaving the summit at South Pass, it would run as a new road near the base of Wind River Mountains. It would go in a direct line to Soda Springs on Bear River, after crossing Green River near New Forks. Leaving Soda Springs, it would go by way of Thousand Spring Valley north of the Humboldt to Mud Lake. The object of the new road was to avoid the Salt Lake trouble spot.

Besides, it would shorten the distance and afford better grass and a greater and more permanent supply of water than the already traveled road. Also it would avoid the Green River Desert from which starvation had caused Washakie's Indians to move, although they still claimed that country.

After Lander had arrived at South Pass on July 16, 1857, he had divided his crew into three groups, which thoroughly explored the area from the Wasatch Mountains into the upper basin

175

of Green River. Superintendent of construction William M. F. Magraw, who had arrived in September, had stayed only long enough to establish winter quarters on the Popo Agie; then he, among others, had left to join Johnston's army. Lander, who succeeded him, remained in the Shoshoni country to see his road a reality. Meanwhile, he served as agent-at-large and furnished detailed accounts of the Indians and their problems.

Lander found Washakie and his once-proud buffalo hunters on an antelope surround near the headwaters of Green River. This must have been as galling as digging roots, since the antelope were considered the "big game" of the Shoshokos. In lieu of other supplies, as the train had not arrived, Lander presented the chief with a fine "herding" horse.[1] Then he broached the subject of his new road.

Washakie replied in characteristic fashion. He maintained that it was never the intention of his tribe to fight the white man. Before the emigrants passed through his country, buffalo, elk, and antelope could be seen upon all the hills. Now, when he looked for game, he saw only wagons with white tops and men riding upon their horses. He admitted that his people were very poor, that they had fallen back into the valleys of the mountains to dig roots and hunt what meat they could find for their little ones. He was not complaining, he said, for he and his Indians knew that they could not conquer the whites or drive them out of the country. They did not even propose to fight, notwithstanding the fact that this new road would destroy many of their root grounds and drive off their game.

Other Indians had told him that if he killed some whites the Great White Father would send many presents to keep him from killing more. He assured Lander that he had no intention of following such advice, but he did want the Great White Father to know that his people were waiting to hear from him. They did not stand "with open hands" begging for presents, but they hoped that he would be just. The Snakes wished to be treated as the Great White Father's children, as they had so often been promised.

[1] Lander's report (984), 68–69.

Lander listened sympathetically, for he was aware that the Indians had suffered greatly at the hands of the emigrants and that the new road would cause further difficulty. In his report he commented that the Shoshonis had probably suffered more than any other tribe from the passage of emigration along the narrow valleys of their rivers, where the white men had relentlessly driven out their game. C. H. Miller, one of the engineers with Lander, further stressed the fact that the cutoff would bring nothing but added misery to the Indians:

> The new road in many instances follows the summer and fall trail of the Shoshonee tribe. The animals of the emigrants will destroy the grass in the valleys where the Indians have kept the pine timber and willows burnt out for years as halting places in going and coming from their great annual buffalo hunts, and I believe, even beyond the mere question of policy, that it would be very unjust and cruel course of action for the government to pursue should we take the use of the land without reimbursement to the tribe.[2]

After leaving the Shoshonis, Miller went to the Bannock country. Here he described the natives as "dangerous, cruel, and vindictive." At the time, they had no regularly constituted head chief, but they respected "the great Washakie," with whom they often went on hunting trips or war excursions against the Crows. When the Miller party fell in with some Bannocks, the Indians, believing them to be Mormons, wanted to shoot them; but their band leader, "a quiet and temperate man," dissuaded them. He thought that it was possible that the white men were "Americans." He maintained that he loved the children of the Great Father and would allow no harm to befall them, but his heart was bad toward the Mormons.

Miller enlisted the services of "Shoshone Aleck" (Isaac Frapp, a half-blood) as interpreter before going to the camp of Pocatello, whose heart was bad toward all whites in general. Although he apparently had no use for a "paleface," he said that Miller "had come to him like a man; and he would meet him like a man." The

[2] Miller's report (984), 69–72.

surveyor made an unusual analytical statement regarding the mixed bands of Shoshonis and Bannocks, whom he considered the most dangerous of all of the Indians he had met:

> I do not think the term "treacherous," as usually applied to Indians tribes, is always just. We can hardly say that a tribe is treacherous which definitely asserts, through its chief, that it will not permit the passage of white men through their country. It has been in the most manly and direct manner that these Indians have said that if emigrants, as has usually been the case, shoot members of their tribes, they will kill them when they can.
>
> They undoubtedly use all the means and appliances of Indian warfare, and, as barbarians, torture their prisoners; but if met with the true spirit of American energy, with kindness and justice, there is no difficulty whatever in approaching and subduing the worst elements of the Indian character; that is my opinion, after an experience of several years among them.

Miller made no attempt to distinguish between Bannocks and Shoshonis. Nor was Jacob Forney, Young's successor as superintendent of Indian affairs in the Utah Territory, able to tell one tribe from the other. In his eagerness to learn more about the natives under his jurisdiction, he wrote to the Indian office requesting a book pertaining to the "general and special history of all of the Indian tribes in the U. States."[3] If the history arrived, it must not have contained the desired information, for the new superintendent was at his post a year before he discovered that the Bannocks comprised a tribe separate and apart from the Shoshonis. Meeting five hundred of them when they came to a treaty council held between the Shoshonis and Utes, he gave them gifts and assigned them temporarily to Washakie's loosely organized territory.

The Western Shoshonis along the Humboldt River and in the Goose Creek Mountains were intermittently at war with the emigrants along the trail. Attacking from the willows in Humboldt Valley, they were known to destroy small groups of overland travelers. The Honey Lake Paiutes, on the other hand, were generally friendly. Occasionally minor difficulties arose, causing

[3] Forney to Acting Commissioner of Indian Affairs, February 10, 1858, I.O.R.

IDAHO'S TERRITORIAL GOVERNOR CALEB LYON points to the treaty signed at the Idaho Council of 1866. The Indians in this oil painting by Charles Christian Nahl are probably Western Shoshonis.

Courtesy Thomas Gilcrease Institute of American History and Art

THESE POCATELLO BRAVES were photographed by C. W. Carter's Photographic Gallery and View Emporium, Salt Lake City.

Courtesy Bureau of American Ethnology

RABBIT TAIL, a Shoshoni, was a scout for the United States Army. Notice the brass-studded mirror which he carries.

Courtesy Frank Phillips Collection, Division of Manuscripts, University of Oklahoma Library

CHIEF WINNEMUCCA, the Paiute who helped bring an end to the Shoshoni uprisings.

Courtesy Nevada Historical Society

SHOSHONI TRIBAL LEADERS: *front row*, Dick Washakie, Chief Washakie, and Tigee; *standing*, Per-na-go-shia, Pan-Zook, So-pa-gant, and Mat-ta-vish.

Courtesy Western Archives, University of Wyoming Library

WAR DANCE at Fort Washakie. The Chief stands at left with a tomahawk in his hand.

Courtesy Western Archives, University of Wyoming Library

"THEY CAME WITH PIPES TO SUE FOR PEACE." Arapaho chief and sub-chiefs with James Irwin, superintendent at Fort Washakie. Note Black Coal's right hand with fingers missing. *Front row*, White Horse, Chief Black Coal, and Little Wolf; *standing*, Iron, Irwin, and Sharp Nose.

Courtesy J. K. Moore, Jr.

THIS DELEGATION waits to see President Arthur on his journey through Wyoming in August, 1883. The Arapahoes are standing, with their chief, Black Coal, at the far right; the Shoshonis are on the front row.

Courtesy J. K. Moore, Jr.

troops to be called temporarily from near-by posts. No permanent military installation was necessary, although the Pacific Wagon Road terminated in the Paiutes' country. They were prepared for the coming of the white man by an old shaman, who, singing four or five nights, predicted the arrival of the "white-skinned people." Naturally the Indians were not surprised to see them, although they were afraid of the armed soldiers who appeared first.[4]

Miller believed that a small gift of a thousand dollars to the Shoshonis of Utah, Nevada, and southern Oregon would put a stop to depredations along the trail. The old men in the tribes could then impress upon the young braves the fact that the Great Father had paid for the passage of the emigrants through their country. Trouble was brewing throughout the Shoshoni area.

Forney, in his September report to the Office of Indian Affairs, stated that there was no tribe of Indians in Utah Territory that had been discommoded as much by the whites as the Shoshonis. He said that for the past five years they had been compelled to live in the mountains, where snows had been so deep in winter that they were destructive "to man and beast." He continued: "The Eastern Snakes are under Washakie, though they rarely stay where they belong. . . . Washakie has perfect command over them and is one of the finest looking and most intellectual Indians I ever saw."[5]

Forney took no chance of being attacked when he went to Gravelly Ford (near Beowawe, Nevada) in September, 1858. He had an escort of 150 soldiers, requisitioned by his friend Governor Cumming. After reaching the ford, 100 miles beyond the first crossing of the Humboldt, he went on to Carson Valley to establish an agency.[6]

In compliance with his theory that the Indians could be won over with gifts, Lander, the following March, asked for what he considered necessary articles to supply Washakie's band (150

[4] Francis A. Riddell, "Honey Lake Paiute Ethnography," *A.P.* No. 4 (1960), 3–5.

[5] (Hereinafter cited as Forney's report), *Sen. Exec. Doc. 1*, 35 Cong., 2 sess. (974), 561–66.

[6] Forney to Acting Commissioner of Indian Affairs, September 6, 1858. I.O.R.

lodges); the Northern Bannocks, Shoshonis, and Sheep Eaters (100 lodges); the Bannocks (150 lodges); and the Western Shoshonis (150 lodges). He even requested a "uniform jacket" (value, $50) for Washakie.[7]

On March 25, 1859, the Secretary of the Interior instructed the Commissioner of Indian Affairs to place a sum, not to exceed $5,000, at Lander's disposal. This amount was supposed to assure safe passage through the country, but we have no knowledge of whether or not Washakie's band received the gifts intended for them. They may have been out of the area at the time, and the gifts may have been given to the troublesome bands.

Had Washakie not tried to hold his warriors in check, hostilities would probably have broken out sooner among the Indians. As it was, the Bannocks were the first to make a large-scale move. They began in the spring of 1859 in the Flathead country by driving off one hundred head of horses from Bitterroot Valley (Montana) while Agent John Owen, of Fort Owen, was on his way back to the agency after a trip to Salt Lake.[8] About the same time some Bannocks and Shoshonis, attacking from a canyon in the Utah-Idaho Goose Creek Mountains, killed seven people and wounded several others in an emigrant train which they pillaged. Miller, learning of this incident through a Salt Lake correspondent, stated that the attack had been made by the same Indians who befriended him a short time before.

> Their good faith and kindness was manifested by the first tribe or band sending runners the whole length of the Humboldt Valley, a distance of 400 miles, in order that thirteen of my men, unprotected and imperfectly armed, might on their arrival, be passed through various bands of this tribe in safety to Honey Lake valley.[9]

Forney requested that troops be sent from Camp Floyd in search of the marauders. Major Isaac Lynde established headquarters at Bear River Crossing, while Lieutenant E. Gay at-

[7] For Dale L. Morgan's reference to this jacket, *see Annals of Wyoming*, Vol. XXVII, No. 2, 198.

[8] John Owen, *The Letters and Journals of Major John Owen*, 191–93.

[9] Miller's report (984), 72–73.

tempted to track down the culprits. He found a large camp of Bannocks at Devil's Gate Canyon. Assuming these to be the guilty Indians, he attacked, killing twenty Indians and capturing an equal number of horses.[10] While on his way back to Bear River Crossing, he captured Pocatello, but Major Lynde released him because he did not want to arouse the Indians by bringing charges that he could not prove.[11] Lynde was severely criticized by the *Deseret News* for allowing the hostile chief to escape punishment.[12]

Other attacks were made with alarming frequency. Among them was one reported by Lander, who said that four emigrants had been killed near the Fort Hall road by some renegade subchiefs of the Bannocks and Shoshonis. He listed them as Saw-witch, Jah-win-pooh, Jag-en-up, and Jag-e-oh. He added that the head chiefs did not approve of their action. Forty lodges of Bannocks accepted gifts distributed to them, but the Camas Prairie and Fort Boise Bannocks, refusing to come in, said that their hearts were bad.[13]

About this time an incident, even more shocking than the Goose Creek Massacre, occurred. It was known as the Otter Massacre.[14] A party of emigrants on Snake River were attacked by the hostile Bannocks and their Shoshoni allies. Of the forty-five men in the party, eighteen were killed outright, and five others who died of wounds were eaten by starved survivors. Four children in the party were captured by the Indians, and two were lost in the mountains. Although a feeble effort was made to recover the children, we find no record to indicate that they were ever located.

Realizing that it was impossible to police the entire territory inhabited by the illusive natives, General Johnston, who had been stationed in Utah after the Mormon War, recommended that troops be placed at Bear River Crossing, Fort Hall, and the Goose Creek Mountains. He emphasized the urgency of pushing the

[10] Lander's report (1033), 19–25.
[11] *Ibid.*, 32.
[12] *Deseret News* (September 14, 1859).
[13] Lander's report (1033), 28–29, 31.
[14] Indian Depredations in Oregon and Washington, *House Exec. Doc. 29*, 36 Cong., 2 sess. (1097), 79–85; also Madsen, *The Bannock of Idaho*, 124.

Bannocks and Shoshonis back from the emigrant roads and the advisability of keeping traders out of the Indian area. As another precautionary measure, he suggested that the jurisdiction of the Military Department of Utah be extended to reach into the troubled area of Idaho.[15]

Referring to the many depredations that took place during 1859, Forney stated that he was convinced that the Bannocks of Oregon had been primarily responsible, with the Shoshonis of Utah Territory taking part only to a minor degree.[16] Reports are meager concerning the Shoshokos to the south. In October, Major Lynde had met and talked with about fifteen of them, sixty-five miles above Gravelly Ford on the North Fork of the Humboldt. He found them friendly, but very poor, nearly naked, and subsisting on squirrels or nuts dug from the ground. They would beg the emigrants for cattle that died from disease so that they might have them for food.[17]

Lynde said that a small band of Snakes, known as Box Elder Indians, had attacked emigrants on the Lander Road and that such attacks were sometimes led by white men painted as Indians. The country was so rough that the redskins could manage to escape when the soldiers were within twenty-five miles of them.

Judge D. R. Eckels, of Utah Territory, agreed with Forney that the Bannocks were the ring leaders in the attacks, although he did not specify that they were from Oregon. He also agreed with Major Lynde that the war parties were sometimes under the leadership of white men, disguised as Indians.[18] Such was the case in the Mountain Meadows (Utah) Massacre, in September, 1857.[19] Though the Paiutes were blamed for this massacre by the Mormons, the perpetrator, John D. Lee, was apprehended some years later. He was tried, convicted, and taken to the scene on March 23, 1877. As he was shot, he fell back into his coffin. He is said to

[15] Johnston's report (1033), 25–27.
[16] Forney's report (974), 634.
[17] Shoshone Depredations, *Sen. Exec. Doc. 2*, 36 Cong., 1 sess. (1024), 243–44.
[18] Indian Depredations (1033), 111.
[19] J. P. Dunn, *Massacres of the Mountains*, 237–83.

have been survived by nineteen wives and sixty-four children. The Mountain Meadows incident is sometimes cited as the reason for building the Lander Cutoff. Undeniably the speed-up in construction was brought about by difficulties in the Salt Lake area, but it should be pointed out that plans were laid and in execution before the massacre occurred.

After an attack upon a wagon train on the Sublette Cutoff, on September 22, 1859, Forney talked to Little Soldier, whom he considered reliable.[20] The chief assured him that the bad Indians had left his band as well as Washakie's. This would indicate that the restless warriors, thirsting for action, were leaving to join the malcontents. There were at this time fourteen regularly organized bands under the Utah Superintendency, with the Green River Snakes—one of the largest—numbering about twelve hundred.[21] Added to this, there were about five hundred Bannocks, presumably those under Taghee, in Washakie's domain. The head chief of the Shoshonis was assisted by four to six subchiefs in his own band, while the other bands recognizing Washakie as their chief each had one principal band leader and several subchiefs.

Five of the bands, numbering about one thousand, roamed through Salt Lake, Weber, Ogden, Bear River, Cache, and Malad valleys and the adjacent mountains and canyons. One band confined itself to the region along the road from Bear and Malad rivers to the Goose Creek Mountains. Seven bands roamed in the valleys of the Humboldt and down into the Paiute country, one hundred miles south of the river. The Gosiutes, whose leader had died four years before, were scattered, although some were by now (1859) settled on Deep Creek Indian farm. Others, in roving bands, ranged from forty to two hundred miles west of Salt Lake City.

Lander, reporting one of the attacks led by renegade chiefs, said that a Western Shoshoni boy brought in the story of the massacre of a small group of emigrants by "Southern Snake Indians" under the direction of Chief Jag-e-oh (The Man Who

[20] Forney's report (1033), 34.
[21] Forney to Commissioner of Indian Affairs, September 29, 1859, I.O.R.

Carries the Arrow).[22] Ah-gutch (The Salmon) also took part. Although the lad carried one of blankets taken from the emigrants, he seemed more afraid of the natives than of the whites. Snag said that he could point out the guilty Indians.

The portion of the Honey Lake Road between South Pass and Point of Rocks was known from the time of its opening as the Lander Cutoff. Emigrants soon began streaming along it, to the annoyance of the Indians. Their hostility was increased by the influence of a mysterious leader, about whom little is known. He was an oracle or high priest, and his power was more widespread even than Washakie's. His influence was felt by Indians who roamed the vast territory comprising what is now eastern Washington, Oregon, and California, throughout Idaho, Utah, and Nevada, and into western Wyoming.

Although we are not sure who this redskin was, Little Soldier identified him as War-i-gika, "the great Bannock prophet," living in the Walla Walla region. In his report of February 11, 1860, Lander said that Pash-e-co, medicine man and head of all the Bannocks, was considered "a wonderful prophet by the Snakes." He was chief of the War-are-ree-kas (Sunflower Seed Eaters).

It seems unlikely that these Digger Bannocks should produce two great prophets at the same time, both with such widespread influence. Since War-i-gika, is so vague a character, we feel that it is reasonable to assume that the oracle, prophet, and chief who was able to wield such an influence over the Indians throughout the entire West was none other than Pash-e-co. C. H. Miller did not mention him by name, but he was obviously referring to him in his report when he said:

> These Indians [the Bannocks and Shoshonis] are very much under the influence of a celebrated prophet of the Western Snake tribe, who resides in the vicinity of the old Hudson Bay Trading Post of Fort Boise.[23] Should I receive your instructions to do so, during the next season I desire very much to visit this noted prophet and confer with him through a good interpreter. He is a man of

[22] Lander's report (1033), 29–30.
[23] John McLaughlin of the Hudson's Bay Company established Fort Boise in 1834.

great influence among these dangerous tribes west of the Wasatch mountain range, and perhaps this influence may be gained in behalf of the whites.

I consider him one of the most dangerous and desperate men now living west of the Rocky Mountains, for the Indians have a superstitious reverence for him. He is extremely hostile to the Mormons. This noted partisan was the chief cause of the expedition against the Mormon settlement of Salmon River.[24]

Attacks were reported by Edward R. Geary of the Washington and Oregon Superintendency in October, 1860. He expressed the opinion that military protection might be needed in his area against "the Snake Indians":

These Indians, though known as Snakes, are by no means to be confounded with the Bannocks and Shoshonees of the Rocky Mountains. The latter are well mounted and annually hunt the Buffalo on the headwaters of the Yellowstone, while the former are a miserable race, clad in skins, without houses or inclosures, hiding like wild beasts in the rocks or cowering beneath the sage brush and deriving a precarious subsistence from roots and insects, except when their predatory forays afford them better fare.

Stealthy as the fox and fierce as the wolf, they seize the unguarded moment to pounce on their prey and bear it away in triumph. Their country has no indication they are numerous; few trails and seldom an old camp are found.

Having but few guns and being generally armed with bows, they cannot be formidable, yet they are the terror of the surrounding tribes, and alike a mystery to the red man and the white. As to the declevities of the Blue Mountains, it is barren desert. Our government could well afford to permit them to possess it without molestation, would they but cease their incursions into more favored regions and suffer the traveler to pass unmolested.

To this, however, they will not consent, till overtaken and taught by sincere chastisement the white man's power, then made the recipients of our bounty, they may be brought to appreciate and enjoy the benefits of peace and honest labor.[25]

[24] Miller's report, (984) 70–71.

[25] Edward R. Geary, *Report,* October 1, 1860, I.O.R.; *Report of Commissioner of Indian Affairs,* 1860, 176–77.

Pash-e-co may have been responsible for the Ward Massacre, one of the most tragic incidents in Idaho's history. The attack, said to have been carried out by a band of "Snake Indians," occurred twenty-five miles from old Fort Boise. All of the men in the wagon train were killed, while the women and children (with the exception of two boys who escaped in the brush) were captured and tortured fiendishly. The unspeakable horror of the scene was reported by the rescue party sent out from the fort.[26]

The vast alliance, masterminded by the chief of the War-are-ree-kas, gradually extended eastward. Hostilities along the road between the Walla Walla country of Pash-e-co and Fort Bridger in one year necessitated a vigorous campaign which cost the government a half-million dollars. Meanwhile, the Nevada Indians broke into open hostility in a series of skirmishes called the Paiute War of 1860.[27] In a fight near Pyramid Lake, Major W. M. Ormsby and Henry Meredith, a California lawyer, were killed. Since Pash-e-co later proved to be a great friend of Winnemucca, he may have had a hand in the Paiute War.

Disturbances in Nevada made it necessary to place troops at Camp Ruby (later Fort Ruby) in Ruby Valley in September, 1862. From there an attempt was made to put a stop to Gosiute and Western Shoshoni depredations. Soldiers patrolled the trail from Deep Creek Station on the Utah line to Austin, Nevada. Then other soldiers at Fort Churchill (erected on the Carson River in 1860) policed the road from Austin to Honey Lake.[28]

William H. Rogers, the agent at Fort Bridger, was so concerned over the situation in the Shoshoni country that he went over the head of Superintendent Benjamin Davies and wrote to

---

[26] Idaho Writer's Project, *Idaho*, 22–23. It should be noted that the term "Snake" during this period was used as loosely as it was by the first explorers and fur traders. It applied to any hostiles east of the Cascades. This makes it difficult to distinguish Shoshonis, Bannocks, and Paiutes. Miller adds to this confusion by calling the celebrated character "Bannock Digger Pash-e-co, a prophet of the Western Snake tribe."

[27] Mack, *Nevada*, 303–34; George D. Lyman, *The Saga of the Comstock Lode*, 106–16.

[28] Mack, *Nevada*, 313–14.

the Office of Indian Affairs. Receiving no response from that source, he frantically appealed to William H. Russell, of Russell, Majors and Waddell, then operating the Pony Express. In his letter, he urged Russell to use what influence he might have with the Commissioner because of the gravity of the situation:

> I have had frequent appeals from the "Snake Indians" to make them a visit and give them a few presents; but I have no means to do so; and I now think if some thing is not done there will be trouble this summer, and I take this opportunity of informing the Department through you that if these Indians, who are the best in the Rocky Mountains and who pride themselves that they have never spilled the blood of a white man are not looked after, the Department must answer for it; they [the Indians] have been deceived by promises from both [Superintendents] Forney and Davies and have received nothing since the winter of '57, and then only a small quantity of goods—they are a large band—Washakie is their chief, they are the bravest and most intelligent Indians in the territory—his tribe have deserted him, or as they say they have thrown him away, and he has always ruled them and could hold them in complete subjection until now.
>
> He told me last summer that his Indians lost Confidence in him that he had made them promises of good[s] on the word of the Superintendent to him, there is no Indian in the Tribe who can manage things so well as Washakee—he should be restored to his former position as Chief, this can be done at present with but little trouble, the Snakes say they do not intend to let the Mail or Emigrants pass through their Country if they do not get some presents this Spring; it should be attended to without delay; they seem to think that the bad Indians, who kill & steal get presents while they get only promises, and seem to have come to the conclusion that bad Indians are the only ones who are rewarded, which is very near the truth as far as this Territory is concerned.[29]

The situation was made more alarming by the fact that the Civil War was drawing forces from the territory. There were not enough United States troops in Utah "to whip the Snakes," Rogers declared. He concluded his urgent message to Russell by saying

[29] W. H. Rogers to W. H. Russell, April 18, 1861, I.O.R.

187

that if the department would send eight or ten thousand dollars by Pony Express to buy goods for the Eastern Shoshonis, there would be no question but that Washakie could be reinstated and serious trouble averted.

Rogers' statement that the Indians had "thrown away" or abandoned Washakie was reaffirmed by James D. Doty, superintendent of Indian affairs in Utah. He was informed by Little Soldied that Washakie had been "set aside" by his warriors.[30]

Although the chief of the Shoshonis had threatened to release his warriors upon a number of occasions, he remained firm in his pledge not to make war against the white man. By stubbornly standing by his word, he lost his following. The usually friendly Shoshonis were ready to join the Bannocks under their great Pash-e-co. If Rogers' charges were true—that Washakie and his Indians had received nothing since 1857—it is evident that they did not receive the goods distributed by Lander. Just what Washakie was given other than a fine herding horse we do not know.

Benjamin Davies, who succeeded Forney, tried to feed the hundreds of Indians who came to him when he found himself bogged down in the deep snows at Fort Bridger.[31] When weather permitted, he had "made liberal distribution of presents" to all bands in his territory except those at Carson Valley and at the head of the Humboldt River and Goose Creek. While the Indians were in his care during the starvation period in the winter, he had tried without apparent success to get them to eat pork when beef was not available.

Through his interpreter, Huntington, who had spent twenty years in direct contact with the Indians, Davies discovered that they were suspicious of the white man's policy. They thought that the paleface intended to drive them into the "Big Waters west of them." Because of this attitude, Davies predicted that the whites would have difficulty purchasing their land by treaty or other-

[30] *Report of Commissioner of Indian Affairs,* 1862, 213.

[31] Rogers, in his letter to Russell, had complained of Davies' supplying the drones who hung around the agency and consumed the food that should have been distributed among the more worthy. Benjamin Davies to Commissioner of Indian Affairs, June 30, 1861, I.O.R.

wise. He observed that the Indians were by nature herdsmen. If given a few cattle, they would accept the idea of caring for them in preference to "the more civilized labor of the farm."

The various Utah Indian agents, as well as Major Owen of the Flathead Agency, Superintendent Geary of Portland, and Governor Cumming of Utah, urged repeatedly that a treaty council be called in order to solve the difficulties among the Indians. Another agent, Henry Martin, in the fall of 1861, held talks with Washakie, Sho-kub (Nevada Shoshoni chief), and their sub-chiefs.[32] The Indians expressed themselves as favoring a treaty council as "the effectual way to check the stealing propensities" of some of their number.

Depredations gained tempo until it seemed apparent that the Indians were bent on a war of extermination. Realizing that the situation was crucial, Charles E. Mix, acting commissioner of Indian affairs, issued a proclamation warning of possible hostilities on the part of the Bannocks and Shoshonis, as well as of the Indians upon the Plains and along the Platte River.[33]

Pash-e-co was by now the recognized leader of the Shoshonean people of Oregon, Utah, and Nevada. His band normally ranged in the region of the Blue Mountains of Oregon, where they subsisted on roots and plunder. He had 150 lodges and only a few horses, stolen from the Cayuses. Nevertheless, he accomplished what Pocatello had tried to do without success, for he managed to win Washakie's warriors to his cause. Unlike Tavendu-wets, who had succeeded in claiming a following from the great chief's band, he was able to control his warriors. He had the advantage of being a prophet as well as a chief.

Fortunately Washakie had cleared the hostile Crows from the Wind River country. There he was free to don his new "uniform jacket" (if it ever arrived) and take his troubles to "the Healing Waters," as he called the Hot Springs at present Thermopolis,

---

[32] Henry Martin to Commissioner of Indian Affairs, October 1, 1861. The agents and superintendents did not remain at their posts long enough to know the Indians or the country, much less to know how to solve the Indian problem.

[33] *Report of Commissioner of Indian Affairs*, 1862, 215.

Wyoming. There he would not be disturbed by either the Crows or the Indian agents, who seemed to have little idea of what was transpiring. Then, too, he could keep from being involved. Washakie was a stubborn man; his word, once given, was not to be broken.

During the time Pash-e-co was lining up the Eastern Shoshonis under his banner, Chief Qui-tan-i-an (Foul Hand), who managed to stay out of trouble, was serving as leader of the Lemhis.[34] He had two subchiefs who were not beyond suspicion. They were Old Snag (Shoshoni) and Le Grand Coquin (Bannock), who had previously caused trouble in the Lemhi Valley. Snag had been known to commit depredations, at the same time claiming to be an Eastern Shoshoni.

The Bannocks had a peace chief, the little-known Tash-e-pah, who like Washakie was half-Flathead and a friend to the Americans. Their more powerful chief (aside from the temporary Pash-e-co) was Mopeah or Horne (Horn of Hair on the Forehead). Lander was favorably impressed by Mopeah when he talked to him in 1859, but knowing the Bannock nature, Lander realized that he and his tribe would not long be at peace.

Po-e-ma-che-ah (Hairy Man), the chief in charge of the Bannocks near Fort Boise, was reported to have a large number of horses, while the Salt Lake Diggers (Lower or "Southern" Snakes), under Mosen (Long Beard), and the Western Shoshonis, under Am-a-ro-ko (Buffalo Meat Under the Shoulder), had few. The last mentioned, ranging over Camas Prairie, included Pocatello's Indians, who were at the time in the Goose Creek Mountains and at the head of the Humboldt River.

The Shoshonis to the east seemed to be awaiting a signal from Pash-e-co. Finally it came. In March, 1862, they went on the warpath by striking simultaneously at every station between Platte and Bear rivers. In a swift, well-planned stroke, they paralyzed all communication on the Overland Trail. The Overland Stage drivers, station attendants, and guards—caught completely by surprise—allowed them to capture every horse and mule belonging

[34] Lander's report, *Sen. Exec. Doc. 46*, 36 Cong., 2 sess. (1099), 121–37.

to the company through their country. Stages, with their passengers, and wagons, heavily loaded, were left standing on the road where the Indians took their toll in horses and mules. Two hundred horses and five mules belonging to Jack Robertson, then interpreter at Fort Bridger, were run off during the surprise attack.

Captain Jesse A. Gove, who had come west with Johnston's troops, was placed in command of the reconstructed post briefly in 1861. Then most of the soldiers were withdrawn because of the Civil War. Before he left, Colonel Philip St. George Cooke, Gove's commanding officer, ordered that all unnecessary property be sold. This was done in spite of the efforts of Brigham Young's agent Lewis Robinson, who tried to prevent the sale on the grounds that the property belonged to the Mormon leader. The only soldiers left were an ordinance sergeant and several privates.

After Cooke's forces had gone, the fort was threatened alternately by Indians and Mormons. William A. Carter, who had accompanied Johnston to Bridger to become post sutler, found it necessary to organize a company of sixty volunteers, made up of the employees and near-by settlers. This was the state of affairs at Fort Bridger at the time the Eastern Shoshonis, under Pash-e-co, went on the warpath. The volunteers searching for Robertson's horses and mules were able to recover only about forty of the number.

Just why the buildings were not burned at Fort Bridger, this time by the Shoshonis, is a mystery. Perhaps they still viewed the fort with a certain amount of sentiment. Jack Robertson had urged Bridger to build it in the first place, and although Blanket Chief had gone his way, Robertson had remained, closely associated with his wife's tribe. This may have had something to do with the Indians' sparing the fort. Then, too, the first agent to visit the Shoshonis had suggested that a permanent agency be placed there. The Indians may not have forgotten, for this had been the common ground upon which they had met representatives of the Great White Father.

The only murder committed in the Eastern Shoshoni region

was at Split Rock Station on Sweetwater. There the Indians ordered a Negro to prepare a meal for them. As he had lived among the Pennsylvania Dutch all his life, he did not understand their sign language. They proceeded to kill him and help themselves to his food. They could still boast that they had not "spilled the blood of a white man." Their reluctance to do so might have been attributed more to the teaching of Washakie than to the preaching of Pash-e-co.

Little Soldier paid an unexpected call at the home of Huntington in Salt Lake City, at midnight on August 2, 1862.[35] He came with the startling news that the Bannocks and Shoshonis inhabiting the northern part of Utah and those in the southern part of eastern Washington had already joined forces for the purpose of making war and committing depredations on the emigrants and settlers. The Indians were moving their families to the Salmon River area out of the danger zone. Meanwhile, they were trying to enlist the Gosiutes, Weber Utes, and other Shoshonis in the war band. He gave as a reason for the Indians' leaving Washakie to join Pash-e-co that the Bannock Digger was "a man of blood." We recall that anyone who would not fight was considered a "squaw." Apparently a chief who would fight was referred to as "a man of blood."

"When the leaves turn red," said Little Soldier, the Bannocks and Shoshonis would assemble. "When the leaves turn yellow and begin to fall," they would break into open warfare against the whites and destroy them. The Weber Ute chief advised the white men to carry their guns with them at all times.

Word reached Superintendent Doty in August that the Indians of Tuilla and Brush valleys who had joined in the organized depredations were entering homes and demanding that food be cooked for them.[36] Doty wrote to the Commissioner of Indian Affairs, frantically urging that Colonel P. E. Connor be sent a telegraph order to speed up his march. The Colonel was at the

[35] James D. Doty, *Report* (hereinafter cited as Doty's report) *House Exec. Doc. 1*, 37 Cong., 3 sess., II (1157), 357–58.

[36] Doty to Commissioner of Indian Affairs, August 13, 1862. I.O.R.

time six hundred miles west of Salt Lake; General James Craig was five hundred miles east. The latter had no authority to enter Utah or Washington territories. With two thousand Shoshonis and Bannocks on the warpath in northern Utah, the situation seemed desperate.

Ben Holladay, of the Overland Mail, stated in a letter to the Postmaster General that a war with nearly all of the tribes—Shoshonis, Bannocks, and Paiutes—was close at hand.[37] He called for prompt and decisive action on the part of the government to prevent delay in the mail service. He also recommended that soldiers be stationed at one-hundred-mile intervals along the line. Connor and his forces, at the time Holladay wrote, were four hundred miles west of Salt Lake and "traveling slowly."

The Massacre Rocks incident, which occurred on Snake River in Idaho, caused great apprehension throughout the West.[38] A large war party attacked an emigrant train, consisting of eleven wagons. The horses were taken and most of the white men were killed before the Indians were forced away by the arrival of a large, well-armed wagon train. When forty of the emigrants in the second train went in search of the stolen stock, they had to turn back after losing three of their number. They reported that they had encountered a band of three hundred Indians. Consequently, the emigrants corralled and waited for the arrival of more trains. When they had increased their number to almost seven hundred, they proceeded westward but were harassed along their way.

While depredations continued, Colonel Connor, who had by now reached Salt Lake with his California-Nevada Volunteers, made every effort to protect the mail and the telegraph. He established a post (later known as Fort Douglas) overlooking the city. It was maintained until the end of the Civil War. The fact that Connor kept guns trained on the Lion House (Young's residence) no doubt caused the Mormon leader to minimize the Indian trouble so that no additional troops would be sent into Deseret. He

[37] (1157), 358.
[38] Byron Defenbach, *Idaho: The Place and Its People*, I, 405–406.

maintained that his militia was ready and able to handle any trouble that might develop.

In an attempt to stop further depredations, Connor sent Major Edward McGarry with two companies after a white boy who was abducted when his parents and sister were killed by Bear Hunter's band.[39] Although this group was made up of Bannocks and Shoshonis, the leadership of the mixed bands during this period of unrest was assumed by Shoshonis, with Bear Hunter as one of their most active war chiefs. The troops were accompanied by the boy's uncle, who had previously instigated a fruitless search for the captive.

McGarry was under orders not to shoot unless necessary. Besides, he was instructed to take three hostages if the Indians would not give up the prisoner. When the troops located the band in Cache Valley, they found that many of the hostiles had moved elsewhere. Armed with bows, arrows, and rifles, thirty or forty warriors made their appearance between the camp and the hills. They shouted and rode in circles. The soldiers, dividing into thirds, drove the Indians into a canyon. By now the order was to kill every one they could.

Chief Bear Hunter appeared on a hilltop with a flag of truce, which was not recognized but thought to be a warlike demonstration. A civilian with the soldiers convinced McGarry that the Indians no longer wanted to fight. When hostilities ceased, Bear Hunter and four of his men came forward for a medicine talk. They were held as hostages until the boy was brought in next day. Three Indians were killed and one wounded in the fray, but there were no casualties among the soldiers.

The appearance of Connor and his soldiers may have awed the Indians into delaying their all-out war. The leaves fell, but still there was no concerted drive on the part of the warriors, though they kept up their depredations.

In December, McGarry conducted an expedition for the purpose of recovering stolen livestock. After capturing four Indians

---

[39] P. E. Connor, *Report, Sen. Exec. Doc. 70,* 50 Cong., 2 sess., II (2611), 66–67, 127.

from the Shoshoni-Bannock camp near Bear River, he sent word to the chief that he would shoot the prisoners if the horses that they had stolen were not returned. Instead of complying with the orders, the Indians broke camp. McGarry carried out his threat by executing the hostages.[40] As a consequence, the Indians determined that they would kill every white man who set foot north of Bear River until they had avenged the death of their tribesmen.

The first victims were two dispatch carriers from Bannock City, Montana.[41] Then the warriors wiped out a group of ten men enroute to Salt Lake. In the third attack they killed a man named John Smith, who with his companions was leaving the Salmon River mines. Charges were filed against the Indians by the surviving members of the Smith party. Subsequently, the Chief Justice of Utah Territory issued a warrant for the arrest of Bear Hunter, San Pitch, and Sagwitch—the Shoshoni chiefs believed to have been responsible for the atrocity.

While depredations were being committed along the trails, brutal murders were being perpetrated near the southern boundary of Washington Territory, Pash-e-co's area.[42] The Indians had not been confronted by the real power of the army. In fact, they had managed to elude Major Lynde's forces. As a result, they exhibited their self-assurance by being saucy and demanding. The settlers, instructed in Young's policy, "It is better to feed the Indians than fight them," were at their mercy.

Colonel Connor's fighting spirit was so aroused by memory of the Goose Creek and Otter massacres and the more recent Massacre Rocks incident that his mind was set on a determined course of action. He vowed to put an end to leniency and subdue the Indians at all cost. When Isaac L. Gibbs, marshal, asked for a military escort so that he could serve a warrant for the arrest of the hostile chiefs, Connor informed him that he had made his plans for an all-out drive, and he would not change them. Gibbs, how-

[40] *Deseret News* (December 10, 17, and 31, 1862).

[41] *Ibid.* (January 14, 21, and 28, 1863).

[42] *The War of the Rebellion*, Ser. I, Vol. L, Pt. 1, 185–87; also Mann to Superintendent of Indian Affairs, September 20, 1862, and January 21 and 28, 1863, I.O.R.

ever, was permitted to accompany him on his expedition in search of Bear Hunter's band.

Connor attempted to keep his plans secret, but the chief was forewarned. He had given a War Dance in front of the home of Preston Thomas, the Mormon bishop at Franklin, Idaho.[43] When Bear Hunter became impudent in his attitude, one of the Mormons inadvertently told him that the army was on the way to settle with him. "Maybe so soldiers get killed too," he is quoted as replying. In spite of his carefree remark he hastened to warn his people. When the troops arrived, they found them entrenched and barricaded in a ravine, about a mile from Bear River.

Connor had sent ahead a small detachment "to fool the Indians." Then he followed with more men. In substantial numbers, they took up their position near the hostile camp during the night. At daybreak on January 29, 1863, some of the warriors ran out, taunting the soldiers and waving "white women's scalps." The troops, who had just completed a 140-mile march through deep snows, were in no mood to prolong the battle. Even though their hands were so cold that they could scarcely pull the triggers of the guns and more than 75 men were suffering from frozen feet, they fought relentlessly.

The Indians, little dreaming of the force of the white man's army, had never experienced such an onslaught. Several fled into the hills by swimming the river, but the avenues of escape were under such heavy fire that few had a chance to save themselves. As a consequence, the battle turned into a massacre. Bear Hunter was believed to have been killed while he was making bullets at the campfire; Sagwitch was wounded. Pocatello and San Pitch, who had left the scene the day before, were still at large, although their striking power was broken. In the 4-hour battle in which Bear Hunter's band was annihilated, the army casualties amounted to 14 killed and 49 wounded. The aftermath is told in Connor's report of February 26:

[43] Franklin, Idaho (1860), was the first permanent settlement in the state. As it was on the line, the Mormons settling there were unaware that they were not in Utah.

At this date, owing to wounds and injuries received on the march and at the Bear River battle, the morning report shows 70 sick in quarters and 22 in hospital; 1 officer and 6 men have died of their wounds, all being shot in a vital part; 4 men have had their toes amputated and 2 have lost a finger each.

Indian losses, according to the official army estimate, amounted to 224 killed, 175 horses taken, 70 lodges destroyed, 160 women and children captured. The lodges, women, and children were found hidden in the willows after the battle. Connor also found about 1,000 bushels of grain and plunder which the Indians had apparently taken from emigrant trains. He left some of the grain for the women and children who remained at the battlefield.

Mormons who were sent out by Bishop Thomas in search of survivors reported a gruesome sight.[44] They counted the dead eight feet deep in one place, and three to five feet deep in several others. This might substantiate the estimate of one of the men in the attacking force that there were as many as four hundred Indians killed. The Mormons found surviving among the dead two badly wounded women and three small children.

While Connor's method of solving the Shoshonean problem was open to criticism, it had the desired result of bringing an end to the large-scale raids. The relentless slaughter of the Indians, for the first time, served as an object lesson. The natives now realized that the army had the power to deal them a crushing defeat.

[44] Madsen, *The Bannock of Idaho*, 137.

CHAPTER TWELVE

Medicine Talk

The Battle of Bear River solved the Indian problem in the immediate area and opened the way for added colonization northward by the Mormons, although there was still scattered resistance. In March, 1863, the Gosiutes, about two hundred miles west of Salt Lake, killed a stage driver on his box, seriously wounded a passenger, and killed two station keepers.[1] Besides that, they burned two stations, took twelve horses owned by the Overland Company, and ran off thirty head of stock belonging to settlers.

Superintendent Doty, viewing the situation with alarm, declared, "I hope soon to hear that they [the Gosiutes] have been overtaken by the troops, and punished. It is a wanton aggression on their part, and was without the slightest provocation." This was the opinion of the average white man of the day. The provocation was not in the form of an overt act, but it was there nevertheless. It was gradually brought about by the encroaching white man and precipitated by starvation.

An Idaho writer, looking back on events a century ago, aptly comments:

> The Indians, fighting to retain what they had owned for ages, were unmitigated rascals, but the whites, fighting to possess what did not belong to them, were splendid soldiers of God. The Indians, often driven to actual starvation, and striking back desperately with arrow or tomahawk, the only weapons they knew, were yelping and unvarnished assassins; but the whites, eager to lay the camas meadows under agriculture, were approved by all the centuries of plunder in which right has been on the stronger side. And not only

[1] Doty to Commissioner of Indian Affairs, March 30, 1863, I.O.R.

198

that: those Indians who, deserting their own traditions and people, came to the aid of the whites are today commemorated in monuments; but the few whites who went over to the Indians were held in unspeakable infamy.[2]

John C. Burche, of the Humboldt Agency, believing that trouble of a serious nature again might arise with the Indians "from the cause of their country being made a highway" by the Pacific Wagon Road, called a council in May, 1863, at Stony Point.[3] Among the men of importance who attended was Winnemucca, head of the Paiute nation. The agent told him that he wanted the Paiutes to be friendly to the whites who passed through their lands. Also, he asked the chief to send a messenger to Pash-e-co and urge him to be peaceful. Winnemucca readily agreed. Thereupon, Burche presented him with a Spanish sombrero, a red silk sash, a pair of heavy red blankets, "and sundries," all of which pleased him.

Three weeks later a messenger, riding a handsome horse given him by Pash-e-co, came with word that Winnemucca was calling a council of the Paiutes and Bannocks in a valley about seventy miles north of Paiute Knob Mountain on the Humboldt. According to the messenger, Pash-e-co wanted the agent to meet him there. Burche went alone and had a "heap good talk" with the Indians. Pash-e-co promised that he would keep his people friendly and quiet if the whites would also behave.

The agent reminded him that many valuable horses had been stolen and driven into his country. This Pash-e-co did not deny, but he was now contrite, and he stated that no such acts would happen again. The hostile kept his word. There are no records other than this to show why he chose to smoke the pipe. In fact, no further mention can be found of him. During his active career, he did more to stir up trouble among the Western tribes than any other one man. His change of attitude may be attributed to the influence of Winnemucca.

A month after the Burche council, Commissioner William P.

[2] Idaho Writer's Project, *Idaho*, 11.
[3] *Report of Commissioner of Indian Affairs*, 1864, 288–92.

Doyle gave Doty the authority to make a treaty with the Bannocks and the Utes as well as with the Shoshonis, "if one can be negotiated with the funds appropriated for the purpose of treating with the latter [the Shoshonis] now at your disposal."[4]

By now, Fort Bridger had come into focus for the third and last time.[5] It had served as an emigrant supply station under the ownership of Bridger and Vasquez; and then as a Mormon stronghold, purchased, improved, and burned (1857) before the advancing Army for Utah. After being reconstructed it had then become an important frontier army post. Captain M. G. Lewis, with Company I, Third California Volunteers, had been assigned to the fort in December, 1862, and it was manned by California-Nevada Volunteers until the close of the Civil War.

In June, 1863, Luther Mann, Jr., in the absence of Doty, sent an urgent wire to the Commissioner of Indian Affairs. He asked for instructions concerning what he should do with five hundred Snake Indians who were to visit the fort that day "for the purpose of delivering up the stolen stock in their possession and of pledging themselves to keep quiet in the future."[6]

Washakie's people were anxious to rally once again under his banner. They had been impressed by the serious defeat of Bear Hunter's band and had stopped beating their war drums even before Pash-e-co's surrender. They were aware that further resistance was futile. This meant that the Indians were back where they had been before the uprisings, although probably they were much wiser from their experience. Hunger drove them to seek council with the white man.

Superintendent Doty, at the time, was away on a six weeks' expedition with Connor, who had been promoted to brigadier general (March 30, 1863) because of his victory at Bear River. They were headed toward Snake River Ferry (Idaho), but along the way the two parted, with the General proceeding to Soda Springs to establish Camp Connor on the emigrant trail. The Ban-

---

[4] Doyle, *Report, House Exec. Doc. 1,* 38 Cong., 1 sess. (1182), 514–15.

[5] Robert S. Ellison *Fort Bridger,* 33–60.

[6] Telegram to Commissioner of Indian Affairs, June 2, 1863, I.O.R.

nocks who saw his cavalry were impressed and spoke to Doty of their desire for friendly relations. They informed the agent that Pocatello's band and several others still at large were bent on revenge. Doty's comment was, "They must be left to General Connor's troops."[7]

At Snake River Ferry, Doty learned of impending trouble along the emigrant road to Bannock City. Investigating, he found few Indians left at Camas Prairie, where he had been told that he would be able to locate them. Most of the tribe had gone to the hills to hunt. The ones he talked with told him a strange tale—that Old Snag and two of his men had been murdered at Bannock City by drunken miners. The Indians did not plan to seek revenge, for, they said, all of the white men were drunk at the time.

On his way to the settlement Doty encountered several friendly Snakes, who gratefully accepted the gifts he gave them. At Bannock City he found that the report was true. The Indians had come to deliver a child whom the white men claimed was a captive. They were peacefully sitting at the edge of the street when they were fired upon. Doty, seeing the child, was convinced that he was a half-blood, rightfully theirs, but he was helpless to bring charges against the murderers. There was no law other than that of the miners.

Later Doty and Connor had reason to seek out Little Soldier near Salt Lake. Although Pash-e-co had now become a good Indian, his influence apparently lingered, for Little Soldier had been destroying property for several months. After Connor and Doty had a talk with him, he agreed to remain near Salt Lake where they could supervise his conduct.[8]

Now that the hostiles were subdued, the white man was able to call his treaty councils and name his terms. The first was held at Fort Bridger,[9] on July 2, 1863, with about one thousand Indians (representing three to four thousand Shoshonis) in attendance.[10]

[7] *Report of Commissioner of Indian Affairs*, 1863, 539.
[8] Doty to Commissioner of Indian Affairs, July 20, 1863, I.O.R.
[9] Fort Bridger Treaty, 1863, *Sen. Exec. Doc. 319*, 58 Cong., 2 sess. (4623), I, 848–50.
[10] Doty and Mann to Commissioner of Indian Affairs, July 3, 1863, I.O.R.

Among the bands listed were those of Washakie, Wanapitz, San Pitch, Ashingodimah (a chief killed at Bear River), and Sagwitch (wounded in the same battle). The San Pitch and Sagwitch bands had practically been exterminated, and yet they managed to have a small representation.

All bands in the nation were represented except four. One was in the Humboldt or Ruby Valley area, while the other three were making a last stand against Connor's troops somewhere between Fort Bridger and Snake River. The troops had reduced their numbers to such an extent that Doty felt if he could get messengers to them, he could induce them to talk medicine. By now, the spirit of the buffalo hunter was broken. Even the braves who had smoked the war pipe with Pash-e-co were frustrated, for he had forsaken them. The Shoshonis could do nothing but accept whatever the white man cared to offer. Doty expressed himself as gratified with the terms which he was able to make, as they were more advantageous than he had anticipated.

Beside declaring perpetual peace, the Fort Bridger Treaty guaranteed safe passage along the trail, and the government stipulated its rights to establish settlements necessary for the convenience, comfort, and protection of travelers. After assuring the safety of the emigrants and the Overland Stage and Telegraph Line, the treaty further made it clear that provisions had been made by the government to construct a railway from the Plains west to the Pacific Ocean. It was stated that said railway and its branches were to be "located, constructed, and operated without molestation" from the Indians through any portion of the country desired.

The boundaries of the Eastern Shoshoni country, roughly designated, extended from the Snake River Valley on the north to the Uinta Mountains on the south, and from the North Platte River westward to an unidentified limit, as there were no representatives from that part of the country in attendance. The bands present claimed that their land was bounded on the west by Salt Lake. The annuity payments in suitable goods were to amount to $10,000 a year for twenty years in such articles as the President might deem "suitable to their wants and conditions either as hunters or herdsmen." Washakie, Wanapitz, and eight of the leading men of their nation signed the treaty, with Jack Robertson serving as their interpreter.

The next medicine talk—not considered a treaty council—was conducted by General Connor and Superintendent Doty on July 7, with Little Soldier and his Weber Utes at their camp, about twenty miles from Salt Lake. Several unnamed bands, on hand to accept presents and see what happened, agreed to talk peace if favorable arrangements could be made. Before the meeting adjourned, all of the Indians present promised to maintain friendly relations with the whites.[11]

General Connor, writing from Salt Lake City, under date of July 18, 1863, observed that the Shoshoni nation was once again united under the leadership of their peace chief Washakie, and that his band was living "in quiet contentment near Bridger." In his report, he told of receiving a message from Pocatello begging for peace and asking for a conference. The chief declared that he was tired of war, and he had been effectually driven from the territory with only a small remnant of his once powerful band left. Connor stated that he would soon conclude a peace which he was sure would be permanent. The General ended his report by stating: "Thus at last I have the pleasure to report peace with the Indian on all hands, save only a few hostile Gosiutes west and north of Deep Creek."[12]

Doty, perhaps as much for effect as anything else, requested the presence of Connor at the treaty councils which followed. He gave as his reason for wanting him that he was instrumental in making the Indians acknowledge for the first time that the Americans were "the masters of the country."[13]

The treaty with the Northwestern band under Pocatello was signed at Box Elder, Utah, on July 30.[14] The object was to assure

11 Doty's report, *House Exec. Doc. 1,* 38 Cong., 1 sess. (1182), 513–14.
12 *The War of the Rebellion,* II, 527–31.
13 Doty's report, *House Exec. Doc. 1,* 38 Cong., 2 sess. (1220), 317; also Charles J. Kappler, ed., *Indian Affairs: Laws and Treaties,* II, 649–52.
14 Box Elder Treaty (4623), 850–51.

the protection of travelers on the road to the Beaverhead gold mines of Montana. More than that, it hoped to protect transportation on the roads leading to northern California and southern Oregon through Pocatello country.

The one thousand Indians who attended the Box Elder Council were representatives of the following bands: the Pocatello, Toomontso, San Pitch, Toso, Bear Hunter (all but seven Indians of this band had been killed at Bear River), and Sagwitch. Although a few of their Indians had been present at the council at Fort Bridger, Sagwitch and San Pitch had been unable to arrive in time. A widely circulated report that they had fled beyond Snake River had proved untrue. Sagwitch also missed the Box Elder council because he was shot by a white man a few days before. He was too badly wounded to leave his lodge, but he assented to all of the stipulated provisions. Several smaller bands, known as "Sheep Eaters," were present but otherwise unidentified.

Like the treaty at Fort Bridger, the one at Box Elder proclaimed friendly relations between the white man and the Indian and provided for the maintenance of "perpetual" peace. It also specified the territory claimed by Pocatello and his people as bounded on the west by Raft River and on the east by the Portneuf Mountains. The government agreed to pay $2,000 to relieve immediate difficulties and "to increase the annuity to the Shoshone Nation $5,000 to be paid in the manner provided in said treaty."

The council with the Western Shoshonis was held at Ruby Valley, Nevada, on October 1.[15] Fort Ruby had been established when the Indians, taking advantage of the Civil War, had attempted to drive out the whites. The Snake Diggers present were the Tosawi and Ankoah bands, representing about twenty-five hundred Indians, not counting those on the lower Humboldt and west of Smith's Creek. Doty and Nevada Governor James W. Nye presided. The Shoshonis were represented by Timoak, Moho-a, Buck, and nine other leaders. The mail, the telegraph lines, the railroad (to be constructed), and the citizens of the United States were to be protected. All routes of travel were to remain

[15] The Western Shoshoni Treaty, signed at Ruby Valley, *ibid.*, 851–53.

"forever free and unobstructed." In the event of depredations, all offenders were to be delivered to the proper authorities.

The treaty further specified that the white man could explore for gold and silver, erect mills, and take timber. For the loss of game and other "inconveniences" caused the Indians by this white encroachment, the United States agreed to pay annually for twenty years $5,000 in such articles as the President of the United States should deem suitable. The boundaries of the country claimed by these Indians were described as follows: from the Shoshone River on the north to the Colorado Desert on the south, and from Smith Creek Mountains on the west to Steptoe and the Great Salt Lake valleys on the east.

The next treaty council was held at Tuilla Valley, Utah, on October 12, with only 350 Gosiutes in attendance.[16] In explaining why so few appeared, the Indians said that they were afraid of the soldiers. This was understandable because of the presence of General Connor. Besides declaring "peace and friendship" and assuring safe passage through the country, the treaty established the limits of their territory. It was to be bounded on the west by the Steptoe Valley, on the south by Green Mountains, on the east by the Great Salt Lake and Tuilla and Rush valleys, and on the north by the middle of the Great Desert. The government promised the Indians one thousand dollars annually for twenty years, including cattle for herding and other purposes. Also another thousand dollars in provisions was given them at the council to relieve their immediate needs.

The Soda Springs (Idaho) Treaty, the last of the five with the Shoshoni and Bannocks in the year 1863, was signed two days later.[17] About 150 families from the mixed bands attended the council. Tendoy and several other leaders sent word that they assented to the terms of the treaty—whatever they were—but that hunger had caused them to go in search of game. The principal chief of the Bannocks, Le Grand Coquin, was there together with Taghee, Matigund, and several other band leaders. The total

---

[16] Tuilla Valley Treaty, *ibid.*, 859–60.
[17] Soda Springs (unratified treaty), I.O.R.; also (1220), 318–20.

population of the mixed bands was estimated to be about 1,000 persons.

The treaty provided first, for the usual "friendly and amicable relations"; second, for the acceptance of the stipulations of the Fort Bridger and Box Elder treaties (read and explained), with the bands sharing in the annuities "therein provided for the Shoshone Nation; third, for safe travel in return for three thousand dollars worth of provisions; and fourth, for a territory extending from the lower part of the Humboldt River and the Salmon Falls on the Shoshone (Snake) River eastward to the Wind River Mountains.

By the time this fifth and last treaty was concluded, the white man had violated the terms of the first, which granted $10,000 a year to the Indians at Fort Bridger. For the Soda Springs Treaty specified that the Indians of the mixed bands were to be given a share of the annuities without the consent or knowledge of the signers of the Fort Bridger Treaty. Is it an "Indian giver" who is said to present a gift, then ask it back?

The generous gesture in extending the eastern boundary of the territory to Wind River should be noted. The western boundary of Washakie's country was not stipulated at the Fort Bridger Treaty Council, but it was made clear that the Eastern Shoshonis believed that it extended to Salt Lake and that Snake River was the northern limit. The white man not only took part of the annuities allowed at Fort Bridger, but he also indirectly established the western limit of Washakie's territory at Wind River Mountains. The Soda Springs Treaty was ratified by the United States Senate on the condition that a section be added "defining the character of the Indian title to the land." However, it was never proclaimed by the Congress.

The whole number of Shoshonis, Gosiutes, and Bannocks, parties to the five treaties held at Fort Bridger, Box Elder, Ruby Valley, Tuilla, and Soda Springs in 1863, amounted approximately to 8,650. In summarizing the value of the agreements, Doty said:

> The importance of these Treaties to the Government and to
> its citizens can only be appreciated by those who know the value

of the Continental Telegraph and the Overland Stage to the commercial and mercantile world, and the safety and security which peace alone can give to Emigrant Trains, and to the travel to the Gold Discoveries in the North which exceed in richness—at least in the quality of the gold—any discoveries on this Continent.[18]

The following year a treaty was made with the Klamath Indians of Oregon,[19] and an attempt was made to put the scattered Snakes in the area on a reservation. They, as we have observed, were predatory. But the Klamaths were a formidable force and had displayed a hostile attitude toward the white man for many years. Their animosity stemmed from an incident in 1846 when Frémont was among them.[20] A war party of twenty or thirty Klamaths, finding his camp off guard, made a night attack and clashed with Frémont's Delaware scouts. One of the Delawares was shot down by five arrows, and the Klamath chief was killed by gunfire. Only the day before, the chief had signified his friendly spirit by presenting a salmon to a member of Frémont's party.

The Oregon Council was held at Klamath Lake on October 14, 1864, and the treaty was signed by chiefs of the Klamath and Modoc tribes and by Kile-to-ak and Sky-te-ock-et and other representatives of the Yahuskins (Snakes affiliated with the nomadic Paiutes who roamed the high desert country of southeastern Oregon). The agreement, executed by William Logan, Indian agent, stipulated the sum of $80,000 to be paid over a period of fifteen years in annual payments to the three tribes who agreed to share the same reservation in eastern Oregon. The government also agreed to expend $35,000 for the purchase of teams, farming implements, tools, and seeds; to build a sawmill, flour mill, blacksmith shop, and other improvements; and to pay the salaries of a carpenter, a farmer, a wagon- and plow-maker, a sawyer, a miller, and two schoolteachers for fifteen years. At the same time, the United States reserved the right to place other Indians on the reservation.

18 (1220), 320.
19 Klamath Treaty, *Sen. Exec. Doc. 319*, 58 Cong., 2 sess. (4624), II, 865.
20 Frederick S. Dellenbaugh, *Frémont and '49*, 320–24.

This right was exercised the following year. On August 12, 1865, J. W. P. Huntington, superintendent of Indian affairs in Oregon, held a treaty council with the Walpapi tribe of Snakes at Sprague River Valley.[21] These Indians agreed to relinquish all rights to country occupied by them, largely in the Blue Mountain Range, and move to the reservation with the Klamath, Modoc, and Yahuskin Snake Indians, and remain there, leaving only with written permission. They also agreed to use their influence to restrain the hostile actions of other Indians and not to sell arms to any hostiles. According to the treaty, the Snakes were to receive $2,000 for the next five years and $1,200 annually for the ten years following. The government promised to expend $5,000 for fences, cultivation of land, seed, and farming implements, and to hire teachers, mechanics, a physician, and a farmer.

To return to the Eastern Shoshonis, we find that in the spring of 1864, Washakie was again having trouble with the Crows. While the Shoshonis were buffalo hunting in the vicinity of Wind River, their enemy tried to drive away their horses. Several skirmishes ensued.[22] As Washakie was returning from the hunt, he encountered a small band of Sheep Eaters, who had in their possession nineteen head of horses that they had stolen from the miners at Beaverhead. They gave as their excuse for having the stolen property that they did not know that a treaty had been signed with the whites. Washakie explained the terms of the treaty and talked the Sheep Eaters into giving up the horses, which one of his braves delivered to Fort Bridger.[23]

This incident is an example of Washakie's helpfulness. In recognition of their service to the white men over the years, he and Kanosh, of the Pahvants, were each given a silver medal of honor on which was inscribed a picture of the Great White Father. This honor to Kanosh was unusual in light of the fact that his band of Indians unquestionably murdered Captain Gunnison. The white man apparently exonerated the chief from any complicity

[21] Walpapi Snake Treaty (4624), II, 876.
[22] Doty to Commissioner of Indian Affairs, June 13, 1864, I.O.R.
[23] Mann to Acting Commissioner of Indian Affairs, June 20, 1864, I.O.R.

in the deed. Washakie is mentioned as proudly wearing his medal on a visit to Salt Lake City.[24]

Doty took over his obligations as governor of Utah and O. H. Irish became superintendent of Indian affairs in the fall of 1865. One month after Irish took office he received a wire from an operator at Shell Creek, Utah. The wire stated that the Indians about two hundred miles southwest of Salt Lake were demanding their annuities which were long past due. A dispatch from Fort Bridger informed him that a large number of Shoshonis at Bear Lake, 140 miles north of Salt Lake, were also impatient because they had not "been paid" so that they could go to their hunting grounds in the Wind River country.[25] Governor Doty and General Connor thereupon wrote a joint letter to the Office of Indian Affairs warning that the situation was so delicate in the Shoshoni country that for the sake of preserving the peace the government should "take great care to comply with its obligations to the Indians."[26]

As the "presents" were not shipped from Nebraska City until August 18, they could not reach the Indians before November. Connor and Doty urged that other provisions be made to fulfill the government obligation. Superintendent Irish, at their suggestion, sent a present of tobacco to Washakie and invited him and four of his chiefs to come in for consultation, but the Indians had already started on a hunting excursion at the insistence of Luther Mann, Jr., the agent at Fort Bridger, who had nothing to feed them.[27]

Just where the Indians were overtaken, we do not know, but they were prevailed upon to turn back. At Fort Bridger, Washakie took the stage for Salt Lake. There he was adamant. Thwarted in his original plan, he refused to go over the mountains with his women and children, for it was too late in the season and too cold. Since the Shoshonis were afraid of the Sioux, they planned to

24 Washakie's medal, *House Exec. Doc. 1*, 39 Cong., 2 sess. (1284), 31.
25 Doty's report (1220), 313–17.
26 *Ibid.*, 314.
27 Mann to Superintendent O. H. Irish, October 5, 1864, I.O.R.

THE ROCKIES, HOME

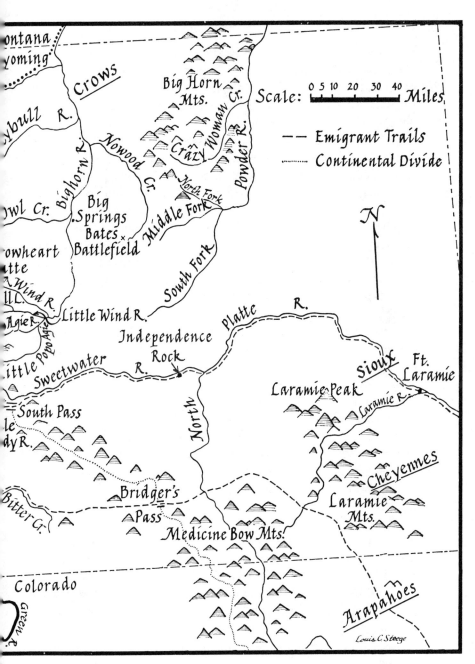

Scale: 0 5 10 20 30 40 Miles

-- Emigrant Trails
...... Continental Divide

ontana
yoming

Crows

Big Horn
Mts.

ybull R.

Nowood Cr.

Bighorn R.

Crazy Woman Cr.

North Fork

Middle Fork

Powder R.

wl Cr.

Big
Springs
Bates x
Battlefield

South Fork

owheart
tte

Wind R.

LL.

Agie R.

Little Wind R.

Little Popo Agie

Independence
Rock

Platte

R.

Sweetwater R.

South Pass

le
dy R.

North

Laramie Peak

Sioux

Ft.
Laramie

Laramie R.

Bitter Cr.

Bridger's
Pass

Medicine Bow Mts.

Cheyennes

Laramie
Mts.

Colorado

Arapahoes

Green R.

Louis C. Steege

SHOSHONIS, IN 1865

leave their families near Fort Bridger for safety and hunt in that neighborhood as best they could. Washakie made it clear that they depended upon their Great White Father to help them now that the white man had driven off their game. He said that if they were not given provisions for the winter they would starve.

The unsatisfactory nature of the council at Salt Lake is clearly shown by Washakie's annoyance when he said he "did not want to hear blankets again." He wanted meat for his people. Irish, promising to lay the matter before the Great White Father, asked the Commissioner of Indian Affairs to send instructions by telegraph.[28] Doyle wired Irish that four thousand dollars was placed at once to his credit in a New York bank, and he instructed him to buy that amount of provisions for the Shoshonis. Goods on the way were to be distributed among non-Shoshonis upon receipt.

During this time, Irish and Mann kept urging the establishment of reservations. Said Mann: "The farmer, with the plough, hoe, and axe, will, if used at the first, be more efficient in keeping peace on the frontier than the soldier with cannon, musket, and bayonets."

Pocatello, as well as Washakie, must have been impatient for the annuities which he had reason to expect. At any rate, he was finding himself once again in trouble. This time he was arrested by General Connor on complaint of Ben Holladay. After an investigation of his own, Holladay stated that the charges (not given) against the offender were "not of the serious character he at first apprehended," and he requested that the matter be dropped. But the arrest of Pocatello caused war clouds to gather.

The impetuous Connor indicated that he intended to hang Pocatello. Word spread rapidly to the Northwestern bands, who began to sound their war drums and assemble a striking force in the mountains. Connor decided "under the circumstances" that it would be proper to turn the chief over to the Superintendent of Indian Affairs.[29] Irish, releasing Pocatello on a promise of meeting him and his band in council at Box Elder the following week,

[28] Irish to Commissioner of Indian Affairs, October 13, 1864, I.O.R.
[29] Connor to Irish, November 4, 1864, I.O.R.

expressed his exasperation by saying, "If the Military authorities will allow me to manage these Indians without any further interference, I am satisfied that by a judicious use of the appropriations made I can maintain peace."[30]

In his annual report for the year, 1864, Irish stated that Washakie's band did not properly belong to the Utah Superintendency.[31] Their country, north and northeast of Utah, was principally in Idaho Territory and Wyoming.[32] With their agency located at Wind River—as they wished and he felt it should be—they would remain away from the white settlements, the mail, and the telegraph lines. The report of Agent Mann gives the following picture of these Indians as they appeared in the 1860's:

> The leggings and breech-cloth are not very soon to be replaced by the pantaloons worn by the whites. I observe a marked improvement each year in their means of protection against the inclemency of the weather. These people have never turned their attention to agricultural pursuits, nor can it be expected of them until they are placed on a reservation where they can have the necessary protection. If they are not provided with such a home, they are destined to remain outside of those influences which are calculated to civilize or Christianize them, as has been done in many parts of our country to tribes not one whit more susceptible of being rendered useful members of society.
>
> Wild Indians, like wild horses, must be coralled upon reservations. There they can be brought to work, and soon will become a self-supporting people, earning their own living by their industry, instead of trying to pick up a bare subsistence by their chase, or stealing from neighboring tribes with whom they hold hostile relations.[33]

Agent Mann assumed that civilizing the Indian was a simple process. Although it is true that the Eastern Shoshonis were more inclined to be peaceful than some of the other bands, it did not

[30] Irish to Commissioner of Indian Affairs, November 9, 1864, I.O.R.
[31] *House Exec. Doc. 1,* 39 Cong., 1 sess. (1248), 310–16.
[32] Even though Wyoming is referred to here, it was not until five years later that it became a territory.
[33] *House Exec. Doc. 1,* 40 Cong., 2 sess. (1326), II, 183.

follow that their acculturation was to be easier than that of others more hostile or less fortunate.

In the spring of 1865 the Crows, Cheyennes, and Sioux tried to enlist the aid of the Shoshonis in ridding the country of the white man, but Washakie steadfastly refused their overtures. When he learned that an expedition was to be made by the white man against the Sioux, he was eager to take part. His only reason for not going was that no military detachment was sent from Fort Bridger, where he was at the time. The Sioux and Cheyennes, infuriated by Washakie's loyalty to the white man, attacked his camp on the Sweetwater during the summer. The Shoshonis lost about four hundred horses. Washakie's favorite son, Nan-nag-gai (Snow Bird), was killed and his body mutilated in his father's sight. The Shoshonis, counterattacking, recovered their horses and routed the Sioux.

Because of their large annuity payments and the fact that they were still able to hunt buffalo, the Eastern Shoshonis were considered wealthy by the other tribes. Since the Northwestern Indians were extremely poor and had no game, an attempt was made to merge them with Washakie's band. The chief good-naturedly allowed Pocatello and Black Beard to accompany him on his annual hunt in 1866. Even so, extra food had to be given to them during the winter to keep them from starving.

The agent lamented the fact that none of these Indians showed any inclination toward agriculture. The Gosiutes, on the other hand, were beginning to prove themselves industrious as herders, employed by the settlers.[34] The roving mixed bands came under the jurisdiction of the Idaho Territory, created in 1863, with Governor Caleb Lyon serving as ex officio superintendent of Indian affairs.

In the fall of 1865, Governor Lyon was directed by the Commissioner of Indian Affairs to appoint the necessary agents and conclude a treaty with the Boise, Bruneau, and Camas Bannocks and Shoshonis of Idaho.[35] The terms of his treaty, signed by the

[34] Economic Conditions (1284), 31.
[35] *Report of Commissioner of Indian Affairs*, 1865, 234; also Kappler, *Indian Affairs*, II, 835–36.

Indians in 1866, were so questionable that their land cession was later renegotiated. Before the matter was settled Lyon was succeeded by Governor D. W. Ballard, who attempted to establish a single agency in southern Idaho rather than the several that were under consideration. He found that the three bands were willing to go to Fort Hall.

Chief Taghee of the Bannocks and four hundred of his band moved temporarily (1866) to Wind River, where they were sure of a welcome by their friend Washakie. There they would be able to subsist until the government should finally provide for them. Taghee ("a very worthy Indian ... in whom I fully repose confidence"—Luther Mann, Jr.) had been living in the vicinity of Soda Springs and along the Snake River.

Ballard was instructed to set aside a reservation in southern Idaho for these Indians.[36] He was more thoughtful of the Eastern Shoshonis than Doty had been, for he favored establishing a reservation including Fort Hall—an area "within the hunting area of the Eastern Shoshones"—if it met with the approval of Washakie.

The chief apparently was not advised when the Fort Hall reservation was created by executive order on the western part of his land, on June 14, 1867. Nor did he seem to raise any objection when he heard of it. Roughly the reservation extended from the mouth of the Portneuf River, then south twenty-five miles to the summit of the mountains dividing the waters of the Snake and Bear rivers; then eastward on the crest of said range seventy miles to a point where the Sublette Cutoff crossed the divide; then north about fifty miles to Blackfoot River, down that stream to its junction with the Snake, and back to the Portneuf.[37]

Agent Mann had concluded by this time that the location of the Fort Bridger Agency was unsuitable.[38] The Indians were obliged to come such a long way from their hunting grounds to receive their annuities that by the time they reached the place, their stock of provisions was virtually exhausted. Also, it was im-

[36] *Report of Commissioner of Indian Affairs*, 1866, 38.
[37] D. W. Ballard to D. N. Cooley, November 18, 1866, I.O.R.
[38] Mann's report (1284), 126–27.

possible for them to remain in the vicinity because of lack of game. This even discouraged some from coming. For the time being, he recommended that a portion of their "presents" be given them in money so that they could buy food during their visit at the agency; but he advised locating the tribe permanently in Wind River Valley and establishing an agency there.

F. H. Head, now superintendent, submitted the following figures in his annual report for 1866: Eastern bands of Shoshonis and the mixed bands of Bannocks and Shoshonis, all of whom recognized Washakie as chief, 4,500 souls; Northwestern bands of Shoshonis, whose principal chiefs were Pocatello, Black Beard, and San Pitch, about 1,800; the Western Shoshonis, about 2,000; the Gosiutes, about 1,000; and the Weber Utes or Cumumbahs, 600 souls.[39]

Superintendent Head and Agent Mann made every effort to remedy the injustice of the still unproclaimed treaty with the mixed bands of Bannocks and Shoshonis, which provided simply that they were to share in the annuities of the Eastern bands. When Taghee, who had no annuity payments, asked that Washakie share his, the latter refused, saying that it was little enough for his own people. The Bannock chief was hurt to think that the Great Father had slighted him. Knowing that all of the other Bannocks and Shoshonis had been provided for by treaty, he was puzzled. His Indians, too, had been good and had kept the peace. Why were they not sent presents? Since their country had been settled by the whites, he felt that they, too, were entitled to compensation.

Luther Mann, Jr., continued to remind the authorities that they had overlooked the mixed or "broken" bands. He offered another argument for the establishment of Wind River as a reservation for the Eastern Shoshonis. While the latter were in the radius of Fort Bridger, the Sioux, roaming unmolested over their beautiful valleys east and north of the Wind River Mountains, were helping themselves to vegetable and wildlife. This encouraged the marauders to come into the country to murder soldiers

[39] F. H. Head, *Report, ibid.*, 122–26.

and emigrants along the trail and to kill "the hardy miners," who were "toiling to develop the mineral resources which constitute the base of our national wealth."[40]

His reference to mining is worthy of note. Although the first gold had been discovered at South Pass as early as 1842, it was not until the 1860's that miners flooded the area. South Pass City came into existence in 1867.[41] That fall Agent Mann accompanied the Snakes and Bannocks to their hunting grounds in the vicinity of the gold mines, as he was afraid that there might be trouble between the miners and the Indians. He reported the miners pleased by the visit and so impressed by Washakie that they favored the establishment of a reservation for the Shoshonis near by for their own protection.[42]

Another Indian greatly respected by the miners in both Wyoming and Montana at this time was Tendoy (The Climber), chief of the Lemhis. He was never known to be unfriendly toward the whites. Although he was usually described as "pathetically poor," such was not always the case.[43] One time when his horse was "rode down," a miner stopped at Tendoy's camp and was hospitably received. The next morning Tendoy drove three hundred horses into the corral and told him to take his pick. A year later the chief had lost almost the entire herd, but he was still optimistic, saying that he was poor but would soon be rich again.

Tendoy was described in 1868 as a fine-looking Indian about thirty-two years of age and over six feet in height. He was light complexioned for a Shoshoni and had a "well shaped brow, Roman nose, and large dark eyes." Dignified and polite, he would lift his hat in greeting.

The Bannock-Shoshoni annuity stipulation was still pending, and the Fort Hall Agency was in name only when the Indian Peace Commission was created by Act of Congress on July 20, 1867, for the purpose of settling all problems with the hostiles. This

[40] Mann's report (1326), II, 182–83.
[41] James Chisholm, "James Chisholm's Journal," ed. by Lola Homsher, in *South Pass, 1868*, 204.
[42] Mann to J. H. Head, September 23, 1867, I.O.R.
[43] Chisholm, "James Chisholm's Journal," *loc. cit.*, 196–97.

matter was given urgency by the fact that the Union Pacific Railroad would soon reach the Shoshoni country. Satisfactory terms with the Indians would be necessary in order to preserve peace. Furthermore, the government would have to extinguish the Indian title before land grants could be made to the railroad builders.

Bannock John and Bannock Jim, brothers-in-law of Taghee, conferred with Governor Ballard at Boise in the spring of 1867. In the absence of Taghee and his subchief Koo-ser-gun, they represented the Boise, Camas, and Bruneau bands of Shoshonis and Bannocks, under the supervision of Agent Charles F. Powell at Boise River. Their answers to the direct questions put to them by the Governor were evasive, for Taghee, who had succeeded Le Grand Coquin as chief, was absent. The leaders refused to speak for the tribe.[44]

At an informal council called by the Indians themselves on August 21, 1867, Taghee was present as spokesman for his people. In his speech he showed considerable frustration over the situation.[45] He began by saying that when the white men had come to Soda Springs they had established a fort to protect him and his people, but now that the soldiers had gone, he did not know "where to go nor what to do." He wanted to know why the settlers had come into his country without asking his consent, and why no government agents had been sent to him before. He would not vouch for the Sheep Eaters who were not his people, but he would answer for all of the Bannocks.

He said that the Boises and Bruneaus were poor and could not travel far. They had no horses to hunt the buffalo, but he stated that they were good Indians and his friends. The Horse Indians had to go farther to the north to hunt the buffalo, for the white people had scared the animals away.

He indicated his willingness to live upon a reservation, but he wanted the privilege of hunting the buffalo for a few years. "When they are all gone far away," he said, "we hunt no more; perhaps one year, perhaps two or three years; then we stay on

[44] Ballard to Commissioner of Indian Affairs, August 3, 1866, I.O.R.
[45] *Report of Commissioner of Indian Affairs*, 1868, 657–58.

the reservation all the time." He wanted a reservation large enough for all his people, "and no white man on it, except the agent and other officers and employees of the government." He insisted on a right of way for his people to travel when going to or coming from the buffalo country, and when going to the white man's market with their furs and skins. He continued:

> I want the right to camp and dig roots on Canyon [Camas] prairie when coming to Boise City to trade. Some of my people have no horses. They can remain at Camas prairie and dig roots while others go on. Our hunting is not so good as it used to be, nor my people so numerous.
>
> I will go from here to the buffalo country, where I will meet all my tribe, and will tell them of this talk and of the arrangements we may make. I am willing to go on to a reservation as you propose, but when will you want me to go? We can go next spring.

Although the Indians formally agreed to move to the Fort Hall Reservation by June 1, no provision was actually made to settle them there. When word reached Fort Bridger that the Indian Peace Commissioner was to arrive on June 4, Agent Mann hastily began rounding up natives. By the end of the second week in May, there were already in the radius of Fort Bridger ninety-six lodges of Shoshonis and forty-nine lodges of Bannocks. Washakie's band was expected momentarily.

The Great Treaty Council, officially known as the Fort Bridger Treaty Council of 1868, was highly significant as it was the last treaty council called for the purpose of establishing a reservation.[46] Thereafter, all reservations were created by executive order.

Two legends, neither of which can be substantiated, grew out of this council. The first is that Porivo (the Wind River Sacajawea) spoke. The elders present insisted that she was there and that she arose and addressed her remarks to Washakie's subchief Bazil. According to a Wyoming theory, Sacajawea lived for many years with the Comanches after leaving Charbonneau. There, known as Porivo, she became the wife of a Comanche and the

---

[46] Fort Bridger Treaty of 1868, Kappler, *Indian Affairs*, II, 1020–23.

mother of a number of children. Following his death, she found her way to her people, then in Bridger Valley.

On the reservation her affiliation with Bazil (an adopted son) and Baptiste (her son, the "Pomp" of the Lewis and Clark journals) was accepted. She died in 1884 and was buried at Fort Washakie, not as Porivo or Sacajawea, but simply as *Bazil Umbea* (Bazil's Mother), for, like Bazil, she seemingly preferred to live in the white man's way in a house at the agency rather than the Indian's way in a skin lodge occupied by Baptiste some distance away.

An opposing theory regarding Sacajawea is that she died at Fort Manuel Lisa (South Dakota) in 1812, with the place of burial unknown. Since the document cited to prove this does not mention her by name, it cannot be considered conclusive.[47] Strenuous efforts have been made to substantiate both theories regarding her death, but the controversy will not be settled until more definite contemporary evidence comes to light. Tourists who visit the grave of Wyoming's Sacajawea at Fort Washakie pay homage to a truly great woman, no matter when she died or where she was buried. Where could a shrine be better placed than on the Wind River Reservation in the land of her people, the Shoshonis?

The second legend concerns General C. C. Augur, who had been authorized by the Peace Commission at Fort Laramie to go to Bridger for the purpose of negotiating with the Indians. While he was attempting to explain to Washakie the meaning of latitude and longitude as determined by the sun and the stars, the chief maintained a respectful silence. Then Washakie said that he hoped someday to learn more about the sun and stars, but for the present he preferred to have the boundaries of his reservation explained to him in terms of rivers and mountains.

His reservation, to be temporarily shared with Taghee and his band, consisted of about 2,774,400 acres. It began at the mouth

[47] John C. Luttig, *Journal of a Fur-trading Expedition on the Upper Missouri.* Miss Drumm, editor of Luttig's *Journal* and librarian at the Missouri Historical Society at St. Louis, was the chief advocate of the South Dakota theory while Grace Raymond Hebard, for many years head of the History Department in the University of Wyoming, was the leading exponent of the Wyoming theory.

of Owl Creek and ran due south to the crest of the divide, between Sweetwater and Popo Agie; along the crest and the summit of Wind River Mountains to the North Fork of Wind River; due north to the mouth of the North Fork and up its channel to a point twenty miles above the mouth; then in a straight line to the headwaters of Owl Creek and along the middle of its channel to the place of the beginning. Thus the boundaries of the Wind River Reservation were defined in a language which Washakie could understand.

The bulk of the treaty concerned the details of establishing and operating the reservation—the buildings to be constructed, the personnel to have charge, and the land allotments for purpose of cultivation. The treaty recognized the fact that education is necessary "to insure the civilization of the tribes." It made school attendance for all children, male and female, between six and eighteen years of age compulsory, while another article provided awards for outstanding farmers. These two clauses show that the white man intended to lose no time in forcing the acculturation of the Indian. The treaty did not take into consideration the fact that the average Indian girl was usually a mother at sixteen, nor the fact that the buffalo hunter had never handled a plow.

It assumed that clothing civilized the Indian. The government agreed to provide, on the first day of September for thirty years, the following articles:

> For each male person over fourteen years of age, a suit of good substantial woollen clothing, consisting of coat, hat, pantaloons, flannel shirt, and a pair of woollen socks; for each female over twelve years of age, a flannel skirt or the goods necessary to make it, a pair of woollen hose, twelve yards of calico, and twelve yards of cotton domestics.
>
> For the boys and girls under the ages named, such flannel and cotton goods as may be needed to make each a suit as aforesaid, together with a pair of hose for each.

While the Indian was being civilized, he did not have an extra pair of socks. Nevertheless, the dawn of a new era had arrived.

The red man was now to give up his nomadic life and settle in one place to become a tiller of the soil.

The head of a family was entitled to 320 acres, to be occupied and held in exclusive possession "as long as he or they may continue to cultivate it." Any person over eighteen years of age, who was not head of a family, could hold a quantity of land not to exceed eighty acres for purposes of cultivation. The tracts were to be certified and recorded in a "land book."

With the X marks which the chiefs and leading men placed on the treaty, they signed away their way of life for one prescribed for them by the white man. Yet Washakie, who was always ready to meet the paleface more than halfway, was jubilant. Speaking in council, he declared:

> I am laughing because I am happy. Because my heart is good. As I said two days ago, I like the country you mentioned, then, for us, the Wind River valley. Now I see my friends are around me, and it is pleasant to meet and shake hands with them. I always find friends along the roads in this country, about Bridger, that is why I come here. It is good to have the Railroad through this country and I have come down to see it.

> When we want to grow something to eat and hunt I want the Wind River Country. In other Indian countries, there is danger, but here about Bridger, all is peaceful for whites and Indians and safe for all to travel. When the white man came into my country and cut the wood and made the roads my heart was good, and I was Satisfied. You have heard what I want. The Wind River Country is the one for me.

> We may not for one, two or three years be able to till the ground. The Sioux may trouble us. But when the Sioux are taken care of, we can do well. Will the whites be allowed to build houses on our reservation? I do not object to traders coming among us, and care nothing about the miners and mining country where they are getting out gold. I may bye and bye get Some of that myself.

> I want for my home the valley of Wind River and lands on its tributaries as far east as the Popo-agie, and want the privilege of going over the mountains to hunt where I please.[48]

[48] Gen. C. C. Augur to President of Indian Peace Commission, October 4, 1868, I.O.R.

CHAPTER THIRTEEN

Friendlies and Hostiles

Tʜᴇ Bᴀɴɴᴏᴄᴋs, with whom Washakie refused to share his annuities at Fort Bridger, were in such poor condition that General Augur allowed them $4,000 worth of goods from the treaty funds.[1] The Boise, Camas, and Bruneau Indians, who considered Taghee their leader, could not understand why he and the small band with him should receive presents when they had none. In order to avoid trouble, Governor Ballard and Agent Charles F. Powell lost no time in moving them to Fort Hall. Powell escorted 1,150 Boise and Bruneau Shoshonis and 150 Bannocks to Fort Hall on April 12, 1869. Without delay, he began to erect buildings to house the supplies soon to arrive. Taghee, with about 800 Bannocks, was away at the time buffalo hunting with Washakie.

To the north, Tendoy's Indians were finding sustenance difficult. They came into notice when Governor Thomas F. Meagher, of Montana Territory, reported their "misery, filth, and dire want." Stirred by his report, the Commissioner of Indian Affairs sent Agent Mann to investigate. Verifying the report, Mann found about one hundred lodges of Bannocks and a few lodges of Shoshonis residing in the same area occupied by a tribe of Sheep Eaters.[2] Just where the remaining Lemhi Shoshonis were, he did not say. They comprised a sizeable number compared to the Sheep Eaters. It is possible that in their poverty he was unable to distinguish one Lemhi from another.

Agent Alfred Sully, of Montana Territory, solved the diffi-

[1] J. A. Campbell, *Report, House Exec. Doc. 1,* Pt. 3, 41 Cong., 2 sess. (1414), 712–15.

[2] *Report of Commissioner of Indian Affairs,* 1867, 189.

culty in terminology by calling all of the Lemhis Bannocks. Although the Sheep Eaters were accused of various depredations as a band, Tendoy's Indians had a surprisingly good reputation. Like Taghee, Tendoy disclaimed any responsibility for their misdemeanors. When Taghee spoke of "all the Bannock" he included the Northern or Lemhi band, consolidated with the Shoshonis. Tendoy's father "Old Bonaparte" came originally from the main Bannock tribe; his mother was a Shoshoni. No record can be found to indicate when the Bannocks left the Fort Hall band and joined the Lemhis. Agent Sully, who said that they boasted they had never shed the blood of the white man, found that they did not like Fort Hall.[3]

The Lemhis signed a treaty at Virginia City, Montana, on September 24, 1868, but it was not ratified nor was a reservation provided for them until February 12, 1875, when the Lemhi Valley Indian Reservation was created by executive order. The one-hundred-square-mile reserve was shared by about seven hundred Indians.[4]

Washakie, meanwhile, was constantly being threatened by his traditional enemies and as a result was finding it difficult to settle with his tribesmen in the area assigned to him. He refused to move to Wind River until he had some assurance that he would be well protected against the encroaching tribes. In the spring of 1867 he and his band had been compelled to leave their hunting grounds before they could prepare their usual supply of dried meat for summer use. The Sioux and Cheyennes, surprising them, had caused them to move southward. When they arrived at Fort Bridger, they were destitute.[5]

The next year the marauding tribes proved even more troublesome. En route to the agency, Washakie's band was attacked by about three hundred Sioux, Cheyenne, and Arapaho warriors,

[3] *Ibid.*, 1869, 731–32.
[4] *Report of Commissioner of Indian Affairs*, 1877, 241. Previously, Tendoy had distinguished himself by forcing a war party of Bannocks to give up a large number of stolen horses and mules. He was honored by the governor of Idaho, who presented him with a flag. *Ibid.*, 1872, 292.
[5] Economic Conditions (1326), 182–84.

led by a son of Red Cloud. In the ensuing battle, young Red Cloud and several of his warriors were killed, while four Shoshonis lost their lives and several were wounded. The enemy captured eighty head of horses. Agent Mann felt that the battle would be a "temporary setback" to the peaceful occupation of the reservation.

Washakie received a runner from the Crows saying that they wanted to sue for peace, but he was not to be misled. He stated that he would be willing to hold a medicine talk with them only if a government official were present. The agent expressed his hope that the Platte River Indians could be forced to stay in their territory so that the Eastern Shoshonis and Bannocks could move to Wind River in safety and settle down to reservation life.

Mann found some of the Indians unwilling to risk their lives to follow Washakie into the danger zone. They chose to remain under the leadership of the half-blood Norkuk in the Green River area. Consequently, Washakie suffered a "diminution of his strength." The agent instructed all able-bodied Indians to follow their chief. He reminded them that Washakie alone was recognized as their head and that if they expected to share the rewards they must be willing to risk the dangers.[6]

The Eastern Shoshonis had shown no inclination to settle down long enough to till the soil. The white man's plan to force education and farming was a treaty stipulation only. Although no special efforts had been made to engage the Northwestern Shoshonis (Pocatello's band) in agriculture, they were already expressing a desire to have cattle for purposes of building up a herd. Superintendent F. H. Head gave fifteen cows to their most reliable chiefs, and the Indians promised faithfully that they would keep them and their increase until they had a large herd of their own. When he visited them some weeks later, he found that the cows had not been eaten.

The Western Shoshonis at Deep Creek and Ruby Valley were showing "a commendable zeal" in their farming operations. They put to good use the work oxen, plows, and seed grain given them by the Superintendent, who reported that they had planted forty

[6] Mann's report, *House Exec. Doc. 1,* 40 Cong., 3 sess., II (1366), 116–19.

acres. He was sure that the crop from this would aid in their support during the coming winter.[7] The agricultural efforts were being made by Indians in small settlements, for the Western and Northwestern bands were still without reservations.

To the east, the Shoshonis continued to hunt in their country where there were still buffalo. In fact, their annual harvest in robes amounted to about twenty thousand dollars. As the Union Pacific Railroad approached, there was an increased demand for buffalo meat, which would further deplete the dwindling supply.

After the creation of Wyoming Territory (July 25, 1868), the Eastern Shoshonis were transferred to the Wyoming Superintendency, with the Territorial Governor, John A. Campbell, serving as ex officio superintendent of Indian affairs. He had under his jurisdiction the Eastern Shoshonis and the Bannocks who were temporarily assigned to the Wind River Reservation.

When Taghee returned from his annual hunting trip with Washakie, he tarried at Fort Bridger only long enough to get his annuities. Then he and his band went to Fort Hall where he said he wanted to live with his people. Since the reservation created at Fort Bridger included Camas Prairie (incorrectly called "Kansas Prairie" in the treaty), Governor Ballard and Agent Powell favored letting them stay.[8] The Bannocks were subsequently granted a permanent home on the Fort Hall Reservation, by executive order on July 30, 1869. When annuities were finally ordered to be delivered at Fort Hall, the Bannocks no longer found it necessary to go to Fort Bridger.[9]

General Augur preceded Mann to Wind River Valley to establish an agency there, on June 11, 1869. Protection was necessary as hostiles had lately killed twenty-five Shoshonis and four white men.[10] Earlier in the season it had been reported that Washakie's warriors had met with disaster before leaving their hunting grounds. They had been trying to recover stolen horses when

[7] *Ibid.*, 608–14.

[8] *Report of Commissioner of Indian Affairs,* 1869, 728.

[9] *Ibid.*, 1872, 270.

[10] Campbell to Commissioner of Indian Affairs, June 10, 1869, I.O.R.

an overwhelming number of Sioux had engaged them in battle and defeated them.

Following this, forty-five of Washakie's most fearless young warriors went in search of the enemy. After driving off several hundred head of their horses, they started home. The Platte River Indians tracked them through the heavy snow and surrounded them. The old-style army revolvers carried by the Shoshonis became useless when wet. As a result, the enemy, using bows and arrows, left them all for dead. Three of the wounded ultimately reached camp, one having crawled eighteen miles on his hands and knees.

In compliance with Washakie's wishes, a sub-post to Fort Bridger—Camp Augur—was established on the site of the present town of Lander, Wyoming, on July 28. It was located on the Big Popo Agie. Laid out in the form of a quadrangle, it was surrounded by a ditch and fortified by earthwork. The camp was primitive, as there were neither floors nor bunks in the building occupied by the infantry, while the cavalry camped outside the stockade. The dirt-roofed buildings, parallel to the sides of the enclosure, surrounded a small parade ground. Major James S. Briskin was placed in command.

Camp Augur was later moved to Little Wind River. There the name was changed to Camp Brown by general order, on March 28, 1870, in honor of Captain Frederick Brown who was killed in the Fetterman Massacre (1866).[11] In this massacre eighty-two officers and men under the command of Colonel William J. Fetterman were wiped out by the Sioux six miles from Fort Phil Kearny in the Big Horns, near Buffalo, Wyoming.[12]

The Northern Arapahoes, looking wistfully toward Washakie's reservation, signified their desire to make it their home not long after it was created. Governor Campbell also was anxious to place them there where they could be kept under surveillance. But the Shoshonis were highly suspicious of the enemy, known

[11] The Camp Brown *Post Surgeon's Record Book* (hereinafter cited as *Post Record*) has the chatty style of a small-town newspaper.

[12] Fort Phil Kearny (1866–68) was known to the Sioux as "the hated fort on the Little Piney."

to have been guilty of atrocities in the area. Washakie did, however, allow them to share his reservation temporarily—until permanent arrangements could be made—in the winter of 1868–69. On March 31 a party of Indians, variously reported as Arapahoes, Sioux, and Cheyennes, made a raid on the Sweetwater mining settlement, where they murdered 8 persons, then made an escape with their livestock.

The settlers organized a force of 250 armed men and started to the Arapaho camp. Along the way, they met 13 members of the tribe, under Black Bear. They proceeded to kill the chief and 10 of his braves. The citizens claimed that the Arapahoes killed the miners; the army believed that the Sioux were guilty.

On May 7 the Arapahoes, who had by now left the reservation, asked to be allowed to occupy the country near old Fort Caspar and to be given an agent.[13] Their request was refused, as this would have placed them too close to the trail and the Sweetwater mining region. The government then decided to send the Arapahoes to the Gros Ventre Agency on Milk River (Montana). Refusing to go, they settled themselves in the vicinity of Fort Caspar, where they continued to cause trouble.[14] Finally, Fort Stambaugh had to be established near South Pass for the protection of the mining camps. It was named for Lieutenant Charles B. Stambaugh, who had recently been killed by the hostiles.

Many of the Western Shoshonis, who had shown a tendency to settle down, were still without reservations. Those who wished to farm were unable to find good tillable land, as most of it had already been settled. The Gosiutes remained the poorest of the lot, but it was predicted that if the Western Shoshonis continued to work as they were doing, someday they would "be rich."[15]

[13] Fort Caspar, near present Casper, Wyoming, was located at the Platte River Crossing on the Oregon Trail. A bridge was built there (1858–59) and the military post was maintained from 1859 until 1867. Young Lieutenant Caspar Collins, for whom the post was named, was one of twenty-six soldiers to lose his life when about three thousand warriors attacked the soldiers at the bridge on July 25, 1865.

[14] Campbell to Commissioner of Indian Affairs, October 11, 1870, I.O.R.

[15] Western Shoshones, *House Exec. Doc. 1*, Pt. 4, 41 Cong., 3 sess. (1449), 567.

By 1872, James Irwin, the second agent at Fort Washakie, reported that the dangers of starvation were removed and that a school had been established, with ten students enrolled. Even so, he felt that the Eastern Shoshonis were still "in a wild state, having learned little from white men except vices."[16]

By act of Congress, on June 1, 1872, the President of the United States was authorized to negotiate with the Shoshonis for the south portion of the Wind River Reservation.[17] Congress was especially anxious to gain title to Miner's Delight, which had been built on the reservation, and to clear title to certain lands that had been taken up by white settlers prior to the Fort Bridger Treaty. Felix Brunot, chairman of the Board of Indian Commissioners, was sent to talk the Shoshonis into an agreement. Their reward was to be an equal number of acres to the north of their reservation.

Brunot, who had little regard for the welfare of the Indians, maneuvered the Shoshonis into an agreement which many years later was to be termed "unconscionable." The proceedings of the council are revealing:

> BRUNOT: . . . If the white men had grown up without learning to farm they would be like the Indians; they would not know how to read and write. Washakie understands all these things as well as I do. Perhaps some of the others do not understand them as well; for that reason I am saying these things, although he knows them. We take the small children and send them to school; we have many school houses so that all the children can go. They learn but little at first, but learn more and more, and when they are grown up they know a great deal. It is too late for men who are grown up to learn. That is why the President and the Indians' friends are anxious to have a school, so that the children will begin to learn. Then when the game is gone the children will know enough to live like white men. . . . I want to hear what Washakie and others wish to say.
>
> WASHAKIE: I have nothing to say. We want you to tell us what you came here to say.
>
> BRUNOT: I came to hear your words and to carry them to the

16 *House Exec. Doc. 1,* Pt. 5, 42 Cong., 2 sess. (1505), 966.
17 Felix Brunot, *Report,* "Negotiations with the Shoshone Indians," *Fourth Annual Report,* Board of Indian Commissioners, 1872, 51–68.

Great Father. But there is another matter of business about the reservation that I will talk about tomorrow. Have you nothing you wish to say about the agency, the buildings, or the farms?

WASHAKIE: I would like to have houses here; I do not like to live in lodges; I am afraid of the Sioux. They come here and hunt for scalps in this valley. I would like to have houses. We would like to talk about the land.

BRUNOT: We will talk about the land now if you wish. The President has heard for a good while that there are miners on the reservation, and Congress has heard about it also. They heard some of these miners were here before the reservation was set apart, and that there were also some people living on the farming land before the reservation was marked out. So they passed a law to send a man to see Washakie and the Indians, to see what arrangements could be made to settle all these troubles. They passed this law to try and settle the whole question, so that there would never be any more trouble about it. [He read the law.]

TOOP-SE-PO-WOT: I did not know there were any whites here when the buffalo were here.

BRUNOT: I have been sent here to tell you about this land and to make a bargain with you for it. . . . It is your land, and you have a right to do what you please about it. . . . I think that Wash-a-kie is wise and that he sees what is best. I think he has considered the matter a great deal, and I think the other men have been thinking of it. You can see that white men have mines on the reservation. You know that you cannot eat the rocks or the gold, and that the Indians cannot dig it out; and if you can get rid of trouble by cutting it off you know that it is best to do so.

The Commissioner then read a letter from the President, directing him to make arrangements. The plan was to exchange acre for acre. Washakie was thoughtful a moment.

WASHAKIE: In that valley [proposed to be ceded] there is plenty of grass, berries, prairie squirrel, and fish—plenty of everything. It is good land. I do not know what to do about it. I have two hearts about it. This land is good; that in the north [proposed as exchange] is poor, and I think it belongs to the Crows. When you were at the Crows did the chief tell you to trade this land off?

BRUNOT: I did not say anything to the Crows about it. It was none of their business. The land does not belong to them.

WASHAKIE: The Shoshones think it belongs to the Crows.

BRUNOT: I will show Wash-a-kie by the map that it does not belong to the Crows.

WASHAKIE: That land belongs to the Crows, the Sioux and everybody. If we went there, then the Sioux might come in and scalp us. I do not want that land. If the whites want to buy this land it is all right, but I do not want to trade it for land anywhere.

The chief was firm. He would not trade, but he would sell for cattle the portion that the government wanted. When asked if the Indians knew how many cattle their land was worth, Wisha, a subchief, answered that it would be good to have cows and drink the milk. He felt that the land might be worth "about a thousand cattle." When the Commissioner asked what they would do if they had cows, Wisha replied that they would corral them and milk them.

WASHAKIE: If we get the cattle, we would keep them here and herd them like we do our horses.

BRUNOT: If you had cattle would some of you stay here all the time and herd them?

WASHAKIE: Whenever we move up Wind River we would have to take them with us. We would like to have cattle. The Utes and all the other Indians have cattle; we are poor and have none.

TO-AS-HOUT: We have nothing; we are poor.

BRUNOT: If a man gambles with another and loses his things, he can't have any left. Will not the Indians gamble for their cattle, and lose them and after a while some will have a great many and others none?

WASHAKIE: The Indians gamble a great deal.

BRUNOT: Would the white people get the cattle away from you, or would you take care of them and keep them?

DEGONDA: We would take the same care of them we do our horses. The whites do not beat us out of them.

WASHAKIE: The Sioux, Cheyennes and Arapahoes might come in and kill them and eat them. . . . Some mean Sioux are over at the Powder River Mountains. They are the ones who are coming in, making trouble around here. You can find them there at almost any time.

The number of acres involved was not specified, but the Shoshonis agreed to relinquish all of their reservation south of the North Fork of the Big Popo Agie for the sum of $25,000, to be paid in the form of $5,000 worth of cattle annually for five years. Washakie was to be given a salary of $500 a year for the same period. Most of the signers of the treaty used their Indian names. Some of them in translated form are eloquent of Indian nomenclature: Dirty-Back, Sweating-Horse, Horse's Grandfather, Rabbit Crying, Grab You and Throw You Down, Topknot-Rooster, Lots of Dogs, Stand and Look, Humpty-Fish, and Emigrant Road.

The Commissioner later went to Fort Hall. There he was shown two hundred acres under successful cultivation, with plantings of wheat, oats, potatoes, turnips, and other crops.[18] The agent believed that there would be enough harvested to subsist the Indians who wintered on the reservation.

In spite of this outward show of adjustment, trouble had been building up among the Bannocks and Shoshonis of Idaho over annuities. It had seemed to the agent and Indians at Fort Hall that the government had failed to meet the terms of the Fort Bridger treaty in every respect. Bitterness over the loss of game and the failure of the government to keep its promises—the most recent one, to send a supply of badly needed blankets—had caused Taghee upon one occasion to lose patience. In exasperation, he had shouted that he would not stand for any more such treatment.

In order to avoid possible war, $3,000 had to be supplied from the Idaho Territorial funds to buy blankets. Although the government had created reservations to keep the Indians under control, mismanagement, failure to live up to treaty terms, and general indifference defeated the purpose for which the reservations were intended.

The death of Taghee while on a buffalo hunt in 1871—the year before Brunot's visit—had been a loss to the white men as well as to the Indians. Through the strength of his influence he had held

18 *Ibid.*, 82–89.

the Bannocks in check over a period of many years. He left only a minor son, Tew-yu, and no one else seemed to want the responsibility of his office. The mixed bands of Bannocks and Shoshonis were temporarily without a chieftain when Brunot arrived. Tendoy still was the only recognized chief of all the Bannocks at the time. He had, according to the resident agent, expressed a willingness to join the Fort Hall Indians.

Brunot was especially impressed by Captain Jim, a Shoshoni chief, who could speak English reasonably well. He had several acres of ground planted in potatoes and had the entire care of them. Also, he expressed a desire for a house and piece of ground on which he could raise all kinds of crops. He wanted to buy cows with the proceeds and stop going for camass and buffalo. Furthermore, he wanted to see "Washington" (the President).

Pocatello, who had but recently arrived at the reservation, had insisted upon staying. He and his band were considered "willing workers," although he admitted to Brunot that he had never tried farming. The agent asserted that if they were encouraged, Pocatello and Captain Jim could bring to the reservation a thousand Indians who had no settled homes. We learn something of the political and economic condition of the mixed bands through Captain Jim:

> CAPTAIN JIM [to the Commissioner]: Your words I put into my ear and take into my heart. Some of the Indians are bad, and ought to be made to stay upon their reservation. They [the Bannocks] have no chief, and ought to have one who would take care of them. I am only a little chief. All the big chiefs are dead. There are only little chiefs and young chiefs left. Taghee, the great Bannock chief, is dead. Tin-a-dore [Tendoy] is the greatest chief of the Bannocks. Washakie is a big chief. I am no big chief. My words are all true.
>
> BRUNOT: Suppose Wash-a-kie came to Fort Hall to live, would he be the big chief?
>
> CAPTAIN JIM: That depends upon what Washington [the President] says. Captain Jim is the great chief, or Washakie is the great chief, just as Washington says about it.

BRUNOT: Suppose Washington should say that Washakie is chief of all the Indians; would that be all right? Or if Captain Jim is chief over all, would Pocatello stay?

CAPTAIN JIM: You can judge that as well as I can.

BRUNOT: Would Tin-a-dore like to come here?

CAPTAIN JIM: He wants to stay at Lemhi, just as Wash-a-kie wants to stay at Wind River. They get their annuity goods there. How many reservations of Shoshones and Bannocks are there?

BRUNOT: Washakie's [Wind River], Tin-a-dore's [Lemhi], and this one [Fort Hall].

The Commissioner sounded out the Shoshoni chief on the subject of education. Captain Jim had never heard of anything like it.

BRUNOT: Do you know what the white man's school is?

CAPTAIN JIM: We do not know what it is.

BRUNOT [after explaining]: If the agent opens a school will you send your children?

CAPTAIN JIM: I have only one little boy, and I do not wish to send him now.

BRUNOT: When your boy is old enough you must send him to school, and he will learn and will have good sense.

CAPTAIN JIM: I do not understand fully about the school. When it is opened I will know more about it and will understand it.

Meanwhile, encouraging reports were coming from the Klamath Agency.[19] The superintendent affirmed that while the Indians had been savages in skins, paint, and feathers two years before, they were now operating a sawmill, and a great reformation had taken place. They had donned the white man's costume. This meant a great deal because of the agents' obsession that clothing civilized the Indian.

The year after Brunot's visit, Irwin reported that the Wind River Shoshonis had resolved to settle down and cease their migratory habits. Their improved attitude was indicated by their raising approximately twelve hundred bushels of wheat and between two and three hundred bushels of potatoes, carrots, beets,

[19] Klamath *Report, House Exec. Doc. 1,* 40 Cong., 2 sess., II (1326), 7–8, 71–73.

234

onions, and other crops. Forty boys were attending school, and the Indians were asking that houses be built.

Coupled with this was an improvement in their appearance. They looked "tidy, cheerful, and healthy," instead of "dirty, squalid, and sickly." According to the agent, neighboring tribes had sent runners to see if the Shoshonis had actually settled down. Even the Crows had sent congratulations on their improved condition. Forty-six lodges (comprising wandering Shoshonis) had drifted in to make the reservation their home.

The optimistic pattern of the agent's report was in contrast to the sardonic opinion of Dr. L. S. Tasson, the first post surgeon to record his observations in the Post Record Book.[20] Pessimistic regarding the acculturation of the Shoshonis, he said that during the summer Washakie's Indians would go north on their annual hunt, with the length of their stay proportionate to their success. In the year 1873, with a great deal of help from the employees of the agency, the Indians had managed to plow and plant a small quantity of grain, but "as a rule they were shiftless, lazy, and dirty." When not upon their annual hunt, small bands visited the railroad and the Salt Lake country. With the Mormons, Tasson stated, "they were fast friends, visiting their little towns, and spending their time begging and gathering up gossip to be retailed upon their return to the tribe."

The Eastern Shoshonis' failure to adjust could be attributed for the most part to the frequent incursions of the Sioux and Arapahoes. Although the presence of troops may have discouraged a large-scale war, sneak attacks were made and the hostiles were out of the country before their presence was detected. Attempts to drive off the government livestock were usually thwarted. Upon one occasion the warriors recklessly dashed by the Indian encampment at the agency. In this daring venture they got no stock but killed one boy.

Early in 1873 two attacks were made upon travelers along the road to the reservation. In the first, the Indians captured four horses, which they deliberately unharnessed and led off, but they

[20] *Post Record*, 9–10.

235

did not harm the drivers nor did they take their arms. In the second, they accomplished nothing. They disappeared as rapidly as they had made their appearance, after receiving a volley from the teamsters in charge of the wagon train.

In spite of the nearness of the garrison, the hostiles made an attack on a small settlement at the original site of Camp Augur (now Lander, Wyoming) about eleven o'clock one morning. After killing two white women, they plundered their house and destroyed all that they did not want. Taking with them a horse and a mule, they quietly rode away without molesting anyone else in the valley. The few white settlers who had not gone to the mountains to cut timber were too scattered for concerted action against the marauders.

A month later an Indian from Washakie's band reported that he had been on a small hunt of his own and that sixty or seventy miles from the post he had discovered an encampment of about two hundred lodges, from which the hostiles were thought to have come. He reported that they were having a grand Scalp Dance. As no scalps had been claimed at the agency, the Indians had apparently attacked elsewhere.

The story created great excitement, and one of the lieutenants and fifteen men were directed to encamp near the reservation Indians every night until the alarm was over. The agent then sent runners to Washakie, who was about sixty miles away on a buffalo hunt. They instructed him to return at once, both to attend to his crops and to help protect his people.

Lieutenant James Wheelan with his command, which had just returned from an expedition sent after the raiders at the settlement, proceeded from Little Popo Agie until he struck a trail of a war party, numbering about three hundred. He followed this trail to Wind River Canyon, some one hundred miles away. When he found no further signs except the continuing trail, he returned to the post to seek reinforcements and authority to resume the search.

The Shoshonis returned from their hunt on the afternoon of the twenty-fifth. The next morning Washakie, regardless of the crops that needed tending, started on the warpath. He hoped to pick up the trail and follow it some distance, whatever direction it might lead. On the following day, the Indians began to filter back to Camp Brown. About twenty-five returned with the excuse that they were sick or hungry or that they had only one horse. The unsympathetic Tasson was inclined to believe that they were afraid of losing their scalps.[21] Evidently the hostiles managed to elude Washakie, as no further mention is made of his excursion.

The next spring (1874), the troops found themselves unable to cope with the hostiles. When raiders drove off several horses and fired upon a white man, soldiers and Indians took to the trail which was found to lead in the direction of Beaver, a small stream on the western slope of the Big Horn Mountains. Reaching there, they found that the hostiles, seventy miles ahead, were fleeing eastward. Abandoning the trail, Captain A. E. Bates, the commanding officer, returned to Camp Brown. He cited Washakie for meritorious service.

Raids of this sort were so upsetting that apparently the government officials became discouraged. At least they formed a plan to remove the tribe to a safer location. Tasson substantiates this by saying:

> The government has been parleying with them (the Wind River Shoshones) for some time in the hopes of gaining their consent to a change of reservation, it being the desire of the Govt. to remove them to Indian Territory, but just as long as Washakie remains in his present position as chief of the tribe, his consent will never be gained. Upon his demise,[22] there being several factions among them, it is hard to conjecture who will succeed him. To any lesser chiefs, however, the idea of moving is not so distasteful.[23]

Meanwhile, the Basin Indians were having troubles. Many of them were being forced from their little farms by white men who seized their property. Pi-an-nump, brother of Kanosh, the

21 *Ibid.*, 34–39.
22 Washakie's death did not occur until February 20, 1900.
23 *Post Record,* 10–11.

Pahvant chief, was one of the few Indians in the entire area who could boast that he was making his own living.[24] The Western Shoshonis were now divided into thirty-one groups or bands. Only about one-fourth of these had derived any benefits from the Ruby Valley Treaty (1863). While waiting for the government to solve their problem, many of the Shoshokos were hiring out as farm laborers to keep from starving.[25]

Thomas G. Maghee, Tasson's successor, wrote of the Shoshonis with a sympathetic understanding, perhaps for the reason that he worked with them more closely than Tasson did. He accompanied them on many of their excursions. The entire camp was aroused when two soldiers, helping build a road on Upper Wind River (probably in the vicinity of Dubois, Wyoming), were captured by the hostiles. By putting up a bold front, the white men managed to escape.[26] The raiders, however, robbed a cache of corn belonging to the road-building crew, not far from Dinwoody Lake. Maghee and Washakie were among the contingent sent to apprehend the guilty Indians. After crossing Big Wind River, they found twelve abandoned wickiups, indicating about 120 warriors. Their trail went east toward the Big Horns.

Maghee was impressed by the elaborate accouterments of Washakie and his warriors as their "gay beaded clothing and brightly gleaming trappings shone in the sunshine." Continuing the march to Dry Creek, they found an abandoned camp with a fire still smoldering. Coup sticks and other items scattered about suggested that the Indians might have left in haste. The soldiers and Shoshonis were again in the saddle early in the morning and on their way to Muddy Creek. As the trail continued over the mountains to the east, they returned to the mouth of Lake Fork, crossed Big Wind River again, and returned to Camp Brown after completing a fruitless march of 110 miles.

While the march may have been futile from the army's point of view, several Shoshoni braves—including Dick Washakie (son

[24] Western Shoshones, *House Exec. Doc. 1*, Pt. 5, 43 Cong., 1 sess. (1601), 425.
[25] *Ibid.*, 428.
[26] *Post Record*, 38–39.

of the chief), Barney, and Snaggletooth Pete—did not turn back. They followed the enemy to their camp.[27] Climbing to the summit, they looked down upon a large Arapaho encampment, "where there were beautiful meadows of grass, abundant springs, and creeks of water with surrounding mountains and precipitous cliffs"—somewhere in the Big Horns. The tipis of the enemy were closely grouped, and about two thousand horses were grazing near by. Each brave managed to capture a fresh mount without being noticed.

It was later found that the Sioux had held a great Sun Dance at their reservation in the Dakotas in June, when the Cheyennes and Arapahoes agreed to join them in a drive against the Wind River Shoshonis. The expedition started and all went well until they crossed the Big Horns. Then a disagreement arose concerning the object of the raid. Some of the Indians claimed that it was for murder and the spoils of war; others, that it was for stealing horses. The Arapahoes refused to accompany the expedition because of the disagreement. The Sioux and Cheyennes then went their way, leaving the Arapahoes in their camp.

The Shoshoni scouts, returning to their reservation, called upon Agent Irwin, whom they told of their experience with wild gesticulations. At Camp Brown they found "all hustle and bustle and military in the extreme," for General P. H. Sheridan and General E. O. C. Ord had just arrived. As soon as the military was appraised of the Indians' findings, a council was called. General Sheridan, General Ord, the army officers at the post, the Shoshoni chief and subchiefs, and Irwin were in attendance. A decision was reached to go against the raiders at once.

Captain Bates was placed in charge of the striking force, and 125 Shoshonis were selected to accompany the troops then available for active service. Besides the soldiers and Shoshonis, there were several civilians, including Maghee and Tom Cosgrove (a Civil War veteran from Texas) who had charge of the Indian scouts while Washakie was assisted by Norkuk, Wanapitz, Rota, Toashshur, and Wesaw.

[27] *Ibid.,* 50–57.

Bates proposed to move his command early in the day, but General Sheridan objected. The weather was dry and hot. He said that if they marched in the daytime, the hostiles could see the dust rising forty miles away. Therefore, they marched by night, and the Indians in advance would give "a peculiar sonorous call" in order to acquaint their scouts with their whereabouts.

At length the scouts returned to say that the village had moved. They showed articles that they had picked up at the abandoned campsite. Again the scouts left, and the Indians and soldiers held council. Washakie was insistent that the foe was near at hand. A few hours before, the Shoshonis had found two Arapaho ponies running loose. "With finger uplifted and eyes fixed in rapt attention, and with his flowing hair and swarthy countenance, mingled with the eager faces and costly uniforms of the officers," the chief presented a striking picture, according to Maghee.[28]

The scouts soon returned to announce that the village had been sighted in a gorge only a short distance away. All was activity. It was July 4, 1874. Captain Bates, advised of the lay of the land, gave orders to his small army. The soldiers were to make a direct attack, and the Shoshonis were to go up the side of the hill and come over the bluff in order to cut off the enemys' retreat.

The warriors, already stripped and painted for battle, mounted their ponies and waited for a word from their chief. Bates ordered his men to charge on the run to keep from losing the advantage of surprise. But the Shoshonis did not go up the side of the hill as ordered. Perhaps they had misunderstood.[29] This is possible, as the interpreter (Norkuk) complained that Bates talked so fast that he could not understand, or he may even have purposely misinterpreted the orders. It has been suggested that the Shoshonis became confused in the desperate charging and firing. As they wore no distinguishing garb, they were afraid that the soldiers would mistake them for the enemy and fire upon them. This may have been Norkuk's reason for failing to interpret the orders correctly.

[28] Thomas G. Maghee, "The Bates Battle," *ibid.*, 126.
[29] Irwin to Commissioner of Indian Affairs, September 18, 1874, I.O.R.

The 112 lodges in the Arapaho village were located in a position calculated for defense. Alarmed by the tumult, many of the enemy rushed from their blankets and clamored up the face of the bluff. Others took to the gorge, where the fighting was sharp and effective. The village seemed to fall so completely into the hands of the attackers that the surgeon established his field hospital in a tipi and proceeded to administer to the wounded.

In the gorge, seventeen Arapaho braves and two women were slain. Five were killed in the village and three on the hill in plain sight. Pe-a-quite, one of the Shoshoni braves, fought his way into the hottest part of the battle, where he received a fatal wound. He cooly planted his coup stick and sang his death song. Another Shoshoni fell in a hand-to-hand fight in front of the lodges, while three others were wounded. The brave warrior Aguina was shot in the wrist, the ball passing through the palm of his hand and cutting off his middle finger, leaving him with a battle scar of which he could boast the remainder of his life.

By now the Arapahoes had gained the heights, from which they began raining lead down upon the soldiers and Shoshonis. A young lieutenant was severely wounded while trying vainly to take the bluff which the Shoshonis had failed to occupy. Cosgrove prevented him from falling into the hands of the hostiles by rushing to his side. Captain Bates immediately headed a column, and with the aid of Washakie, Tigee, and several other warriors, succeeded in bringing him to safety. After James M. Walker and Peter T. Engell (two civilians) were killed and three other white men were wounded, Bates ordered the surgeon to move to safer grounds.

Smoke signals were now being made by the enemy to summon aid from the Cheyennes and Sioux. The soldiers were aware that there were probably two hundred Arapahoes still unharmed and ammunition was running low. Captain Bates was informed that some of the Shoshonis, "who had persistently kept aloof during the fight at Norkuk's advice," were determined to leave.

With the Arapahoes now in a strategic position, Bates was forced to order a retreat, which became general as soldiers and

Indians headed for home. This was fortunate as the Arapahoes, although severely punished, felt in view of the withdrawal that the battle might have gone their way. Hastily assembling, they made plans to pursue the enemy, but they were unable to do this as the soldiers and Shoshonis had succeeded in driving away their horses.

A roll of bedding, containing all of the force's medical supplies and surgical instruments, was needlessly abandoned during the retreat. Discovering this, Bates sent one of his men after the vitally needed supplies, but the hostiles drove him off and took possession of them. The surgeon, deprived of everything but a pocket case and a linen handkerchief, brought the wounded on horseback sixty miles to the mouth of Little Wind River, where he was met by an ambulance with medical stores.

The Arapaho losses were undetermined, but it was learned some time afterward that Black Coal (then an equal chief with Sharp Nose) was severely wounded. Besides having his horse shot from under him, he sustained a chest wound, and three of his fingers were shot off. He was later known on the Wind River Reservation as Tag-ge-tha-the (Shot-off-Fingers).

A courier brought news of the outcome of the battle first to the post; then it spread to the Indians. A Shoshoni woman, weeping and waving her arms, came to the agency gate; "Mah-bake; mah-bake!" she wailed.[30] "Shoshone mah-bake, shourd Pampazim-in-a!" ("They have killed; they have killed: those Sioux have killed Shoshones!")

Washakie's personal regret was the loss of a handsome gray horse which he had captured. He had loaded a gunny sack containing the Arapaho scalps on his back. The horse broke away and, returning to the enemy, took the war trophies with him.

Maghee and others who were at the battle reported that the Shoshonis "did good execution," but Bates gave them no credit. Irwin, who stoutly defended them, claimed that from all reports given him he was convinced that they fought as well as any white

---

[30] James I. Patten, "Bates' Famous Battle," *The Rustler* (October, 1899), 1–5. Patten came to the agency as teacher and lay missionary in 1873.

man. He thought that the reason Bates did not appreciate their efforts was that he was young, and this was his first battle. A logical reason may have been that he could neither forgive nor forget the breach of faith shown by Norkuk, who thwarted him in his ambition to gain personal glory through a decisive victory.

James Patten, who was on the reservation as teacher at the time of the engagement and later served as agent, gave a sequel to the battle. He said that after the Sioux and Cheyennes left the Arapahoes, they went in a northerly direction as if returning to their agency. Instead, they slipped around to the west, apparently determined to give the Shoshonis and whites of the Wind River country "a deal at all hazards." At Tensleep[31] they cut across country and came up Owl Creek Mountains to the vicinity of Black Mountain. From there they went straight to the Shoshoni Indian Agency.

The warriors came to the top of the hill west of Camp Brown, "not over a mile from the flagstaff in the parade ground." Then they held council, during which they saw something which seemed a bad omen. The consultation abruptly ended, and the hostiles fled homeward. They did not falter in their march until they encountered the discomfited Arapahoes. From them they learned of the battle and its results. Instead of sympathizing with their allies, they jeered them for holding out and not making the onslaught which had originally been intended.[32]

Two weeks after the Bates Battle, smoke signals were observed on the hills. Following General Sheridan's suggestion of night marching, Captain Bates and his command went to an old rendezvous site, about sixty miles east of Pacific Springs. There they found evidence of a recent large encampment. Looking up the trail, the scouts discovered eight Sioux. They gave chase and managed to intercept them. When the scouts returned, they had seven ponies, one mule, and a scalp.

[31] Tensleep means that it is a ten-day (or -night) journey from Fort Laramie to that point.

[32] Patten obviously gained his facts from the Arapahoes who were later placed on the Wind River Reservation.

CHAPTER FOURTEEN

'Red Allies of the White Man

WASHAKIE AND HIS INDIANS returned from their annual hunt in February, 1875, with little meat and few robes. They were discouraged; some were sick. Many of their horses had died—from what cause, we are not informed. The chief reported that he had returned to the Bates Battlefield not long after the engagement and that he had found three tipis still standing. He had counted thirty dead Arapahoes. The odor was so bad at the bluff that he did not examine it. He was convinced that there were at least eighty killed in the battle. Robes and other property, including some plantation hoes issued by the government, were strewn about.[1]

In July, J. K. Moore, the proprietor of the trading post; two officers; and Maghee were on a fishing excursion on the North Fork of the Popo Agie when they were surprised by hostiles. The white men could see them driving off the livestock belonging to a settler. A fourteen-year-old boy dashed out unarmed to stop them. The boy's uncle, seizing a gun, went to his assistance. Then the boy's sister, knowing that the two had but a small number of cartridges, gathered about a hundred rounds in her apron and rushed to the scene. This disconcerted the Indians, who fled, taking the settler's livestock with them.

This incident took place so near Camp Brown that shots could be heard; then the marauders came in sight some distance away. Racing around the base of a butte, the soldiers surprised them. In fact, one of the raiders was in the process of patting another on the back in a congratulatory manner.

The hostiles made every effort to keep the stock, but upon

[1] *Post Record,* 40–41.

reaching a crossing of the Popo Agie, they found it expedient to change mounts and abandon the other horses and cattle to save themselves. The cavalry had to give up the chase. Upon making a scout next day, it was found that the party was at least forty strong.

At Camp Brown, thirteen log houses—sixteen by eighteen feet, and one and a half stories high—had been built, with old-style, nine-plate plantation stoves for cooking. Although Superintendent Irwin had given encouraging reports before, he reluctantly admitted that the school on the reservation was not a success and that, at the time, there was neither a minister nor a missionary.[2]

Many disgruntled Wind River Shoshonis had drifted to Utah to be baptized by the Mormons. According to Irwin, the Saints had advised them to leave their reservation and drive out the gentiles, but "timely intervention stopped the trouble." He did not specify the nature of the intervention. He said merely that after the Indians had returned to their reservation they were ashamed of the affair.[3]

By the mid-seventies, open hostilities had broken out in the Sioux country. As a result, all tribes were ordered to their reservations in January, 1876. When the Sioux chiefs Sitting Bull, Crazy Horse, and some of their allies ignored the summons, soldiers were sent to round them up and force them back upon their reservations. General Sheridan ordered General Alfred Terry and General George Crook to close in on them. In order to understand the nature of the difficulties and the attitude of the Shoshonis, we need turn back for a moment to 1866.

A council had been called that year at Fort Laramie to treat with the Sioux for a road (the Bozeman Trail) through their hunting grounds in the Powder River country. While the Indians were assembled, supply trains made an untimely arrival. As one of the Sioux said, "Great Father sends us presents and wants new road, but white chief [Colonel Henry B. Carrington] goes with soldiers to steal road before Indian can say yes or no." The Sioux, declaring vengeance, stalked out of the council. The new road,

2 Irwin's report, *House Exec. Doc. 1*, Pt. 5, 43 Cong., 2 sess. (1639), 578–79.
3 Irwin's report, *House Exec. Doc. 1*, Pt. 5, 44 Cong., 1 sess. (1680), 877.

northward to the gold mines of Montana, was to cost the government more than a fine herding horse, for the three forts—Phil Kearny, Reno, and C. F. Smith—that were established along the route were under constant pressure by the Sioux.

In July, 1867, Superintendent F. H. Head discussed the matter with Washakie, whom he considered "the most sagacious, honorable, and intelligent Indian among the uncivilized tribes."[4] The chief, who was able to appraise the matter at a distance, made several significant remarks. In fairness to the Sioux, he said that the Bozeman Trail would ruin their hunting grounds. It was an old story to him, for he would never recover from the effects of the various trails and cutoffs through his land.

He said that the Sioux had entertained a friendly feeling toward the whites until the opening of the road. Knowing full well what the consequences would be, they threatened the lives of all who ventured upon it. Yet hostilities did not begin at once, for the white men said that there was no other way to reach the Montana gold fields. The Sioux soon found that this was not true, as few civilians passed along the road. Soldiers were sent to man the three forts on the supposition that they must protect the "travelers," but traffic consisted mainly of wagons supplying the forts. Furthermore, the soldiers gave whisky to the braves and seduced their women. Counciling among themselves, the Indians came to the conclusion that the road was made to give employment to the soldiers and to destroy their hunting grounds. Therefore, they decided that they would rather die fighting than starve to death.

Head amplified Washakie's statements by saying that the road was secured by speculators, owning or expecting to own certain lucrative toll bridges, roads, and ferries thereon. Although claims were made for the road, light-draft steamboats were carrying the bulk of the freight to Montana up the Missouri River. He labeled the Bozeman Trail as "one of the most complete and expensive humbugs of the day."

The Trail proved more expensive than anyone realized at the time. It was estimated that about two hundred white men lost

[4] Head to Commissioner of Indian Affairs, July 30, 1867, I.O.R.

their lives in the Phil Kearny area before the road was ordered closed (1868) and troops were withdrawn. The immediate reason for the withdrawal was that the Union Pacific was being built through southern Wyoming, and it was necessary to keep the Sioux north of the Platte, out of the way of the construction crew.

It was easier to keep the red men in their area than to keep the white men out of Sioux country after gold was discovered in the Black Hills of South Dakota. The resentment engendered by the Bozeman Trail was brought to a climax by the influx of reckless gold seekers. The result was the Indian wars of 1876, in which the Shoshonis played a minor though significant role.

Although Washakie had defended the Sioux in their indignation over the Bozeman Trail, he stood steadfastly by the white man when hostilities broke out. Learning that General Crook was planning a campaign during the summer of 1876, he determined to help. He sent word that he hoped to join the soldiers at Fort Fetterman, the supply station for the forts along the Bozeman Trail. But when a contingent of 120 Shoshonis left Camp Brown, he was not with them. He had been told by runners that the Utes and Bannocks wanted to join him; hence, he awaited their arrival.

A band of 176 Crow warriors, with their chiefs Old Crow, Medicine Crow, and Good Heart, arrived at Crook's camp on June 14. They were anxious to fight the Sioux, who had robbed them of the Powder River hunting grounds. Through the eyes of John G. Bourke, a captain in Crook's command, we can see them with "their grotesque head-dresses, variegated garments, wild little ponies, and warlike accoutrements."[5]

The battalion commanders and staff officers were assembled in front of Crook's tent when the Shoshonis, temporary allies of the Crows, came upon the scene. "Glittering lances and brightly polished weapons of fire" heralded their approach as they galloped up to headquarters and came left-front into line. "No trained warriors of civilized arms ever executed the movement

[5] The above account is based primarily on Captain John G. Bourke's first-hand account of the showing which the Shoshoni warriors made while serving with Crook. *On the Border with Crook*, 303–57.

more prettily," said Bourke. Admiration was voiced even by their traditional enemies, the Crows.

The Shoshonis, "resplendent in all the fantastic adornment of feathers, beads, brass buttons, bells, scarlet cloth, and flashing lances," passed in review before the General. Aware of the favorable impression they made, they responded to the order to file off to the right by proudly moving with clockwork precision. During the "big talk" that evening, Old Crow expressed the feelings of his people toward the Sioux:

> The great white chief will hear his Indian brother. These are our lands by inheritance. The Great Spirit gave them to our fathers, but the Sioux stole them from us. They hunt upon our mountains. They fish in our streams. They have stolen our horses. They have murdered our squaws, our children. What white man has done these things to us? The face of the pale face has ever been red to the Crow. ("Ugh!" "Ugh!" "Hey!")
>
> The scalp of no white man hangs in our lodges. They are thick as grass in the wigwams of the Sioux. ("Ugh!") The great white chief will lead us against no other tribe of red men. Our war is with the Sioux and only them.
>
> We want back our lands. We want their women for our slaves —to work for us as our women have had to work for them. We want their horses for our young men, and their mules for our squaws. The Sioux have trampled upon our hearts. We shall spit upon their scalps. ("Ugh!" "Hey!" and terrific yelling.) The great white chief sees that my young men have come to fight. No Sioux shall see their backs. Where the white warrior goes, there shall we be also. It is good.[6]

The council was dismissed early so that the Shoshonis, who had ridden sixty miles that day, might have their rest. However, the Indians were too busy preparing for battle to feel fatigue. Bourke described the nocturnal scene:

> A long series of monotonous howls, shrieks, groans, and nasal yells, emphasized by a perfectly ear-piercing succession of thumps

[6] John F. Finerty, of the *Chicago Times,* was one of five correspondents with Crook. *War-Path and Bivouac,* 103–104.

upon drums improvised from "parfleche" (tanned buffalo skin), attracted nearly all the soldiers and many of the officers not on duty to the allied camp. Peeping into the different lodges was very much like peeping through the key-holes of Hades.

Crouched around little fires not affording as much light as an ordinary tallow candle, the swarthy figures of the naked and half-naked Indians were visible, moving and chanting in unison with some leader. No words were distinguishable; the ceremony partook of the nature of an abominable incantation, and as far as I could judge had a semireligious character.

One of the Indians, mounted on a pony and stripped almost naked, passed along from lodge to lodge, stopping in front of each and calling upon the Great Spirit (so our interpreter said) to send them plenty of scalps, a Big Sioux village, and lots of ponies. The inmates would respond with, if possible, increased vehemence.

According to Bourke, a patient in the infirmary died with the "wild requiem" ringing in his ears. The army's small herd of beef cattle became frightened and broke for the hills while the ceremony continued unabated.

The next day, as the white soldiers prepared for battle, the Indians made their preparations in their own way.[7] Squads of young warriors devoted their attention to their rifles, the Shoshonis being armed with the latest .45-caliber models, which they "kept with scrupulous care in regular gun-racks."

Some were sharpening lances or adorning them with feathers and paint; others were making "coup" sticks, which are long willow branches about twelve feet from end to end, stripped of leaves and bark, and having each some distinctive mark, in the way of feathers, bells, fur, paint, or bright-colored cloth or flannel. These serve a singular purpose: the great object of the Shoshones, Crows, Cheyennes, and Dakotas in making war is to set the enemy afoot. This done, his destruction is rendered more easy if not more certain. Ponies are also the wealth of conquerors; hence, in dividing the spoils, each man claims the animals first struck by his "coup" stick.

Tom Cosgrove, leader of the scouts, demonstrated that he had learned his lesson well while serving as captain in the Civil War.

[7] Bourke, *On the Border with Crook*, 319–20.

The discipline and good order in his command caused his men to show up to a better advantage than the Crows, according to Bourke. Accompanying Cosgrove when Crook's forces began their march were two fellow Texans (Yarnell and Eckles), the only other white men with the Shoshoni contingent.

When Crook crossed Tongue River on June 16, the Indians who had been marching on the flank passed his column and took the lead, with their medicine men in front. One of them kept up a chant, as he proclaimed the wrongs that had been done by the enemy.

During the afternoon, the Indians gave a frenzied War Dance, while scouts went ahead to examine the country. They returned at great speed to report that they had spotted a large herd of buffalo, running away from a Sioux hunting party. During the time when General Crook was arranging the details of the march, the excited warriors were racing their ponies to put them out of breath. After their breath was regained, the ponies were said to be able to endure a day-long battle. Also during that busy afternoon thirty buffalo were killed, and the choicest pieces were packed away for future use. Bourke described the feast that accompanied the butchering:

> The Indians ate the buffalo liver raw, sometimes sprinkling a pinch of gall upon it; the warm raw liver alone is not bad for a hungry man, tasting very much like a raw oyster. The entrails are also much in favor with the aborigines; they are cleaned, wound round a ramrod or something akin to it . . . and held in the hot ashes until cooked through; they make a palatable dish.[8]

Crook's command bivouacked that night on the headwaters of the Rosebud (Montana). At daylight next day (June 17, 1876) they began marching down the stream. Suddenly they heard shots fired in the valley to the north. Two Crow scouts—one badly wounded—returned. "Sioux! Sioux!" they cried. Thus began the famous Battle of the Rosebud.

Immediate plans were made to strengthen the lines, the Shoshonis taking up position with Major A. B. Cain's forces in the

[8] *Ibid.*, 310.

hills to the left. Crazy Horse, said to have been emboldened by a superior strength, covered the hills to the north with about fifteen hundred warriors, the others remaining concealed. The Sioux, advancing at full run, were repulsed by Cain's forces. After regrouping, they charged again. Bourke, who was in a position to see what was going on, tells of the way in which the Shoshonis distinguished themselves:

> . . . this second advance was gallantly met by a counter-charge of the Shoshones, who, under their [war] chief, "Luishaw," took the Sioux and Cheyennes in flank and scattered them before them. . . . There was a headlong rush for about two hundred yards, which drove the enemy back in confusion; then there was a sudden halt, and very many of the Shoshones jumped down from their ponies and began firing from the ground; the others who remained mounted threw themselves alongside of their horses' necks, so that there would be few good marks presented to the aim of the enemy. Then, in response to some signal or cry which, of course, I did not understand, we were off again, this time for good, and right into the midst of the hostiles, who had been halted by a steep hill directly in their front.

Tigee, who had gained distinction at the Bates Battle, was credited with bravery when he risked his life to keep Captain Guy V. Henry from falling into the hands of the enemy. Henry had been dangerously wounded in the head. During the fight, an unnamed Shoshoni boy obtained the permission of his chief to return to a spring to prepare himself for his first battle. He had painted only one side of his face when he was struck by a Sioux who lifted his scalp.

Meanwhile, Major George M. Randall was leading an attack against the Sioux on the opposite flank. Crook reached the heights, from which he could observe the enemy. Although able to withstand the onslaught, his troops were not strong enough to prevent the Sioux and their Northern Cheyenne allies from carrying away their dead and wounded. When the General ordered a final advance of his whole line, the Sioux and Cheyennes left him in undisputed possession of the battlefield.

The Shoshonis reportedly suffered "large" casualties and lost a "tremendous number" of their best warriors.[9] This is largely supposition, as there is no definite record to show how many red allies of the white men were killed. We know that the boy who wanted to be a warrior was one.

During the night-long lamentation, the Shoshonis vengefully cut two Sioux bodies to pieces in retaliation for a similar act committed by the Sioux upon the body of one of the soldiers. Then they buried the boy with the dead white men in a deep trench dug in the bank of the Rosebud, near the water line. The bodies, laid in a row, were covered with earth and stones.

When camp broke, the soldiers marched over the graves to obliterate them so that they would not be discovered by the hostiles. As the soldiers looked toward the battlefield, they saw several Sioux riding back to the site. Then the warriors dismounted, sat down, and bowed their heads. When asked the meaning of the strange conduct, the Shoshoni and Crow scouts explained that they were weeping for their dead. They were not molested.

The care taken of the Shoshoni wounded pleased Bourke. He observed that the medicine men knew how "to make a fair article of splint from the twigs of the willow, and that they depended upon such appliances in cases of fracture fully as much as they did upon the singing which took up so much of their time, and was so obnoxious to the unfortunate whites whose tents were near it."

Bourke characterized the behavior of the Shoshonis and Crows during the battle as excellent. Luishaw, the war chief, appeared to great advantage, "mounted on a fiery pony, he himself naked to the waist and wearing one of the gorgeous head-dresses of eagle feathers sweeping far along the ground behind his pony's tail."

By a quirk of circumstance, Washakie was not even present at the Battle of the Rosebud, although most writers give him credit for taking part.[10] The error may be attributed to the somewhat

[9] Robert B. David, *Finn Burnett*, 350.

[10] Hebard, *Washakie*, 180–91; J. W. Vaughn, *With Crook on the Rosebud*, 23, 58, 62; and Sidney O. Reynolds, "The Redskin Who Saved the White Man's Hide," *American Heritage*, Vol. XI, No. 2 (February, 1960), 50.

doubtful word of Frank Grouard, scout, who affirmed that the Crows arrived at three o'clock in the afternoon on June 15 (Bourke gave the date as June 14), and the Shoshonis two hours later.[11] When an alarm signal was sounded, Grouard said that he went out to learn the cause.

> I found it was the Snake Indians with Tom Cosgrove as their interpreter coming to join the command. I think he had one hundred sixty-four or one hundred eighty-two Indians. I am not certain which. Their chief Washakie was with them.

No official documents place Washakie with Crook at the time of the battle. The Post Record, indicating that he did not leave with the first contingent but waited for the Utes and Bannocks, is substantiated by both Captain Bourke and James Finerty, a newspaper reporter with Crook. The latter gave the names of the Shoshoni chiefs at Rosebud as Wesha and Nawkee (perhaps Norkuk). Although Wesha has been identified as Washakie,[12] he was probably Wisha, a subchief or headman who was a spokesman at the Brunot Council and a signer of the treaty of 1872. Although Luishaw was described as war chief, Cosgrove, in command of the scouts, had obviously drilled the Indians, as they appeared in excellent military form. "Washakie's two sons"[13] were mentioned, but the chief of the Shoshonis was not mentioned until after a second contingent arrived from Camp Brown (July 11), twenty-four days after the battle of the Rosebud.

Soon after the battle the Shoshonis and Crows left their white comrades to return to their reservation for a Scalp Dance, following which they planned to return. Five remained with Crook to help in any way needed.[14] When Cosgrove and his men reached Camp Brown on June 25, they confirmed the report that had been brought back three days before that Crook had been worsted.

Although the Rosebud had been a drawn battle, it was, nevertheless, a strategic defeat for Crook because he was unable to take

[11] Frank Grouard, *Frank Grouard, Life and Adventures,* 221.
[12] Hebard, *Washakie,* 183.
[13] Hebard identifies Washakie's sons as Dick and Bishop.
[14] Bourke, *On the Border with Crook,* 319–20.

the offensive and strike a decisive blow at the enemy camp.[15] He did, however, succeed in driving the enemy from the battlefield, though he was unable to pursue them. Crook and some of his men claimed a victory, but even so the General was effectively kept in his place while the hostiles assembled their striking force elsewhere.

Early in July forty Utes arrived at Camp Brown, only to find that Washakie, tired of waiting for them, had left with his warriors.[16] Bourke and Finerty, seeing Washakie for the first time on July 11, were impressed by his dignified appearance.

Messengers finally brought an explanation for the Utes' delay. They had been prevented by their agent from taking part in the campaign. General Robert Williams, of Omaha, learning of the matter, appealed to the Department of the Interior, which directed their enlistment. Tardiness of the Utes was all that prevented Washakie from taking part in the Battle of the Rosebud. This must have been a grave disappointment to him.

No reason can be found for the Bannocks' failure to arrive as planned. It is possible that they were too busy trying to find sustenance to make such an extensive trip. Rations had been completely exhausted at their agency in April. When the children cried for bread, and they had to be told there was none, the Indians left "with sad and sorrowful hearts."[17]

While Washakie was with Crook, he would go each morning to a hilltop to scan the country through powerful field glasses. Then he would report his observations to the General. His braves would drill daily under his orders, while he bore the banner of the tribe—a standard of eagle feathers attached to a lance-staff twelve feet in length. The warriors, wearing a small piece of white material in their headdress as a distinguishing mark, were accompanied by Bourke and several soldiers so that recruits who were arriving would not mistake them for hostiles.

While drilling, the warriors moved in a double column. Riding

[15] George E. Hyde, *Red Cloud's Folk*, 263–65.
[16] *Post Record*, 11.
[17] *Report of Commissioner of Indian Affairs*, 1876, 42–43.

proudly, they were quiet until their leaders broke out in a war song. Then away they would go down the valley about three miles, while the sound of more than two hundred lusty voices would fill the air. According to Bourke:

> . . . at a signal from Washakie, the column turned, and at another, formed front into line and proceeded slowly for about fifty yards. Washakie was endeavoring to explain something to me, but the noise of the ponies' hoofs . . . and my ignorance of his language were impediments to a full understanding of what the old gentleman[18] was driving at. I learned afterwards that he was assuring me that I was now to see some drill such as the Shoshones alone could execute.[19]

The drill was the "charge" for which the Shoshonis were famous, the maneuver they had proudly executed when the first missionaries had come along the trail. It was a wild and yet orderly demonstration of speed and control:

> He [Washakie] waved his hands; the line spread out as skirmishers took about two yards' interval from knee to knee. Then somebody—Washakie or one of the lieutenants—yelled a command in a shrill treble; that's all I remember. The ponies broke into one frantic rush for camp, riding over sagebrush, rocks, stumps, bunches of grass, buffalo heads—it mattered not the least when they went over it—the warriors all the while squealing, yelling, chanting their war-songs, or howling like coyotes.
>
> The ponies entered into the whole business and needed not the heels and "quirts" which were plied against their willing flanks. In the centre of the line rode old Washakie; abreast of him the eagle standard. It was an exciting and exhilarating race, and the force preserved an excellent alignment.
>
> Only one thought occupied my mind during this charge, and that thought was what fools we were not to incorporate these nomads— the finest light cavalry in the world—into our permanent military force. With five thousand such men, and our aboriginal population

---

[18] Washakie at this time was believed to be either seventy-two or seventy-eight. The Shoshonis did not keep accurate record of their ages, but there is evidence that he was born either in 1798 or in 1804.

[19] *On the Border with Crook*, 337–44.

would readily furnish that number, we could harass and annoy any troops that might have the audacity to land on our coasts, and worry them to death.[20]

Not wearied by the daily drill, the braves would join in pony races during the evening. They proved themselves adept also in gambling, fishing, and hunting. On clear nights they held serenades. Again Bourke said:

> Once when the clouds had rolled by and the pale light of the moon was streaming down upon tents and pack-trains, wagons and sleeping animals, the Shoshones became especially vociferous and I learned from the interpreter that they were singing to the moon. This was one of the most pronounced examples of moon worship coming under my observation.[21]

Washakie's warriors had their own method of fishing. They would make an improvised net or dam, which allowed the water to pass through but stopped all solids. Then two or three braves, mounting their ponies, would lash the water with long, forked poles while they sang their medicine song and drove the fish upstream into the net. The frightened fish, darting forward, would be held at the dam until the Indians had caught enough to fill their gunny sacks.

General Sheridan, in over-all command, had ordered Crook to await the arrival of reinforcements under General Wesley Merritt. Then the two were to make connections with General Alfred Terry, who with a strong force was coming from the east. Only by their combined strength could they chastise the Sioux. After the arrival of Merritt, Washakie is quoted as saying to Crook, who was impatient to meet Terry:

> The Sioux and Cheyennes have three to your one, even now that you have been reenforced; why not let them alone for a few days? They cannot subsist the great number of warriors and men

---

[20] *Ibid.*, 340–41.

[21] According to Lowie ("Notes on Shoshonean Ethnography," *loc. cit.*, 309), the Shoshonis thought that the moon died and came to life again. This may have been during a change of the moon.

in their camp, and will have to scatter for pasturage and meat; they'll begin to fight among themselves about the plunder taken on the battlefield, and many will want to slip into the agencies and rejoin their families.[22]

Two scouting parties were sent out (one made up of Shoshonis under Washakie) which went as far as the head of Little Bighorn and thence to the Canyon of the Bighorn. They found that the hostiles had hundreds of lodges and that, as the chief suspected, they were hard pressed for food. This was indicated by the fact that dog and pony bones were found scattered at their abandoned campgrounds. The hostiles had by now moved northeast toward Powder River.

General George A. Custer, with General Terry's command, might not have led his troops so recklessly to their deaths had he been similarly advised. Terry, hoping to round up the Indians and return them to their reservation without bloodshed, had told Custer not to follow the Indian trail if it led in the direction of the Little Bighorn, but to await the arrival of reinforcements. Custer disobeyed orders, and as a result his entire command of 268 men lost their lives in the resulting massacre, in Montana, June 25, 1876.

Among the recruits in Crook's command was an Indian called Ute John, said to belong to the Ute tribe. Since he was a well-known character at the Wind River Reservation before and after the Indian wars, he may have been a Weber Ute Shoshoni. He boasted that he had been "washed" by the Mormons three times in a single year and that they had given him "heap biled shirt." He was on the friendliest terms with General Crook, whom he would address without hesitancy by saying, "Hello, Cluke, how you gettin' on? Where you tink dem Crazy Hoss en Settin' Bull is now, Cluke?"[23]

The Shoshonis and the Utes delighted in tearing down the burial scaffolds that were found in the Sioux country. There they sometimes acquired fine bows and arrows and even nickel-plated

[22] Bourke, *On the Border with Crook*, 341.
[23] *Ibid.*, 349.

revolvers. One scaffold, supposed to be full of bad medicine, was feared by all but Ute John, whose reward was a nest of field mice.

After Crook, Merritt, and Terry had joined forces, Washakie took exception to the slow-moving mule-driven supply trains and threatened to leave. Besides, it was annuity time, and he wanted to return to the reservation. Even though he had missed the Rosebud battle, his services to Crook had proved invaluable. As a consequence, the government saw fit in 1878 to change the name of Camp Brown to Fort Washakie in his honor. Also, President U. S. Grant, recognizing Washakie's helpfulness, presented him with a handsome saddle with silver mountings, a token of appreciation for his loyalty.[24] At the presentation service the agent prompted Washakie to express a word of appreciation which might be sent back to Washington. The old chief was thoughtful a moment. Then he made his most famous statement:

> Do a kindness to a Frenchman [white man], he feels it in his head and his tongue speaks; do a kindness to an Indian, he feels it in his heart. The heart has no tongue.

Washakie, like Captain Jim, often expressed a wish to visit the nation's capitol, but there are no records to prove that his wish was ever realized. He did, however, have the honor of being visited by President Chester A. Arthur in 1883. Upon that occasion he did not go with the other leaders of his tribe to greet the President. Instead, dressed in his best attire, Washakie stayed in his lodge and waited for the President to call.

After returning from Crook's camp, the Shoshonis received $5,000 worth of cattle at the agency; then they continued on to Owl Creek. Louisant (probably Luishaw) developed a case of rheumatism along the way and had to be taken to the post hospital. Soon returning to his tipi, he gave as his excuse for leaving the hospital that he could not stand the bedbugs.

In October, Captain Randall, of Crook's staff, came to Camp Brown in quest of Shoshoni scouts. He pronounced them "far the

[24] J. K. Moore, Jr., of Lander, Wyoming, recalls seeing this saddle.

most serviceable of any to be found on the plains." Again Tom Cosgrove started lining up recruits. On the fourteenth, nearly one hundred Shoshonis reported ready to enlist. Armed and equipped, they left, this time without Washakie, who sent word to his friend General Crook that he was sending two of his sons, but he did not like to run the risk to his own health of a winter campaign. He promised that he would come later if needed. Ko-na-ya, Washakie's oldest son, was captain and Sar-a-gaunt, color sergeant, according to the Post Record. Numbering ninety-five, the warriors marched in twos, forming an excellent line to receive their guidon. Several, including Cosgrove, took their Indian wives.

After the recruits had left to join Crook, and the Shoshonis under Washakie had moved camp, word reached the agency that the Crows, Bannocks, and Nez Percés intended to break into open hostility in the spring. Two scouts, Edmo LeClair and Tom Harris, were sent in search of the Shoshoni encampment to find out if the chief could verify the report. When Edmo returned a week later, he said that he found Washakie and his Indians north of Point Rock with two hundred lodges of Crows. Now professing their friendship, the Crows were trying to ascertain what part Washakie would take in case of an outbreak in the spring. They claimed that they had enough arms and ammunition to fight a long war. Washakie gave them no satisfaction, for he stated that he would not fight against the white man.

Although Sitting Bull had fled into Canada following the Custer massacre, Crazy Horse and many Sioux warriors were still roaming the country. In November, Humpy (a Shoshoni scout) rushed to Camp Brown at two o'clock one morning to report more than one thousand Sioux lodges in Hidden Canyon at Point Rock. Tig-a-in-dum, a band leader, with fifty lodges had inadvertently camped near their rendezvous. As a result, the Shoshonis were attacked early one morning. After a day-long fight, they lost seven scalps but managed to take two.

Five days later signal smokes were seen north of the post, and it was supposed that Washakie might be corralled. Fifty men with their howitzer were sent to investigate. Tom Harris met them along the way, and he assured them that there was no cause for alarm as Washakie was safe on Owl Creek.

Harris was convinced that the Crows had been raiding, for he had observed a number of beef cattle and some shod horses in their village. He felt that they needed to be chastised; and he declared that if the military would help, he would settle with them, as he predicted an easy victory. The Harris plan did not materialize, as he was killed a few nights later at Lander by a drunken Mexican, Francisco Franco.

Cosgrove and his Shoshonis, returning to Camp Brown with about one hundred Cheyenne ponies and many scalps, gave an account of the attack on Dull Knife's camp.[25] They told that the village was destroyed in a savage fight. The Shoshonis had reason to look with satisfaction upon the defeat of Dull Knife. The preceding October, while on the annual hunt, Washakie's band was attacked by the Cheyenne chief and about four hundred of his warriors. The battle lasted until sundown, when the hostiles withdrew. The Shoshonis put up good resistance, as their casualties amounted to only one man, two women, and two children.[26]

Not long after the Dull Knife Battle, Camp Brown was alerted to be on the watch for raiding parties. Hostiles opened fire on six white men on Popo Agie. Barney Hill, the only survivor, was badly wounded. He told of a crawling fight that had taken place after the white men's horses were killed.

On May 6, 1877, Red Cloud induced Crazy Horse to give himself up at Fort Robinson, Nebraska. A month later Generals Sheridan and Crook and their staff of officers arrived in Wind River Valley. They camped just below the post. Two months later General Merritt arrived to organize an expedition against the hostile Nez Percés. They had gone on the warpath because of "unauthorized intrusion of lawless whites on lands which the

---

[25] George Bird Grinnell gives the Cheyenne point of view regarding the destruction of Dull Knife's village in *The Fighting Cheyennes*, 259–82.

[26] Patten's report, *House Exec. Doc. 1*, Pt. 5, 45 Cong., 2 sess., VIII (1800), 605–606.

Indians claimed as theirs by virtue of occupancy from time immemorial."[27]

Washakie may have been in sympathy with the Nez Percés, but he gave no indication of it. The Bannocks who took part with the soldiers were encouraged by the army to do so in order to give their aggressive spirit an outlet so that it would not be directed against the whites. Buffalo Horn, a rising young Bannock warrior, took an active part in the campaign, where he made a reputation for himself by his daring. Indians not serving with the expedition against the Nez Percés were forced to remain on their reservations so that they would not take sides against the troops.

This did not prevent war hysteria from spreading. The Bannocks, who had been without a strong chief since the death of Taghee, were quick to rally around the fearless Buffalo Horn. Tyhee had been induced to become chief when Tendoy refused to leave the Lemhi Valley. But now the Bannocks were casting him aside in favor of a more warlike leader. A number of incidents costing the lives of white men followed. Agent W. H. Danilson, at Fort Hall, called for help to prevent an anticipated war.

Three companies of infantry were temporarily ordered to the fort in December, 1877. Authorities arrested one of two Indians believed to have been guilty of murdering settlers, but they were unable to force the Bannocks to turn over the other, Tambiago. They finally apprehended him, arrested him along with certain members of his family, and sentenced him to be hanged. About fifty of the Shoshonis, foreseeing trouble, moved away from Fort Hall.

In the spring of 1878 threat of starvation again caused the Bannocks to leave the reservation for their hunting ground. Buffalo Horn, who had proved his dependability as a scout, was issued ammunition—for hunting purposes. The Indians became infuriated when they found settlers' hogs rooting up their precious camass bulbs. There were also about 2,500 head of the white man's

[27] James Mooney, "The Ghost Dance Religion and the Sioux Outbreak of 1890" (hereinafter cited as "The Ghost Dance"), *Fourteenth Annual Report*, B.A.E.

cattle grazing at Camas Prairie. This incensed Buffalo Horn and his people, who were now definitely intent upon war. They killed a number of settlers and drove out others.

Before his execution Tambiago cited as a reason for the disturbances that the settlers were destroying the food supply at Camas Prairie. He also said that the Bannocks objected to the agent and the missionary at Fort Hall. Thoroughly aroused by the execution of Tambiago, the hostiles tried to enlist the aid of the Paiutes and Western Shoshonis. Chief Winnemucca, of the Paiutes, flatly refused to give any assistance. As a result, he was later said to have been held a virtual prisoner.[28]

Captain Sam, of the Western Shoshonis, not only refused to help, but he also gave valuable information to his agent. He reported that the Bannocks were bent on destroying the railroad. After killing all the whites in the area, they planned, he said, to exterminate all Indians who had opposed them. Then they would divide their world among their allies.

The Shoshokos "felt bad" over the uncertainty of their future, but they did not show their resentment by joining the hostiles. The land set aside for them was already claimed by the white man, who took most of the irrigation water. Old Timoak, the only recognized chief of the tribe, was their spokesman in council. He was determined to remain in Ruby Valley, but he wanted good water and land for his people. He recommended that Duck Valley be set aside as a Shoshoni reservation for all of the tribe south of the railroad.

When Timoak refused to join the hostiles, the Bannocks threatened to kill him if he tried in any way to interfere with their alliance with the Paiutes. He had his scout, Bruno John, ready to spread the alarm among the ranchers if hostilities broke out, and his Indians later served as guides and assisted the army in many ways.[29]

[28] Sarah Winnemucca Hopkins, in an impassioned account of the Bannock War (*Life among the Piutes*, 146–90), claimed that her people were forced to fight.

[29] Levi A. Ghem, *Report, House Exec. Doc. 1*, Pt. 5, 45 Cong., 3 sess. (1850), 600–602.

Tendoy tried to keep his Northern Bannocks in check, but he could not prevent them from raiding. There were a few Umatillas who saw fit to join the hostiles, who consisted mostly of Buffalo Horn's Bannocks and Northern Paiutes. The latter were so discontented with their agent, W. V. Rinehart of the Malheur Agency, that they welcomed a chance to go on the warpath.

The Bannocks set out to raid the countryside while the Paiutes assembled. Killing settlers and driving off their horses along the way, 150 warriors crossed the Snake River and proceeded toward Bruneau Valley on June 2, 1878.

Before Captain R. F. Bernard and his forces from Fort Boise could catch up with the warriors, a group of volunteers from Silver City, Idaho, clashed with about sixty Bannocks on June 8. In the fierce fighting which followed, Buffalo Horn was mortally wounded, whether by the white men or by a Paiute scout we are not sure.[30] The death of their leader caused the Bannocks to be all the more determined to wage a ruthless war.

Oytes, a Paiute prophet, advised Egan, the war chief, to join the Bannocks, contrary to his better judgment. The latter gave as his reason for fighting not that he expected victory but that he thought the Great Father at Washington might give him more supplies, the way he had when Egan quit fighting during the Paiute War (1860). Besides he thought that the Father in Washington might not try to make his people work.[31] Egan, convinced that his people wanted war, joined the Bannocks and assumed leadership of the hostile forces. Moving northward, they burned and pillaged as they went.

Their destination was the Umatilla Reservation, which they finally reached after several battles with the soldiers who were ordered by General O. O. Howard, in command of the field troops, to intercept them. The hostiles succeeded in enlisting the aid of some of the Umatillas, but most of the tribe refused to leave the agency.

As General Nelson A. Miles's troops were at breakfast one

[30] Hopkins, *Life among the Piutes,* 146.
[31] *Report of the Commissioner of Indian Affairs,* 1878, 103–104.

morning, the hostiles — about four hundred strong — attacked. There were losses on both sides in the day-long battle that resulted. Before Miles had left the general area, some of the Umatillas joined his ranks. According to Sarah Winnemucca's account of the battle, the Umatillas had been secretly helping the Bannocks. Then someone led them to believe that one thousand dollars had been offered for the capture of Egan. U-ma-pine, the Umatilla chief, wanted the reward. He sent about forty of his warriors to capture Egan on July 15, under the guise of joining his cause. They tolled Egan and seven of his men outside their camp to discuss terms. Quickly they overpowered them and attempted to take them to the army camp. Egan and three of his men who tried to escape were killed and scalped.

Staggered by the loss of another leader, the hostiles began breaking up and scattering in small but still dangerous groups. Most of the Paiutes were heading back toward the Malheur Reservation, but the Bannocks seemed intent upon trying to reach Sitting Bull, who had not been brought under military control. Every effort was made to intercept these Indians as they went through the buffalo country.

Lieutenant H. S. Bishop, who had launched his expedition against the hostiles from Camp Brown, took with him 25 soldiers and 160 Shoshonis and Arapahoes.[32] They marched to the head of Big Wind River and sent scouting parties into the Yellowstone Park area to ascertain the whereabouts of the Bannocks. Two days later the Shoshoni scouts of Bishop's command returned with 7 Bannock prisoners, whom they captured at the head of Dry Creek, a tributary of Big Wind River, about 5 miles north of the post. Later Lieutenant Bishop surprised a small party of Bannocks and killed 1 man and captured several prisoners, including women and children.

The last large-scale attack upon the Bannocks took place near Clark's Fork of Yellowstone River, where Miles overtook a camp of 20 lodges. While a cannon massacred the hostiles, the Crow scouts drove away 250 of their horses. Lieutenant Bishop captured

[32] *Ibid.*, 103–105.

some of those escaping from the battlefield, the paths from which were described as "slippery with blood" as many of the wounded had been dragged away.

Those who were not killed by Miles or captured by Bishop managed to lose themselves in the rugged country or drift unnoticed back to Fort Hall. Hostile action came to an end in October, thus concluding the Bannock War which cost the government more than $556,000. The dead amounted to nine soldiers and thirty-one civilians, while eighteen were wounded. Known Indian casualties, listed by the government, were seventy-eight killed and sixty-six wounded, although the number may have been three times that great.[33]

[33] George F. Brimlow, *The Bannock Indian War of 1878*, 197–99.

CHAPTER FIFTEEN

Reservations

THE LAST OF THE RESISTANCE in the Shoshonean territory was broken with the defeat of the Bannocks, who were so reduced in numbers that they could no longer cause trouble. They were fortunate, nevertheless, in being given reservations in their original homeland, even though confinement was naturally resented by the roving bands. As some of the natives had already begun farming before the slow-moving government machinery could produce satisfactory reservations, they were permitted to remain where they were.

Some of the Northwestern Shoshonis of Box Elder County, Utah, for example, had homesteaded approximately 17,500 acres of land before the reservations were created. Taking up land at what became known as Washakie Indian Village, they improved their acreage and began to raise good crops under the supervision and direction of early Mormon settlers.[1] This settlement claims the distinction of being the only all-Indian Mormon bishopric in existence. Long served by Bishop Moroni Timbimboo, the Indians have fulfilled missions for their church in foreign lands. Yeagah Timbimboo, one of the natives, claimed that his tribesmen were dressed in full regalia when they trudged behind their oxen and ponies as they plowed the prairie, back in 1855.

Although the less settled bands had signed the Box Elder Treaty, they remained outside the control of the Indian office as late as 1871. That year Agent M. P. Berry succeeded in persuading some of the wanderers to settle at Fort Hall.[2] This did not include Indians under San Pitch and Sagwitch who chose to live on Ban-

---

[1] *Box Elder News Journal* (September 14, 1943).
[2] Berry, *Report, Sen. Exec. Doc. 24,* 43 Cong., 1 sess. (1580), 12–34.

nock Creek or the small following of Chief Tav-i-wun-shear who preferred Wind River.[3] When Berry made his report, there were only 400 Northwestern Shoshonis, though they had numbered 1,200 in 1869. There are now about 145 at Washakie (Utah), the others having lost their identity at Fort Hall and elsewhere.

The 1,945 Western Shoshonis of Nevada stubbornly refused to be moved to Fort Hall, in spite of attempts on the part of the government. Timoak had been among the dozen headmen who had signed the Ruby Valley Treaty, but he and his Indians looked with no more favor on the location—Duck Valley—that was finally set aside for them than they did upon Fort Hall. It was Timoak, we will recall, who had originally proposed that Duck Valley be made a reservation for his people.

The Duck Valley, or Western Shoshoni, Reservation, one of the largest and most significant in the state of Nevada, is in country over which the Basin Indians ranged before the coming of the white man. In their economic extremity, they covered over twenty-five hundred square miles in their quest for food. In the more fertile localities, the population density amounted to one person to every two square miles; in the desert area, one to fifteen or twenty.[4]

Since 1886 the Paddy Kap band of Paiutes from Oregon (comprising about 50 per cent of the reservation's present population of 740) have occupied the northern end of this reservation, located at Owyhee, Nevada. As the Shoshonis and Paiutes have always been friendly, they live together amicably. Little adjustment was necessary for either tribe.

A study made of these Indians in the late 1930's showed them adaptable not only to agriculture but also to stock-raising.[5] Their chief handicap was that the Owyhee River would dry up during the summer and they would be without irrigation water for their livestock. Family income in the thirties amounted to no more than

[3] Berry's report, *House Exec. Doc. 1*, Pt. 3, 41 Cong., 2 sess. (1414), 445–85.

[4] Julian H. Steward, "Linguistic Distribution and Political Groups of the Great Basin Shoshoneans," *A.A.*, N. S., Vol. XXXIX (1937), 625–34.

[5] Harris, "The White Knife Shoshoni," *loc. cit.*, 105.

$1,500 a year at the most, with an average between $350 and $600. The Indians could afford little beyond the necessities of life.

Since the completion of the Wild Horse Dam, bringing an additional ten thousand acres under irrigation, a surprising improvement has taken place.[6] There are no longer houses without floors or bedsteads. The Indians, like other Americans in the West, own good automobiles and live in comfortable houses. The family income ranges up to a maximum of $15,000 to $20,000, with the average around $3,000, and the lowest around $1,000. Approximately 20 per cent of the high-school graduates attend trade school or college.

The harsh life of the Shoshokos once caused the population to remain stable. Popular sanction did not permit more than two or three children to a family, but in 1963 the average number per family was five. With the death rate low, the population is steadily on the increase.

The early attempts of the Mormons and Catholics to proselyte were not lasting, and the Indians only halfheartedly accepted their reservation church—Presbyterian. And yet, they have shown no greater enthusiasm for either the Sun Dance or the Peyote Cult, which will be discussed in detail later. Peyotism was introduced at one time, but it was suppressed by the Indians themselves. Since prehistoric times, the Buhagant has taken care of spiritual needs. One old Shoshoko, defending his native religion, is quoted as follows: "In the Bible it says that the old men will dream dreams and the young men will see visions. In the same way, God directed the Shoshoni in the old days. Didn't God give Moses a dream, just like He gives our own Buhagants dreams?"[7]

Although many of the old taboos remained with the Western Shoshonis in modified form, the Indians soon learned property values after locating on their reservation. They no longer buried the hunter's gun with the deceased, nor did they continue to kill his horse and destroy his lodge, even though they did not reoccupy

[6] Statistics and other data regarding the Owyhee Agency furnished by the Nevada Indian Agency, Stewart, Nevada.

[7] Harris, "The White Knife Shoshoni," *loc. cit.*, 107.

the dwelling for at least six months, allowing time for his *mugua* (spirit) to leave.

The Western bands were in possession of the horse for so short a time that it did little to change their way of life. In fact, many of the Indians did not possess a horse until after going on the reservation. Yet the acquisition of the horse furthered the formation of bands, usually for the purpose of depredation.

In the early history of these people there were two factions: the progressives, the educated, white-talking Indians; and the conservatives, whose resentment toward the white man caused the split. Factionalism has flared up from time to time, with charges and countercharges being hurled from one group to the other. With the resentment toward the white oppressors fading and stirring issues lacking, little evidence of factionalism can be found today. As one authority says, factionalism is an issue which the Indians must handle for themselves.[8] The Western Shoshonis have proved this to be true.

In the far Northwest, the Snakes of Oregon, under Chief Wewa-we-wa, seemed to adjust surprisingly well to reservation life and to work harmoniously with the Walpapis and Yahuskins.[9] In fact, the term "Snake," by official usage, has come to include both the Yahuskins and Walpapis.[10]

The Shoshonean people of California, who once occupied the most extensive area of any of the twenty-one nations represented there, are difficult to trace. In fact, the entire population of California Indians has diminished so greatly that only one Indian can now be found where there were eight when the white man arrived. Authorities attribute this decline of nearly 90 per cent in part to new diseases and to changes in diet and clothing.[11] Cultural as well as physiological factors also enter into the final analysis.

The Northern Paiutes, Eastern Mono Paiutes, and Western Mono Indians are located east of the mountains down through

[8] Sven Liljiblad, "The Indians of Idaho," Idaho State Historical Society.

[9] *Sen. Exec. Doc. 24,* 43 Cong., 1 sess. (1580), 34.

[10] *Bulletin 30,* B.A.E., 557.

[11] R. F. Heizer and M. A. Whipple, *The California Indians,* 74–75.

Mono and into Inyo County. The Shoshonis are in the Death and Panamint valleys farther east and over the Inyo and Panamint Mountains but still in Inyo County.

Estimates in 1870 showed sixty-five Shoshonis in Saline Valley and forty-two in Death Valley, with no available statistics on the Panamints.[12] The Department of the Interior reports (1960) only one reservation in California, where the Shoshonis are mentioned as "a major tribe." It is Lone Pine, where the Indians, only ninety-eight in number, are considered as Paiutes for the most part, and Shoshonis.[13]

> The few Indians who come to live in Death Valley during the winter can hardly be called members of any one tribe. They have intermarried with so many cultural groups that they have about lost any tribal identity. Some of the older Indians who live here speak a Shoshonean dialect.[14]

The Death Valley Indians, whose small reservation is near Furnace Creek Ranch, usually go into the mountains in the summer, then up to Beatty, Nevada. While they are locally considered Shoshonis because of their dialect, they are mixed with Paiutes, among other cultural groups. Even those who know them well have difficulty telling the Shoshonis from the Paiutes. Their dialectic difference, although slight, is attributed to their being separated by a mountain range.[15]

The Lemhi Valley Indian Reservation, which was created by executive order for the mixed bands of about seven hundred Bannocks, Shoshonis, and Sheep Eaters, proved impractical.[16] The government sought vainly to close the reservation and move the Indians to Fort Hall, but even though poor and victimized by dishonest agents, they still refused to leave. Learning of an executive

[12] Steward, "Basin-Plateau Groups," 12, 48–49.
[13] "U.S. Indian Population and Land," *Report,* Department of the Interior, 1960, 8.
[14] Granville B. Liles to Virginia Cole Trenholm, October 30, 1961.
[15] Dorothy C. Cragen to Virginia Cole Trenholm, October 25, 1961.
[16] *Report of Commissioner of Indian Affairs,* 1877, 241.

order, in 1879, forcing their move, Tendoy protested strenuously; and his subchief, Pegge, vowed that he would go to war before he would move.[17]

Tendoy of the Lemhis, Tyhee of the Bannocks, and Gibson Jack and Captain Jim of the Fort Hall Shoshonis were sent to Washington in 1880, so that they might be impressed with the power of the government.[18] Six years previously, Captain Jim had told Brunot that he had heard that three Nez Percé chiefs had seen "Washington" (the President) and that he, too, wished to see him. Tendoy's delegation also included Grouse Pete, Jack Tendoy, and Tsidimit. On May 14, 1880, these Indians signed a treaty in Washington which provided among other things for the removal of the Lemhis to Fort Hall. However, "Tendoy's Indians" flatly refused to move. The Indian Commissioner, therefore, recommended to Congress that the portion having to do with the Lemhis be deleted from the treaty. This caused them to forfeit any benefits which they might have received.

Thirty-two Lemhis voluntarily moved to Fort Hall two years later. But the benefits specified in the treaty still were not forthcoming. Consequently, a delegation headed by Chief Tyhee was permitted to go to Washington in 1888 to find out the cause of the delay. The treaty was ratified with amendments the following year, but the Lemhis did not abandon their home country until 1907, when they voluntarily trekked to Fort Hall. All went but Tendoy, who died in his beloved Lemhi Valley on May 9, 1907. He was succeeded by his son Tu:pombi (Black Hair), who played an insignificant role in tribal affairs. He in turn was succeeded by his English-speaking brother Winc.[19]

Just why the Lemhis of Idaho and the Shoshokos of Nevada had an aversion for Fort Hall is not quite clear. It is true that the reservation was far from harmonious, for factionalism was strong. This might be expected in Wind River, where traditional enemies

[17] *Ibid.*, 1879, 54.
[18] *Ibid.*, 1880, 30.
[19] Steward, "Basin-Plateau Groups," 40–45.

were forced to reside side by side, but the Shoshonis and Bannocks of Fort Hall had lived together throughout their history. Their factionalism was largely the result of difference in temperament. Also the Shoshonis were more adaptable to the white man's cultural demands than were the Bannocks. The white man's practice of rewarding the more deserving often aroused antagonism.

The early attempts to civilize the Fort Hall Indians were largely on an economic level, as the white man hoped to make the Indians self-sustaining. At first the Bannocks balked, but they looked more favorably upon the idea of farming after Tyhee built a house and showed his desire to live like the white man.[20]

The complexities of their troubles, involving agents as well as Indians, kept the Bannocks and Shoshonis in a state of excitement which hindered farming efforts. Cattle-raising on a small scale was attempted. Although the Bannocks were better adapted to stock-raising than to farming, they killed and ate the cattle allotted to them the first year. The Shoshonis, who managed to save fifty out of two hundred head, had shown little interest in the Bannock War for the reason that they were beginning to see reward for their efforts in goods produced and in certain favors from the agents.[21]

After Brunot's visit the Shoshonis indicated their good faith by adopting the white man's attire and accepting the non-Indian names bestowed upon them. The Bannocks, defiantly wearing their native costumes, continued to use their Indian names. The action of unscrupulous white men both on and off the reservation, the building of the town of Pocatello, and the creation of a military post at Fort Hall (May 27, 1870) contributed to unsettled conditions on the reservation.[22]

The Act of May 27, 1878, whereby Congress made an attempt to deal with reservation law enforcement, provided a force of Indian police to keep order and stop liquor traffic among the Indians. Although the police were subject to the will of their chiefs, they

[20] *Report of Commissioner of Indian Affairs,* 1876, 42.
[21] *House Misc. Doc. 340,* Pt. 15, 53 Cong., 1 sess. (3016), 237.
[22] Madsen, *The Bannock of Idaho,* 310, 313.

managed to put a stop to the practice of plural marriage on the reservation and to suppress the Scalp Dance.[23]

No hospital was built at Fort Hall, on the advice of the resident physician who knew the nature of the Indians. When a young Bannock boy was accidently killed at the mill, the Bannocks set fire to the building in which the Shoshonis had stored fifteen thousand bushels of wheat and twelve thousand bushels of flour. The loss was complete.[24] As the doctor pointed out, a similar act might occur if one of the Indians were to die at the post hospital.

The missionary work, other than that carried on by the Mormons at near-by Corinne, Utah, was under the sponsorship of the Methodist church, which seemed indifferent to its opportunities. The minister, who received no compensation from the church, was hired as a teacher. Like the Western Shoshonis of Nevada, the Fort Hall Indians showed little interest in the white man's religion. The ineffectual missionary effort left the Indians ripe for the acceptance of the Ghost Dance religion, which later took hold with fervor at Fort Hall.

E. A. Stone, who became the Fort Hall agent in 1881, lamented the fact that a teacher was costing the government $1,700 annually besides food and clothing furnished the pupils, but not one single Indian on the reservation could yet read or write.[25] The impractical nature of the clause in the 1868 treaty requiring compulsory education of girls under eighteen years of age was illustrated in a dramatic incident recounted in the *Pocatello Tribune*.[26] The husband of a fourteen-year-old girl protested to the agent when she was forced to attend school, but the agent ruled that she must stay. Consequently, the irate husband formed a band of young braves and took his wife by force. The band also released all of the other girls, as they claimed they, too, were married.

The Indians who had depended for their livelihood upon the chase were far more concerned over the dwindling buffalo herds

[23] *Report of Commissioner of Indian Affairs*, 1884, 63.
[24] *Ibid.*, 1883, 53.
[25] *Ibid.*, 1881, 63.
[26] *Pocatello Tribune* (September 29, 1877).

than they were over their inability to read and write. Blaming the white man for the extermination of game animals, Dick Washakie claimed that the Indians hunted but once a year, while the white men hunted the year around.[27] After the white man came, the Shoshonis could see the animals rapidly disappear. Young Washakie said that the Indians did not know whether the white men had the right to hunt on their reservation, but maintaining the chief's peaceful attitude, they did not interfere.

An authority on Indians gives evidence to prove that the Sioux were "born wasters."[28] The Shoshonis may also have slaughtered recklessly for commercial purposes, as hides were their chief source of income. Finn Burnett, the first agricultural agent for the government at Fort Washakie (1871–85), said that the Indians never sold green hides. A bale of twelve would bring from twelve to fifteen dollars per hide. Buffalo, elk, and deer meat brought from fifteen to twenty-five cents a pound, according to his recollection. Another writer of the period remembered the meat's selling for as little as five cents.

Louis Ballou, who lived on the reservation from 1879–81 as carpenter and sometimes special agent, confirmed Dick Washakie's belief that the white man was largely responsible for the disappearance of the wild game:

> We [Ballou and his companions] were ascending the mountains on the north side that lie between Owl Creek and Wind River in late November 1879 when the first heavy fall of snow came, where we were forced to lay over a day unable to see in what direction to travel. It was while in camp here that we met one of the three hunters who the day before admitted having shot over sixty elk in a little basin near our camp, and he told with much pride that not a single animal had got away. All the meat these three hunters had taken were two hindquarters, one of which was given to us, and the tongues, these evidently to be shown in Lander as proof of their skill.[29]

[27] Dick Washakie's testimony was entered into Shoshoni Case No. H–219.
[28] George E. Hyde, *Spotted Tail's Folk*, 18.
[29] Louis L. Ballou to E. O. Fuller, November 14, 1929.

TENDOY

Courtesy Bureau of American Ethnology

TYHEE

Courtesy Bureau of American Ethnology

CHIEF WASHAKIE was photographed at his cabin
by J. K. Moore, Jr., in 1899.

Courtesy J. K. Moore, Jr.

CHIEF WASHAKIE'S BIOGRAPHY was recorded in this hide painting by Charley Washakie.

Courtesy J. K. Moore, Jr.

A SHOSHOKO (Kolmako, Elko, Nevada, 1898) wears white man's clothing but retains tribal hairdressing and feathers. Note the facial
tattoo, sometimes used by Basin Shoshonis.

Courtesy Nevada Historical Society

A MEDICINE MAN, Gro-wot (Man without a Wife), blesses a young Shoshoni Sun Dancer, about 1904.

Courtesy J. K. Moore, Jr.

Wovoka, the Paiute prophet whose influence was felt especially at
Fort Hall, which became a point of diffusion for his
Ghost Dance religion.

Courtesy Nevada Historical Society

CHIEF TRUCKEE, from a photograph taken by C. W. Irish at
Pyramid Lake Agency in 1887.

Courtesy Nevada Historical Society

Ballou went on to say that in the spring of 1881 he looked over an immense pile of buffalo robes being baled for J. K. Moore at Fort Washakie. He selected four that Moore sold him at cost. He gave four dollars each for two calf robes, five dollars for a two-year-old size, and eight dollars for a large bull robe. When he wrote to the Moore Trading Post asking that they express to him three robes four years later, he was told that they no longer carried them, as all the buffalo that could be reached by the Indians were gone.

While game was still plentiful, the government (1875) issued 5,000 head of Texas cattle, consisting of cows and calves, to the Shoshonis at Wind River. About 75 per cent of these were lost, most of them being stolen by white men, according to Burnett. In subsequent years there were 500 issued at a time, these to be divided between the Shoshonis and Arapahoes.

The once large Bannock tribe had shrunk to 450 persons by 1900, while the Shoshonis affiliated with them had increased in population to more than 1,000 souls. That year the residents of Fort Hall were listed as Shoshoni-Bannock, both tribes having lost their identity largely through intermarriage.[30] One cannot help wondering if the great Eastern band of Shoshonis might someday face the loss of their identity, for they, too, have become greatly outnumbered.[31] Their reservation is listed by the Department of the Interior as Arapaho and Shoshoni. As factionalism is tribal rather than political and as intermarriage is still a rarity, the amalgamation may not take place for several generations.

In order to appreciate the situation at Wind River, one must turn back briefly to 1870, when the Northern Arapahoes were "urged and invited" by the government to make a treaty with the Shoshonis, with a view to a permanent location. The year before, Washakie had made a treaty with the Crows in order to strengthen his forces "with reliable allies," but he had shown no desire to be on friendly terms with the Arapahoes.[32] The fact that Friday, the

---

[30] *Report of Commissioner of Indian Affairs*, 1900, 215.
[31] Tribal rolls as of July 1, 1964, showed 1,910 Shoshonis and 2,532 Arapahoes.
[32] G. W. Fleming to Commissioner of Indian Affairs, July 11, 1870, I.O.R.

adopted son of Thomas Fitzpatrick, had been Washakie's friend as a youth may have caused him to indicate a willingness to hold council with the Arapahoes. "When I see their faces, I can understand their intentions," he had stated.[33]

Norkuk, whose failure to co-operate at the Bates Battle had resulted in needless loss of life, had again been causing trouble. He was convinced that the only way to obtain presents from the white man was to steal a few horses and kill a few men. Washakie gave as his reason for not wanting to council with the Arapahoes that he was "sick and cold," indicating that he was troubled. Furthermore, he was afraid that if he left his camp, it might be invaded by the Sioux.

The first of the two Arapaho groups that went to Wind River to discuss terms with the Shoshonis included Medicine Man, Sorrell Horse, Friday, Little Wolf, and Cut Foot. When a runner was unable to locate Washakie after twelve days, they left. The second delegation included Medicine Man, Knock Knees, Little Wolf, Black Bear, Little Robe, and Sorrell Horse. Their object, according to Washakie, was to enjoy the privileges accorded the Shoshonis at the Fort Bridger Treaty Council of 1868.

Angered by their demands, he not only refused to allow them to settle on his reservation, but he also accused them of all of the murders that had taken place in the Wind River Valley and at the mining camps the summer before. The Arapahoes did not deny the charges, but they claimed that they wanted to be good. Washakie, skeptical of their intent, said that they were even then laying up a supply of ammunition, for which they had offered large amounts in trade. He was sure that they planned to unite with the Sioux to make war against his camp, a statement which later proved to have foundation.

The Arapahoes, who had formerly roamed freely in northern Colorado, had concentrated in Wyoming following the Sand Creek Massacre on November 29, 1864.[34] On that occasion about

[33] Campbell to Commissioner of Indian Affairs, September 23, 1869, I.O.R.
[34] Stan Hoig, *The Sand Creek Massacre*, 129–82.

five hundred Indians—mostly women and children—had been killed. The attack was made by Colonel John M. Chivington against an encampment of Cheyennes and Arapahoes on Sand Creek, near Fort Lupton, Colorado. Although Black Kettle, the chief, waved an American flag, nothing could stop Chivington, who was bent on destruction.

The nomadic Arapahoes repeatedly attacked miners, settlers, and Indians in the Sweetwater, Bridger, and Wind River areas. Not knowing what else to do with them, the government temporarily placed them on the Wind River Reservation in 1872. After staying only a short time, they returned to Pine Ridge to join their allies, the Sioux.

While the Arapahoes were looking covetously toward the Wind River Reservation as a permanent home, the white man, as early as 1870, was demanding that titles to lands for them on the Shoshoni Reservation be cleared. Forces seemed to be closing in on the aging Washakie.

There was never a more impressive array of war bonnets than when Crazy Horse finally surrendered at Fort Robinson.[35] The Platte River tribes were represented by their well-known chieftains. Red Cloud and Spotted Tail were there with the Sioux, and Dull Knife was with the Cheyennes. The Arapahoes were under Sharp Nose and a lesser chief, Washington, so named because he wanted "to walk in the new road," after having seen the wonders of the capitol. Black Coal, White Horse, and Six Feathers were also numbered among the Arapahoes. Sorrel Horse—a medicine man, magician, and a ventriloquist—entertained the officers and chieftains as they awaited the arrival of Crazy Horse.

Six Feathers (Arapaho) should not be confused with Six Feathers (Shoshoni) who was killed by Washakie some time later. The agent had told the chief that wife-beating was a cruelty. Therefore, when he caught Six Feathers beating his wife he reproved him and advised him not to do it again. The second time Washakie caught Six Feathers abusing her, he effectively put a stop to it

---

[35] Bourke, *On the Border with Crook*, 407–408.

by killing him. Ethelbert Talbot, bishop of the Episcopal church and a great friend of Washakie's, quipped that it cost only "one buck" to get rid of wife-beating on the reservation.[36]

Friday, peace chief of the Arapahoes, spoke fluent English. While at Fort Robinson he explained to the officers the meaning of his various names, the last translated to mean "The-Man-Who-Sits-in-the-Corner-and-Keeps-His-Mouth-Shut." Most Indians of any importance had at least three names, earned in one way or another. Friday had four. To him partly goes the credit for Washakie's allowing the Arapahoes to be placed temporarily on his reservation, on March 18, 1878. They were in a starving condition when 938 of them were conducted en masse to the Wind River Agency under military escort.

Why Washakie would allow the Arapahoes to be placed on the most productive portion of his land is puzzling. There are two possible explanations—the first that he was on a hunting excursion at the time and had no say in the matter. The other is that he did not want to be separated from his beloved Wind River Mountains, home of Tamapah, the Sun-Father.[37]

He believed that from the heights he could see the land that he would someday occupy, the land after death. He could see it with its pure mountain streams stocked with fish and its grassy glens abounding in deer. There would be beautiful Indian women to wait upon him, and he would have horses that never tired. The lodges would all be new and comfortable, and meat would be so plentiful that his people would never again know hunger.

Is there any wonder that Washakie withdrew with his dreams to the higher level? The arrangement, so he thought, was but temporary. As he later said, he did not realize that the Arapahoes by visiting upon his land would have any claim upon it.

When the Arapahoes arrived at the reservation, they were reported to be "in such indigent circumstances as to be wholly un-

---

[36] Ethelbert Talbot, *My People of the Plains*, 28–29.

[37] Albert G. Brackett, "The Shoshone or Snake Indians, Their Religion, Superstitions, and Manners," *Annual Report*, Board of Regents, Smithsonian Institution, 1879, 328–33.

able, without generous assistance from the government to speedily emerge from their present state of mendicity."[38] The once proud tribe, now "rich only in horses" (two thousand) had been reduced in number to 198 warriors, the rest being women, children, and old men.

In the spring of 1878, Agent Patten expressed the opinion that the government would not experience much difficulty in settling the Arapahoes permanently. At the same time he urged that the Shoshonis be duly compensated for the lands occupied by any Indians placed on their reservation. Patten stated that although Washakie and his headmen disliked to divide their property with other tribes, they had "too great hearts to say no."[39]

To Washakie's repeated questions concerning when the Arapahoes were to be moved, the government remained silent. The arrangement proved distasteful to both tribes, for they had nothing in common except a bitter hatred. Governor John W. Hoyt, Campbell's successor, made a special trip to the reservation in response to Washakie's urgent plea. There he conferred with him and with Black Coal, then head chief of the Arapahoes. Hoyt was impressed by the dignity of the Shoshoni chief and his subchiefs when they appeared in council.

Granted an opportunity to speak into the sympathetic ear of the Governor, Washakie seemed to lose track of the issue in his effort to express his feelings. He spoke first of the wretched lives of the Indians who had once roamed over the country from sea to sea, and reminded the Governor that every foot of what he now proudly called "America" had belonged to the red man not very long ago. Then came the whites—hordes of them from beyond the sea—who finally cornered the "sorry remnants of tribes once mighty in little spots of earth, where they were watched over by men with guns who were more than anxious to kill them all." Referring to the Treaty of 1868, he said:

> The white man's government promised that if we, the Shoshones, would be content with the little patch allowed us, it would

[38] *Report of Commissioner of Indian Affairs*, 1878, 148.
[39] Patten to Commissioner of Indian Affairs, April 18, 1878, I.O.R.

keep us well supplied with everything necessary to comfortable living, and would see that no white man should cross our borders for our game, or for anything that is ours. But it has not kept its word!

The white man kills our game, captures our furs, and sometimes feeds his herds upon our meadows. And your great and mighty government . . . does not protect us in our rights. It leaves us without the promised seed, without tools for cultivating the land, without implements for harvesting our crops, without breeding animals better than ours, without the food we still lack . . . without the many comforts we cannot produce, without the schools we so much need for our children.

I again say, the government does not keep its word. And so, after all we can get by cultivating the land, and by hunting and fishing, we are sometimes nearly starved, and go half naked, as you see us! Knowing all this, do you wonder, sir, that we have fits of desperation and think to be avenged?[40]

Governor Hoyt was so moved by Washakie's eloquence that he pledged himself to see that justice was done. The chief cordially shook hands and expressed his personal confidence in the Governor. When Hoyt telegraphed the Secretary of the Interior, he stated: "The hand of the red man has surely been stayed." Furthermore he affirmed that all would be well if the government would but send assurances of good will, followed up promptly by material goods. Hoyt's next annual report concluded with the statement that carloads of supplies were sent and provision was made for the instruction of the children. He said, "A new happiness was by these same means conferred upon two to three thousand of the most deserving of the nation's wards."

Some of the Shoshoni warriors may have left the reservation at this time because of the presence of the unwanted guests, the Arapahoes. Washakie maintained that his warriors went to Utah "to get washed." This was probably the same group mentioned earlier by Governor Campbell. He said that a strong party had separated from Washakie to follow the leadership of a half-blood "of good character but nevertheless crafty and somewhat am-

[40] J. W. Hoyt to Secretary of the Interior, July 17, 1878, I.O.R.

bitious."[41] He was presumably referring to Norkuk, although he did not mention him by name.

The separation between the Shoshonis and Arapahoes today is not as much from hostility as from the feeling that each is a distinct social unit. The first break through the tribal barrier occurred when one of Washakie's sons married an Arapaho. At the time when a study was made of the acculturation of the Arapahoes in the 1930's, there had been only four intermarriages. Today, while such marriages are infrequent, they are more numerous; intermarriage is not as much frowned upon as it is irregular. As the number of satisfactory marriages increases, there seems to be a gradual breakdown of hostile attitudes. The young people of today are embarrassed when one of their elders spitefully calls an Arapaho "Dog Eater" to his face.

James K. Moore, Jr., of Lander, Wyoming, recalls a dramatic occasion which took place in his home many years ago.[42] His mother served roast beef and mashed potatoes to three distinguished guests, Washakie, Black Coal, and Red Cloud, who had come to visit the Arapahoes. Washakie, who possessed a keen sense of humor, reminded Black Coal of the time he had shot his horse from under him at the Battle of Bates Hole. These three veterans of the Indian wars had a great time reminiscing.

The demoralization of the Arapahoes was almost complete before they were even placed on the Wind River Reservation:

> The loss of their food supply, the losing battle for their hunting territories, the failure of the whites to keep the first treaties, the first free access to liquor, prostitution of their women, disease, and the general harassing that led to their placement in Pine Ridge Reservation as prisoners of war to be fed and kept in idleness, broke much of their morale and the harmonious functioning of their tribal life.[43]

[41] Campbell to Commissioner of Indian Affairs, September 23, 1869, I.O.R.

[42] Moore, interview, Lander, Wyoming, June, 1961.

[43] "History and Economy of the Indians of the Wind River Reservation, Wyoming" (hereinafter cited as "History and Economy of Wind River Indians"), Missouri River Basin Investigations, Mimeographed Report 106, 1, 6, 7.

The Arapahoes had little left but their dreams. They were naturally susceptible to Peyotism, for through the use of the drug their dreams could be self-induced. The Peyote Cult, which we will discuss later as it relates to the Shoshonis, was accepted by the Arapahoes at Wind River a decade before it found its way into the Shoshoni tribe.

During the 1870's and 1880's, the chief object of the Department of the Interior was to settle the Indians upon reservations and provide for their basic needs. In attempting economic acculturation, the white man began by trying to acquaint the natives with the intricacies of farming. Finn Burnett, later recounting some of his experiences, said that it was difficult to tell which knew less about the plow, the Indian or his horse.

Old-timers in the Lander area supplement this with an anecdote regarding the first farming endeavor of Wild Man. Burnett helped him plant his grain and lay out his irrigation ditches. There was a promise of a fine crop, but each time the agent asked why he did not irrigate, Wild Man would not answer. Knowing the old saying, "Indian time; no time," Burnett thought the crop might be irrigated next time he came around.

Soon the young grain began to fire at the roots, and it looked as if it might burn up for lack of water. When the government farmer scolded the Indian for not running water in his ditch, Wild Man looked at him in alarm.

"You want me to die?" he asked.

"Of course not," Burnett replied.

"You want my family—my children to die?"

Again the white man answered in the negative. "What has that to do with irrigating your crop?"

"I run water in ditch. Gopher come out of hole. He look at Indian and he die—maybe all family die."

Some years after that, scientists discovered that Rocky Mountain spotted fever is caused by the bite of an infected tick that has fed upon dead rodents. The sight of a dead gopher has caused more than one Indian camp to be moved, though the natives associated the fever with the gopher rather than with the tick, the transmitter.

As Indian lands were held in common, there was little incentive in communal farming.[44] A need for individually owned tracts to challenge the initiative of the native farmer resulted in the Allotment Act of 1887. The law authorized the President of the United States to issue land allotments in severalty when he was convinced that a reservation was suited to agriculture. Allotments to heads of families were to amount to 160 acres; to single persons over eighteen or orphan children under eighteen, 80 acres; and to other single persons under eighteen, 40 acres to be doubled when land was adaptable for grazing only.

The Indian could not sell his alloted land for at least twenty-five years. Those receiving their allotments were granted full citizenship, which was also offered to Indians taking up residence off the reservation but within the boundary of the United States. Surplus lands were to be sold to the government, and the funds therefrom were to be used for the welfare of the Indians.

Settlement on the Wind River Reservation was determined largely by allotments, with the Shoshonis to the west and northwest and the Arapahoes to the east and southeast. To say that the Shoshoni settlements are at Fort Washakie, Burris, and Crowheart and the Arapaho at Ethete and Lower Arapaho is misleading, for the people of both tribes are rural. Except for Fort Washakie, a meeting ground for both tribes, the points named above consist for the most part of a post office, a grocery store, and a filling station.

In June, 1934, the Indian Reorganization Act was passed,[45] primarily to keep Indians from selling their lands granted to them under the Allotment Act. It also gave the Indians a form of tribal self-government with legal powers. They could incorporate, elect officers, and handle their local matters through tribal councils and

[44] Lawrence F. Schmeckebier, "Institute of Government Research, Service Monographs of the U. S. Government, No. 48," 78–80, I.O.R.

[45] *U.S. Statutes at Large,* 73 C, 1933–34, 48, Pt. 1, 984.

Indian officials. The Shoshoni and Arapaho tribes did not accept all the provisions of the Act; consequently, they are not chartered tribes. Each tribe has two councils—the business and the general, with the former made up of six members elected by popular vote every two years. The Arapaho and Shoshoni business councils meet together as a joint council to discuss intertribal matters.

CHAPTER SIXTEEN

Healing Waters

Wᴀsʜᴀᴋɪᴇ, the great chief of the Shoshoni Nation, was a remarkable man, whose longevity may be attributed to his strong constitution and his will to live. When one of his friends tried to explain to him the concept of immortality, he replied, "I want to stay here with my friends, and I do not want to go to another world."[1]

He possessed a great dignity and pride in his simple but significant possessions. The walls of his cabin were covered with pictures of his exploits in battle, which with the help of his son Charlie he painted with great relish as he relived the days when he was a famous warrior. He is said to have worn on his high-crowned hat a silver casket plate, reading "Our Baby," which he purchased from the son of a furniture dealer for a bow and arrow.[2] He was proud to the last of the medallion and the handsome saddle which the Great White Father had given him.

Above all, he liked his enormous, framed photograph that graced the wall at "Jakie's" store. He, too, had pictures of himself but none as fine as this one. He would stand before it and silently admire it.[3]

The picture shows Washakie wearing his favorite ornament, described by J. K. Moore, Jr., as "a beautiful pink sea shell," which he used as a kerchief-necktie holder. It apparently had some significance, but no one knows what. His face shows dignity, strong character, and an unmistakeable scar left there by a Blackfoot

[1] Hebard, *Washakie*, 236–37.
[2] *Ibid.*, 233–34.
[3] The picture now hangs on the wall in J. K. Moore's apartment in Lander, Wyoming. It is large for the room, but "Jimmie," as his friends call him, likes it there for sentimental reasons.

arrow which pierced his nose. A. C. Jones, missionary-teacher, described him in 1885 as having a "fine open countenance" which became so animated and expressive when he spoke that it was a real pleasure to look at him. When he smiled, it was "like casting a ray of soft light on a pretty picture." A profusion of silver gray hair, hanging over his shoulders, gave him a venerable appearance.[4]

If Washakie was remarkable in 1885, he was even more so eleven years later when he met in council with the white man to discuss the matter of the Great Hot Springs. Then in his nineties, he had outlived all of those who had at one time planned to move the Shoshonis to Indian Territory following his death. He was permitted to live in his wonderland of dreams until the end of his days.

Since the arrival of the first explorer, the white man had been intrigued by mineral deposits, a natural phenomenon in the northwestern corner of Wyoming. John Colter had described sulphurus deposits and mineral springs in such fantastic terms that his friends considered him demented. To them it was unbelievable that conditions such as he described could exist.

In 1875, Thomas Maghee, the post surgeon at Camp Brown, went on a reconnaissance trip to the Great Spring (Thermopolis, Wyoming) for a firsthand inspection of the wonders that he had heard of so often. He proceeded down the Bighorn over a well-used Indian trail until he arrived at the spring at the mouth of Owl Creek. He found that it had formed a deposit of some age, from four hundred to six hundred yards in extent, divided by the Bighorn River. The main part on the east included the enormous spring which gushed from the butte, seventy-five yards to the stream. The mineral deposit from the spring sloped both to the north and to the south from its middle, along which an artificial conduit was formed.

The deposit sounded hollow beneath the horses' hoofs, but it was found to be solid enough to bear a much greater weight. Examining the huge spring, Maghee found on its northern and east-

---

[4] A. C. Jones to Nellie Quackenbush, January 7, 1885, courtesy Evelyn Corthell Hill, Laramie, Wyoming.

ern sides a high bluff of red and white clay and standstone, while immediately over the crater were some large blocks of sandstone which seemed to receive their support from the edges of the spring. They were cemented to each other by the deposit from the water which practically covered them. Stepping upon one of these blocks, he found himself over an immense caldron of boiling, seething water, which seemed to be trying to escape from the heat below.

Large volumes of carbonic acid gas and other gasses found their way to the Bighorn by many subterranean channels of large size as well as by "the aqueduct," through which flowed a stream three and one-half feet deep and four feet wide, at the rate of eight miles an hour. The caldron at the butte was of great but unknown depth, about thirty feet wide and circular in form. The water was "limpid" and clear, although in the caldron it had the characteristic emerald tint, slightly acidulous to taste, and it possessed the genuine geyser odor.

Flowing through the aqueduct in a single stream till about five yards from the river, it divided and ran in two streams to the edge of the precipice, over which it leaped and broke into spray upon great white fantastic forms. Despite the rapid current of the Bighorn, these shapes arose from its bed to meet the waters that daily increased their size instead of wearing them away.

Maghee found the deposits so plentiful that any break of continuity at the edge was repaired in a few hours. He procured some specimens of the formation and some bottles of water. At the same time, he commented that an unfortunate rattlesnake had fallen into the reservoir and had been thoroughly cooked.[5] There is no record of Colter's description of the wonders he saw at the sulphur spring between Shoshone River and Heart Mountain, but to an unbelieving listener Maghee's account could well have sounded like the fire and brimstone of hell. Yet the bottles of water which he later analyzed were found to possess important mineral qualities. Washakie had frequently boasted of his great "healing waters" where he and his Indians had spent much time.

[5] *Post Record*, 187.

They drank it and bathed in it to relieve their joints, aching from the infirmities of age.

The white man, too, had rheumatism and other muscular ailments that could be relieved. Again he cast a covetous glance at Washakie's "little piece of land," particularly the northeastern corner of the reservation. He hoped to whittle off another slice—this time an area ten miles square.

In 1896, James McLaughlin, United States Indian inspector, was sent to negotiate with the Shoshonis and Arapahoes. Washakie had written a letter to the President of the United States on January 31, 1891, in which he stated:

> This Reservation belongs solely to the Shoshone Indians and we do not concede that the Arapahos have a right to one foot of the land on this Reservation. We are willing to sell a part of this Reservation to the Govt for the Arapahos but until such arrangements are made we protest against any improvements that will in any way give the Arapahos a right to any of the land.
>
> At the time the Arapahos came to this Res. we did not tell them they could come here and to stay nor did we give them any land. They and the Sioux had been fighting the soldiers and got whipped; they came up here and we have allowed them to live here since, thinking they could not hurt the land by living on it, we do not think that this would give them any right to the land.[6]

Oddly enough the Arapahoes had much to say on the subject, even though their title to the land upon which they were still visiting had never been cleared. They had been there so long that the government now dealt with the two tribes as a single people. McLaughlin found the weather so inclement and the roads so "wretchedly bad" that it took him three days to make the 150-mile trip from Rawlins, Wyoming, by stage to Fort Washakie. From there he was accompanied by three Shoshonis, three Arapahoes, two interpreters, and the agency miller on his visit to the Big Spring, and incidentally to the one thousand acres of fertile bottom land to be included in the Treaty. McLaughlin gave the following description:

[6] I.O.R.

The main or principal spring is on the east side of the Big Horn River, and the mountain scenery at this point is magnificent. This spring is truly wonderful; the surface is about 30 feet across, circular in form, a seething, boiling cauldron, with a temperature of 132° F., and discharging a volume of water estimated at 1,250,000 gallons every twenty-four hours . . . it [this water] is not unpleasant to drink, and with salt and pepper added it tastes very much like fresh chicken broth.[7]

A complete analysis of the water had been made by Professor Schutzenberger, of the College of France, at the insistence of Dr. J. A. Schulke, of Lander, Wyoming. Felix Brunot, in 1872, had admittedly paid the Indians less than they were entitled to for the southern end of their reservation, but when they took him up on the small offer, he saw no reason for upping it. McLaughlin, after inspecting the Big Spring and surrounding area, felt that the $50,000 which he was not to go over in his offer was not enough. He raised it to $60,000, which he considered "a fair evaluation, not excessive, and only just and reasonable," for the tract to be ceded.

Businesslike in council, McLaughlin explained to the Indians the object of his visit, to pay liberally for the ten square miles which the government wished to purchase. When he had finished, Washakie arose and said:

Now you will hear what I have to say. A good many years ago I used to live near Fort Bridger, called Piney. Then there was a man like you came to see me and asked, "Where is your country? Where is your country? Is it here, or there, or is it over the mountains, where the hot springs are?" (meaning both hot springs)[8]

After I got here I stayed here. After the game was gone then I told my agent to write to Washington. I want to sell those springs. I used to go to the hot springs on Owl Creek [where the creek opens into the Bighorn] when the game and buffalo were there,

---

[7] James McLaughlin, *Report, Sen. Exec. Doc.* 247, 54 Cong., 1 sess. (3354), 2–3.

[8] By "both hot springs," the chief included a smaller spring ("Washakie's Plunge") at the agency. It was made into an attractive swimming pool with modern facilities, in 1957, at a cost of approximately $250,000.

and stay there. When buffalo were plenty I wintered there. Now I have moved away from there and have come over in this country. I was afraid to stay there when there was nothing to eat. I came here to farm a little. One hot spring [the one near the agency] is enough for me, my people, and the soldiers.

After the chief concluded his speech, in which he sought reassurance that he had never done anything wrong, the inspector called upon Sharp Nose. The Arapaho chief replied, "If you tell me how much this offer is, then you will hear after awhile what we want. That is what we are all here for—about the spring."

When McLaughlin said that he felt after examining the area that the Indians should be entitled to $60,000 instead of the $50,000, Washakie said that he had tried all the day before to count $50,000 without success. McLaughlin asked if he had talked with Dick, Bishop, and other leaders in the tribe about the transaction. The chief stated, "I am chief and whatever I do the others will agree to. The other tribe [the Arapaho] has too many chiefs."

It was evident that he was childish and short of patience. At various times he spoke up, saying, "I would like to know when the money will be paid"; "I am getting old and may not live to enjoy it, unless it comes soon"; and "I would like to see some of the money."

Sharp Nose was more practical, as he wanted rations and cattle rather than cash. The Shoshoni chief replied that he was afraid that it would be as it had been in former times—the two tribes would not agree. He said, "I have always thought the land belonged to me, but I think now that somebody always gets ahead of me. I was the first to come here, and I think I would be the first to get what I want."

Pinning McLaughlin down to figures, Washakie discovered that a cash settlement would amount to only $5.73 per capita for the 1,744 Indians then on the reservation, annually for a period of ten years. When an agreement such as Sharp Nose proposed had been made, Washakie said, "I have given you the springs; my heart feels good."[9]

[9] McLaughlin's report (3354), 3–4.

Sharp Nose's comment was:

I am very glad to hear what you [McLaughlin] have to say, and whatever you do I like it. I wish a copy of this agreement, as I have never had one before. I want this right and straight. I never tell lies. I want to help the Great Father, and everything is done now. After this I want each man's rations weighed; no more scoops or shovels to be used. I always liked the Great Father, and wish to do what he wants. If he wants me to work I will do so.

Washakie also requested a copy of the treaty. Then the old man who had suffered so acutely from the white man's trails and railroads asked if the government were going to "hurry cars in there." To this McLaughlin replied that the railroad would possibly build a branch line in that direction. Washakie's reply to this is not recorded, but it made little difference, for his days were numbered and no one knew it better than he. As he signed his X for the last time to the white man's paper, he commented, "I sign this; I never tell lies."

Sharp Nose made his X mark after Washakie's, Black Coal having died in 1893.[10] There were a few old Indians left—Norkuk, Lone Bear, Tigee, and John Enos among them. Sprinkled among the English names—for example, William Shakespeare and Fremont Arthur—were Wallowing Bull, Sitting Eagle, Little Shield, Gun, Runs Across the River, Bear's Backbone, Hungry Wolf, Runs Behind, Mountain Sheep, Shoulder Blade, Big Grasshopper, and Charlie Little Ant.

On Washakie's last trip to see "Jakie" at the trading post, J. K. Moore, Jr., had to help him mount his horse. The old chief left in a windstorm that filled his eyes with fine particles of grit, causing him to lose his eyesight. He could no longer see his beloved mountains or the healing waters.

It is fitting that Bishop Talbot and the Reverend John R. Roberts, who knew Washakie for so many years, should speak

[10] Roberts considered Black Coal "the unsung hero of Wyoming." W. H. Ziegler, *Wyoming Indians*, 42. Black Coal succeeded Sharp Nose because of his popularity. Then Sharp Nose again became the leading chief following Black Coal's death.

of his last days. When Roberts visited him in the hospital where he was confined after a stroke, Washakie complained that his bed was too soft. At his insistence the missionary removed a door from its hinges and put it where the mattress had formerly been.[11]

When it came time for the old chief to die, his heart was heavy, for he feared that he had offended the Great Spirit by accepting the white man's religion. As a result, he might not be permitted to join his people who had gone before him. One of his friends explained that Dam Apua and God were the same, which gave him some comfort. One of his last messages, in sign language when he became too weak to speak, was for Bishop Talbot: "Tell the good friend who has gone East that Washakie has found the right trail."[12]

[11] Hebard, *Washakie*, 276.

[12] Talbot, *My People of the Plains*, *38–39*. Washakie, who died on February 23, 1900, was given a military funeral. The Reverend John R. Roberts officiated at the service, with burial in the Fort Washakie cemetery.

CHAPTER SEVENTEEN

Forced Acculturation

THE NORTHERN SHOSHONIS, as we have pointed out, brought from the Basin the native religion, involving simply the spirit and the ghost. Then the Nez Percés taught them the white man's doctrine—perhaps the most distinctive influence of the Plateau—but the most lasting concept came from the Plains in ritualistic forms and symbols. Three religious trends are observable among the Shoshonis: first and most important, the Sun Dance, which we have mentioned at a Plains innovation; second, the Ghost Dance, a Basin contribution; and third, the Peyote Cult, of Mexican-Indian origin.

Many changes have taken place in the Sun Dance ritual over the years, but all have been for the definite purpose of making the sacred ceremony more acceptable to the white man. The Indian, in fear that his religious rite might be permanently suppressed, has done everything in his power to conform without an outright sacrifice of the ritual. Whatever the original symbols in the sacred lodge might have meant, they now signify Christian principles. The forked uprights that dot the countryside to show where Sun Dances have taken place in previous years point to the two roads to travel—the good and the bad. Thus the Indian is reminded that he must make his choice. Red willows represent tranquillity; the buffalo skull, blessings; a beaverpelt, industry; a long braid of hair (rather than a scalp), sacrifice.[1]

The Sun Dance has three integral parts, namely: the Hunt, which originally involved the quest for the buffalo, but now only the search for the poles for the sacred medicine lodge; "Making

[1] At the time when Lynn St. Clair was last interviewed, the ceremony "Making the Ground Sacred" was in progress.

the Ground Sacred" (four days in duration), when the Lodge is prayerfully assembled; and the Dance of Thirst, lasting three days and nights, during which time the dancers abstain from food and water.

When the evening star appears on the opening night (Friday), the dancers, with their medicine man and sponsor, congregate back of the lodge. Then with whistles blowing, they circle it single file two or three times, depending on the wish of the leader. As they enter, they take their places to the west, opposite the entrance.

On the south sit the musicians who sing in unison and beat the large drum, around which they are seated. Near by sit women with willow branches, significant of the first vision when the dancers' tracks were erased. When all have taken their places, the leader stands by the center pole and prays. Lynn St. Clair, a well-remembered tribal leader, gave the following as his opening prayer:

> Our Father, bless me now that my people and I have built this place, a gift from you, Our Father, a gift which you have [given] to our forefathers, which through them you gave to us. Bless us, that all of these men who came in to dance with me, be well, that the sick ones may be made well through this Sun Dance.
>
> Bless us, even though we may become dry and weak from thirst and hunger. Protect us through these days and nights, so that at the end of three days, when we get out, with your blessing, we may take of your precious gifts, water and food, and receive our strength back and become healthy, and the sick and weak grow strong; that the old and young may be protected from diseases. Bless us, I pray to you Our Father that all my people who are sick may be made well through you, Our Father. Amen.[2]

After the singers have chanted their four prayer songs four times—the magic number of the Shoshonis—the sacred fire is lighted and the dancers take positions in their stalls. Then the singers begin beating the drum and singing, while the dancers breathe their prayers through the medium of eagle-bone whistles.

[2] St. Clair, "Sun Dance," *loc. cit.*, 4.

St. Clair interpreted these prayers as asking that this earth be clean like the air and the skies where Thunderbird (the eagle) flies. As the dancers flex their knees, sound their whistles, and move with a limping dance step to and from the center pole, their eyes are constantly fixed upon the buffalo head, high above them.

The sunrise service brings a temporary lull to the dance. It is said to commemorate the two visions which brought the Sun Dance to the Indians.[3] Just before sunup the dancers form in rows behind the center pole and face east, the only time they pray directly toward the sun. The first rays that touch them are said to bring inspiration. The flag ceremony, which takes place at eight o'clock, necessitates another intermission.

The sick and the lame are brought into the sacred lodge on the second day. Barefoot, they approach the center pole where they are met by the medicine man, who administers to them. He does this in accordance with mystic rites. On the second day there are sometimes those who faint. St. Clair explained this by saying:

> The one who falls down or faints sees a vision. He is shown in his vision a way to help his people. It is said he is given a power to press or lay his hand on a sick person and the sick one is helped. This has been a secret. The Indian is afraid to tell because he has been made fun of so much. The writer wishes his white friends to understand this Indian way of worshiping and understand the symbols.[4]

At ten o'clock on Monday morning the dance comes to an end. Two young men are instructed to bring buckets of water, which are blessed in the final prayer. The water is then passed to the dancers, who for the first time are allowed to drink. Thank offerings are made when the Indians bring clothing, blankets, or other goods and tie them around the center pole. An authority on the Shoshoni culture states:

> The Sun Dance today is a vital emotional and cultural force affecting not only the Shoshones but also their neighbors. Elements

[3] Marie Montabé, *This is the Sun Dance*, 8.
[4] "Sun Dance," *loc. cit.*, 6.

of disintegration do exist within the ceremony: rivalries between religious leaders, jealousy of the Sun Dance Committee, and the threat of commercialization. Yet these appear minor, and it appears virtually certain that the Sun Dance will retain its vitality and exercise profound influence on Shoshone life for some years to come.[5]

This prediction has proved true, and yet the Sun Dance in the 1960's is more commercialized than it was even a decade ago. While it may not have lost any of its spiritual significance for the dedicated advocates, to the onlooker it seems to be surrounded by distracting elements, tending to lessen its solemnity.[6]

The Sun Dance was not opened to the public until 1938, when an enterprising cameraman broke the barrier by promising twenty-four watermelons for the feast which always follows. Since then it has become a tourist attraction. Although this native religious ceremony was carried to the Eastern Shoshonis at an early date, it did not reach Fort Hall until about 1900.[7]

The Ghost Dance religion was started in the 1880's by the humble Paiute prophet Wovoka (The Cutter), known locally in Nevada as Jack Wilson, a full-blood Indian who had acquired his name while working for a settler, David Wilson.[8] Wovoka had learned of Jesus, his Crucifixion, and his return to life through Bible-reading and family prayer in the Wilson home. He mingled this knowledge with the native concepts taught him by his father, a Paiute prophet.

In 1888, during an eclipse of the sun, Wovoka "died for a time." In his dream or vision, he talked with God, who told him that he should return and preach the doctrine of love and peace. The essence of his theory was happiness. He taught the simple truths: "Do no harm to anyone. Do right always. Do not tell lies. When your friends die, you must not cry. You must not fight."[9]

Wovoka claimed that God gave him new words for the old

[5] Shimkin, "Wind River Shoshone Sun Dance," *loc. cit.*, 33–34, 474.
[6] Bonnie Hunter, *These Americans in Moccasins*, 31–54.
[7] Madsen, *The Bannock of Idaho*, 26.
[8] Paul Bailey, *Wovoka*, 22.
[9] Mooney, "The Ghost Dance," *loc. cit.*, 653–1110.

Naroya or Ghost Dance songs. The Indians were to sing as they danced five consecutive nights. If they followed his teachings, used a sacred paint he prescribed, and repeated the Ghost Dance at intervals, the white man would disappear and dead Indians would return to life.

The Bannocks and Shoshonis of Fort Hall who became converts were the intermediaries between the prophet and the Plains tribes to the east. When the messiah craze was flourishing in 1889, a Bannock who had been among the Paiutes and who had been instructed by Wovoka went to the Wind River Reservation to spread the word that the dead were coming back to life—the messiah would come once again. Nevertheless, as late at 1892, Washakie was still skeptical of the new faith. On February 25 of that year, he dictated a letter to a "dear old time friend, Hank Brownson," from Washakie Mansion, Fort Washakie, Wyoming, in which he said:

> I have got something to ask you and I want you to write me and tell me what you know about this new profit that we hear about in the west, and if he is truely a great medicine man, we have heard a great deal about him. The Sioux believe him but we do not know what to think.[10]

Porcupine, a Cheyenne, and Short Bull and Kicking Bear, two Sioux leaders, seeking knowledge of the new religion, came to Fort Hall. After the agent had issued passes to the Bannock interpreters who had accompanied them, they went by train to Nevada to be instructed by Wovoka.[11]

His doctrine of humility, when carried to the Plains tribes, assumed ominous proportions. Love and tolerance gave way to hatred and revenge as the new religion spread. The warriors, now carrying weapons and wearing bulletproof Ghost Dance shirts, began dancing with messianic frenzy—not just five consecutive nights, but until they fell in exhaustion and recounted dreams of

[10] Washakie to Hank Brownson, February 25, 1892, Hebard Collection, University of Wyoming Library.
[11] Madsen, *The Bannock of Idaho*, 319–20.

an ideal world with hunting grounds stocked with vast herds of buffalo. Inspired by a new hope, they envisioned a world in which the Indian was once again lord of the Plains.

The new craze had the zeal of a war dance, filling the white man with terror. In the belief that it must be suppressed at all costs, the army threw its military might against the Sioux, among whom the craze had reached its most menacing state. Sitting Bull, Big Foot, and their followers were annihilated at Grand River and Wounded Knee.

Following the death of the two leading exponents of the abortive doctrine, the Indians gradually became disillusioned. The millenium did not take place on the date prophesied by Wovoka; the messiah did not come to alleviate the wrongs that had been done to the natives. Furthermore, it was found that the Ghost Dance shirts would not deflect bullets. The disillusioned Plains Indians, now without hope, gradually returned to their dreary existence. Wovoka's religion became but a memory everywhere except in Nevada, where it lingered in its original inoffensive form.

The Plains tribes, who were forced to discard the Ghost Dance as a religious concept, may be gradually turning from the Sun Dance to the Peyote Cult. This seems true of the Comanches, who have shown far more enthusiasm for Peyotism than for the Sun Dance religion.[12] Can it be that the Indians are finding that the sun and other power-giving agencies have been unable to turn back the tide of progress and preserve their way of life? This may account for the growing popularity of Peyotism, which serves as a religious solace, removed from outside interference. An authority on the Bannock-Shoshonis of Idaho says: "The new faith (Peyotism) is so shrouded in ritualistic forms, so subdued and so quiet that it could never be commercialized or become a spectacle."[13]

Although the Bannocks served as a center of diffusion for the Ghost Dance and the Wind River Shoshonis for the modern Sun

[12] Ernest Wallace and E. A. Hoebel, *The Comanches: Lords of the South Plains*, 331–32.

[13] Sven Liljeblad, "The Indians of Idaho," *loc. cit.*, 131.

Dance, the Comanches were both directly and indirectly responsible for the spread of the Peyote Cult. They taught it to the Kiowas and several other neighboring tribes before the turn of the century. These tribes caused the complex to spread throughout the Plains and finally into the great Basin and desert country of the Southwest. It has proved to be one of the most important cultural contributions which the Comanches have made to the way of life of their fellow Indians.[14]

Many Wind River Shoshonis believe Jesse Day was the first of their number to use peyote for medicinal purposes. His opinion on the use of peyote represents the usual Indian point of view:

> The Barefooters [Indians of Mexico] were the first to use Peyote; second were the Apaches, and third the Comanches.[15] It stayed with them a long time. Quanah Parker, chief of the Comanches, introduced it to other tribes. . . . He went to Washington to defend the Peyote religion.[16]
>
> I'll say it is good medicine to use. I've been through the mill. White people usually call it mescal. Some say it is a drug; I say it ain't a drug. It is a herb. For myself I went blind. I had my eyes operated five times. The last doctor I went to said nothing could be done for me. I had no hopes to see the mountains again.
>
> So I was using this medicine. But it took a long time—I never gave up on the peyote and finally I got my sight back. I went to Oklahoma and took it with the Comanches. . . . Some people say it makes you crazy. I know it won't. I've been taking it over thirty years and still got my head.

Visions once gained through fasting and prayer can be self-induced by the use of the button, or the dried top of the peyote plant. Because of the unpleasant taste and the fact that it is difficult to chew, it is used only for the effect which it produces. The peyote plant is a small, bulb-shaped, spineless cactus found in the

14 Wallace and Hoebel, *The Comanches*, 337.

15 Molly P. Stenberg, "The Peyote Cult among Wyoming Indians," (hereinafter cited as "The Peyote Cult") 1945, Western Archives, University of Wyoming Library, 143–45.

16 Alice Marriott gives Quanah Parker's "Peyote Way" in *The Ten Grandmothers*, 165–72.

arid hills along the Río Grande and southward into Mexico. The top, all that appears above the ground, resembles a pincushion, the bottom a radish in size and shape. The word *peyote* is a Spanish derivative from *peyotl* (caterpillar), referring to the downy center of the button.[17]

Among the Shoshoni, Arapaho, and other Plains tribes, peyote is used as a part of a ceremony of prayer and quiet contemplation, usually performed as a supplication for the recovery of someone who is ill. Persons taking part in the ritual for the most part are middle aged, although the medicine is given to children and even babies.

The rites are held in a tipi erected specifically for the purpose. The objects used in the ceremony resemble the Plains ritualistic paraphernalia. They consist of a small kettle-shaped drum; a special pipe, used by the leader during the midnight ritual; and a gourd rattle, a staff, and a feather. The ceremony is of night-long duration. As many men as can sit comfortably within the tipi circle may take part. Women as a rule are too busy preparing the feast which follows to participate. Whenever they attend, they do not take an active part in the singing.

Before the ritual begins, a bundle of sage is passed around. Everyone strips the leaves from a branch and rubs it over his body as a purification rite. To begin with, four peyote buttons are usually distributed to each participating member.

The meeting opens when the leader offers peyote on the altar, a crescent-shaped mound within which a fire is kept burning. He explains the purpose of the gathering and prays for the recovery of the one who is ill—the one for whom the prayers are to be offered. Then with his right hand the drum chief shakes the rattle for the opening songs. In his left hand he holds the staff and feather. After the leader has sung his opening songs, the drum is passed to the left so that each may play his own accompaniment as he sings his four prayer songs. This process, varied only by special intervals of prayer and distribution of peyote, is kept up throughout the night.

[17] Frederick W. Hodge, ed., *Handbook of American Indians*, II, 237.

The number of buttons consumed by an individual at Wind River during a ceremony is said to vary from ten to forty. The herb produces a form of spiritual exultation, differing entirely from that resulting from any other drug. The effect is heightened by the weird songs, the constant sound of the drum and the rattle, and the flickering glare of the fire, the "center of life in the tepee and the only moving thing."[18]

During her study of Peyotism at Wind River, Molly P. Stenberg was the first white woman ever to take part in the ceremony there. After partaking of peyote—half the amount given to the Indians—she recorded her reactions:

> The throbbing of the drum beats through me; my heart is beating and my blood flowing in time to its rhythm. It is exhilarating; it reaches into one and carries one's spirit on its pulsations. I find myself wanting to beat the drum, and notice that my hand and arm are keeping time with the drummers, my pen serving as a drumstick.

Some of the prayers were in English for her benefit. All were long and "delivered with many gestures, great humility, and deep reverence." She was impressed by the sight of the leader on his knees imploring heaven to bless and pity him. His voice was choked, and tears streamed down his cheeks. His humility and his desire to merit the blessing of the Creator were unquestionably sincere. It was a time in which he could give full expression to his innermost feelings.

At midnight, when the woman appointed to bring in the water entered, she poured four small portions on the ground to signify "the benefits coming from God's gifts." Following this, four morning songs were sung and the woman prayed, asking "Friend Peyote" to carry her pleas up to God. After the leader's concluding prayer, breakfast was served. It consisted merely of the four symbolic foods: water, corn, meat, and fruit. Translations of the period-marking songs in the ceremony are given by Mrs. Stenberg:

[18] Stenberg, "The Peyote Cult," *loc. cit.*, 69.

THE STARTING SONG

We start this meeting,
We sing this song to the Creator,
Asking Creator to pity him, the leader,
And pity the people in this meeting.
God help us.

THE MIDNIGHT WATER SONG

The water travels down below to us,
It travels down.
Whatever is moving, whatever is traveling.
It is always traveling.

THE QUITTING SONG

God have mercy upon us
That the cause of this meeting
May be granted.[19]

The Starting Song, though a prayer, is more in the nature of an explanation addressed to the people. The last line of it is directed to the Creator. Stylistically, the Quitting Song more closely resembles the pattern of the Shoshoni public prayer, which almost without exception begins with an invocation. Each of the prayers rendered in the Sun Dance by Lynn St. Clair began with "Our Father."

The Peyote Cult, which was firmly established on Oklahoma reservations by 1890, has spread through the Shoshoni tribes in recent years. Extreme poverty and uncertainty over land allotments caused the Indians in despair to turn to the new faith. Sam Lone Bear,[20] a dedicated missionary, is presumed to have brought the cult to Fort Hall in 1915.[21] He is also thought to have intro-

---

[19] *Ibid.*, 67–71, 75.

[20] Sam Lone Bear is said to have been a Sioux, and yet a Lone Bear Ute is believed to have held meetings among the Washo Indians of California in 1932. The name Lone Bear is well known at Fort Washakie, where the agent changed it to Lon Brown. Many Browns among the Arapahoes claim descent from a Lone Bear.

duced it to the Gosiutes of Utah between 1921 and 1925.[22] The Deep Creek and Skull Valley Indians had two "peyote ways"— the "tipi way" and the "Sioux way."

The Northern Arapahoes received the worship in the middle 1890's from their kinsmen, the Southern Arapahoes of Oklahoma. About a decade later when some of the hostile feeling between the Shoshonis and the Arapahoes had died down, Jock Bull Bear, a medicine man of the Southern Arapahoes, began to instruct the Wind River Shoshonis. He met Charley, son of Washakie, while he was visiting at Wind River, and he invited him to Oklahoma to learn "the right Peyote way."[23] Young Washakie spent three months during the winter of 1916 with the Southern Arapahoes, while he received instructions from Bull Bear. Many individual leaders of both tribes have traveled to Oklahoma to receive training in the ritual from recognized Kiowa and Comanche leaders.

The strength of the Peyote Cult no doubt rests on three basic principles: Indian pride in its being a native religion; faith in the healing properties of the herb; and the social nature of the meetings, with the accompanying entertainment and feasting. The visiting that takes place during the time when the Indians are waiting for food to be served is soul satisfying to the friendly natives.

While the Peyote meetings are religious in nature, the doctrines are few and vague. "Friend Peyote" has come to the Indians to lead them to God as Jesus came to the white race. In their monotheistic concept, they consider Peyote as an intermediary. Even though some authorities may brand the meetings as idolatrous, they have unquestionably helped a downtrodden people in group recovery.

Although the Indians have found their natural approach to God, they have had difficulty gaining official recognition. Peyotists in Oklahoma, defending their religious liberties, in 1918

[21] Liljeblad, "The Indians of Idaho," *loc. cit.*, 132.

[22] Carling Malouf, "Gosiute Peyotism," *A.A.*, Vol. XLIV (1942), 93.

[23] Charley Washakie met an untimely death some years later. While under the influence of the white man's liquor, he drove down a railroad track in Idaho and was killed by a train.

organized the Native American church, which has received inter-tribal recognition by most groups from Canada to Mexico. Instead of causing unnatural dissensions among the Indians as the white man's whisky does, peyote is conducive to a feeling of peace. Some members of the cult are convinced that there would be no wars if people would resort to the use of the drug as a tranquilizer.

There has been native as well as white reaction against the cult, for it has threatened the power of the Buhagants. Also, church bells are unable to toll the Indians to Sunday morning Mass when a Peyote meeting is in progress. The Arapahoes are predominantly Catholic and the Shoshonis Episcopalian. This, however, has little to do with the lack of unity. In each case, it has been a matter of who got there first.

The ritualistic service of the Catholic church has a definite appeal to the Indians. Sensing this, the Episcopal church at St. Michael's (Ethete, Wyoming) introduced the formality of the High Church among the Arapahoes, who learned of the Protestant church through Sherman Coolidge, the Reverend John R. Roberts' assistant. When Coolidge, a full-blood Arapaho and ordained minister, told his people of the proposed mission at St. Michael's, they labeled it "e-th-te!" ("good!").[24]

A stigma against the white man's religion had apparently been forgotten. It had originated at the Horse Creek Treaty Council in 1851, when De Smet "regenerated" more than fifteen hundred Indians, about three hundred of whom were Arapahoes. Shortly afterwards, many died from a plague which the Indians believed was in some way connected with the white man's religion.[25]

When the Most Reverend Bishop James O'Connor of Omaha, in the 1880's, learned that the government was building a boarding school for the children on the Wind River Reservation, he raised $5,000 and offered it for the purpose of fitting out the school. According to Catholic records, the offer was accepted.

[24] Helen Butler's novel, *A Stone Upon His Shoulder*, 49. This novel is based on the life of Sherman Coolidge.

[25] McGovern, *History of the Diocese of Cheyenne*, 196–98.

Father John Jutz was appointed to take charge, and the Franciscan sisters at Buffalo, New York, were selected to be the teachers.

When Jutz arrived at Lander in 1884, he was told that the government school had been given over to the Reverend John Roberts, an Episcopalian. Roberts had been teaching some of the Shoshoni children at his home near the school. As soon as the building was ready, the agent gave him full charge. Patrick A. McGovern's comment, in his record of the Catholic church, was: "First come, first grind."

Roberts, a Welshman, came to Wyoming by way of southern Colorado during the winter of 1883, one of the coldest in the state's history. When he arrived at the post that had been assigned to him by the Right Reverend J. F. Spalding, Episcopal bishop of Colorado and Wyoming, the thermometer registered 60° below zero. Four people froze to death at Wind River. The 150-mile trip from Green River to Lander required eight days.

The stage line had been discontinued because of the severe weather. Consequently, the young minister accompanied the mail clerk at his own risk.[26] Government requirements made it mandatory that mail be delivered, as a heavy penalty was exacted in the event of delay. According to members of the Roberts family, the young minister had asked to be sent to establish a mission "among the wildest Indians in America." After his initial experience, he found the Indians tame compared to the weather.

Jutz reminded the agent of the Catholic Bishop's offer. The agent in turn expressed regret and suggested opening another school wherever the priest chose. Knowing that the Arapahoes occupied the eastern part of the reservation and that they had already shown interest in education by sending some of their children to the government school, Jutz decided to begin his missionary efforts among them. With Father Moriarty, the first priest at Lander, he set out early one morning, after he had decided to locate his new mission (St. Stephen's) on the delta formed by the Little and Big Wind rivers. He gave the following account of his new venture:

[26] Olden, *Shoshone Folk Lore,* 65–66.

My belongings and a few old boards found behind the store were piled up in a wagon. On the way, we picked up my pony (bought from one of the soldiers) and the tent (bought from an army surgeon) and reached the country of the Arapahos shortly after midday.

My chattels were unloaded and after brief respite the priest returned to Lander by short cut, leaving me all alone with my Indians. I began at once to pitch my tent and to put up an altar for Mass on the following morning. Chief Black Coal was my next door neighbor, so I invited him and his two wives and two children to watch me during the Mass. He and his family sat down upon the ground before my tent and witnessed with awe the celebration of the Divine Mysteries.

The Mass was my only spiritual missionary occupation as I did not understand the Indian language, nor they mine. I next enlarged my habitation by making another tent out of the extra canvas which is usually spread over the tent itself. My sleeping apartment was in a corner of the tent and my bed a mattress made of hedge branches covered with buffalo hide.

My kitchen was a hole in the ground into which I laid a few stones. During the first night I was awakened by the sound of a big bass drum and the ghostly incantations of the medicine men who were plying their skill at the home of a sick woman. I can hear that wierd incantation to this very day, it left such an indelible impression upon my memory.[27]

The same pessimistic attitude expressed by Agent Stone at Fort Hall is found in the letters of A. C. Jones, missionary-teacher at Wind River. Since Washakie was not a Christian until a few years before his death, it was difficult to convert the Shoshonis, as Jones found:

My work is not exactly what I had hoped it would be: it is more secular than religious . . . it being almost an absolute necessity to teach the pupils English in order to explain the many things connected with religion, that heathen people have not words to try and teach the adults. They are too old to learn our language or at least would not do so, and anything beyond the common

[27] McGovern, *History of the Diocese of Cheyenne*, 199-200.

incidents of their daily life cannot be readily explained to them even in their own language: they have just enough words to meet their wants; useless ones would soon be forgotten as they have no means of perpetuating them.

There are about two thousand Indians on this reservation and all of them are greatly in need of religious enlightenment from a Christian's point of view, though I am sure that they are perfectly contented with their limited knowledge on such subjects: but if a person has anything to instruct them in that will help their finances, all are willing to be pupils. They know the value of a dollar just as much as white people do.

Some of them are wealthy for Indians, possessing perhaps from fifty to one hundred and fifty horses. A few of them have cattle, but they are the exception. Government supports all, whether rich or poor; it allows each individual a certain amount of flour, beef and a few other articles each week. . . . [The Indians] have many good points and traits of character, and according to my judgment, are not nearly as bad as they are represented to be. They fight and are probably quick to shed blood. . . . The Indian steals cattle when hungry (occasionally) which sometimes leads to the sacrifice of human life, but hunger is an extenuating circumstance. They sometimes give presents to each other but always expect the equivalent in return.[28]

The missionary-teacher, in a second letter, still found little reason for optimism.

A lady living in Philadelphia sent two dozen Gospel Hymns. . . . The children can sing eight or ten of them very nicely, but are ignorant of their meaning; however, I hope the time is coming when they shall understand and rejoice in the truths they contain. Nevertheless, the prospect is not very encouraging. . . .

Before taking up such a work as this, one is inclined to believe that very soon the effect of religious teaching will be seen, but after giving it a trial of some months and finding that little change has been wrought; there is a feeling created which if expressed would be somewhat like the following: Well, I see there is no use in trying to teach the Indians anything, for they don't seem to

[28] Jones to Quackenbush, September 11, 1884.

have any desire to be guided by our religious teaching, although they listen very attentively to the parables and miracles of our Lord and to the story of the cross told to them through an interpreter. Great patience and a religious faith in Our Heavenly Father are very necessary in a work of this kind if one is laboring to win souls to Christ.[29]

In January, 1897, there occurred an incident that gave Washakie a new impression of the white man's religion.[30] The chief was especially fond of a wild young son who was killed in a tavern. After word reached him, he vowed that when he came down from the mountain, he would kill the first white man he met, and he would continue to shoot until he himself was killed. Later that night the Reverend John Roberts, hearing of this, went to Washakie's lodge and offered to forfeit his life for the son's. The chief refused his offer. At the same time, he asked what medicine the missionary possessed that made him more courageous than a chieftain. At three o'clock the following morning (January 24), Washakie was baptized.

Many converts were made by Roberts following this. He further endeared himself to the Indians by editing and publishing two pamphlets in their native language.[31] Rare copies of these are still prized at Wind River.

While there were many obstacles in the way of religious acculturation among the Shoshonis, the educational problems were also difficult to solve. Irene Kinnear Meade, a native of Wind River Valley, gives an account of educational acculturation of the Shoshonis from the Indian point of view.[32] She was so keenly interested in school that, after finishing college in California, she

[29] *Ibid.*, January 7, 1885.

[30] Ziegler, *Wyoming Indians*, 10.

[31] *The Shoshone Prayer Service*, translated by Charles Lajoe, a Shoshoni student of Roberts, 1883–1890; *Questions and Answers*, translated, 1900, into the native language by Enga-Barrie, also a Shoshoni. Both out-of-print publications were courtesy of Delmer Wesaw, son of Allasandra (Tom Wesaw), Fort Washakie, Wyoming.

[32] Irene Kinnear Meade, "Some Early-Day School Events in the Wind River Valley," courtesy Mrs. Charles Snyder, Crowheart, Wyoming.

dedicated her life to teaching children on the reservation. She is also remembered as the first woman to become a member of the Shoshoni business council. The following is an excerpt from her account:

At Fort Washakie, a steam whistle at the government school proclaimed the beginning of morning sessions, the noon hour, and closing time. The whistle was so loud and clear that it could be heard seven or eight miles away. People at the Kinnear ranch on the Big Horn River could set their time by it.

The government school at Fort Washakie and the two missions (the Roberts School for girls and the St. Stephens Catholic School) were boarding schools where Indian children entered in the fall and remained throughout the school term. Their board, room, and clothing were furnished. There were no plumbing facilities in any of these schools. Water was placed in basins in the dormitories for the morning face and hand cleansing period. At the government school, the children took their Saturday baths in large square tubs in the laundry building. In addition to their introduction to the classroom, the Indian children were taught cleanliness—how to keep their hands, faces, and noses clean—and particularly how to comb and brush their hair. They also learned to keep their shoes polished.

The most difficult problems the Indian children faced were the discarding of their native tongue for the English language and changing from the soft comfort of the moccasin to the confining stiffness of the shoe. This was as hard to bear as the homesickness from which they suffered acutely. Some of the Indian parents were reluctant to part with their children and tried to evade the rule by camping in out-of-the-way places along Big Wind River before school started.

School attendance was compulsory, and when some children did not report, the Indian police were sent out to bring them in. Often the police were seen taking children behind them on horseback. The children would be crying and their hair tousled. The policemen were full blood Indians who wore blue uniforms, carried guns and quirts, and looked fierce, especially to the children. It was usual for the little boys to have on only a shirt and a pair of moccasins on the momentous ride to school.

As administration changed, the government school took on the appearance of a public school. Busses transported students to and from, and excellent hot lunches were served at the noon hour. Education and religion progressed among the Indians in Wyoming until today special schools are no longer needed.

Perhaps Washakie was more farsighted than anyone realized by keeping less desirable lands toward the mountains—the Wind River, the Absaroka, the Teton Mountains. His Indians were not fenced in as completely as the Arapahoes, who were given no choice but to farm. Their first efforts were discouraging, and when famine threatened, they ate the seed which they were supposed to plant. As the cattle issued to them were unbranded, those that did not find their way into the herds owned by white cattlemen were eaten by the Indians.

Comparatively speaking, the Shoshonis have a far better economy than many Indian tribes today.[33] Besides being able to make use of their natural resources, they have wages and salaries from seasonal off-reservation work and moneys earned through arts and crafts and other means. They also receive "unearned income" as dividend (per capita) payments from tribal funds derived from oil, gas, and minerals; grazing unit assignments; and farm and pasture leases.

As of August 1, 1963, the monthly dividend payments came to sixty-four dollars for each Shoshoni and forty-five dollars for each Arapaho on the tribal roles.[34] The assets are held in common, and the returns therefrom are equally distributed to the two tribes, with the difference in individual payments resulting from the fact that there are fewer Shoshonis than Arapahoes.

The same pattern of mobility is observable among both the Arapahoes and Shoshonis, who still enjoy their long trips, now in automobiles. The Shoshonis visit back and forth with the Bannocks and other bands of their people and sometimes with the Comanches, while the Arapahoes enjoy prolonged visits with

[33] "History and Economy of Wind River Indians," 3–4.

[34] Data supplied by Clyde W. Hobbs, superintendent of the Wind River Reservation, Fort Washakie, August 9, 1963.

the Southern Arapahoes and Cheyennes in Oklahoma or with the Northern Cheyennes and Crows in Montana. Sometimes they visit their old allies, the Sioux in the Dakotas.

At Wind River Agency today the average person might not be able to tell the Shoshonis and Arapahoes apart, although the former, when full blood, are shorter, stockier, and darker complexioned. One of the old-timers in Lander vows that he can tell an Arapaho horse from a Shoshoni horse at a hitching post, but it is more difficult to distinguish between their automobiles.

The Indians dress alike, the men in typical Western attire, with Levis, shirts, and shoes. Only the older women wear the out-sized calico dresses, shawls, and moccasins. Although some of the women cling to their braids, long hair is seen only among the older full-blood men. Most of the Arapahoes are full blood but there are few full-bloods among the Shoshonis. The men and women of both tribes like decking out in their native costumes with lavish beadwork for their tribal dances, which are gaining in favor. In their ceremonial dress the beadwork—floral designs for the Shoshonis and geometric designs for the Arapahoes—is not always consistent. Sometimes a wide girdle may be typical of Shoshoni work, while a headband may show the Arapaho influence.

The Wyoming Shoshonis find self-expression in various forms of pageantry, including the "Gift of the Waters," held annually at Thermopolis, Wyoming. This is purely a Shoshoni affair, as it depicts the relinquishment of the Big Spring to the white man in the McLaughlin Agreement, or the Treaty of 1896. The Shoshonis and Arapahoes held their first joint tribal fair in August, 1963.

"All American Indian Days," an annual event held in Sheridan, Wyoming, in August, draws Indians from throughout the country. Here the natives have a chance to lose themselves momentarily in their old tribal ceremonies and dances. They often enter into the spirit of their unrehearsed performances with such intensity that it is difficult for them to stop. Briefly, they are again the Indians of the Plains, the Basin, the coastal region, or the High Plateau. They are oblivious to the white man who watches them.

Their campground, many years ago, was a common meeting place for the Plains Indians who once accepted warfare as a recognized way of life. A few miles to the north is the famous Custer Battlefield, to the south the site of Old Fort Phil Kearny, "the hated fort on the Little Piney."[35] The old animosities are gone as the tribes visit back and forth and talk over "the good old days" in English. Some of the Indians arrive by train, bus, or airplane, but most of the tribes trek across country in small bands very much as their fathers did before them. Only today cars, trucks, and trailers take the place of horses and travois.

Since the turn of the century all residents of the Wind River Reservation have had double names, given to them by Herman G. Nickerson, agent. It took him two years to Anglicize more than two thousand names. Forty-nine of the signers of the Treaty of 1904 affixed their full names to the document.

As we have observed, the forced acculturation of all Shoshonis has been slow but effective under favorable conditions. The Indians are proud not only of their American citizenship but also of the culture which they have had to accept. Now firm believers in education, the Wind River Indians alone have contributed about $27,550 to their scholarship funds. While they enjoy modern conveniences, they are aware of the farsightedness of their great statesman Washakie, who steadfastly maintained that the white man's way of life was superior to their own.

There is one note of discouragement. Since the tribal council voted to allow liquor to be sold on Wind River Reservation, the fatal accident and crime rate has been alarmingly high. No definite study of criminality has been made among the Shoshonis, but newspaper accounts indicate that they, like other Indians, have a problem which cannot be readily solved. In an over-all study, Omer C. Stewart, an authority on behavior science at the University of Colorado states:

> Nationally the Indian rate for all types of arrests is nearly three times that of Negroes and about eight times that of Whites. An examination of the causes for arrests indicates the Indians are par-

[35] Fort Phil Kearny was designated a national landmark in 1963.

ticularly vulnerable to arrests for drunkenness and other crimes involving alcohol. In fact, drunkenness alone accounted for 71% of all Indian arrests in 1960. The Indian arrests for all alcohol-related crimes is twelve times greater than the national average and over five times that of Negroes.[36]

Stewart, in summarizing the problem, expresses his opinion that "the Indians must acquire standards and values which are so important to them that they will have good reasons not to drink to excess. They need personal experience which can only be acquired in time."[37]

Liquor, like factionalism, seems to be a tribal matter which the Indians must work out for themselves. Meanwhile, the elders shake their heads sadly and agree in their hearts with the wisdom of the old chieftain who said long ago:

> Send it [liquor] not to us; we would rather die by the arrows of the Blackfeet. It unmans us for the hunt and for defending ourselves against our enemies; it causes unnatural dissentions among ourselves; it makes the Chief less than his Indians; and by its use, imbecility and ruin would come upon the Shoshone tribe.[38]

[36] "Questions Regarding American Indian Criminality" (mimeographed), lecture given in Denver, Colorado, December 29, 1961.
[37] Stewart to Virginia Cole Trenholm, February 4, 1963.
[38] Farnham, *Travels*, I, 264.

CHAPTER EIGHTEEN

Retribution

Lᴇɢᴀʟʟʏ ᴛʜᴇ Aʀᴀᴘᴀʜᴏᴇs were not entitled to share with the Shoshonis in the amount paid for the Big Hot Spring in 1896, nor should they have had any part in the second McLaughlin Reservation Relinquishment Agreement in 1904, ceding to the United States 1,346,320 acres lying north of Big Wind River. They did not even have squatters' right to the land. The government remained indifferent to the situation until 1927, when Congress passed an act enabling the Shoshonis to sue in the Court of Claims for having to share their reservation with the Arapahoes.[1] The Shoshonis also sought compensation for losses through white encroachment. This became Case Number H–219. The petition, or bill of complaint, was filed on May 27, 1927.

The Shoshonis were represented by four able attorneys: George M. Tunison, Albert W. Jefferis, Francis S. Howell, and Charles J. Kappler, all of Omaha except Kappler, who specialized in Indian cases in Washington, D.C. On the local scene, E. O. Fuller, of Laramie, Wyoming, an early-day land agent for the government, was called upon to appraise the land and to secure evidence to support the case in other ways.

From the beginning, there was a question concerning the date when the land was "taken" from the Shoshonis. The historical date would have been March 18, 1878, when the Arapahoes, under escort of the United States Army, were placed on lands ceded to the Shoshonis by treaty. However, the attorneys for the Indians acted upon the theory that the "taking" was in 1927, the year when Congress passed the act authorizing the Indians to sue the

[1] 144 (Pt. II) Stat. 1349, March 3, 1927.

government. It would not have been difficult to arrive at the value of the land on that date.

The Court of Claims decided that the land was "taken" on August 13, 1891, because at that time the Commissioner of Indian Affairs definitely stated that the Arapahoes had equal rights with the Shoshonis on the reservation.[2] The court accordingly ruled that the value should be fixed as of that date. Upon appeal, the United States Supreme Court held that the date should be 1878.[3] This made it difficult to determine the value, since there was no land title in the Lander area at that time. Before the case was concluded, values had to be shown as of 1927, 1891, and 1878, all of which necessitated long-drawn-out court action, costly for the Indians.

Specifically the items at issue were oil, minerals, and lands, which included the standing timber, a part of the realty until it had been cut. Each of these assets required separate appraisers.

The written reports are dated over a period from October, 1929, to March, 1938. The volume of evidence is shown by the fact that the land appraiser alone submitted thirty-one such reports, of lengths varying up to as high as 396 pages. Printed evidence, amounting to 1,873 pages, is now on file with the Indian Claims Commission in Washington, and hundreds of pages introduced as exhibits were not printed. Included in the records is testimony concerning the value of the use of the lands by the Arapahoes, loss of game, use of public facilities, reservation boundaries, trespass by stock and settlers, water power, reservation schools, value of game and hunting rights, summer and winter ranges, and government accounting records.

More than eight hundred questionnaires were sent out for information that might be of use in the suit. One of the most significant of these is a questionnaire on game animals, filled out by Dick Washakie and Quentin Quay, leaders on the reservation at the time. Through their interpreter, they told of seeing hundreds of buffalo lying out on the range after being killed by white men.

[2] 82 Ct. Cl. 23, December 2, 1935. [3] 299 U.S. 476, January 4, 1937.

They maintained that it was not hearsay as they had seen them with their own eyes. They also told of cases in which the white men killed buffalo and poisoned their carcasses to bait coyotes for their pelts.

The United States appealed from the valuation fixed by the Court of Claims. It maintained that the Indians had a right to the surface of the land, "limited to those uses incident to the cultivation of the land and the grazing of livestock but that such right did not include ownership of the timber and mineral resources." This brought the case a second time before the Supreme Court, a rather unusual procedure. The Court rejected the government contention, and the valuation stood as fixed by the Court of Claims.[4]

The value of the land as of March, 1878, was finally placed at $1.35 an acre, and a judgment was rendered against the government for the value of one-half the reservation—that part occupied by the Arapahoes.[5] The Shoshonis lost their claim for damages from white trespassers and the destruction of game by white hunters.

The cases of other Indian tribes against the government about the same time did not turn out as well, for their lands were valued much lower. The Blackfoot and Assiniboin lands of Montana were valued at $.50 an acre, as were also the Mandan lands in North Dakota and Montana. This low value gave the Indians little or no recovery after government offsets were deducted. Had the Shoshoni lands been valued so low, nothing would have been left after deductions. As it was, they were awarded $6,364,-677.91 for the value of one-half the reservation, less offsets (including the cost of operating the reservation since its creation) of $1,956,233.68, leaving a balance of $4,408,444.23. From this sum, the attorneys' fees and other court costs of the suit were deducted. The government paid the interest since 1878 "as just compensation."

From the local standpoint, the case was especially important

[4] 304 U.S. 111 (October, 1937, term), April 25, 1938.
[5] 85 Ct. Cl. 331, 333, June 1, 1938.

to the state of Wyoming because it cleared the title to 1,171,770 acres of land belonging to the Arapahoes. It also gave legal status to these Indians, who became citizens of the state.

The award would have given Washakie great satisfaction had he lived to see it. He had been willing, we recall, to relinquish a part of his reservation for a price. It was not a sale but a court order that finally brought recompense to his Indians. When the expenses accrued from 1868 to the time of the court action were tabulated, ironically the Shoshonis were charged for the famous saddle presented to Washakie during Grant's administration.[6]

The appropriation for the payment of the judgment was made on June 25, 1938, and the next year the method of payment was prescribed.[7] Under the terms of the Shoshone Judgment Act of July 27, 1939,[8] a per capita allocation of $2,450, credited on the books of the Office of Indian Affairs, was made to the Shoshonis on the rolls as of that date.[9] A payment of $100 was made in cash, and the remaining $2,350 was to be expended under planned programs. Minors' shares were held in the Treasury, although each was allowed $500 to help in a family program. After reaching the age of eighteen, the young Shoshonis were entitled to the remaining $1,850 with accrued interest. This money, however, had to be spent in programs approved by the superintendent and the tribal council.

The Shoshonis, under an agreement for reimbursement from joint tribal funds (including oil and gas royalties and permits), allowed $1,000,000 of their judgment money to be used in a joint tribal land acquisition program, their major project.[10] Practically all of the remaining alienated and allotted lands on the reservation were restored to Indian tribal ownership.

6 In list of offsets, "Presents and Provisions," $125.00, 82 Ct. Cl. 23, 56.

7 52 Stat. 1156.

8 53 Stat. 1128.

9 The decision to place only quarter-bloods or more on the tribal rolls was approved by the Joint Business Council on April 24, 1940, and approved by the Secretary of the Interior on November 23, 1949, ten years after the Judgment Act.

10 "Missouri River Basin Investigations," *Report*, 106, Bureau of Indian Affairs, July 31, 1950.

A second case—this time tried before the Indian Claims Commission—sought restitution for the government offset deductions in Case No. H–219.[11] The Shoshonis claimed that of the estimated $1,956,233.68 only $400,000.00 was actually Indian expense. Furthermore, the case sought to right another wrong—that done in 1872 when Felix Brunot negotiated a treaty claimed to be "inadequate and unconscionable." The petition in this case, Number 63 (unofficially known as the Brunot Case), was filed on May 20, 1950.

The background is more significant than the case itself because it indicates the extent of the aboriginal domain. In the Treaty at Fort Bridger in 1868, the Eastern Shoshonis gave up their rights to 44,672,000 acres of land lying in Colorado, Wyoming, Utah, and Idaho, to settle peacefully on their reservation of only 3,054,182 acres. Salt Lake City, Utah; Pocatello, Idaho; and Evanston and Green River, Wyoming, are now on lands relinquished. Apparently to gain Washakie's consent (1872) to a surrender of 710,642 acres of ceded land, the chief was granted under the Brunot Agreement $2,500—or a "salary" of $500 a year for five years.

Case Number 63 did not reach the Court of Claims, much less the Supreme Court.[12] While it was before the Indian Claims Commission, the attorneys for the Indians and the government came to terms. Their agreement, filed with the Indian Claims Commission on April 19, 1957, awarded the Shoshonis $533,013.60, from which offsets were taken to the amount of $100,000.00. Accordingly, the Indian Claims Commission issued its "Order of Final Judgment" on April 22, 1957, specifically awarding the Indians $433,013.60 for the land acquired through the Brunot Agreement, referred to as Brunot land.[13] This amounted to $377.00 for each Shoshoni on the tribal rolls. No consideration was given the

[11] Indian Claims Commission, created by Act of Congress, August 13, 1946. 60 (Pt. I) Stat. 1049.

[12] For background material on the case, see 82 Ct. Cl. 23, 46–47, 77.

[13] Agreement and Order for Final Judgment furnished by Jean R. Hanna, clerk, Indian Claims Commission, Washington, D.C., July 17, 1961 and July 9, 1963. Money to pay the award was appropriated on June 21, 1957.

claim that much of the offset deduction in Case Number H–219 was not Indian expense.

In 1960 the *Wyoming State Journal* (Lander) carried a sequel to the story of H–219.[14] It stated, under the heading "SHO-SHONES GET $500 EACH NOV. 1," that payments totaling $901,303 were to go to 1,777 Shoshonis on the rolls. The payment comprised the unpaid balance ("Tunison money" from H–219) due the Indians, who had asked for it in lump sum so that it could be used in improving their homes and buying items beyond the reach of their monthly per capita payments. The request met with the approval of the Commissioner of Indian Affairs.

Noticeable changes have taken place as the result of improved economy. Many of the Indians have remodeled their houses and bought station wagons and late-model cars. Television aerials loom above even the most humble dwellings. But the most outward sign of acculturation is an absence of tipis. When this study was started a decade ago, many of the Indians had summer lodges in their yards. Most of these have now been replaced by trailer houses, some obviously expensive.

Other changes are in store for the Shoshonis, as the Indian Claims Commission has accepted two important cases (Numbers 326 and 367) as justifiable, with the amount of the claims to be paid in each still to be determined. The former concerns gold taken from South Pass, the latter the aboriginal domain of the nation. Since the Shoshonis have proved that they respond well to the demand of the white man's culture under favorable conditions, the future looks bright not only for the Wind River band but also for the Lemhis, the Gosiutes, and the Western Shoshonis who will share in the award in the more important of the two cases, Number 367.

Alcoholism is still a major problem, but perhaps by the time the final judgments are rendered the Shoshonis as a tribe may have acquired those standards and values necessary to prevent drinking to excess. There is still a package liquor store at Fort Washakie, but the two bars which once flourished are now closed, one on

[14] October 13, 1960.

the voluntary part of the owner and the other through purchase. Herman and Daisy St. Clair, now owners of the latter, have converted it into a popular restaurant and gift shop. A prominent sign back of the lunch counter reads: "No Intoxicants Allowed."

Herman St. Clair, whose picture is being used on a poster by the United States Travel Service to encourage European travel in America, is deserving of the honor, but neither as a medicine man nor as a resident of Thermopolis as he is reported to be. He is a tribal leader, residing on his farm west of Fort Washakie, where he has worked consistently over the years for the betterment of his people.

Bibliography

I. UNPUBLISHED MATERIALS

Bragg, W. F., Jr. "Sacajawea's Role in Western History." University of Wyoming, Laramie, 1953.

Carter, William A. "Pocket Vocabulary of the Shoshone Language." W. C. Castro Collection, Western Archives, University of Wyoming, Laramie.

Collier, Donald. "The Sun Dance of the Plains Indians," Indians of the United States. Office of Indian Affairs, Washington, 1940.

Crawford, Jacke Newton. "Fort Supply, or Wyoming's First Agricultural Settlement." University of Wyoming, Laramie, 1955.

Daines, W. H. "Journal." Latter-day Saints Church Historian's Office, Salt Lake City.

Dupont, Mrs. August. "Recollections." (Tape recording.) Lander, Wyoming.

Eastman, Charles A. "Special Report on Sacajawea," to Commissioner of Indian Affairs, March 2, 1925. Western Archives, University of Wyoming, Laramie.

Forbis, Richard G. "Religious Acculturation of the Flathead Indians." Montana State University, Bozeman, 1950.

Fuller, E. O. "Notes Regarding the Shoshone Indian Case No. H–219." Western Archives, University of Wyoming, Laramie, December 15, 1938.

———. Shoshone Indian Case No. H–219 and the Brunot Case, No. 63, with Letters, Exhibits, Questionnaires, and Other Materials Pertaining Thereto. Personal files, Laramie, Wyoming.

Green, A. F. C. "Fremont County." Wyoming State Museum, Cheyenne, 1941.

Holihan, Delores. "Shoshoni Indians in Wyoming through 1868." University of Wyoming, Laramie, 1959.

Hyde, Orson. To "Washakeete," Fort Supply, December 10, 1853.

Lyman Stake Unpublished Historical Records, entry May 9, 1854, Latter-day Saints Church Historian's Office, Salt Lake City.

Indian Office Records. Central Superintendency, 1851–56; Idaho Superintendency, 1863–80; Nevada Superintendency, 1861–80; Oregon Superintendency, 1842–80; Utah Superintendency, 1849–80; and Wyoming Superintendency, 1869–80. National Archives, Washington.

Jones, A. C. To Miss Nellie Quackenbush. Two letters in the possession of Mrs. Evelyn Corthell Hill, Laramie, Wyoming. Photocopy courtesy Clarice Whittenburg.

"Journal History." Latter-day Saints Church Historian's Office, Salt Lake City, Utah.

Liljeblad, Sven. "The Indians of Idaho." Idaho State Historical Society, Boise, 1960.

Meade, Irene Kinnear. "Some Early Day School Events in the Wind River Valley." In the possession of her daughter, Mrs. Charles Snyder, Crowheart, Wyoming.

Moore, David. "Salmon River Mission Journal" and "Salmon River Mission Record." Latter-day Saints Church Historian's Office, Salt Lake City.

Moore, J. K., Jr. "Recollections of Early Days at Fort Washakie." (Tape recording.) Lander, Wyoming.

Murphy, Mrs. E. V. A., and others. "Desert Friends." Nevada Historical Society, Reno, 1939.

Overholt, Helen. "The Warm Valley Folk." Wyoming State Museum, Cheyenne.

Post Surgeon's Record Book. Camp Augur, 1869–70; Camp Brown, 1870–78; Fort Washakie, 1878–1909. In the possession of J. K. Moore, Jr., Lander, Wyoming.

Powell, J. W. "Outlines of the Philosophy of the North American Indians." Read before the American Geographical Society, December 29, 1876, Colorado State Museum, Denver.

Richards, William. "History of Brigham Young." Latter-day Saints Church Historian's Office, Salt Lake City.

Riddell, Francis A. Unpublished field notes on the Lone Pine Indians of California. Sacramento, California.

St. Clair, Lynn. "The So-called Shoshone Sun Dance, *Dagoo Winode.*" Western Archives, University of Wyoming, Laramie, 1936.

Shimkin, D. B. "Some Interactions of Culture, Needs, and Personality among the Wind River Shoshone." (Ph. D. dissertation.) University of California, Berkeley, 1939.

Sides, Johnson. Biographical tape recording. Nevada Historical Society, Reno.

Siebert, Roger D. "A History of the Shoshoni Indians of Wyoming." University of Wyoming, Laramie, 1961.

Smart, George W. "Mission to Nevada." Office of Religious Activities, Haskell Institute, Lawrence, Kansas, 1958.

Steege, L. C. "Petroglyphs of Dinwoody." Wyoming State Museum, Cheyenne, 1954.

Stenberg, Mollie P. "The Peyote Cult among Wyoming Indians." Western Archives, University of Wyoming, Laramie, 1946.

Stewart, Omer C. "Questions and Answers Regarding Indian Criminality." Courtesy Dr. Stewart, University of Colorado, Boulder, December 29, 1961.

———. To Virginia Cole Trenholm, concerning Indian criminality, February 4, 1963.

Stone, Forrest R. "Indians at Work and Play." University of Wyoming, Laramie, n.d.

———. "Proposed Ten Year Program." Fort Washakie, Wyoming, 1944.

Sowers, T. C. "Petroglyphs and Pictographs of Dinwoody." University of Wyoming, Laramie, 1939.

———. "Petroglyphs of West Central Wyoming." University of Wyoming, Laramie, 1940.

Walker War. Letters and other manuscript materials. Military Records Division, Utah State Historical Society Archives, Salt Lake City.

Washakie. To Hank Brownson, concerning Wovoka, the Paiute prophet, dated and dictated at "Washakie Mansion," Fort Washakie, Wyoming, February 25, 1892. Western Archives, University of Wyoming, Laramie. (Washakie's name affixed by person writing the letter.)

"Washakie." Typed excerpt from General Ray's manuscript (original of which is in the Pennsylvania Historical Society Library). University of Wyoming, Laramie.

2. NEWSPAPERS

Box Elder (Utah) *News Journal* (September 14, 1943).

The Shoshonis

Deseret News (Salt Lake City) (August 8, 1851; June 30, July 20, and September 30, 1854; September 19, 1855; August 17 and 24, September 14, 1859; and December 10, 17, and 31, 1862).
Lander (Wyoming) *Evening Post* (April 1, 1935).
Pocatello (Idaho) *Tribune* (September 29, 1897).
Republican-Boomerang (Laramie, Wyoming) (July 11, 1950).
Riverton (Wyoming) *Ranger* (March 24, 1960).
St. Louis (Missouri) *Republican* (September 26–November 30, 1851).
St. Louis Weekly Reveille (March 1, 1847; July 17 and 24, 1848).
Worland (Wyoming) *Grit* (February 19, 1920).
Wyoming Churchman (Laramie, Wyoming) (Centennial Edition—May, 1959, and January, 1960).
Wyoming Eagle (Cheyenne) (July 28, 1961).
Wyoming State Journal (Lander, Wyoming) (October 13, 1960).

3. GOVERNMENT DOCUMENTS AND LEGISLATIVE REPORTS

Berry, M. P. "Report," 41 Cong., 2 sess., *House Exec. Doc. 1.*
———. "Report," 43 Cong., 1 sess., *Sen. Exec. Doc. 24.*
Board of Indian Commissioners. Annual reports, 1872 and 1896.
Bureau of Indian Affairs. "History and Economy of the Indians of the Wind River Reservation, Wyoming," in *Missouri River Basin Investigations*, Department of the Interior, Area Office, Bureau of Indian Affairs, Billings, Montana, July 31, 1950.
———. "The Montana-Wyoming Indian," in *Missouri River Basin Investigations*, Department of the Interior, Area Office, Bureau of Indian Affairs, Billings, Montana, June, 1961.
Brunot, Felix R. "Negotiations with the Shoshone Indians for the Relinquishment of a Portion of Their Reservation in Wyoming," in *Report*. Washington, Government Printing Office, 1873.
Campbell, J. A. "Report," 41 Cong., 2 sess., *House Exec. Doc. 1*, Pt. 3.
Commissioner of Indian Affairs. Annual Reports, 1851 to 1906.
Connor, P. E. "Report," 50 Cong., 2 sess., *Sen. Exec. Doc. 70*, II.
Department of the Interior and General Land Office. Decisions. "Opening of Shoshone Reservation," *Cases Relating to the Public Lands*, July, 1905–June, 1906, Vol. XXXIV. Washington, Government Printing Office, 1906.
Doty, James D. "Report," 37 Cong., 3 sess., *House Exec. Doc. 1*, II.
———. "Report," 38 Cong., 1 sess., *House Exec. Doc. 1.*
———. "Report," 38 Cong., 2 sess., *House Exec. Doc. 1.*

324

Doyle, William P. "Report," 38 Cong., 1 sess., *House Exec. Doc. 1.*

Ficklin, B. F. "Report," 35 Cong., 2 sess., *Sen. Exec. Doc. 1,* II.

Forney, Jacob. "Report," 35 Cong., 2 sess., *Sen. Exec. Doc. 1.*

Fort Bridger Treaty, 1863. 58 Cong., 2 sess., *Sen. Exec. Doc. 319,* I.

Ghem, Levi A. "Report," 45 Cong., 3 sess., *House Exec. Doc. 1,* Pt. 5.

Indian Depredations in Oregon and Washington. 36 Cong., 2 sess., *House Exec. Doc. 29.*

Irish, O. H. "Report," 39 Cong., 1 sess., *House Exec. Doc. 1.*

Irwin, James. "Report," 42 Cong., 2 sess., *House Exec. Doc. 1,* Pt. 5.

————. "Report," 43 Cong., 2 sess., *House Exec. Doc. 1,* Pt. 5.

————. "Report," 44 Cong., 1 sess., *House Exec. Doc. 1,* Pt. 5.

Jones, William. "Report upon the Reconnaissance of Northwestern Wyoming." Washington, Government Printing Office, 1877.

Kappler, Charles J. (ed.). *Indian Affairs: Laws and Treaties.* 3 vols. Washington, Government Printing Office, 1903, 1913.

"Klamath Report," 40 Cong., 2 sess., *House Exec. Doc. 1,* II.

Klamath Treaty. 58 Cong., 2 sess., *Sen. Exec. Doc. 319,* II.

Lander, W. F. "Report," 36 Cong. 1 sess., *Sen. Exec. Doc. 42.*

————. "Report," 36 Cong., 2 sess., *Sen. Exec. Doc. 46.*

————. "Report," 36 Cong., 2 sess., *Sen. Exec. Doc. 36.*

McLaughlin, James. "Report," 54 Cong., 1 sess., *Sen. Exec. Doc. 247.*

Mann, Luther, Jr. "Report," 40 Cong., 2 sess., *House Exec. Doc. 1,* II.

————. "Report," 40 Cong., 3 sess., *House Exec. Doc. 1,* II.

Miller, C. H. "Report," 36 Cong., 2 sess., *Sen. Exec. Doc. 36.*

"Pacific Wagon Road Report," 36 Cong., 2 sess., *Sen. Exec. Doc. 40.*

Patten, James. "Report," 45 Cong., 2 sess., *House Exec. Doc. 1,* Pt. 5, VIII.

"Shoshone Depredations," 36 Cong., 1 sess., *Sen. Exec. Doc. 2.*

Stansbury, Howard. "Report," 32 Cong., spec. sess., *Sen. Exec. Doc. 3,* II.

U.S. Bureau of Census. *Report of Indians Taxed and Not Taxed.* Eleventh Census Report, Washington, Government Printing Office, 1894.

U.S. Court of Claims. Case No. H–219, "Shoshone Tribe of Indians of the Wind River Reservation in Wyoming, Petitioner, vs. The United States of America, Defendant." (Published portion of the case), Western Archives, University of Wyoming, Laramie.

U.S. Department of Health, Education, and Welfare. Public Health Service. *Indians on Federal Reservations in the U.S.* (1) Albuquerque Area (Arizona, Colorado, New Mexico, and Utah), 1960; (2) Billings Area (Wyoming and Montana), 1958; and (3) Phoenix Area (Arizona, California, Nevada, and Utah). Washington, Government Printing Office, 1961.

U.S. Department of the Interior. "U.S. Indian Population and Land." Washington, Government Printing Office, 1960.

U.S. Statutes at Large, XI. December 3, 1855, to March 3, 1859. Boston, Little Brown & Co., 1859.

U.S. Survey of Conditions of Indians. Hearings authorized by 70 Cong., 2 sess., *Resolution 79*, Committee on Indian Affairs, July 22–August 2, 1929. Washington, Government Printing Office, 1933.

(The) War of the Rebellion. Ser. I, Vol. L, Pts. I and II. Washington, Government Printing Office, 1897.

"Washakie's Medal," 39 Cong., 2 sess., *House Exec. Doc. 1.*

"Western Shoshones," 41 Cong., 3 sess., *House Exec. Doc. 1*, Pt. 4.

———, 43 Cong., 1 sess., *House Exec. Doc. 1*, Pt. 5.

4. BOOKS AND PAMPHLETS

Allen, A. J. *Ten Years in Oregon*. Ithaca, New York, Andrus, Gauntlett Company, 1850.

Allen, W. A. *The Sheep Eaters*. New York, Shakespeare Press, 1913.

Alter, J. Cecil. *James Bridger*. Salt Lake City, Shepard Book Company, 1925.

Andrews, Ralph W. *Indians as the Westerners Saw Them*. Seattle, Superior Publishing Company, 1963.

Bailey, Paul. *Walkara, Hawk of the Mountains*. Los Angeles, Westernlore Press, 1956.

———. *Wovoka, the Indian Messiah*. Los Angeles, Westernlore Press, 1957.

Bancroft, Hubert Howe. *History of Utah, 1540–1887*. San Francisco, The History Company, 1890.

———. *Native Races*. (Vol. I of *Works of Hubert Howe Bancroft*) San Francisco, The History Company, 1886.

Bartlett, Richard A. *Great Surveys of the American West*. Norman, University of Oklahoma Press, 1962.

Biddle, Nicholas (ed.). *The Journals of the Expedition under the Command of Captains Lewis and Clark*. New York City, Heritage Press, 1962.

Billington, Ray Allen. *Westward Expansion: A History of the American Frontier.* New York, Macmillan Company, 1949.

Bischoff, W. N. *The Jesuits of Old Oregon.* Caldwell, Idaho, The Caxton Printers, Ltd., 1945.

Bonner, T. D. (ed.). *The Life and Adventures of James P. Beckwourth.* New York, Macmillan, 1892.

Bonney, Orrin H. *Guide to Wyoming Mountain and Wilderness Areas.* Denver, Sage Books, 1960.

Bourke, John G. *On the Border with Crook.* New York, Charles Scribner's Sons, 1896.

Brackenridge, Henry M. *Journal of a Voyage up the River Missouri in 1811.* Ed. by R. G. Thwaites. In *Early Western Travels, 1748–1846.* Cleveland, The Arthur H. Clark Company, 1904.

Brimlow, George F. *The Bannock Indian War of 1878.* Caldwell, Idaho, The Caxton Printers, Ltd., 1938.

Brooks, Juanita. *The Mountain Meadows Massacre.* Norman, University of Oklahoma Press, 1962.

Brosnan, Cornelius J. *History of the State of Idaho.* New York, Charles Scribner's Sons, 1935.

Brown, James S. *Life of a Pioneer.* Salt Lake, George Q. Cannon & Sons Company, 1900.

Brown, Jennie B. *Fort Hall.* Caldwell, Idaho, The Caxton Printers, Ltd., 1932.

Bryant, Edwin. *What I Saw in California; Or, Rocky Mountain Adventures.* Philadelphia, Appleton & Company, 1848.

Burroughs, Raymond D. *The Natural History of the Lewis and Clark Expedition.* East Lansing, Michigan State University Press, 1961.

Burton, Richard F. *The City of the Saints.* New York, Harper and Brothers, 1862.

Butler, Helen. *A Stone on His Shoulder.* Philadelphia, Westminster Press, 1953.

Carson, Christopher (Kit). *Kit Carson's Autobiography.* Ed. by Milo M. Quaife. Chicago, The Lakeside Press, 1935.

Catlin, George. *George Catlin: Episodes from "Life Among the Indians" and "Last Rambles."* Ed. by Marvin C. Ross. Norman, University of Oklahoma Press, 1959.

———. *North American Indians.* 2 vols. Edinburgh, John Grant, 1926.

Chalfant, W. A. *Story of Inyo.* Bishop, California, The Author, 1933.

Chisholm, James. "James Chisholm's Journal of the Wyoming Gold

Rush. In *South Pass, 1868.* Ed. by Lola Homsher. Lincoln, University of Nebraska Press, 1960.
Chittenden, Hiram M. *The History of the American Fur Trade of the Far West.* 2 vols. New York, The Press of the Pioneers, Inc., 1935.
Clark, William Philo. *The Indian Sign Language.* Philadelphia, L. R. Hammersly, 1885.
Clayton, William. *William Clayton's Journal.* Salt Lake City, Clayton Family Association, 1921.
Clyman, James. *James Clyman, American Frontiersman, 1792–1881.* Ed. by Charles J. Camp. San Francisco, California Historical Society, 1928.
Coke, Henry John. *A Ride over the Rocky Mountains to Oregon and California.* London, Richard Bentley, 1852.
Cook, John R. *The Border and the Buffalo.* Ed. by Milo M. Quaife. Chicago, The Lakeside Press, 1938.
Coutant, Charles G. *The History of Wyoming.* Vol. I. Laramie, Chaplin, Spafford & Mathison, 1899.
Cox, Ross. *Adventures on the Columbia River, Including the Narrative of a Residence of Six Years on the Western Side of the Rocky Mountains.* New York, J. and J. Harper, 1832.
Crawford, Medorem. "Journal of Medorem Crawford." Ed. by F. G. Young. In *Sources of the History of Oregon,* Vol. I, No. 1. Eugene, Oregon, Star Job Office, 1897.
Crook, George. *General George Crook, His Autobiography.* Ed. by Martin F. Schmitt. Norman, University of Oklahoma Press, 1946.
Dale, Harrison C. *The Ashley-Smith Explorations and the Discovery of a Central Route to the Pacific.* Cleveland, The Arthur H. Clark Company, 1918.
David, Robert B. *Finn Burnett.* Glendale, California, The Arthur H. Clark Company, 1937.
Defenbach, Byron. *Idaho: The Place and Its People.* 3 vols. Chicago, New York, The American Historical Society, Inc., 1933.
———. *Red Heroines of the Northwest.* Caldwell, Idaho, The Caxton Printers, Ltd., 1930.
———. *State We Live In, Idaho.* Caldwell, The Caxton Printers, Ltd., 1933.
Dellenbaugh, Frederick S. *Frémont and '49.* New York, Putnam and Sons, 1914.

Del Monte, H. D. *Life of Chief Washakie and Shoshone Indians.* Lander, Wyoming, privately printed, 1945.

De Smet, Pierre Jean. *Letters and Sketches, with a Narrative of a Year's Residence among the Indian Tribes of the Rocky Mountains.* Ed. by R. G. Thwaites. Vols. XXVII and XXVIII of *Early Western Travels.* Cleveland, The Arthur H. Clark Co., 1906.

———. *Life, Letters, and Travels of Father Pierre-Jean De Smet.* Ed. by Hiram M. Chittenden and Alfred T. Richardson. 4 vols. New York, F. P. Harper, 1905.

De Voto, Bernard A. *Across the Wide Missouri.* Boston, Houghton Mifflin, 1947.

———. *Course of Empire.* Boston, Houghton Mifflin, 1952.

———. *The Journals of Lewis and Clark.* Boston, Houghton Mifflin, 1953.

Dickson, Albert J. *Covered Wagon Days, Journal of Albert Jerome Dickson.* Cleveland, The Arthur H. Clark Company, 1929.

Dodge, Grenville M. *Biographical Sketch of James Bridger.* New York, Unz & Company, 1905.

———. *How We Built the Union Pacific Railway.* Washington, Government Printing Office, 1910.

Dodge, Richard I. *Our Wild Indians.* Hartford, Connecticut, A. D. Worthington & Company, 1882.

Douglas, F. H. *The Ute Indians.* (Leaflet 10). Denver Art Museum, 1930.

Drannan, W. F. *Chief of Scouts Piloting Emmigrants across the Plains of Fifty Years Ago.* Chicago, Rhodes & McClure Publishing Company, 1910.

———. *Thirty-one Years on the Plains and in the Mountains.* Chicago, Rhodes, 1900.

Driggs, B. W. *History of Teton Valley, Idaho.* Caldwell, Idaho, The Caxton Printers, Ltd. 1926.

Driggs, Howard R. *The Pony Express Goes Through.* New York, Frederick A. Stokes Company, 1935.

———. *Westward America.* New York, Putnam and Sons, 1942.

Dunn, J. P. *Massacres of the Mountains, 1815–1875.* New York, Archer House, n.d.

Dunraven, W. T., 4th Earl of. *Hunting in the Yellowstone.* (Reprint of *The Great Divide,* 1876). London, Chatto & Windus, 1878.

Eells, Myron. *Marcus Whitman*. Columbus, Ohio, Harriman Publishing Company, 1909.

Elkin, Henry. "The Northern Arapaho of Wyoming." In *Acculturation in Seven American Indian Tribes*, ed. by Ralph Linton. New York, Appleton Century, 1940.

Ellison, Robert S. *Fort Bridger, Wyoming*. Casper, privately printed, 1931.

———. *Independence Rock*. Casper, privately printed, 1930.

Ewers, John C. *The Blackfeet: Raiders on the Northwestern Plains*. Norman, University of Oklahoma Press, 1958.

Farnham, Thomas J. *Travels in the Great Western Prairies*. Ed. by R. G. Thwaites, Vol. XXVIII in *Early Western Travels*. Cleveland, The Arthur H. Clark Company, 1906.

Favour, Alpheus H. *Old Bill Williams, Mountain Man*. Chapel Hill, University of North Carolina Press, 1936.

Ferris, Warren Angus. "A Diary of the Wanderings on the Sources of the Rivers Missouri, Columbia, and Colorado from February, 1830, to November, 1835." In *Life in the Rocky Mountains*, ed. by Paul C. Phillips. Denver, Old West Publishing Company, 1940.

Finerty, John F. *War-Path and Bivouac*. Chicago, M. A. Donohue & Company, 1890.

Fourt, Judge E. H. *A Sanctuary*. Privately printed, n.d.

Frémont, John Charles. *Memoirs of My Life*. New York, Belford, Clarke & Company, 1887.

———. *Report of an Exploring Expedition to the Rocky Mountains, 1842*. Washington, Blair & Rivers, 1845.

Gass, Patrick A. *A Journal of the Voyages and Travels of a Corps of Discovery under the Command of Captain Lewis and Captain Clark*. New York, F. P. Harper, 1897.

Gebow, Joseph A. *A Vocabulary of the Snake or Sho-sho-nay Dialect*. Green River, Wyoming, privately printed, 1868.

Gottfredson, Peter. *History of Indian Depredations in Utah*. Salt Lake City, Skelton Publishing Company, 1919.

Gove, Jesse A. *The Utah Expedition, 1857–1858*. Ed. by Otis G. Hammond. Concord, New Hampshire Historical Society, 1928.

Grinnell, George Bird. *The Fighting Cheyennes*. New York, Charles Scribner's Sons, 1915.

Grouard, Frank. *Frank Grouard, Life and Adventures*. Ed. by Joe de Barthe. St. Joseph, Missouri, Combe Print Company, 1894.

Bibliography

Hafen, Le Roy R., and W. J. Ghent. *Broken Hand, the Life Story of Thomas Fitzpatrick.* Denver, Old West Publishing Company, 1931.

——, and A. W. Hafen. *Colorado.* Denver, Old West Publishing Company, 1943.

——. *The Overland Mail, 1849-1869.* Cleveland, The Arthur H. Clark Company, 1926.

Haines, Francis. *The Nez Percés.* Norman, University of Oklahoma Press, 1955.

Hamilton, William T. *My Sixty Years on the Plains, Trading, Trapping, and Indian Fighting.* Ed. by E. T. Siebert. New York, Forest and Stream Publishing Company, 1905.

Harris, Burton. *John Colter, His Years in the Rockies.* New York, Charles Scribner's Sons, 1952.

Harris, Jack. "The White Knife Shoshoni of Nevada." In *Acculturation in Seven American Indian Tribes,* ed. by Ralph Linton. New York, Appleton Company, 1940.

Hart, Shiela, and Vida F. Carlson. *We Saw the Sun Dance.* Concord, California, 1948.

Hastings, Lansford W. *The Emigrant's Guide to Oregon and California.* Princeton, Princeton University Press, 1932.

Hebard, Grace Raymond. *Sacajawea.* Glendale, California, The Arthur H. Clark Company, 1957.

——. *Washakie.* Cleveland, The Arthur H. Clark Company, 1930.

Heizer, R. F., and M. A. Whipple. *The California Indians.* Berkeley, University of California Press, 1957.

Hill, George H. *Vocabulary of the Shoshone Language.* Salt Lake City, 1877.

Hodge, Frederick Webb (ed.). *Handbook of American Indians North of Mexico.* 2 vols. *Bulletin 30,* Bureau of American Ethnology. Washington, Government Printing Office, 1912.

Hoig, Stan. *The Sand Creek Massacre.* Norman, University of Oklahoma Press, 1961.

Hopkins, Sarah Winnemucca. *Life among the Piutes: Their Wrongs and Claims.* Ed. by Mrs. Horace Mann. Boston, Cupples, 1883.

Howard, Oliver Otis. *Nez Percé Joseph.* Boston, Lee and Shepard, 1881.

Humfreville, J. Lee. *Twenty Years among our Hostile Indians.* Hartford, Connecticut, Worthington and Company, 1903.

331

Hunter, Bonnie. *These Americans in Moccasins*. New York, Vantage Press, 1959.

Huntington, D. B. *Vocabulary of the Ute and Sho-sho-ne or Snake Tribe*. Salt Lake, Salt Lake Herald Office, 1872.

Hyde, George E. *Indians of the High Plains*. Norman, University of Oklahoma Press, 1959.

———. *Red Cloud's Folk*. Norman, University of Oklahoma Press, 1937.

———. *Spotted Tail's Folk, a History of the Brulé Sioux*. Norman, University of Oklahoma Press, 1961.

Idaho Writer's Project. *Idaho*. New York, Oxford University Press, 1950.

Irving, Washington. *The Adventures of Captain Bonneville*. New York, J. B. Miller & Company, 1885.

———. *Astoria*. Philadelphia, Carey, Lea and Blanchard, 1836.

Jackson, W. Turrentine. *Wagon Roads West*. Berkeley, University of California Press, 1952.

James, Thomas. *Three Years among the Indians and Mexicans*. Ed. by Walter B. Douglas. St. Louis, State Historical Society of Missouri, 1916.

Johnston, William G. *Overland to California, 1849*. Oakland, Bio Books Publishers, 1948.

Jones, Daniel W. *Forty Years among the Indians*. Salt Lake, Juvenile Instructor Office, 1890.

Jones, William. *Report upon the Reconnaissance of Northwestern Wyoming, 1873*. Washington, Government Printing Office, 1877.

Kelly, Luther S. *Yellowstone Kelly*. Ed. by Milo M. Quaife. New Haven, Yale University Press, 1926.

Kroeber, A. L. *Handbook of the Indians of California. Bulletin 78*, Bureau of American Ethnology. Washington, Government Printing Office, 1925.

Langford, Nathanial P. *Diary of the Washburn Expedition to the Yellowstone*. St. Paul, Minnesota, N. P. Langford, 1905.

Larpenteur, Charles. *Forty Years a Fur Trader on the Upper Missouri*. 2 vols. Ed. by Elliott Coues. New York, Francis P. Harper, 1898.

Leonard, Zenas. *The Adventures of Zenas Leonard*. Ed. by John C. Ewers. Norman, University of Oklahoma Press, 1959.

Lewis, Meriwether, and William Clark. *Original Journals of the Lewis and Clark Expedition*. 8 vols. Ed. by R. G. Thwaites. New York, Dodd, Mead, 1904–1905.

Lowe, Percival D. *Five Years a Dragoon*. Kansas City, Missouri, Franklin Hudson Publishing Company, 1906.

Luttig, John C. *Journal of a Fur-trading Expedition on the Upper Missouri*. Ed. by Stella M. Drumm. St. Louis, State Historical Society of Missouri, 1920.

Lyman, George D. *The Saga of the Comstock Lode*. New York, Charles Scribner's Sons, 1934.

McGovern, Patrick A. *History of the Diocese of Cheyenne*. Cheyenne, Wyoming Labor Journal, 1941.

Mack, Effie Mona. *Nevada, a History of the State from the Earliest Times through the Civil War*. Glendale, California, The Arthur H. Clark Company, 1936.

McLaughlin, James. *My Friend the Indian*. Boston, Houghton Mifflin Company, 1910.

McNickle, D'Arcy. *They Came Here First*. New York, J. P. Lippincott, 1949.

McWhorter, L. V. *Hear Me, My Chiefs!* Caldwell, Idaho, The Caxton Printers, Ltd., 1952.

Madsen, Brigham D. *The Bannock of Idaho*. Caldwell, Idaho, The Caxton Printers, Ltd., 1958.

Manly, William Lewis. *Death Valley in '49*. San Jose, California, Pacific Tree and Vine Company, 1894.

Marriott, Alice. *The Ten Grandmothers*. Norman, University of Oklahoma Press, 1945.

Marsh, James B. *Four Years in the Rockies*. Newcastle, Pennsylvania, W. B. Thomas, 1884.

Mattes, Merrill J. *Indians, Infants, and Infantry*. Denver, The Old West Publishing Company, 1960.

Mayhall, Mildred P. *The Kiowas*. Norman, University of Oklahoma Press, 1962.

Miles, Nelson A. *Personal Recollections and Observations of General Nelson A. Miles*. New York, The Werner Company, 1896.

Miller, Alfred Jacob. *The West of Alfred Jacob Miller*. Ed. by Marvin C. Ross. Norman, University of Oklahoma Press, 1951.

Montabé, Marie. *This Is the Sun Dance*. Privately printed, 1951.

The Shoshonis

Morgan, Dale L. *The Great Salt Lake.* New York, Bobbs-Merrill Company, 1947.
———. *Jedediah Smith and the Opening of the West.* Indianapolis, Bobbs-Merrill Company, 1953.
Mumey, Nolie. *The Life of Jim Baker, 1818-1898.* Denver, The World Press, Inc., 1931.
Oglesby, Richard Edward. *Manuel Lisa and the Opening of the Missouri Fur Trade.* Norman, University of Oklahoma Press, 1963.
Olden, Sarah Emilia. *Shoshone Folk Lore.* Milwaukee, Wisconsin, Morehouse Publishing Company, 1923.
Owen, John. *The Letters and Journals of Major John Owen.* Ed. by Seymour Dunbar, with notes by Paul C. Phillips. 2 vols. New York, Edward Eberstadt, 1927.
Palmer, Joel. *Journal of Travels over the Rocky Mountains to the Mouth of the Columbia River, 1845-1846.* Ed. by R. G. Thwaites. Vol. XXX in *Early Western Travels.* Cleveland, The Arthur H. Clark Company, 1906.
Parker, Samuel. *Journal of an Exploring Tour beyond the Rocky Mountains.* Auburn, New York, J. C. Derby & Company, 1846.
Pattie, James O. *Personal Narrative.* Ed. by R. G. Thwaites. Vol. XVIII in *Early Western Travels.* Cleveland, The Arthur H. Clark Company, 1906.
Phillips, Paul C., and J. W. Smurr. *The Fur Trade.* 2 vols. Norman, University of Oklahoma Press, 1961.
Preuss, Charles. *Exploring with Frémont.* Norman, University of Oklahoma Press, 1958.
Putnam, George Palmer. *Death Valley and Its Country.* New York, Duell, Sloan & Pearce, 1946.
Raynolds, William F. *Report on the Exploration of the Yellowstone River.* Washington, Government Printing Office, 1868.
Reese, John E. "The Shoshone Contribution to Lewis and Clark." In *Idaho Yesterdays.* Vol. II. Boise, Idaho State Historical Society, 1958.
Reid, Russell. *Sakakawea, The Bird Woman.* Bismarck, North Dakota Historical Society, 1950.
Remington, Frederick. *Frederick Remington's Own West.* Ed by Harold McCracken. New York, Dial Press, 1960.
Remy, Jules, and Julius Brenchley. *A Journey to Great Salt Lake.* Vol. I. London, W. Jeffs, 1861.

334

Replogle, Wayne F. *Yellowstone's Bannock Indian Trails*. Yellowstone Interpretive Series, No. 6. Yellowstone, Yellowstone Library and Museum Association, 1956.

Roberts, John. *Questions and Answers*. Trans. by Enga-Barrie, a Shoshone Indian. Privately printed, 1900.

———. *Shoshone Prayer Service*. Trans. by Charles Lajoe, a Shoshone, 1883–90. *Privately printed*, n.d.

Rockwell, Wilson. *The Utes, a Forgotten People*. Denver, Sage Books, 1956.

Roe, Frank G. *The Indian and the Horse*. Norman, University of Oklahoma Press, 1955.

Rollins, Philip Ashton. *The Discovery of the Oregon Trail, Robert Stuart's Narratives*. New York, Charles Scribner's Sons, 1935.

Ross, Alexander. *Adventures of the First Settlers on the Oregon or Columbia River*. Ed. by R. G. Thwaites. Vol. VII in *Early Western Travels*. Cleveland, The Arthur H. Clark Company, 1904.

———. *The Fur Hunters of the Far West*. 2 vols. London, The Smith, Elder & Company, 1855.

Russell, Osborne. *Journal of a Trapper; Or, Nine Years in the Rocky Mountains, 1834–1843*. Boise, Idaho, The Syms-York Company, Inc., 1921.

Ruth, Kent. *Great Day in the West*. Norman, University of Oklahoma Press, 1963.

Ruxton, George F. *Adventures in Mexico and the Rocky Mountains*. London, John Murray, 1847.

———. *Life in the Far West*. London, John Murray, 1849.

Sabin, E. L. *Building the U.P.* Philadelphia, Lippincott, 1917.

Sage, Rufus B. *Scenes in the Rocky Mountains*. Glendale, California, The Arthur H. Clark Company, 1956.

Sandoz, Mari. *The Buffalo Hunters*. New York, Hastings House, 1951.

———. *Cheyenne Autumn*. New York, McGraw-Hill, 1953.

Schoolcraft, Henry R. *Information Respecting the History, Conditions, and Prospects of the Indian Tribes of the United States*. 5 vols. Philadelphia, Lippincott, Grambo and Company, 1852–1860.

Schultz, James W. *The Bird Woman*. Boston, Houghton Mifflin Company, 1918.

Scott, Mary Hulbert. *The Oregon Trail through Wyoming*. Aurora, Colorado, Powder River Publishers, 1958.

Shinn, George Hazen. *Shoshonean Days.* Glendale, The Arthur H. Clark Company, 1941.

Simpson, J. H. *Report of Explorations across the Great Basin.* Washington, Government Printing Office, 1876.

——. *The Shortest Route to California.* Philadelphia, J. B. Lippincott, 1861.

Slattery, Charles L. *Felix Reville Brunot.* New York, Longmans, Green & Company, 1901.

Slotkin, J. S. *The Peyote Religion, a Study in Indian-White Relations.* Glencoe, Illinois, Free Press, 1956.

Smith, Jedediah. *Travels of Jedediah Smith.* Ed. by Maurice Sullivan. Santa Ana, California, Fine Arts Press, 1934.

Smucker, Samuel J. *Life of Colonel John Charles Frémont.* New York, Miller, Orton and Mulligan, 1856.

Stansbury, Howard. *An Expedition to the Valley of the Great Salt Lake of Utah.* Philadelphia, Lippincott, Grambo & Company, 1852.

Steege, L. C. *Stone Artifacts of the Northwestern Plains.* Colorado Springs. The Northwestern Plains Publishing Company, 1961.

Stone, Elizabeth A. *Uinta County.* Laramie, Wyoming, Laramie Printing Company, 1924.

Strahorn, Robert E. *The Handbook of Wyoming and Guide to the Black Hills and Big Horn Region.* Chicago, The Western Press, 1877.

Stratton, Fred D. *Early History of South Pass, Wyoming.* N.p., n.d.

Stuart, Granville. *Forty Years on the Frontier.* Ed. by Paul C. Phillips. Cleveland, The Arthur H. Clark Company, 1925.

Stuart, Robert. *The Discovery of the Oregon Trail.* Ed. by Philip Ashton Rollins. New York, Charles Scribner's Sons, 1935.

Swanton, John R. *The Indian Tribes of North America. Bulletin 145,* Bureau of American Ethnology. Washington, Government Printing Office, 1952.

Talbot, Ethelbert. *My People of the Plains.* New York, Harper & Brothers, 1906.

Talbot, Theodore. *The Journal of Theodore Talbot, 1843 and 1849–1852.* Ed. by Charles H. Carey. Portland, Oregon, Metropolitan Press, 1931.

Thompson, David. *David Thompson's Narrative of His Explorations in Western America, 1784–1812.* Ed. by J. B. Tyrrell. Toronto, Canada, Champlain Society, 1916.

Topping, E. S. *The Chronicles of the Yellowstone*. St. Paul, Minnesota, Pioneer Press, 1883.

Townsend, John K. *Narrative of a Journey across the Rocky Mountains to the Columbia River, 1832–1834*. Ed. by R. G. Thwaites. Vol. XXI in *Early Western Travels*. Cleveland, The Arthur H. Clark Company, 1905.

Trenholm, Virginia Cole, and Maurine Carley. *Wyoming Pageant*. Casper, Wyoming, Bailey School Supply, 1954.

Underhill, Ruth. *Red Man's America*. Chicago, University of Chicago Press, 1953.

Vaughn, J. W. *With Crook at the Rosebud*. Harrisburg, Pennsylvania, The Stackpole Company, 1956.

Victor, Frances F. *The River of the West*. Hartford, Columbia Book Company, 1870.

Vinton, Stallo. *John Colter, Discoverer of Yellowstone Park*. New York, Edward Eberstadt, 1926.

Wallace, Ernest, and E. A. Hoebel. *The Comanches: Lords of the South Plains*. Norman, University of Oklahoma Press, 1952.

Warren, Eliza Spalding. *Memoirs of the West*. Portland, Marsh Printing Company, 1916.

Webb, Walter Prescott. *The Great Plains*. Boston, Houghton Mifflin, 1931.

Wedel, Waldo R. *Prehistoric Man on the Great Plains*. Norman, University of Oklahoma Press, 1961.

Weeks, Rupert. *Pachee Goyo, The Bald One*. New York, Vantage Press, Inc., 1963.

Welch, Charles A. *History of the Big Horn Basin*. Salt Lake City, Deseret News Press, 1940.

Wellman, Paul I. *The Indian Wars of the West*. Garden City, New York, Doubleday, 1954.

Wheat, Carl. *Trailing the 49'ers through Death Valley*. San Francisco, Fields, 1940.

Williams, Joseph. *Narrative of a Tour from the State of Indiana to the Oregon Territory in the Years 1841–1842*. New York, The Cadmus Book Shop, 1921.

Wilson, E. N. *The White Indian Boy*. Ed. by Howard R. Driggs. New York, World Book Company, 1919.

Wissler, Clark. *Indians of the United States*. New York, Doubleday, Doran & Company, 1940.

Wislizenus, F. A. *A Journey to the Rocky Mountains in the Year 1839.* St. Louis, State Historical Society of Missouri, 1912.

Woodruff, Wilford. *Journal and Life History.* Ed. by M. F. Cowley. Salt Lake City, Deseret News Press, 1909.

Wyeth, John B. *Oregon, or a Short History of a Long Journey.* Ed. by R. G. Thwaites. Vol. XXI in *Early Western Travels.* Cleveland, The Arthur H. Clark Company, 1905.

Wyeth, Nathaniel J. "Indian Tribes of the South Pass of the Rocky Mountains." Ed. by H. R. Schoolcraft. In *Indian Tribes of the United States,* Vol. I. Philadelphia, Lippincott, Grambo and Company, 1851–1857.

Ziegler, W. H. *Wyoming Indians.* Privately printed by the Episcopal Church of Laramie, Wyoming, n.d.

5. ARTICLES AND SPECIAL REPORTS

Auerback, Herbert S. "Father Escalante's Itinerary," *Utah Historical Quarterly,* Vol. IX, No. 4. Salt Lake City, Utah State Historical Society, October, 1941.

Ball, John. "Across the Continent Seventy Years Ago," *Oregon Historical Quarterly,* Vol. III, No. 4. Eugene, Oregon Historical Society, 1902.

Brackett, Albert G. "The Shoshoni or Snake Indians, Their Religion, Superstitions, and Manners," *Annual Report.* Board of Regents, Smithsonian Institution. Washington, Government Printing Office, 1879.

Bragg, William F., Jr. "Feed 'em in the Winter; Fight 'em in the Summer," *The Westerner's Brand Book.* Boulder, Johnson Publishing Company, 1945.

Brooks, Juanita. "Indian Relations on the Mormon Frontier," *Utah Historical Quarterly,* Vol. XII, Nos. 1 and 2. Salt Lake, Utah State Historical Society, January and April, 1944.

Chamberlin, Ralph V. "The Ethno-botany of the Gosiute Indians," *Memoirs,* Vol. II, No. 5. Menasha, Wisconsin, American Anthropological Association, 1911.

Clark, E. E. "George Gibb's Account of Indian Mythology in Oregon and Washington Territory," *Oregon Historical Quarterly,* Vol. LVII, No. 2. Portland, Oregon Historical Society, 1935.

Coville, Frederick V. "The Panamint Indians of California," *American*

Anthropologist, Vol. V. Menasha, Wisconsin, American Anthropological Association, 1892.

Crampton, C. G. "The Discovery of the Green River," *Utah Historical Quarterly*, Vol. XX, No. 4. Salt Lake City, Utah State Historical Society, October, 1952.

Culin, Stewart. "Games of the American Indians," *Twenty-fourth Annual Report*, Bureau of American Ethnology. Washington, Government Printing Office, 1907.

Davenport, T. W. "Recollections of an Indian Agent," *Oregon Historical Quarterly*, Vol. VIII. Portland, Oregon Historical Society, December, 1907.

Delacy, Walter W. "A Trip up the South Snake River in 1863," *Contributions*, Vol. I. Helena, Historical Society of Montana, 1876.

Denig, Edwin T. "Indian Tribes of the Upper Missouri." Ed. by J. N. B. Hewitt. *Forty-sixth Annual Report* (1928–29), Bureau of American Ethnology. Washington, Government Printing Office, 1930.

Dibble, Charles E. "The Mormon Mission to the Shoshone Indians," *Utah Humanities Review*, Vol. I, Nos. 1, 2, 3. Salt Lake City, January, April, and July, 1947.

Dorsey, George A. "The Shoshonean Game of Nă-wá-tă-pi," *Journal of American Folk-Lore*, Vol. XIV. Philadelphia, Bennett Hall, University of Pennsylvania, 1901.

Dutcher, B. H. "Piñon Gathering among the Panamint Indians," *American Anthropologist*, Vol. VI. Menasha, Wisconsin, American Anthropological Association, 1893.

Gatschet, Albert S. "The Klamath Indians of Southwestern Oregon," *Contributions*, North American Ethnology, Vol. II, No. 1. U.S. Geological Survey, Washington, Government Printing Office, 1890.

Gebhard, David S., and H. A. Cahn. "The Petroglyphs of Dinwoody, Wyoming," *American Antiquity*, Vol. XV, No. 3. Society for American Archaeology, Salt Lake City, University of Utah Press, 1950.

Hafen, LeRoy R. "Fraeb's Last Fight and How Battle Mountain Got Its Name," *Colorado Magazine*, Vol. VII, No. 3, Historical Society of Colorado, May, 1930.

Haines, Francis. "How the Indian Got the Horse," *American Heritage* (February, 1964).

———. "Where Did the Plains Indians Get Their Horses?" *American Anthropologist*, Vol. XL, No. 3. Menasha, Wisconsin, American Anthropological Association, 1938.

Hamilton, William T. "A Trading Expedition among the Indians in 1858," *Contributions*, Vol. III. Helena, Historical Society of Montana, 1905.

Harrington, J. P. "The Origin of the Names Ute and Paiute," *American Anthropologist*, N. S., Vol. XIII. Menasha, American Anthropological Association, 1911.

Harris, Jack. "The Western Shoshoni," *American Anthropologist*, N. S., Vol. XL. Menasha, Wisconsin, American Anthropological Association, 1938.

Hill, Joseph J. "Spanish and Mexican Exploration and Trade Northwest from New Mexico into the Great Basin," *Utah Historical Quarterly*, Vol. III. Salt Lake City, Utah State Historical Society, 1930.

Hilyer, M. Inez. "Arapaho Child Life and Its Cultural Background," *Bulletin 148*, Bureau of American Ethnology. Washington, Government Printing Office, 1952.

Hoebel, E. A. "Bands and Distributions of the Eastern Shoshone," *American Anthropologist*, N. S., Vol. XL. Menasha, American Anthropological Association, 1938.

———. "Comanche and Hekandika Shoshone Relationship Systems," *American Anthropologist*, N. S., Vol. XLI. Menasha, American Anthropological Association, 1939.

———. "The Sun Dance of the Hekandika Shoshone," *American Anthropologist*, N. S., Vol. XXXVII. Menasha, American Anthropological Association, 1935.

Hoffman, W. J. "Poisoned Arrows," *American Anthropologist*, Vol. IV. Menasha, American Anthropological Association, 1891.

Hoffman, W. T. "Miscellaneous Ethnographic Observations on Indians Inhabiting Nevada, California, and Arizona," *Tenth Annual Report*, U.S. Geological and Geodetic Survey (Hayden Survey). Washington, Government Printing Office, 1878.

Hornaday, William T. "The Extermination of the American Bison," U.S. National Museum *Report, 1887*. Washington, Government Printing Office, 1889.

Hultkrantz, Ake. "The Indians in Yellowstone Park," *Annals of Wyo-*

ming, Vol. XXIX, No. 2. Cheyenne, Wyoming State Archives and Historical Department, 1957.

———. "The Shoshones in the Rocky Mountain Area," *Annals of Wyoming*, Vol. XXXIII, No. 1 Cheyenne, Wyoming State Archives and Historical Department, 1961.

Kelly, Isabel T. "Ethnography of the Surprise Valley Paiute," *American Archaeology and Ethnology*. Berkeley, University of California, 1932.

Kroeber, A. L. "The Bannock and Shoshoni Language," *American Anthropologist*, N. S., Vol. XI. Menasha, American Anthropological Association, 1909.

———. "Indian Myths of South Central California," *American Archaeology and Ethnology*, Vol. LV, No. 4. Berkeley, University of California, 1906–1907.

———. "Shoshonean Dialects of California," *American Archaeology and Ethnology*, Vol. IV, No. 3. Berkeley, University of California, 1961.

Lee, Jason. "Diary of Reverend Jason Lee," *Oregon Historical Quarterly*, Vol. XVII. Portland, Oregon Historical Society, June, September, and December, 1916.

Leidy, Joseph. "Remains of Primitive Art in the Bridger Basin," *Hayden Sixth Annual Report*, U.S. Geological Survey. Washington, Government Printing Office, 1873.

Loud, L. L., and M. R. Harrington. "Lovelock Cave," *American Archaeology and Ethnology*. Berkeley, University of California, 1929.

Lovejoy, A. L. "Lovejoy's Own Story." Ed. by Henry E. Reed. *Oregon Historical Quarterly*, Vol. XXXI, No. 3. Salem, Oregon Historical Society, 1930.

Lowie, Robert H. "The Cultural Connection of California and Plateau Shoshonean Tribes," *American Archaeology and Ethnology*, Vol. XX. Berkeley, University of California, 1923.

———. "Dances and Societies of the Plains Shoshone," *Anthropological Papers*, Vol. XI. New York, American Museum of Natural History, 1915.

———. "Indians of the Plains," *Anthropological Handbook*, Vol. I. New York, McGraw-Hill, 1954.

———. "The Northern Shoshone," *Anthropological Papers*, Vol. II, Part 2. New York, American Museum of Natural History, 1909.

341

———. "Notes on Shoshonean Ethnography," *Anthropological Papers*, Vol. XX, Part 3. New York, American Museum of Natural History, 1924.

———. "Shoshone and Comanche Tales" (collected by H. H. St. Clair), *Journal of American Folk-Lore*, Vol. XXII. Philadelphia, Bennett Hall, University of Pennsylvania, 1909.

———. "Shoshone Tales," *Journal of American Folk-Lore*, Vol. XXXVII. Philadelphia, Bennett Hall, University of Pennsylvania, 1924.

———. "Sun Dance of the Shoshone, Ute, and Hidatsa," *Anthropological Papers*, Vol. XVI, Part 5. New York, American Museum of Natural History, 1919.

Lyman, Albert R. "Pahute Biscuits," *Utah Historical Quarterly*, Vol. III. Salt Lake City, Utah State Historical Society, 1930.

McLeod, William C. "The Distribution Process of Suttee in America," *American Anthropologist*, Vol. XXXIII. Menasha, American Anthropological Association, 1931.

Mallery, Garrick. "Picture-Writing of the American Indians," *Tenth Annual Report*, Bureau of American Ethnology. Washington, Government Printing Office, 1893.

Malouf, Carling. "Gosiute Peyotism," *American Anthropologist*, Vol. XLIV. Menasha, American Anthropological Association, 1942.

Marsden, W. L. "The Northern Paiute Language of Oregon," *Archaeology and Ethnology*. Berkeley, University of California, 1923.

Mason, J. Alden. "Myths of the Uintah Utes," *Journal of American Folk-Lore*, Vol. XXIII. Philadelphia, Bennett Hall, University of Pennsylvania, 1910.

Mason, O. T. "Aboriginal Skin Dressing," *Report*, U.S. National Museum, 1888–89. Washington, Government Printing Office, 1891.

———. "The Human Beast of Burden," *Report*, U.S. National Museum. Washington, Government Printing Office, 1889.

Mattes, Merrill J. "Behind the Legend of Colter's Hell," *Mississippi Valley Historical Review* (reprint). Cheyenne, Wyoming Historical Department, September, 1949.

Mooney, James. "The Ghost Dance Religion and the Sioux Outbreak of 1890," *Fourteenth Annual Report*, Bureau of American Ethnology (1892–93), Vol. XIV, Pt. 2. Washington, Government Printing Office, 1896.

Morgan, Dale L. (ed.). "Washakie and the Shoshoni" (A Selection of Documents from the Records of the Utah Superintendency), *Annals of Wyoming*, Vol. XXV, No. 2 (July, 1953), to Vol. XXX, No. 1 (April, 1958). Cheyenne, Wyoming State Archives and Historical Department.

Mulloy, William. "Archaeological Investigations in the Shoshone Basin of Wyoming," *University of Wyoming Publications*, Vol. XVIII, Nos. 1, 2, 3. Laramie, University of Wyoming, July 15, 1954.

————. "A Preliminary Historical Outline for the Northwestern Plains," *University of Wyoming Publications*, Vol. XXII, No. 1. Laramie, University of Wyoming, July, 1958.

Munger, Asahel. "Diary of Asahel Munger and Wife," *Oregon Historical Quarterly*, Vol. VIII. Portland, Oregon Historical Society, 1907.

Nelson, E. W. "The Panamint and Saline Valley Indians," *American Anthropologist*, Vol. IV. Menasha, American Anthropological Association, 1891.

Nickerson, Hiram G. "Early History of Fremont County, 1886," *Bulletin*, Vol. II, No. 1. Cheyenne, Wyoming Historical Department, 1924.

————. "Indian Depredations in Sweetwater County," Wyoming Historical Society *Collections*, Vol. I, No. 1. Cheyenne, Wyoming Historical Society, 1897.

Ogden, Peter Skene. "The Peter Skene Ogden Journal, Snake Expedition, 1825–1826," *Oregon Historical Quarterly*, Vol. I, No. 4. Portland, Oregon Historical Society, December, 1910.

Palmer, W. R. "Utah Indians Past and Present," *Utah Historical Quarterly*, Vol. I. Salt Lake City, Utah State Historical Society, 1929.

Park, Willard Z. "Paviotso Polyandry," *American Anthropologist*, N. S., Vol. XXXIX. Menasha, American Anthropological Association, 1937.

————. "Paviotso Shamanism," *American Anthropologist*, N. S., Vol. XXXVI. Menasha, American Anthropological Association, 1934.

Patten, James I. "Bates' Famous Battle," *The Rustler* (Newspaper). Bonanza, Johnson County, Wyoming, October, 1899.

Powers, Stephen. "Centennial Mission to the Indians of Western Nevada and California," Smithsonian *Annual Report*, 1876. Washington, Government Printing Office, 1877.

Ray, Verne F., and others. "Tribal Distribution in Eastern Oregon and Adjacent Regions," *American Anthropologist*, Vol. XL, No. 3. Menasha, American Anthropological Association, 1938.

Reagan, Albert B. "The Gosiute or Shoshoni-Goship Indians of the Deep Creek Region in Western Utah," *Proceedings*, Utah Academy of Sciences, Arts & Letters, Vol. II. Salt Lake City, 1934.

Reed, Verner Z. "Ute Bear Dance," *American Anthropologist*, Vol. IX. Menasha, American Anthropological Association, 1896.

Renaud, E. B. "Archaeological Survey of Eastern Wyoming," *Bulletin*, Department of Anthropology. University of Denver and University of Wyoming. Denver, University of Denver, May, 1932.

Reynolds, Sidney O. "The Redskin Who Saved the White Man's Hide," *American Heritage*, Vol. XI, No. 2. New York, American Heritage Publishing Company, Inc., February, 1960.

Riddell, Francis A. "Honey Lake Paiute Ethnography," *Anthropological Papers*, No. 4. Carson City, Nevada State Museum, 1960.

Robinson, Doane. "Sac-a-jawe vs. Sa-kaka-wea," *Collections*, Vol. XII. Pierre, South Dakota Historical Society, 1924.

Robinson, W. G. "Sa-ka-ka-wea—Sa-car-ja-wea," *The Wi-Iyohi*, Vol. X, No. 11. Pierre, South Dakota Historical Society, February, 1957.

———. "Sa ka ka we—Sa ca ja wea," *The Wi-Iyohi*, Vol. X, No. 6. Pierre, South Dakota Historical Society, September, 1956.

Ross, Alexander. "Journal of the Snake River Expedition, 1824," *Oregon Historical Quarterly*, Vol. XIV. Portland, Oregon Historical Society, December, 1913.

Russell, Carl P. "Trapper Trails to the Sisk-ke-dee," *Annals of Wyoming*, Vol. XVII, No. 2 (reprint). Cheyenne, Wyoming Historical Department, July, 1945.

Shimkin, D. B. "Childhood and Development among the Wind River Shoshone," *Anthropological Records*, Vol. V, No. 5. Berkeley, University of California, 1947.

———. "Dynamics of Recent Wind River Shoshone History," *American Anthropologist*, N. S. Vol. XLIV. Menasha, Wisconsin, American Anthropological Association, 1942.

———. "Shoshone and Comanche Origins and Migrations," *Proceedings*, Sixth Pacific Science Congress, Vol. IV, Toronto, Canada, 1941.

———. "Wind River Geography," *American Anthropologist*, N. S., Vol. XL. Menasha, American Anthropological Association, 1938.

———. "Wind River Shoshone Ethnogeography," *Anthropological Records*, Vol. V, No. 4. Berkeley, University of California, 1947.
———. "Wind River Shoshone Literary Forms," *Journal*, Vol. XXXVII, No. 10. Washington, Academy of Sciences, October 15, 1947.
———. "Wind River Shoshone Sun Dance," *Bulletin 151*, Nos. 33–34, Bureau of American Ethnology. Washington, Government Printing Office, 1953.
———. "Uto-Aztekan System of Kinship Termonology," *American Anthropologist*, Vol. XLIII. Menasha, American Anthropological Association, 1941.
Shurtliff, Lewis W. "The Salmon River Mission," *Utah Historical Quarterly*, Vol. V, No. 1. Salt Lake City, Utah State Historical Society, 1932.
Snow, William J. "Utah Indians and Spanish Slave Trade," *Utah Historical Quarterly*, Vol. II. Salt Lake City, Utah State Historical Society, 1929.
Sonne, Conway B. "Royal Blood of the Utes," *Utah Historical Quarterly*, Vol. XX, No. 3. Salt Lake City, Utah State Historical Society, July, 1954.
Spier, Leslie. "The Prophet Dance of the Northwest and Its Derivatives: The Source of the Ghost Dance," *General Series in Anthropology*, Vol. I. Menasha, American Anthropological Association, 1935.
———. "The Sun Dance of the Plains Indians, Its Development and Diffusion," Ed. by Clark Wissler, *Anthropological Papers*, Vol. XVI, No. 7. New York, American Museum of Natural History, 1921.
Steward, Julian H. "Aborigines of Utah," *Utah Resources and Activities*. Salt Lake City, Department of Public Instruction, 1933.
———. "Ancient Caves of the Great Salt Lake Region," *Bulletin 116*, Bureau of American Ethnology. Washington, Government Printing Office, 1937.
———. "Basin-Plateau Aboriginal Sociopolitical Groups," *Bulletin 120*, Bureau of American Ethnology. Washington, Government Printing Office, 1938.
———. "Changes in Shoshonean Culture," *Scientific Monthly*, Vol. XLIX. Washington, American Association for the Advancement of Science, 1939.

———. "Ethnography of the Owens Valley Paiute," *American Archaeology and Ethnology*, Vol. XXXIII. Berkeley, University of California, 1933.

———. "Lemhi Shoshoni Physical Therapy," *Bulletin 119*, Bureau of American Ethnology. Washington, Government Printing Office, 1938.

———. "Linguistic Distribution and Political Groups of the Great Basin Shoshoneans," *American Anthropologist*, N. S., Vol. XXXIX. Menasha, American Anthropological Association, 1937.

———. "Native Cultures in the Intermontane (Great Basin) Area," Smithsonian Institution, *Miscellaneous Collections*. Washington, Government Printing Office, 1940.

———. "Nevada Shoshoni," *Anthropological Records*, Vol. VIII, No. 3. Berkeley, University of California, 1941.

———. "Northern and Gosiute Shoshoni," *Anthropological Records*, Vol. VIII, No. 3. Berkeley, University of California, 1943.

———. "Shoshoni Polyandry," *American Anthropologist*, N. S., Vol. XXXVIII. Menasha, American Anthropological Association, 1936.

———. "Some Observations on Shoshonean Distribution," *American Anthropologist*, N. S., Vol. XLI. Menasha, American Anthropological Association, 1939.

———. "The Uinta Ute Bear Dance," *American Anthropologist*, N. S., Vol. XXXIV. Menasha, American Anthropological Association, 1932.

Stewart, O. C. "The Northern Paiute Bands," *Anthropological Records*, Vol. II, No. 3. Berkeley, University of California, 1939.

Stuart, James. "Adventures on the Upper Missouri," *Contributions*, Vol. I. Helena, Historical Society of Montana, 1876.

Swanson, Earl H. "Problems in Shoshoni Chronology," *Idaho Yesterdays*, Vol. I, No. 4. Boise, Idaho State Historical Society, 1957–58.

Taylor, Eli F. "Indian Reservations in Utah," *Utah Historical Quarterly*, Vol. IV. Salt Lake City, Utah State Historical Society, 1931.

Teit, James A. "The Salishan Tribes of the Western Plateaus," Ed. by Franz Boas, *Forty-fifth Annual Report*, Bureau of American Ethnology. Washington, Government Printing Office, 1930.

Underhill, Ruth. "Indians of the Pacific Northwest," *Bulletin*, U.S. Department of the Interior. Washington, Government Printing Office, 1944.

——. "The Northern Paiute Indians of California and Nevada," *Bulletin*, U.S. Department of the Interior. Washington, Government Printing Office, 1941.

Vérendrye, Chevalier de la. "Journal of the Voyage Made by Chevalier de la Vérendrye with One of His Brothers in Search of the Western Sea" (in "Margry Papers," trans. by Anne H. Blegen), *Oregon Historical Quarterly*, Vol. XXVI, No. 2. Eugene, Oregon Historical Society, June, 1925.

Voget, Fred W. "Current Trends in the Wind River Shoshoni Sun Dance," *Bulletin 151*, Bureau of American Ethnology. Washington, Government Printing Office, 1953.

——. "Individual Motivation in the Diffusion of the Sun Dance of the Wind River Shoshoni to the Crow Indians," *American Anthropologist*, N. S., Vol. L. Menasha, American Anthropological Association, 1948.

Wheeler, Col. H .W. "Reminiscences of Old Fort Washakie," *Annals of Wyoming*, Vol. I, No. 4. Cheyenne, Wyoming Historical Department, 1924.

Williams, P. L. "Personal Recollections of Wash-a-kie," *Utah Historical Quarterly*, Vol. I, No. 4. Salt Lake City, Utah State Historical Society, October, 1928.

Wissler, Clark. "The Influence of the Horse in the Development of Plains Culture," *American Anthropologist*, N. S., Vol. XVI. Menasha, American Anthropological Association, 1914.

——. "Population Changes among the Northern Plains Indians," *Anthropology*, Vol. I. New Haven, Connecticut, Yale University, 1936.

"Wyoming Indians" (A Brief History, comp. by the U.S. Census of 1890), *Collections*, Vol. I, No. 1. Cheyenne, Wyoming Historical Society, 1897.

Index

Absaroka Indians: *see* Crow Indians
Absaroka Mountains (Wyoming): 50, 310
Acculturation: viii f., 84, 221–22, 234f., 272, 281 f.
Agaidüka (Salmon Eater) Indians: 22, 150; *see also* Lemhi Indians
Agriculture: 162, 212, 214, 221, 225–26, 243f., 266f., 274f., 282f.
Aguina (Eagle): 241
Ah-ah-why-per-sie (Crow Maiden): 174
Ah-gutch (The Salmon): 184
Alberta, Canada: 18, 38
Allasandra: *see* Wesaw, Tom
Allotment Act: 283
Ama-qui-em (Sherry-dika chief): 38, 54
Am-a-ro-ko (Buffalo Meat Under the Shoulder): 190
American Fur Company: 75, 77, 81, 87, 99, 119
Anker-howitch (Ute chief): 131
Ankoa band: 204
Annuities: 208, 212, 214, 216f., 226, 232f., 258
Antaro (Ute chief): 131, 162
Arapaho Indians: 26, 37, 119, 121, 228f., 237ff.; Shoshoni name for, 3, 22; origin of, 22; demoralization of, 281f.; at McLaughlin council, 288f.; lands of, 314ff.; *see also* Northern *and* Southern Arapaho Indians
Arikara Indians: 26, 61
Armstrong, George: 141
Army for Utah: 157f., 168, 200

Arrapeen (Ar-ra-pine), Ute chief: 134f., 138f.
Arthur, President Chester A.: 258
As-as-to (Blackfoot chief): 72
Ashingodimah (Shoshoni chief): 202
Ashley, William H.: 56f., 60–61, 62ff., 70
Ashley-Henry Fur Company: 56
Assiniboin Indians: 20, 22, 59n.
Astor, John Jacob: 51, 73; scouts of, 75, 109
Astoria, Oregon: 51, 53
Astorians: 51f.
Atkinson, General Henry: 64
Atlantic City, Wyoming: 73
Atrocities: 252; *see also* Warfare
Arsina (Gros Ventre) Indians: 3, 21; *see also* Gros Ventre Indians
Augur, General C. C.: 220, 223, 226f.
Augutasipa (Shoshoni chief): 115
Austin, Nevada: 186

Baker, Jim: 91, 95, 102
Ball, John: 78
Ballard, D. W.: 215f., 218, 223
Ballou, Louis: 274f.
Bands: formation of, 17; significance of: 19, 115; leaders, 100, 183, 204, 218; hostile to Shoshonis, 224f., 244ff.
Bannock City, Montana: 195, 200
Bannock Creek: 266
Bannock Creek Shoshonis: 29, 163
Bannock Diggers: *see* Digger Indians
Bannock Indians (Northern Paiutes): 3, 18, 22, 70f.; affiliation with Shoshonis, 23; cause trouble, 53ff.; fight

348

Gro-se-pene (Ute chief): 127
Gros Ventre Agency: 228
Gros Ventre (Atsina) Indians: 21, 77, 105
Gros Ventres of the Missouri: *see* Hidatsa Indians
Gros Ventres of the Prairies: *see* Atsina Indians
Grouard, Frank: 253
Grouse Creek Indians: 18
Grouse Pete: 271
Guina, "Happy Jack": *see* Tissaguina
Gulf of California: 109
Gunnison, Lieutenant John W.: 112, 135, 208

Hamilton, William T.: 106f.
Ham's Fork: 84, 113
Harris, Tom: 259f., 260
Hastings, Lansford: 103
Head, F. H.: 216f., 225f., 246f.
Heart Mountain (Wyoming): 287
Henry, Andrew: 51, 53, 56
Henry, Captain Guy V.: 251
Henry's Fork: 102, 142
Henry's Lake: 168
Hidatsa Indians (Gros Ventres of the Missouri): 3, 21 f., 42, 48
Hidden Canyon: 259
Hiding Bear (Pah-dasher-wah-un-dah): 85, 97f., 101, 103
Hill, Barney: 260
Hill, G. W.: 150
Hoback, John: 51, 53
Holeman, Jacob H.: 116f., 128f., 156
Holladay, Ben: 193, 212
Honey Lake: 186
Honey Lake Paiutes: 178
Hopkins, Sarah Winnemucca: *see* Winnemucca, Sarah
Horse, The (Bannock chief): 72, 79
Horse Creek (Nebraska): 120
Horse Creek (Wyoming): 87, 91 & n.
Horse Creek Treaty Council: 120f., 127, 167, 304; *see also* Fort Laramie
Hot Springs: 286f., 289n.; *see also* Big Hot Springs

Howard, General O. O.: 95, 263
Howell, Francis S.: 314
Hoyt, John W.: 279f.
Hudson, Wyoming: 173
Hudson's Bay Company: 58, 60, 63, 87
Humboldt Agency: 129, 199
Humboldt Lake: 10
Humboldt River (Nevada): 14f., 62, 111, 129f., 136, 175ff., 190, 204f.
Humboldt Valley: 178
Humpy (Shoshoni scout): 259
Hunt, Wilson Price: 51
Hunt: 23, 28, 58, 67, 111, 212
Huntington, J. W. P.: 208
Hurt, Garland: 136 & n., 140, 162
Hyde, Orson: 142f.

Idaho: viii, 3f., 22, 50, 182
Idaho Territory: 214, 232
Immortality: 8f., 278
Independence Rock (Wyoming): 97, 99–100, 103, 175
Indian Claims Commission: 315f.
Indian John: 145
Indian Office: 114n., 178
Indian Peace Commission: 217, 220
Indian Reorganization Act: 283
Indian Territory: 237, 286
Indian wars of 1876: 247ff.
Ink-a-tosh-a-pop (Red Eagle): 97f.
Inyo County (California): 270
Inyo Mountains: 270
Irish, O. H.: 209f., 212
Iron Point (Nevada): 14
Iron Wristbands (Hiding Bear): 38, 85
Iroquois Indians: 60, 75, 84
Irwin, James: 229, 234f., 239, 245f.

Jackson, David E.: 56, 70
Jackson Hole (Wyoming): 60 n.
Jag-en-up (Crying Shoe): 181
Jag-e-oh (The Man Who Carries the Arrow): 181, 183–84
Jah-win-pooh (subchief): 181
James, Thomas: 53
Jefferis, Albert W.: 314

of which *The Shoshonis: Sentinels of the Rockies* is the seventy-fourth volume, was inaugurated in 1932 by the University of Oklahoma Press, and has as its purpose the reconstruction of American Indian civilization by presenting aboriginal, historical, and contemporary Indian life. The following list is complete as of the date of printing of this volume:

1. Alfred Barnaby Thomas. *Forgotten Frontiers:* A Study of the Spanish Indian Policy of Don Juan Bautista de Anza, Governor of New Mexico, 1777–1787.
2. Grant Foreman. *Indian Removal:* The Emigration of the Five Civilized Tribes of Indians.
3. John Joseph Mathews. *Wah'Kon-Tah:* The Osage and the White Man's Road.
4. Grant Foreman. *Advancing the Frontier, 1830–1860.*
5. John Homer Seger. *Early Days among the Cheyenne and Arapahoe Indians.* Edited by Stanley Vestal.
6. Angie Debo. *The Rise and Fall of the Choctaw Republic.*
7. Stanley Vestal (ed.). *New Sources of Indian History, 1850–1891.* Out of print.
8. Grant Foreman. *The Five Civilized Tribes.*
9. Alfred Barnaby Thomas. *After Coronado:* Spanish Exploration Northeast of New Mexico, 1696–1727.
10. Frank G. Speck. *Naskapi:* The Savage Hunters of the Labrador Peninsula. Out of print.
11. Elaine Goodale Eastman. *Pratt:* The Red Man's Moses.
12. Althea Bass. *Cherokee Messenger:* A Life of Samuel Austin Worcester.
13. Thomas Wildcat Alford. *Civilization.* As told to Florence Drake. Out of print.
14. Grant Foreman. *Indians and Pioneers:* The Story of the American Southwest before 1830.
15. George E. Hyde. *Red Cloud's Folk:* A History of the Oglala Sioux Indians.
16. Grant Foreman. *Sequoyah.*
17. Morris L. Wardell. *A Political History of the Cherokee Nation, 1838–1907.* Out of print.
18. John Walton Caughey. *McGillivray of the Creeks.* Out of print.
19. Edward Everett Dale and Gaston Litton. *Cherokee Cavaliers:*

Forty Years of Cherokee History as Told in the Correspondence of the Ridge-Watie-Boudinot Family.

20. Ralph Henry Gabriel. *Elias Boudinot, Cherokee, and His America.* Out of print.
21. Karl N. Llewellyn and E. Adamson Hoebel. *The Cheyenne Way:* Conflicts and Case Law in Primitive Jurisprudence.
22. Angie Debo. *The Road to Disappearance.*
23. Oliver La Farge and others. *The Changing Indian.* Out of print.
24. Carolyn Thomas Foreman. *Indians Abroad.* Out of print.
25. John Adair. *The Navajo and Pueblo Silversmiths.*
26. Alice Marriott. *The Ten Grandmothers.*
27. Alice Marriott. *María:* The Potter of San Ildefonso.
28. Edward Everett Dale. *The Indians of the Southwest:* A Century of Development under the United States.
29. Adrián Recinos. *Popol Vuh:* The Sacred Book of the Ancient Quiché Maya. English version by Delia Goetz and Sylvanus G. Morley from the translation of Adrián Recinos.
30. Walter Collins O'Kane. *Sun in the Sky.*
31. Stanley A. Stubbs. *Bird's-Eye View of the Pueblos.* Out of print.
32. Katharine C. Turner. *Red Men Calling on the Great White Father.*
33. Muriel H. Wright. *A Guide to the Indian Tribes of Oklahoma.*
34. Ernest Wallace and E. Adamson Hoebel. *The Comanches:* Lords of the South Plains.
35. Walter Collins O'Kane. *The Hopis:* Portrait of a Desert People.
36. Joseph Epes Brown. *The Sacred Pipe:* Black Elk's Account of the Seven Rites of the Oglala Sioux.
37. Adrián Recinos and Delia Goetz (translators). *The Annals of the Cakchiquels.* Translated from the Cakchiquel Maya, with *Title of the Lords of Totonicapán*, translated from the Quiché text into Spanish by Dionisio José Chonay, English version by Delia Goetz.
38. R. S. Cotterill. *The Southern Indians:* The Story of the Civilized Tribes before Removal.
39. J. Eric S. Thompson. *The Rise and Fall of Maya Civilization.*
40. Robert Emmitt. *The Last War Trail:* The Utes and the Settlement of Colorado. Out of print.
41. Frank Gilbert Roe. *The Indian and the Horse.*

42. Francis Haines. *The Nez Percés:* Tribesmen of the Columbia Plateau.
43. Ruth M. Underhill. *The Navajos.*
44. George Bird Grinnell. *The Fighting Cheyennes.*
45. George E. Hyde. *A Sioux Chronicle.* Out of print.
46. Stanley Vestal. *Sitting Bull, Champion of the Sioux:* A Biography.
47. Edwin C. McReynolds. *The Seminoles.*
48. William T. Hagan. *The Sac and Fox Indians.*
49. John C. Ewers. *The Blackfeet:* Raiders on the Northwestern Plains. Out of print.
50. Alfonso Caso. *The Aztecs:* People of the Sun. Translated by Lowell Dunham.
51. C. L. Sonnichsen. *The Mescalero Apaches.*
52. Keith A. Murray. *The Modocs and Their War.*
53. Victor W. von Hagen (editor). *The Incas of Pedro de Cieza de León.* Translated by Harriet de Onis.
54. George E. Hyde. *Indians of the High Plains:* From the Prehistoric Period to the Coming of the Europeans.
55. *George Catlin. Episodes from "Life among the Indians" and "Last Rambles."* Edited by Marvin C. Ross. Out of print.
56. J. Eric S. Thompson. *Maya Hieroglyphic Writing:* An Introduction.
57. George E. Hyde. *Spotted Tail's Folk:* A History of the Brulé Sioux.
58. James Larpenteur Long. *The Assiniboines:* From the Accounts of the Old Ones Told to First Boy (James Larpenteur Long). Edited and with an introduction by Michael Stephen Kennedy. Out of print.
59. Edwin Thompson Denig. *Five Indian Tribes of the Upper Missouri.* Edited and with an introduction by John C. Ewers.
60. John Joseph Mathews. *The Osages:* Children of the Middle Waters.
61. Mary Elizabeth Young. *Redskins, Ruffleshirts, and Rednecks:* Indian Allotments in Alabama and Mississippi, 1830–1860.
62. J. Eric S. Thompson. *A Catalog of Maya Hieroglyphs.*
63. Mildred P. Mayhall. *The Kiowas.*
64. George E. Hyde. *Indians of the Woodlands:* From Prehistoric Times to 1725.

65. Grace Steele Woodward. *The Cherokees.*
66. Donald J. Berthrong. *The Southern Cheyennes.*
67. Miguel León-Portilla. *Aztec Thought and Culture:* A Study of the Ancient Nahuatl Mind.
68. T. D. Allen. *Navahos Have Five Fingers.*
69. Burr Cartwright Brundage. *Empire of the Inca.*
70. A. M. Gibson. *The Kickapoos:* Lords of the Middle Border.
71. Hamilton A. Tyler. *Pueblo Gods and Myths.*
72. Royal B. Hassrick. *The Sioux:* Life and Customs of a Warrior Society. Written in collaboration with Dorothy Maxwell and Cile M. Bach.
73. Franc Johnson Newcomb. *Hosteen Klah:* Navaho Medicine Man and Sand Painter.
74. Virginia Cole Trenholm and Maurine Carley. *The Shoshonis:* Sentinels of the Rockies.
75. Cohoe. *A Cheyenne Sketchbook.* Commentary by E. Adamson Hoebel and Karen Daniels Petersen. Out of print.
76. Jack D. Forbes. *Warriors of the Colorado:* The Quechans and Their Neighbors.
77. Ralph L. Roys (editor and translator). *Ritual of the Bacabs.*
78. Lillian Estelle Fisher. *The Last Inca Revolt.*
79. Lilly de Jongh Osborne. *Indian Crafts of Guatemala and El Salvador.*
80. Robert H. Ruby and John A. Brown. *Half-Sun on the Columbia:* A Biography of Chief Moses.
81. Jack Frederick and Anna Gritts Kilpatrick (editor and translators). *The Shadow of Sequoyah:* Social Documents of the Cherokees.
82. Ella E. Clark. *Indian Legends from the Northern Rockies.*
83. William A. Brophy and Sophie D. Aberle, M.D. (editors). *The Indian:* America's Unfinished Business.
84. M. Inez Hilger with Margaret A. Mondloch. *Huenun Ñamku:* An Araucanian Indian of the Andes Remembers the Past. Preface by Margaret Mead.
85. Ronald Spores. *The Mixtec Kings and Their People.*
86. David H. Corkran. *The Creek Frontier.*
87. Ralph L. Roys (editor and translator). *The Book of Chilam Balam of Chumayel.*

88. Burr Cartwright Brundage. *Lords of Cuzco:* A History and Description of the Inca People in Their Final Days.
89. John C. Ewers. *Indian Life on the Upper Missouri.*
90. Max L. Moorhead. *The Apache Frontier:* Jacobo Ugarte and Spanish-Indian Relations in Northern New Spain, 1769–1791.
91. France Scholes and Ralph L. Roys. *The Maya Chontal Indians of Acalan-Tixchel.*
92. Miguel León-Portilla. *Pre-Columbian Literatures of Mexico.* Translated by Grace Lobanov and the author.
93. Grace Steele Woodward. *Pocahontas.*
94. Gottfried Hotz. *Eighteenth-Century Skin Paintings.* Translated by Johannes Malthaner.
95. Virgil J. Vogel. *American Indian Medicine.*
96. Bill Vaudrin. *Tanaina Tales from Alaska.* Introduction by Joan B. Townsend.
97. Georgiana C. Nammack. *The Iroquois Land Frontier in the Colonial Period.*
98. Eugene R. Craine and Reginald C. Reindorp (editors and translators). *The Chronicles of Michoacán.*
99. J. Eric S. Thompson. *Maya History and Religion.*
100. Peter J. Powell. *Sweet Medicine:* The Continuing Role of the Sacred Arrows, the Sun Dance, and the Sacred Buffalo Hat in Northern Cheyenne History. 2 volumes.
101. Karen Daniels Petersen. *Indians Unchained:* Plains Indian Art from Fort Marion.
102. Fray Diego Durán. *The Books of the Gods and Rites and The Ancient Calendar.* Translated and edited by Fernando Horcasitas and Doris Heyden. Foreword by Miguel León-Portilla.
103. Bert Anson. *The Miami Indians:* Sovereigns of the Wabash-Maumee.
104. Robert H. Ruby and John A. Brown. *The Spokane Indians:* Children of the Sun. Foreword by Robert L. Bennett.
105. Virginia Cole Trenholm. *The Arapahoes, Our People.*
106. Angie Debo. *A History of the Indians of the United States.*
107. Herman Grey. *Tales from the Mohaves.*
108. Stephen Dow Beckham. *Requiem for a People:* The Rogue Indians and the Frontiersmen.
109. Arrell M. Gibson. *The Chickasaws.*

110. *Indian Oratory:* Famous Speeches by Noted Indian Chieftains, compiled by W. C. Vanderwerth.
111. *The Sioux of the Rosebud:* A History in Pictures. Photographs by John A. Anderson, text by Henry W. Hamilton and Jean Tyree Hamilton.
112. Howard L. Harrod. *Mission Among the Blackfeet.*
113. Mary Whatley Clarke. *Chief Bowles and the Texas Cherokees.*
114. William E. Unrau. *The Kansa Indians:* A History of the Wind People.
115. Jack D. Forbes. *Apache, Navaho, and Spaniard.*
116. W. David Baird. *Peter Pitchlynn:* Chief of the Choctaws.
117. *Life and Death in Milpa Alta:* A Nahuatl Chronicle of Díaz and Zapata. Translated and edited by Fernando Horcasitas, with a foreword by Miguel León-Portilla.
118. Ralph L. Roys. *The Indian Background of Colonial Yucatán.* With an introduction by J. Eric S. Thompson.
119. *Cry of the Thunderbird:* The American Indian's Own Story. Edited by Charles Hamilton.
120. Robert H. Ruby and John A. Brown. *The Cayuse Indians:* Imperial Tribesmen of Old Oregon.

The Shoshonis has been printed on a paper which has been developed for an effective life of at least three hundred years. The type chosen for the text is eleven-point Janson with two points of spacing between the lines. Janson is noted for its distinctive character and was selected for this book to reflect the rich western background implicit in the subject of the Shoshonis.

UNIVERSITY OF OKLAHOMA PRESS
Norman